HIDEYOSHI

HARVARD EAST ASIAN MONOGRAPHS, 146

Portrait of Hideyoshi, with an inscription dated the eighteenth day of the eighth month, 1598, in the collection of Kōdaiji, Kyoto

HIDEYOSHI

Mary Elizabeth Berry

Published by
The Council on East Asian Studies
Harvard University
and distributed by
The Harvard University Press
Cambridge (Massachusetts) and London

10 9 8 7 6

The Council on East Asian Studies at Harvard University pub-
lishes a monograph series and, through the Fairbank Center for
East Asian Research and the Reischauer Institute of Japanese
Studies, administers research projects designed to further scholarly understanding of China, Japan, Korea, Vietnam, Inner Asia,
and adjacent areas.

Publication of this book has been aided by a grant from the
Andrew W. Mellon Foundation

Library of Congress Cataloging in Publication Data
Berry, Mary Elizabeth, 1947–
Hideyoshi.

(Harvard East Asian series; 97)
Includes index.
1. Toyotomi, Hideyoshi, 1536?-1598. 2. Generals—
Japan—Biography. 3. Japan—History—Period of
civil wars, 1480-1603. 4. Japan—History—Azuchi-
Momoyama period, 1568-1603. I. Title. II. Series.
DS869.T6B47   952'.023'0924 [B]   82-1056
ISBN 0-674-39026-1

For
D.H.S.

ACKNOWLEDGMENTS

FROM THE BEGINNING of my work on Hideyoshi, Edwin O. Reischauer and Albert M. Craig have been wise and tireless advisers. More recently I have enjoyed the always bracing counsel of my colleagues at the University of California, Berkeley. They must be in a class by themselves as exacting and generous critics who saw, often when I could not, how the book might be made better. They provided and helped me through a "time yet for a hundred indecisions, / And for a hundred visions and revisions." In particular, I am grateful to Thomas C. Smith, Irwin Scheiner, David Keightley, Randolph Starn, Robert Brentano, Paula Fass, Robert Middlekauff, and Susanna Barrows.

During several trips to Kyoto, I received the guidance of Professors Hayashiya Tatsusaburō, Asao Naohiro, Motoyama Yukihiko, and Mr. Kubota Fuyuhiko. Professor Takagi Kiyoko had a decisive influence on my training both in language and intellectual history. I am one of many students of Japan in a new generation who began to realize the satisfactions of our profession under her direction. The late Richard Beardsley of the University of Michigan was a dear friend and counsellor throughout my first years of teaching and writing.

My dissertation research, which formed the basis of chapter seven of this book, was funded by a Danforth Fellowship, a Whiting Fellowship, and a Fulbright-Hays Fellowship. My subsequent work on Hideyoshi, and an ongoing project concerning sixteenth-century Kyoto, has been funded by the Japan Foundation, the Social Science Research Council, the Japan Institute of Harvard University, and summer fellowships from the University of Michigan, Ann Arbor, and the University of California, Berkeley.

Mary Elizabeth Looram Berry and James Fant Berry have always been my best teachers and the best of people. Because we discovered Japan together, it will always feel like home. My greatest debt, one that can be mentioned but never fully acknowledged, is to my mentor, colleague, and husband, Donald Shively. For his sake, "I would be trebled twenty times myself." But that would not be enough.

CONTENTS

xi
Contents

MAPS

FIGURES

The chapter ornament is Hideyoshi's *kaō*, a monogram or emblematic signature
The jacket illustration is one of Hideyoshi's helmets

A Note on Names, Dates, and Measures

I HAVE TRIED to refer to each individual mentioned in the text by a single surname and a single personal name, those that are most familiar to scholars of Japan and can readily be found in standard Japanese reference works. Thus childhood names, adoptive names, and Buddhist names, for example, do not normally appear here. On occasion, I have mentioned official titles, though not—as is sometimes the case in Japan—in substitution for family and personal names. I have referred to our main subject as Toyotomi Hideyoshi throughout the text, but discuss his other names in note 5 to chapter 1. Following Japanese custom, surnames precede personal names in this work.

The Japanese used a lunar calendar prior to the late nineteenth century and numbered years according to a system of era names. *Tenshō* 3.6.12, for instance, is the twelfth day of the sixth month of the third year of *Tenshō* (an era name that might be rendered as "Heaven's Justice"). In general, I have converted the years to their equivalents in the Gregorian calendar, but have not converted the months and the days. Thus I describe *Tenshō* 3.6.12 as the twelfth day of the sixth month of 1575 (which is July nineteenth and *not* June twelfth in the Gregorian calendar).

Because the lunar year ends between twenty and forty days later than the solar year, problems arise in the treatment of dates falling late in the lunar calendar. *Tenshō* 3.12.1, for example, corresponds to January first, 1576. For the sake of consistency, however, and to avoid the use of Western month names, I have adhered to a single system throughout the text: I describe *Tenshō* 3.12.1 as the first day of the twelfth month of 1575. Readers interested in a precise correspondence between Japanese and Gregorian dates should consult Paul Yachita Tsuchihashi, *Japanese Chronological Tables from 601 to 1872 A.D.* (Tokyo: Sophia University Press, 1952).

Linear, area, volume, and weight measures present a much greater problem than the calendar. Although measuring units tended to bear the same names throughout Japan in the sixteenth century, the dimensions of those units varied, even within domains and even after Hideyoshi's attempts to standardize them. Moreover, sufficient evidence does not always exist to permit scholars to establish equivalences between Hideyoshi's "standards" and modern measures. There is no authoritative judgment, for instance, on the weight or purity of the *mai*, a basic unit for weighing gold and silver at the time.

When measures are introduced in the text, a rough modern equivalent is suggested and reference is occasionally made to explanatory notes. The reader should understand, however, that these equivalences are often approximate at best.

HIDEYOSHI

Fig. 1. Hideyoshi's mausoleum, a detail from *Higashiyama meisho-zu*, a screen in the collection of Yoshimatsu Tsuruki, Kyoto

1

THE TOYOTOMI PEACE

ON A PEACEFUL, pine-shaded rise in the land, just north of the Kyoto National Museum, stands a shrine honoring Toyotomi Hideyoshi. It was here, not long after Hideyoshi's death in 1598, that Emperor Go-Yōzei declared him a divinity of the first rank with the title Hōkoku Daimyōjin—Most Bright God of Our Bountiful Country. Men of every station gathered at the shrine to mark the early anniversaries of Hideyoshi's apotheosis with boisterous festivity. Processions of nobles, priests, and mounted warriors opened the commemorative services; dancing by the costumed townspeople of the capital went on for days. Banquets and musical recitals took place under the shade of ornately carved halls finished in lacquer and gold leaf.[1]

Hideyoshi's successor, Tokugawa Ieyasu, closed the shrine in 1615 to discourage these unseemly displays of loyalty to a man he had eclipsed. Long before that time, however, Hideyoshi had become a legend. Storytellers endlessly recounted the tales of a leader who had changed his country more profoundly than any of his predecessors. A general who had unified Japan after a century of civil war, a governor who had laid the foundation for almost three hundred years of peacetime rule, and a showman without peer who had brought a new pageantry to power, Hideyoshi was the most remarkable man in premodern Japanese history.

There was nothing in Hideyoshi's origins to foretell his destiny. Born during 1536 and orphaned seven years later, he was the son of a farmer and part-time soldier from a small village in Owari province, several days' journey from Kyoto. Although his family may have owned some land, it was neither prosperous nor influential enough to bear a surname—a distinction common in the upper stratum of agrarian society by the early sixteenth century. The major legacy left to Hideyoshi was his father's example of military service.

In a country divided by war since 1467, affiliation with one of the scores of provincial magnates competing for domination provided an

1

opportunity for advancement. Thus Hideyoshi left home around the age of fifteen to begin his career as a page in the army of Imagawa Yoshimoto, lord of the two provinces of Suruga and Tōtōmi. After several years, he transferred allegiance to another lord, Oda Nobunaga. It was a prescient choice. Hideyoshi rose in the Oda ranks to become in his mid-thirties one of Nobunaga's chief deputies. He and his fellow commanders extended Oda hegemony across a third of the nation before Nobunaga was murdered in 1582. Within days of the attack, Hideyoshi avenged his dead lord, presented the head of the assassin before Nobunaga's corpse, and began to take charge of the Oda coalition.

During the next fifteen years, Hideyoshi laid the basis for a legend hardly bolder than the life itself. His popular biographers, who produced numerous variants of the *Taikō-ki*, or *Chronicles of the Regent*, concentrated on the spectacular military success.[2] Hideyoshi launched campaigns throughout the country to bring well over one hundred lords, many of them from illustrious houses, under his command. Those campaigns engaged as many as 250,000 soldiers, including infantrymen equipped with muskets, and covered the three major islands. Conquest was as swiftly achieved as it was great in scope: Hideyoshi was lord of all Japan by 1590. To make so large a story accessible to the imagination, Hideyoshi's chroniclers lingered over the vivid, if improbable, details of his encounters. They tell us that Hideyoshi was a tactical genius who took his opponents by surprise after rapid marches, diverted rivers to withhold water from adversaries under siege, and erected mock castles overnight to deepen the enemy's impression of his strength on the battlefield.

Hideyoshi's martial accomplishment assumed particular meaning because of the length and gravity of national suffering before unification. For one hundred twenty years, warlords had fragmented the state, defied traditional authorities, and used national monuments as battle sites. Kyoto itself, capital of emperors and former military leaders, became a symbol of distress. "The Flower Capital of myriad ages is now a lair of foxes and wolves. Even valiant Tōji and Kitano have turned to ash . . . The revolution of the Ōnin years destroys both the law of Buddha and the law of kings . . . The capital we knew, even while gazing upon the evening lark in the fields, brings falling tears."[3] Never, prior to the fifteenth century, had the nation experienced prolonged war or the total collapse of legitimate governing institutions.

Hideyoshi's success was made more striking by the odds against him. Without pedigree or seniority in the Oda league, he was not the obvious successor to Nobunaga. Nor, having mastered the Oda coalition, was he in an invincible position for further conquest. His adversaries were ambitious men who had resisted Nobunaga for years to preserve and expand their own local influence. Some controlled as many as six of Japan's sixty-six provinces, the more powerful could bring tens of thousands of men to war, and all could cooperate to destroy the Toyotomi forces. Instead, numerous warlords entered into alliance with Hideyoshi, and the rest were subdued by a joint army that grew to vast proportions. The story of those alliances, the conditions and shared goals that made them possible, is at the heart of Hideyoshi's achievement.

Military unification, much as it excited the carriers of the Hideyoshi legend, was only the beginning of a career with many facets. For his contemporaries, Hideyoshi's acts of renewal marked his greatness. He restored the dignity of the imperial house, rebuilt the capital and other cities, repaired monasteries and shrines ravaged by battle. Grasping the need to make an unfamiliar peace real in the popular mind, he used the symbols of power in an extravagant fashion to signal the return to normality. Tea parties for thousands of commoners, theatricals, blossom-viewing outings, parades, and princely receptions—all signaled harmonious rule. Hideyoshi went on to erect a colossal statue of the Buddha, and he surrounded himself with material glory: three elegant castles, a tea house finished in gold, boats and palanquins painted by celebrated artists, gardens rich with tropical plants and hundreds of choice rocks.

Hideyoshi set the tone, and the pace, of an age that came to be known as Momoyama, or Peach Mountain, the popular name of his last castle. Women dressed their hair in boyish cuts; they wore robes of daring patterns draped in casual folds. High and low cultures converged as warriors patronized merchant tea men, and the nō theater became an urban amusement. With the expansion of overseas trade, the Ryukyuan samisen enlivened Japanese music. Korean ceramics, heavy and sensuous to the touch, turned tastes away from the refined porcelains of China. Pantaloons, high hats, clocks, and exotic animals carried by the Europeans came into vogue. Even meat eating was a temporary rage. The Portuguese Jesuit João Rodrigues described Hideyoshi's era with enthusiasm: "The laws, administration, customs, culture, trade, wealth and magnificence were restored throughout the kingdom, and populous cities and other buildings were raised everywhere as a result of trade and peace . . . Throughout the kingdom there was a great abundance of money, new mines were opened and the country was well supplied with everything."[4] Architect of renewal and leader of a glamorous era, Hideyoshi used ostentation as a tool of statecraft.

Although pageantry became an end in itself on occasion, it was designed to inspire confidence in a political settlement that became

Hideyoshi's most durable contribution to his successors. The government he created was federal in character, the first of its kind in Japan and a startling departure from the model of administration established by Oda Nobunaga.

Oda Nobunaga was a centrist. As his conquests proceeded, he supplanted the vanquished with a small band of trusted men whom he controlled firmly. He drew once-independent monasteries, cities, and mining resources into his own sphere. He also remained aloof from traditional authorities, lest association with the survivors of an old order compromise his ambitions. Nobunaga's administration was arresting because of the amount of land he commanded, yet it conformed to wartime patterns of rule. Other local lords had tried to govern absolutely the territory they held. All evidence suggested that military unification of Japan, when it finally came, would bring autocracy. What victor could entrust power to rivals, with huge personal armies, who had fought for decades to extend their own hegemony? Peace presumed the elimination of independent, defiant lords.

The peace Hideyoshi achieved, however, was founded upon just such independent lordships. He divided the land of the nation among two hundred daimyo ("great lords"), invested with domains of various sizes. Some of these men were old vassals who had fought under Hideyoshi for Nobunaga. Others were peers in the Oda coalition who had joined Hideyoshi voluntarily after Nobunaga's death. Still others were daimyo—from both within and without the Oda sphere—who had negotiated alliances with Hideyoshi under threat of attack. The last members of the federation were defeated enemies who were permitted to maintain their lands and status.

The allocation of land to outsiders was surprising in itself. Far more surprising were the concessions they received; Hideyoshi neglected opportunities to aggrandize himself and his personal vassals. He not only confirmed the holdings of his allies and most of his vanquished adversaries, he expanded them. Land seized following conquest or recovered through disciplinary attainders was often redistributed to former rivals. Hideyoshi's personal domain was not the largest in the state, nor did men long in his service begin to approach the wealth of their historical enemies. Two daimyo houses, conclusively defeated by Toyotomi armies, numbered among the most powerful families in the nation.

Hideyoshi's involvement in domainal governance remained limited. With some exceptions, the daimyo made local policy themselves. They were not taxed systematically by Hideyoshi. And, most extraordinary, they retained control over their own armies. Their soldiers were never demobilized or brought directly under Toyotomi command. The management of domainal forces was a daimyo concern. Despite, or because of, these concessions, local lords paid Hideyoshi homage and fought his wars.

Further, Hideyoshi depended upon the daimyo—outsiders as well as long-time associates—to undertake his administrative tasks. He created no central bureaucracy, identified no regular corps of career officials to oversee national business. The registration of land and similar projects were delegated to daimyo appointees. The most sensitive assignment ever made by Hideyoshi, guardianship of his child heir, was entrusted to five former adversaries.

Hideyoshi employed none of the tactics long familiar to Oda Nobunaga and his counterparts to preserve control: massive attainder or transfer of vassal domains, stern regulation of vassal behavior, or the promotion of proven deputies to supervise his affairs. A radical and consistent federalist, he respected the domain as the essential, largely autonomous unit of local government. Hideyoshi's daimyo were free from arbitrary seizure of land or capricious interference of central officials in land management.

Such restraint did not proceed from timidity or a misunderstanding of the power attending national conquest. A peasant turned soldier who had spent most of his life at war and who had learned to define authority in terms of the compact between the lord and his man, Hideyoshi nonetheless grasped the role of universal governor. Unlike Nobunaga in his retreat from absolutism, Hideyoshi had a bolder perception than his predecessor of the uses of central power. He emulated Nobunaga in assuming jurisdiction over matters of public interest: the administration of major cities, religious establishments, and mines. He retained final judicial authority in the state and sole control over foreign affairs. Yet he also used his position more broadly, and more inventively, to eliminate what he perceived as the fundamental causes of disorder in his age. In the process, he initiated a social revolution.

Through edicts nearly unparalleled in ambition and effect, Hideyoshi ordered that farmers and townsmen be disarmed, that soldiers be removed from the village to the castle towns of their daimyo, and that all changes of class and residence be halted. Designed to pacify the countryside and stabilize the federation, these laws established the framework for local government. They had a conservative intent, were compatible with daimyo interests, and were not succeeded by further attempts to alter the administration of the domains. The laws reflected the critical assumption, however, that the leader had the right to dictate the principles of society's organization.

This consciousness of a national role transcending lordship over the daimyo led Hideyoshi to seek the loftiest sanction for his rule. To give moral weight to his authority, he appealed to the throne, the traditional source of legitimacy in Japan. After acquiring the highest offices at court, imperial regent and great minister of state, Hideyoshi arranged the promotion of his confederates to prestigious positions as well. He secured his federation within a system of imperial and customary law to transform wartime alliances into a rationalized political order. The emperor himself awarded Hideyoshi the surname Toyotomi, or Bountiful Minister.[5]

Hideyoshi's association with the throne was unusual in several respects. First, his return to the ancient seat of national jurisdiction was unexpected. Not only had imperial authority become purely symbolic, Nobunaga and his peers had remained distant from a court too closely identified with obsolete forms of rule. They were new men, makers of a new settlement, committed to individual contract as the foundation of legitimate power. Military leaders in previous eras, moreover, had served not as regents or great ministers but as shogun. Bestowed by the emperor, the title was a martial commission that signified practical governing responsibility in the state. Shogun was the logical appointment for Hideyoshi—if he was intent upon court promotion at all—yet he eschewed it.

Hideyoshi's imagination as a lawmaker and his original approach to legitimation are not the sole indications of his understanding of his position. It is difficult to find in Japanese history a more self-conscious, self-promoting ruler, impossible to find a more ambitious one. Hideyoshi's temperance toward the daimyo did not proceed from humility or a distaste for great power. He described himself as a man of destiny whose virtue would "illumine the four seas" and relentlessly converted his letters—whether to family members or foreign leaders—into personal panegyrics.[6] He told one correspondent that his government would "be superior to anything since Yoritomo," the founder of Japan's first military administration in the twelfth century; he announced to the king of the Ryukyus that "even if a land be thousands of miles distant," he would "deeply achieve amity and so build with foreign lands the spirit of the four seas as one family."[7] Having commissioned an adulatory biography, the Tenshō-ki, he went on to commission nō plays that memorialized his achievements. Hideyoshi even acted the lead in those plays during performances for his vassals.

Unbounded assurance brought Hideyoshi astonishing success. It also led him into a vainglorious war with Korea. In the first Japanese adventure abroad, Hideyoshi sent 150,000 troops to take control of the peninsula. "Even China," he was convinced, "will enter my grip."[8] He planned to establish the Japanese emperor in Peking and then to distribute China's land among his daimyo. The venture ended in retreat just before Hideyoshi died. One of his early biographers offered a telling commentary on the affair: "He spread his violence across the seas with a lawless pride. Since he disgraced his high office, divine retribution was very deep."[9]

Divine retribution, if it was that, entailed the collapse of the Toyotomi house. Within a few years of Hideyoshi's death, his young son was overpowered by Tokugawa Ieyasu. The Tokugawa would govern until 1868. Hideyoshi's failure was one of succession, however, not of vision. Unable to transfer power to an able and adult heir, Hideyoshi left to his followers a form of government that endured until the modern era. While his legend makers preserved the story of military conquest and unsurpassed pageantry, the Tokugawa explored the meaning of Hideyoshi's political legacy. His federation is our principal subject: the conquest and conciliation that made it possible, the motives that inspired an extraordinarily powerful man to share authority with his daimyo, and the particular expressions that his federal settlement took.

We shall be concerned as well with the unprepossessing farmer turned conqueror who commanded the allegiance of great daimyo and looked to the emperor for a sacerdotal confirmation of his power. Both a healing minister and a parvenu showman, a temperate lord and an arrogant expansionist, Hideyoshi was a flawed governor as capable of virtue as of vice. His distinction was his ability to transcend himself—his vanity and his taste for unchallenged power—to create a federal model of rule that survived him.

2

A WORLD WITHOUT A CENTER

THE VILLAGE OF Nakamura lies in the rich farming country of south-western Owari in the delta of the Kiso River. Cotton, hemp, and rice were cultivated there during Hideyoshi's day by a comparatively well-off community of peasants, many of whom owned their own land. Hideyoshi's father, Yaemon, was a member of this community. Like some of his neighbors, he put in occasional service to the local warlord, Oda Nobuhide, until a battlefield injury brought him home permanently to Nakamura. He died at a young age in 1543, leaving behind the seven-year-old Hideyoshi and an elder daughter. Within the year, his widow married another farmer in the area, a man called Chikuami, who had once been a servant of Oda Nobuhide. She also bore her second hus-band a son and a daughter.

Assembled in the seventeenth century by genealogists and popular biographers, this account of Hideyoshi's beginnings is unpretentious enough to inspire belief. Some chroniclers accord Yaemon the courtesy of a surname, Kinoshita, which his son began to affect years after he left home. Others attribute to him the position of musket-carrying foot sol-dier under Nobuhide, although firearms were introduced into Japan only around the time of Yaemon's death. Many elevate Chikuami to the position of master of protocol to the Oda. Yet these embellishments are notable in their modesty. Even the spare, apocryphal details offered about Hideyoshi's youth—that he was dispatched for an education to a temple, which he fled for headier exploits, for example—are parts of an adventure story rather than a heroic myth.[1]

The only departure from an otherwise simple childhood legend concerns Hideyoshi's conception. A biographer writing about 1625 provides a typical formulation of the event: "One time his mother dreamed that a ray of the sun graciously entered within her. The child was thus conceived and when he was born they gave him the name Hiyoshimaru (The Bounty of the Sun)."[2] Common to the fables of great men, the story of a miraculous conception would be unremarkable had Hideyoshi not inspired it himself in numerous letters and conversations with foreign visitors: "At the time my mother conceived me, she had an auspicious dream. That night, a ray of the sun filled the room as if it were noontime. All were overcome with astonishment and fright and when the diviners had gathered, they interpreted the event saying: when he reaches the prime of life, his virtue will illumine the four seas, his authority will emanate to the myriad peoples."[3] Never did he mention Yaemon or life in Nakamura. Never, while he sponsored the promotions of his mother and siblings to high places at court, did he recall in public their early struggles. Hideyoshi chose instead to overawe his audience with talk of dreams and thus to transform what was painfully plain about himself. He apparently found no pleasure in contrasting his father's lot with his own.

Although Hideyoshi wrapped his youth in silence, the votive portraits completed just after his death—the first we have of him—hold a rare, though fragile, clue to one of its trials. In these paintings, a heavily robed Hideyoshi sits upon a dais framed by damask curtains. The figure is dignified, its transcendent aspect expressed by the exaggeration of the body in relation to the head. Thin and deeply lined, the face has an ascetic quality that conveys the hauteur of authority. Nonetheless, the Hideyoshi of these sympathetic interpretations is an unexpectedly small and ugly man. The body is squat and emaciated, the eyes are cold, the mouth sour. The portrayal gives substance to Oda Nobunaga's reference to Hideyoshi as a "bald rat" and the epithet used in a piece of contemporary graffiti, "monkey regent." While he was eventually able to distinguish himself with the accoutrements of office, as a young man Hideyoshi may have resembled the person beneath the robes—slight, short, and ill-favored of feature. Denied wealth and pedigree, he seems also to have been denied height, beauty, and a powerful body.[4]

Little else can be said of his youth. We are told that Hideyoshi went to the province of Tōtōmi about 1551 to join Matsushita Yukitsuna, a retainer of Imagawa Yoshimoto. The choice is curious since both Hideyoshi's father and stepfather had served the local Oda. We are also told that he returned to Owari in 1558 to support Oda Nobuhide's son, Nobunaga. Not until the early 1570s, however, does Hideyoshi's career enter the light of history, when his own letters, and references to him in Nobunaga's documents, begin to appear. Hideyoshi's official biography, composed by his secretary, opens with the year 1577. To take the measure of Hideyoshi's challenges, then, we must turn from the thin account of his early life to explore the society he entered and the experiences that shaped it.

The Meanings of Sengoku

Hideyoshi came to maturity during the last half of a period historians call *sengoku*—the era of "the country at war," or, "the warring states." Although "warring states" is something of a misnomer for a civil war fought between the lords of many small domains, it suggests the radical difference of the period from any other in Japan's experience: armed conflict became the essential fact of life and resulted in the complete transfer of power from the central administration to local magnates. Neither military action nor local defiance of the government was new to this age. What was new was the descent into seemingly endless, intractable struggle—for no previous country-wide conflict had lasted much longer than five years—and the collapse of all national institutions. With their collapse came the denial of political assumptions that had shaped Japan's development from the eighth to the fifteenth century.

Yet the *sengoku* era encompassed more than rebellion against a traditional concept of rule. The major achievement of the time was the creation of strong institutions of local government. That achievement was of lasting, transforming significance. The rebellion, as well as the direction it took, was born of contradictions in the old political order.[5]

The Political Order before 1467

During the seventh and eighth centuries, the leading family of Japan converted its loose hegemony over competing clans into a national monarchical rule. Legitimated by claims to divine descent and fortified by an already long history of ascendancy in the Yamato Plain, the family modeled the new regime upon the T'ang dynasty of China. Following continental precedents, this powerful house reconceived its head as a universal king, or emperor, who was to govern all inhabitants of the nation on the basis of civil and penal statutes and through the agency of a large, presumptively well-educated officialdom. Holders of higher office became members of a hereditary, carefully graded aristocracy. The country was divided into provinces, subdivided into districts and villages, where local administrators were empowered to allocate and to tax land in conformity with the civil statutes.

Embedded in Chinese practices, of course, were Chinese principles of government. While many of these principles had negligible influence, four of them took deep root in Japan to remain fundamentally undisturbed until the *sengoku* era: that the entire country composed a political unit with an administrative center; that the emperor was the source of authority who bestowed power through official appointment;

that change was to take place within a structure of law; and that officers of state had the right to distribute the nation's resources.

It is difficult to judge the extent to which the philosophy underlying these principles was ever comprehended or accepted in Japan. Certainly the authors of the early imperial histories and legal formularies knew the vocabulary of continental political thought. They could speak of the emperor as representative of heaven who served as trustee of the public good and preserver of earthly harmony. They could portray the ministers of his court as men who exemplified humanity, wisdom, and decorum and who consequently inspired order in social relationships throughout the land. And they could see in government, its laws and its rituals, man's best effort to reflect the symmetry and sense of the cosmos. Such views may rarely have provided more than a rationalization of power, but they defined one ideal of rule that survived as a point of reference for lawmakers, historians, and reformers.

The counterpoint to these views directed political behavior far more compellingly. In practice, government existed to distribute the resources of land among the social and political elites and their clients. Thus once the unwieldy tax system of the imperial regime failed to exploit those resources sufficiently, state control over property devolved to a new pattern. By about the year 1000, substantial landholdings had become private estates (shōen) that were free from public taxation and the legal jurisdiction of public officials. Formed with the collusion of government ministers by members of the imperial house, the high nobility, and religious establishments, the estates arose within the accommodating bounds of the law. Other lands remained technically within the public sphere, although most were used by provincial governors for gain to themselves and the men at the center who appointed them. In sum, the government presided over the transfer of property control from its own hands to the private household administrations of the individuals who had always been the chief recipients of the nation's revenues.

The central administration survived to confirm and mediate land claims as well as to distribute the promotions that continued to generate income. Many of its functions—taxation, policing, reclamation and public works—were taken over by local landholders, while others atrophied or were simply abandoned. The compilation of imperial histories stopped; the national university became a shelter of seedy and generally uninteresting scholars; embassies to China were discontinued; the great buildings of state fell into disrepair while the mansions of estate proprietors took over the capital's landscape. If Chinese conceptions of government remained an inspiration to some, the primacy of land matters to the elite was indisputable.

* * *

The conversion to private property brought its own problems. Because estate and "public" lands were intermingled throughout the provinces, quarrels over boundaries and jurisdiction were endemic. Absentee administration exacerbated the situation. Both estate proprietors and provincial governors entrusted managerial duties to local representatives who acquired rights to the income produced by the lands they oversaw. Disputes between these parties and between their many heirs, who divided claims to revenue over generations, prompted persistent complaints before imperial ministries and occasional conflict between the militias that had grown up to protect "public" as well as private property. Between 1180 and 1185 litigation succumbed to war as armed contests over land erupted across the nation.

The main beneficiary of this upheaval was Minamoto no Yoritomo, a descendant of collaterals of the imperial family who had established a land base in the eastern provinces of the Kantō. His own vendetta against a rival house in the capital of Kyoto, the Taira, helped precipitate the general disruption of 1180. He used the occasion to declare control of the Kantō, to expand an army of personal supporters looking for land concessions, and to order offensives against the Taira in central and southwestern Japan. After Yoritomo achieved his vengeance in 1185 by destroying the Taira house, the imperial court appealed to him for continuing help in the business of pacification. Yoritomo was later named shogun and was authorized to station deputies throughout the country to recover harmony. The *shugo*, or military governors, acted as policemen at the provincial level; the *jitō*, or land stewards, entered estates and parcels of public land in the same capacity. Yoritomo made his capital in the city of Kamakura.

An abbreviation of *sei-i tai-shōgun* ("great general who subdues the barbarians"), the title of shogun was originally awarded to eighth-century warriors who led campaigns against the still-belligerent descendants of Japan's first inhabitants. It was rarely used thereafter and had long become anachronistic. Nonetheless, it served to absorb Yoritomo into the government's structure and to designate the specifically martial nature of his commission. He was charged—first and last—to hold the peace after widespread disturbance had shown the imperial court unable to maintain stability; his officers were charged to shore up the prevailing landholding system. Thus a military administration employed for surveillance was simply imposed upon the cranky and complex order that had encouraged disorder.

The history of the Kamakura shogunate, which lasted until 1333, is the history of a balancing act. As claimants to a portion of local resources in their capacity as peacekeeping deputies, the early *shugo* and *jitō* shared in a vertical system of income rights to property. On the estate, for example, the *jitō* drew the equivalent of a salary from holdings that also supported the *shōen* proprietor and his representatives. But with time, these fiscal pyramids collapsed. Legal and armed actions resulted in the subdivision of lands between traditional holders and military deputies. By the fourteenth century, these deputies had converted themselves from policemen into a new proprietary class. Further, their holdings tended to increase through purchase, foreclosure on loans, reclamation, or outright confiscation. Thus the heads of the shogunate were engaged in a delicate task: to rationalize the incursions of their own men while attempting to defend the rights of the old elite that had appointed them.

Finally unsuccessful in the task, the shogunate founded by Yoritomo came to an end because of the expanding ambitions of the *jitō* and *shugo* on the one hand, and the discontent of the court on the other. In 1333 the Emperor Go-Daigo attempted to slough off the whole shogunal apparatus and so to return to active, and exclusive, imperial rule. He succeeded in his rebellion with the help of disaffected military deputies, only to be ousted by those deputies. After leading Go-Daigo's final assault upon Kamakura, a warrior named Ashikaga Takauji forced the emperor into exile in 1336. He arranged the succession of the more placable heir apparent to the throne and received his own shogunal appointment from the new monarch in 1338.

Although they pressed rebellion at the highest echelons of power, the Ashikaga had a small land base and few personal ties to *jitō* and *shugo* from the previous regime who had become military proprietors. Their principal challenge was to exert control over these men. In the sternest administrative reform since the years of the early imperial state, they attempted to do so by manipulating the *shugo*—some of whom survived from the preceding shogunate, some of whom were newly appointed from the Ashikaga ranks. In theory, *shugo* prerogatives were greatly expanded; they took over civil as well as military powers in the provinces and were gradually vested with the right to appoint their own *jitō*, to assume judicial responsibility at the provincial level, and to tax most categories of land. In practice, *shugo* power was constrained by complex landholding arrangements and by shogunal policy toward them.

The provinces the *shugo* governed were patchworks of many individual properties: the surviving estates of aristocrats and religious proprietors that were, at least in law, protected against entry by military officials; the numerous proprietorships formed by military men before the consolidation of Ashikaga authority; and some tracts of "public" land appropriated after Go-Daigo's exile. Although such diversity was an impediment to provincial rule, the *shugo* could win the allegiance of proprietors by confirming their rights in judicial decisions or exempting them from taxation. He could also develop a cadre of close retainers through the shrewd distribution of public land and certain tax rights. He was able, as well, to coerce absentee proprietors into awarding tax contracts to his men. In these ways the military governors of the Ashikaga could use their legal authority to integrate individual provincial landholders into an orderly political community. This was the goal of the shogun who appointed them, and it also stirred their gravest fears.

If strong *shugo* could subordinate local proprietors, they could just as well use provincial bases to resist the comparatively weak shogun. Hence after enhancing the power of the *shugo*, the Ashikaga resolved to contain their unseemly growth. They did this, ironically, by overextending them. Most *shugo* were appointed to several, noncontiguous provinces where they had few family members or current proprietary interests. Some of the more threatening were transferred from time to time. Many were expected to keep residences in the Ashikaga capital of Kyoto and to remain there for long periods, away from their provinces. A number, in addition to their provincial assignments, were elevated to national office. Lest such diversion of responsibility fail to confuse the *shugo*, the shogun engaged in occasional acts of sabotage: the encouragement of local resistance to the *shugo* or the passage of succession rights to an unpopular heir. But by dividing the interests of the *shugo*, the Ashikaga necessitated the widespread delegation of authority to lower-ranking deputies and the consequent maturation of the very local powers whom the *shugo* were meant to constrain. The shogun provided the *shugo* with the opportunity to rule their provinces well and then undercut them. After 1467, rebellion by the deputies of these military governors opened the period of warring states.

In a sense, the introduction of administration by the military was a turning point in Japanese history. The creation of the Kamakura and Ashikaga shogunates made military men a fixture of government and an increasingly dominant part of the proprietary class. It is also true that the shogunates transcended their police functions to assume most prerogatives of national rule. The Ashikaga built upon the legacy of their Kamakura predecessors to take control of foreign relations, to confirm and mediate land claims, and to assume tax rights. While the once illustrious ministries of the imperial state went into eclipse, a shogunal bureaucracy of archivists, secretaries, judicial assistants, finance officers, and supervisors of appointments grew apace.

Yet the similarities between the imperial and shogunal governments remain most striking. Both served to confirm rights to land that were exercised in a private fashion. Aristocrats had used the ministries of state to legalize the commendations, reclamations, and confiscations that shifted control of property into their household administrations. Similarly, military deputies used the organs of the shogunates first to convert the perquisites of office into hereditary, proprietary privileges and then to expand their land bases in ways already blazed by their courtly predecessors. Continuity existed on a deeper level as well, for the heads of the shogunates adhered to the principles of rule associated with the imperial state: that the emperor was head of a united country ruled by law under a central administration, whose resources were under the control of official appointees. There were assaults upon these principles, to be sure, but until 1467 the center held.

Although the two shogunates came to power after periods of war and grew in influence despite the sometimes fierce opposition of the imperial court, they became an extension of the old regime. Shogunal officials received their commissions from the throne, melded with the aristocracy through marriage and receipt of rank and title, and increasingly assumed the deportment and culture of the court. They guaranteed the emperor's revenues, underwrote the ceremonies of state, and kept the palace in repair. They chose to represent themselves, and were viewed by historians and legal scholars, as loyal deputies of an imperial government that could not maintain order without them.

As the extension, or military counterpart, to the old regime, the shogunates also inherited the jurisdiction of the imperial state. *Shugo* and *jitō* moved through the provinces in an official capacity. And as the police function of the shogunates came to be identified with rights of arbitration, their boards of inquiry became the seats of national justice. To a surprising degree, these boards remained faithful to their original charge to protect religious and noble landholders. If estates were seriously reduced over time, their survival was the result of the vigilance of shogunal judges who limited the inroads of military deputies. The rule of law meant, too, a regard for precedent and a dependence upon documentation and formal litigation in the resolution of land quarrels. So deep was the tradition of legal settlement established by the imperial state that not only did shogunal courts adhere to procedure, those courts were routinely invoked by complainants.

Government and its courts survived, beyond doubt, because they were successful in distributing the resources of land to the powerful—first to the nobility and later to the military deputies of the shogunates. These shogunates were particularly adroit in absorbing armed, often self-proclaimed proprietors into officialdom and thus justifying their land claims. They also made law sufficiently flexible to condone what could only be regarded as land thefts. The history of the military regimes can be read, therefore, as a response to the needs of armed proprietors who used government for their own purposes. Yet the response was agile enough to protect the assumption that land and its resources remained within the purview of a national administration, to be allocated as perquisites of office or as the result of appeals defensible in law.

Some of the more luminous figures in the shogunal administrations, like some of the ministers of the imperial state, transcended a preoccupation with land matters to conceive of government in broader terms. They composed legal formularies and painstakingly codified the rulings of their courts. They attempted to establish national tax systems to rationalize the claims of their officials. They began to regulate commerce, to conduct an orderly foreign trade, to bureaucratize government, to delineate the legal rights of their agents. On occasion, they commissioned official histories, opened institutions of higher learning, and studied Chinese philosophy. In general, they patronized the arts and the church and carried themselves like gentlemen.

But renewed attempts at systematic governance, or even the periodic reaffirmation of a political morality, never broke—and were not intended to break—the pattern of private control of land. Rather, they highlighted the disparate, tenuously reconciled attitudes toward rule that emerged from a combination of Chinese administrative principles and a native presumption that the authorities existed to allocate property. From the eighth until the fifteenth century, rulers saw government both as a national trust and as the guarantor of personal, hereditary privilege; they perceived themselves as public governors confirmed by law, as well as representatives of the family members and clients who supported their legal claims to power; they believed in the exercise of that power through courts and formal appointees, while using judicial decisions and nominations to office to spread networks of patronage; they governed by statute yet found their formularies ever susceptible to reinterpretation. Such dichotomous approaches to rule, though hardly unique to Japan, persisted so long and so intensively there as to provide a frame of analysis for most political developments before 1467.

War and Its Tidings

In 1467, a quarrel over succession in the Ashikaga house, fueled by similar quarrels in two major *shugo* houses, deeply divided shogunal officials. Tens of thousands of soldiers recruited by *shugo* across Japan gathered in the streets of Kyoto to support rival factions. Fighting finally dissipated there ten years later, leaving the capital in ruins, the ninth Ashikaga shogun uneasily installed in office, and much of the nation in rebellion. Military proprietors abjured the authority of the shogunate in order to declare autonomous control over their holdings and to expand their dominion to neighboring areas.

This widespread rebellion of military men had been prefigured in regional uprisings earlier in the century, in attempts by shogunal officials in the Kantō to separate themselves from Kyoto, and in the military's antipathy toward some Ashikaga leaders that led to the murder of the sixth shogun in 1441. The rebellion was given license, however, by the long and bitter succession quarrels that testified to profound rifts within the governing class and a common willingness to revert to armed confrontation. The specter of the Ashikaga and the *shugo* at war with one another for a decade in the Capital of Peace and Tranquillity (Heian-kyō) established lawlessness as the norm.

In the early decades after 1467, the illusion of political continuity was sustained by the survival of the shogun and some of his *shugo*. The local contests between neighboring proprietors that characterized the first stages of civil war could be perceived by men of the day as passing disturbances that would effect a new balance of power. Yet by the time Hideyoshi left home to seek his fortune in the 1550s, all the commonplaces of an earlier day had been discarded: the emperor and his shogunal surrogates had been denied practical authority over the nation; the state was atomized by competing warlords who created their own autonomous domains; land was distributed by local powers in exchange for military service; and law was rewritten by individual lords to declare their primacy and the eclipse of higher tribunals.

In effect, the principles that had undergirded government until 1467 were repudiated as the dichotomy between official, centralized authority over land resources and private management was shattered. Private management of land was the sole certainty by 1550. Accompanying this change was the rise of two assumptions of rule that, though not new to the sixteenth century, had never before been confronted so clearly or to the exclusion of loftier views: that power over land devolved upon those able to muster and control military force, and that the control of military force depended upon stern and independent administration of the lands a lord could take.

We shall look at *sengoku* society from the perspective of the 1550s and in terms of developments at four levels of political power: the court, the shogunate, the village, and the domain. The history of the court and the shogunate is an unhappy one, that of the village and the domain one of critical change.

The Court

Two men succeeded to imperial power during the first half of the *sengoku* era: Go-Kashiwabara in 1500 and his son, Go-Nara, in 1526. Go-Kashiwabara waited twenty-one years before funds could be found to mount his modest enthronement ceremonies in 1521; Go-Nara waited ten years, until 1536, for his enthronement. In both cases, financial assistance came from distant warlords and religious establishments distressed over the embarrassment of the court.[6] Such help was rare, however, and most ceremonies of state—the induction of a crown prince, the retirement of an emperor, New Year's assemblies, and even court burials—were abandoned or stripped of all pomp. Observers found the palace wall "overgrown with briars" and its buildings "indistinguishable from common lodgings in the neighborhood."[7] Imperial poverty was conspicuous enough to give weight to stories that the emperors were reduced to selling their calligraphy.

Records of the court treasurer reveal the problem starkly. Recipient of income from as many as 250 landholdings during the peak of Ashikaga power, the court sporadically collected offerings from no more than 34 holdings in the era of warring states.[8] This decrease indicates both the extent of *sengoku* upheaval and the dependence of the throne on the shogun. They had secured imperial revenues and sustained the dignity of the court for the sake of their own legitimacy. While the nobility lost most of its influence, the pageantry of court remained a symbol of political decorum and the rectitude of the shogun who supported it. Once the shogunate was assailed, the court floundered badly.

Some aristocrats—among them Ichijō Kanera and Kujō Masamoto—left the capital to try to recover their estates or to lecture military men on the literary classics for small stipends. Those who remained in war-torn Kyoto entered more freely into commoner society. They shared in the festivals of the townspeople, invited merchants to their residences for amateur nō recitals and communal dancing (*furyū*), haggled occasionally with tradesmen, and more actively supervised their financial interests in the city—mainly the toll barriers at Kyoto's entrances. Now dependent upon the capital's citizens for diversion, defense, and sustenance, courtiers mingled with commoners to produce an agreeable mix of cultures.[9] The result was new painting idioms and new poetic and theatrical styles. Similarly, the flight of nobles to the countryside disseminated courtly values to the lower ranks of the military. These were salutary developments, to be sure, but the cloud-dwellers had been shaken from their clouds.

The Shogunate

One ceremonial function carried on by the imperial house was the induction of successive shogun from the Ashikaga family. Between the outbreak of war in 1467 and the mid-sixteenth century, five of them assumed office, thus preserving the fiction of Ashikaga ascendancy in the state. A bare outline of their careers, however, illustrates the confusion in Kyoto.

Still a young child, Ashikaga Yoshihisa became the ninth shogun in 1473 when his supporters prevailed in the war of succession raging in Kyoto's streets. He died in 1490, during a campaign against the Rokkaku house of Ōmi province. That campaign had begun after the Rokkaku head, a *shugo*, denied Ashikaga jurisdiction in his territory and confiscated local estates.

Ashikaga Yoshitane, tenth shogun and the uncle of his predecessor, was unseated from office and exiled in 1493. His nemesis was Hosokawa Masamoto, descendant of a *shugo* family whose members had often acted as *kanrei*, chief administrative officers of the shogunate. Intending to use the position of *kanrei* to establish his own hegemony, Masamoto replaced the tenth shogun with Ashikaga Yoshizumi, a cousin who was fourteen years old.

Yoshizumi, the eleventh shogun, was little more than a puppet until his ouster in 1508. The head of the Ōuchi house, a *shugo*, conspired with one of Hosokawa Masamoto's sons to return Ashikaga Yoshitane to office. They removed the eleventh shogun from the capital and presided over the reappointment of the tenth.

Already victim of a coup, Ashikaga Yoshitane fled the capital again after Hosokawa Masamoto's son, Takakuni, became *kanrei* and attempted to deny the shogun all power. Yoshitane died in exile on the island of Awaji.

Ashikaga Yoshiharu succeeded as twelfth shogun in 1521, at the age of ten. He was, to use the word now inevitable in Japanese histories, Takakuni's "robot." And he too abandoned Kyoto to escape Hosokawa domination. He died in Ōmi.

Ashikaga Yoshiteru, ten-year-old son of Yoshiharu, was inducted as thirteenth shogun in 1546. He was not long under Hosokawa influence, however, because in 1549 that family succumbed to its vassals, the Miyoshi. The Miyoshi simply replaced the Hosokawa in Kyoto and, when the thirteenth shogun attempted to declare his autonomy in 1565, saw him murdered by their agent, Matsunaga Hisahide.

Three of the *sengoku* period shogun whom we have seen thus far were exiled, one died in battle, and one was assassinated. Four succeeded as children, preferred to other heirs precisely because of their age, and all but the first were figureheads for their deputies.[10] But what of these deputies? By manipulating the Ashikaga, did they acquire significant influence over national affairs?

The consuming problem facing the Hosokawa was survival itself. Hosokawa Masamoto, who brought the eleventh shogun to office in 1493, was assassinated by the first of his three adopted sons in 1507. That son was promptly destroyed by the second of Masamoto's adopted children. And he, in turn, was eliminated by the third, Hosokawa Takakuni. Takakuni lived to install Ashikaga Yoshitane, and later Ashikaga Yoshiharu, as shogun, but remained preoccupied with familial assaults. One of his nephews raised an army of redress against Takakuni, occupied the capital on at least two occasions, and compelled the beleaguered *kanrei* to spend much of his time outside Kyoto looking for military assistance. Takakuni took his own life in 1531 after a decisive defeat in Amagasaki.

Takakuni's triumphant nephew, Hosokawa Harumoto, faced continuing challenges from his elder brother and from Miyoshi Motonaga, the deputy administrator (*shugo-dai*) of some of the holdings the Hosokawa retained as *shugo*. After mustering a vast army of Buddhist sectarians, Harumoto ensnared Miyoshi Motonaga and went on to govern as *kanrei*. Yet his tenure was interrupted by religious uprisings in the capital, by new family quarrels, and by the loss of provincial holdings to the Miyoshi. In 1549 Motonaga's son, Miyoshi Nagayoshi, drove Harumoto out of the capital for good. He died in a monastery in Settsu.

The Miyoshi dominated Kyoto until 1565, when they were expelled by rebel members of their own house under the leadership of a former vassal, Matsunaga Hisahide. The intervening decades saw attacks from rival warlords throughout the capital area.[11]

These infamous battles for control of the shogunate drained the resources of all concerned, even as they depleted whatever reserves of national influence the institution still held. What, then, were the prizes the Hosokawa and Miyoshi sought so single-mindedly? The material rewards were potentially great. We do not know enough about Ashikaga landholdings and tax revenue from their *shugo* before the war to gauge the income recoverable by their *kanrei* surrogates from these sources. We do know that the Ashikaga profited from trade with China, from fees and forced loans exacted from religious establishments and moneylenders, from guild dues, and from land taxes in the capital and its environs. Although the monopolization of foreign trade by pirates and members of the Ōuchi family cut off that channel of revenue after

1500, the other income remained available to strong administrators of Kyoto.

In fact, the Hosokawa and Miyoshi succeeded in holding the city. Periodic uprisings by peasants demanding cancellation of their debts to moneylenders, battles between religious sectarians, and tax delinquency by the townspeople never broke the shogunate's grip on Kyoto. The *kanrei* collected house and commissariat taxes, enlisted corvée labor, exacted bribes from the commercial elite, and took guild dues. They survived, too, as the effective governors of the capital—policing toll barriers, adjudicating cases brought by commoners, nobles, and religious communities, confirming land sales, issuing city regulations. Their power in Kyoto was the only firm foundation of their claims to wider rule.[12]

The point becomes clear once we assess the fate of the *shugo* in the era of warring states. As the principal agents of the Ashikaga, the *shugo* embodied the authority of the shogunate throughout the provinces of Japan and, in their obedience to the shogun, sustained the principle of national union. Yet warfare destroyed the majority of *shugo* and provoked the remainder to disobedience. The rebellion of and against these military governors defines the meaning of *sengoku.*

Because many *shugo* had appointments to several provinces, there were only twenty-five to thirty of them when war began. All but about twelve fell in the first decades of fighting, most very quickly. The spectacular collapses involved families such as the Shiba, Hatakeyama, and Yamana that had served the shogunate in its highest administrative posts and controlled four or more provinces each. The Shiba, for example, had governed Wakasa, Echizen, Tōtōmi, and Owari; its heads acted as *kanrei* seven times. But one of the quarrels over succession that precipitated the hostilities of 1467 occurred in this house, unleashing opposing factions throughout the family's holdings. Oda Nobunaga's forebears, deputy administrators (*shugo-dai*) of Owari, began to take over that province after the battles of succession in Kyoto consumed the Shiba lords.[13]

The shogun's deliberate distraction and overextension of the *shugo* made many such defeats inevitable, once military power became the critical element in holding territory. Without conscription systems or firm control of local military proprietors, the *shugo* relied upon the dignity of their office, the support of personal deputies (including the errant *shugo-dai*), and noncontractual bonds to those proprietors whom they favored in judicial and tax matters. When the remoteness of the *shugo* precluded contact with local powers, and when general lawlessness opened opportunities for aggrandizement, little was left to secure their authority.[14]

Most *shugo* who survived into the *sengoku* era had escaped the constraints that enfeebled their peers: they held single or adjacent provinces, had seldom been transferred, and were both distant from Kyoto and free of obligations there. Thus they were able to use the powers of *shugo* appointment to unite their provinces. These cases, which we shall examine later, illustrate the soundness of the original Ashikaga conception of the *shugo*. Left unhampered by the shogunate, they achieved the political integration of their territories desired, but feared, by the Ashikaga.

Their loyalty to Kyoto after 1467, however, steadily dissipated. As we have seen, the Rokkaku confiscated the estates of Ōmi, and the Ōuchi initiated a coup against the eleventh shogun. These houses and three other *shugo* families of the warring-states period wrote law codes that supplanted shogunal statutes in their properties. All of the surviving *shugo*, further, fought with one another to expand their own independent jurisdiction. Although some *shugo* houses remained in power, they offered no practical support for Ashikaga pretensions to authority in the provinces.

Persistent demonstrations of their independence were offset by one sign of homage to the shogunate: warriors in as many as forty provinces requested appointment as *shugo* after 1500. Some of these men came from old *shugo* families that were defeated in war but clung to the symbols of power. Many were the still-strong survivors of *shugo* houses who claimed their ancestral honors despite newly professed autonomy. Others were upstarts who sought to rationalize their conquests with a suitable title.[15]

The continuing desirability of *shugo* appointment reflects both the concern of local lords with legitimacy and their assumption that the shogunate remained the source of military authority. In the midst of chaos, the shogunate was a symbol of continuity and national cohesion. And in the absence of an alternative model of rule, most *sengoku* leaders presumed that pacification would finally take place under its aegis. Shogunal government was over three hundred years old and had a distinguished history. Thus pursuit of the *shugo* title, however perfunctory, united several generations of warriors to the only institution likely to integrate the warring states again.

The Hosokawa and the Miyoshi, as well as the shogun who submitted to their manipulation, aspired to far more than control over Kyoto and its resources. Sustained by the memory of great power and encouraged by appeals from warlords for official titles, each envisioned

the restoration of the shogunate. This was the goal that moved the Hosokawa and the Miyoshi to such brutal confrontations with each other.
Indeed, the final phase of the movement to unify the country under one
leader would begin under shogunal auspices. Yet *sengoku* politics were
relentlessly changing the conditions that might make a restoration of
the shogunate, at least in familiar terms, possible.

The Village

For most Japanese in the mid-sixteenth century, there were two, and
only two, poles of power: the village and the larger wartime domain
into which it was integrated. Numbering in the thousands, villages varied in size from several to several score households and served as the
basic units of communal and political association. Village members
shared labor, religious and festive rites, water, and commons. They
generally created formal and less formal governing bodies, often village
councils, to regulate affairs such as public works and the control of access to common resources, adjudication and punishment of miscreants,
tax collection, and representation of the group to proprietors. Such
self-regulation was widespread in the fifteenth century, common in the
sixteenth.[16]

Before the war, villagers paid basic land taxes to a proprietor
whose claims were confirmed by the shogunate—a nobleman or a religious institution, a representative of the province's *shugo*, or a military
man descended from the class of estate managers and *jitō* who had established their dominion through force or legal appeal. The task for
would-be powers in the *sengoku* era was to retain or seize proprietary
rights to villages, the essential source of manpower and revenue, and to
forge these units into a defensible domain.

Although villages were very different in size, organization, and
vulnerability to a warlord's takeover, many shared two characteristics
that help explain their development in the *sengoku* period: economic
stratification and the presence of armed members. One such agrarian
community of the early warring-states era, Kamikuze-no-shō, illustrates these features and provides a basis for discussion of the domain.
An estate controlled by a temple, this community was somewhat unusual. Good documentation of early military proprietorships is rare,
however, and except for its link to a religious institution this example
conforms to much of what we know about others of the time.

Kamikuze-no-shō was an estate in Yamashiro province held by
Tōji temple.[17] A land register of 1507 lists 76 individuals responsible
for working 70.9.180 *chō* of arable land. (One *chō* = 10 *tan* = 3,600 *bu*;
70.9.180 *chō* = 70 *chō*, 9 *tan*, 180 *bu*. One *chō* = approximately 2.45 acres.)
As proprietor (*ryōshu*) of the estate, Tōji levied annual taxes on all regis-

tered property. Additional rights to land and income were of two basic types, de facto ownership rights (myōshu-shiki) and cultivation rights (saku-shiki). Owners paid taxes only to Tōji; cultivators rented land from owners and paid taxes to Tōji as well as rents to the owners of the fields they worked. Both ownership and cultivation rights could be sold, leased, or divided.

Roughly 37 percent of the land of Kamikuze was owned by village residents, the remainder directly by Tōji. Like many aggressive proprietors, Tōji had been tightening its grip on holdings by consolidating ryōshu and myōshu tenures. In addition to proprietary taxes imposed upon all Kamikuze land, then, the temple was collecting rents on the 63 percent of the property it owned and released to tenant cultivators. Although myōshu-shiki were often bought or acquired through foreclosure on loans and tax debts, confiscation occurred as well. In the sengoku era, such rights tended to concentrate in the hands of the few—large and successful village holders and absentee proprietors like Tōji. Thus cultivation rights were often residual claims, retained by agreement when a former owner was forced to yield his privileges to another myōshu.

Of the seventy-six individuals who appear in the 1507 registry of Kamikuze-no-shō, four held ownership rights to all fields listed under their names; fifty held only cultivation rights to fields owned by Tōji; and twenty-two held ownership rights to some fields and cultivation rights granted by Tōji to others. More important to a discussion of economic cleavage are the differences in the sizes of their holdings. Fourteen registrants held rights to land totaling more than one chō each. As a nuclear family could farm no more than one chō, larger holders were releasing surplus fields to others. In the home provinces about the capital, where Kamikuze was located, these subordinate cultivators tended to be tenants with simple financial obligations to their landlords. In the eastern provinces, they tended to be real or fictive relations with the status of servants.

Virtually all of the fourteen larger holders in Kamikuze combined a variety of land rights to make up their substantial portfolios. A certain Tarōzaemon, for example, held ownership rights to 1.2.240 chō of land, and cultivation rights procured from Tōji to another 2.6.300 chō of land. Hence this man and others like him were not only renting out the land they owned, but were renting out their cultivation rights (already subordinate tenures) as well. The Kamikuze register does not describe the manner in which the ownership and cultivation rights retained by larger holders were subdivided. It is likely, though, that their surplus fields went to those of the sixty-two smaller holders who lived near the subsistence level. Such holders, formally registered as renters of Tōji's plots, consequently became tenants of village landlords too.

In sum, the size and status of Kamikuze holdings varied considerably; the linkages between proprietor and farmers, and between farmers themselves, were complex. Fourteen men combined ownership and cultivation rights to become larger holders and landlords. Some of the remainder owned small plots, but all depended primarily upon fields from Tōji or from local landlords with ownership and cultivation rights too great for independent farming.

The cleavages between Kamikuze residents were not purely economic. Twenty-five of the registrants received the designation *kata* after their names, a term of respect indicating some military function. Mainly from the group of larger or self-sufficient holders, these men were part of that colorful and dangerous population of *sengoku* fighters known as *jizamurai*, the soldiers of the land.[18] Armed cultivators capable of acting on behalf of their proprietors, their villages, or themselves, they were the critical variable in the fate of agrarian communities. When allied to their proprietor, they secured his control over village resources. When united in opposition to proprietary impositions, they invited military conflict, the intervention of an outside warlord, or an attempt at village autonomy. Because many *jizamurai* monopolized military, economic, and political power in their villages, they were bound to communal interests but also vulnerable to the inducements of higher powers who could guarantee their privileges.

Despite the diversity of village responses to the *sengoku* situation, two patterns of behavior stand out. On one hand, villagers often made common cause against their proprietors to demand tax relief (particularly in times of natural disaster), independent control of water and forest resources, police rights, and the power to discipline thieves, arsonists, and petty criminals. The frequency of formal petitions, tax withholding, and armed insurrection has led some historians to emphasize the solidarity of the village against outside authorities. On the other hand, cleavages within the village provoked internal disputes and appeals for mediation by the proprietor, the affiliation of larger holders with those proprietors who could protect the holders' land and improve their status, and the toleration by such larger holders of confiscatory tax rates on their less fortunate neighbors. The ease with which certain proprietors used economic and social differences within the village to co-opt its elite moves another group of historians to emphasize the conflict of interest in *sengoku* villages. They note that absconding by peasants—not organized action—was the leading form of protest in this era, signifying splits within the group that made communal support of an individual grievant unlikely.[19]

As the Kamikuze-no-shō case suggests, villages had the potential for unified resistance to, as well as subversion by, a proprietor. Tōji's concentration of *ryōshu* and *myōshu* rights over land and the meagerness of many holdings was surely a provocation to protest, particularly when there were so many armed *kata* on the estate. Yet these prosperous *kata* had much to lose from radical change.

There is little incongruity, however, between the two patterns of village behavior we have mentioned. Collective action when there was a union of interest—over the necessity of water control, for example—hardly precluded internecine struggles over rents and subsequent appeals to a proprietor. Successful daimyo contrived to manipulate the latter development.

The Daimyo and Their Domains

When Hideyoshi came of age during the 1550s, there were roughly 120 domains in Japan.[20] About fifteen extended to a province or more, but most were a fraction of that size. All were controlled by daimyo lords who had absorbed numerous villages and their proprietors into a new political constellation centered upon themselves. A small minority of these mid-century daimyo, about twelve men, were survivors of *shugo* households. While some had lost territory during the decades of war, five had expanded their traditional *shugo* bases to number among the most formidable powers in the country. More important, their histories, experience, and rapid adjustments to the changes taking place made them the ablest governors in the daimyo group. Their administrations became models for their peers. Hideyoshi's first lord, Imagawa Yoshimoto, was a member of this extraordinary *shugo* fraternity.[21]

The overwhelming majority of the daimyo came from that class of *shugo* deputies and local military proprietors whom historians call *kokujin*—men of the province.[22] Unlike armed cultivators, the *jizamurai* or "soldiers of the land," *kokujin* were proprietors with tax rights to part of a village, an entire village, or a group of villages. Some banded into leagues whose leaders emerged as daimyo. Others built slowly from their bases, destroying weaker peers to form sizable domains. Often the most powerful *kokujin* were *shugo* deputies who parlayed their official rights—proprietorship over once "public" land, tax contracts with manorial holders, and the privilege of levying special house and land dues—into independent lordship. Like the Miyoshi and the Oda, they supplanted the *shugo* to take their own places as daimyo. So dramatic was the rise of these *kokujin*, and so colorful are their individual stories, that they have given a name to their age: *gekokujō jidai*, the period of "mastery of the high by the low." Hideyoshi's second lord, Oda Nobunaga, was the most brilliant of these new men.

Both the *shugo* and the *kokujin* who became warring-states daimyo met the same basic challenge: to subordinate villages and their armed cultivators, as well as local military proprietors with rights to those villages, to their own control. The Oda did this through battle, the Imagawa through their courts of law.

In 1554 Imagawa Yoshimoto was thirty-five and at the height of his power. Lord of the two provinces of Suruga and Tōtōmi (map 1), he had also extended his influence into Mikawa as a result of his alliance with the Matsudaira family. Two peace treaties, completed just that year, secured his eastern flank from attack by the Hōjō and the Takeda, large daimyo houses that had regularly assailed the Imagawa boundaries. Yoshimoto used the lull in fighting to initiate a new series of cadastral surveys (twenty-five would occur before 1560), to improve production at the silver mines of Suruga, and to circulate twenty-one regulations supplementing the domainal code. A cultivated man who reputedly perfumed his hair and blackened his teeth in the style of a courtier, he also established a printing press and made his headquarters in Sumpu the most refined city east of Kyoto. There he oversaw the completion of a history, in five volumes, of Imagawa rule.[23]

Imagawa strength in the mid-sixteenth century was the legacy of two groups of household heads, those who had developed the family's power under the Ashikaga shogunate and those who expanded it in the sengoku period. Collaterals of the Ashikaga, Imagawa leaders served continuously as shugo of Suruga after 1337. Some division of responsibility occurred in the fourteenth century—one member represented the Ashikaga in Kyushu, three superintended the shogunate's board of retainers, and several became shugo of neighboring Tōtōmi. As part of the shogunate's vanguard in the east, however, the Imagawa remained at home after 1400 to raise troops for disciplinary maneuvers against the Kamakura kubō, an Ashikaga scion stationed in the Kantō who periodically challenged Kyoto's dominion. Thus military preparedness, a history of continual rule in a single province, and distance from the intrigue of the capital laid the basis for a strong administration.[24]

The prewar shugo of the Imagawa house consolidated power in Suruga by exercising judicial responsibility in the province and by levying taxes (land taxes, or tansen; house taxes, or munebechisen; and commissariat taxes, or hyōrōmai). Because there were very few estates in Suruga (we know of only five), and because the Imagawa confiscated property once held by Emperor Go-Daigo's supporters, the land available for allocation to family agents was relatively plentiful. Such agents could be supported in judicial decisions involving tax and rent claims, property transfers, defaults on loans, and the assignment of cultivation privileges. Further, they could be assigned a portion of the general tax

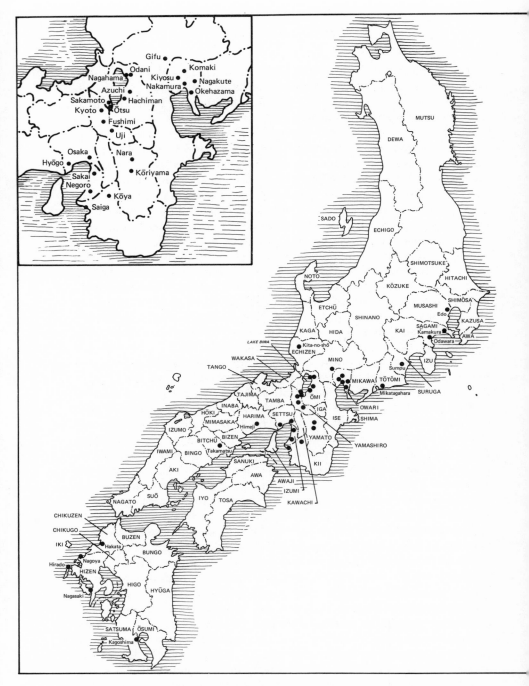

Map 1.   The provinces of Japan and sites associated with Hideyoshi; inset: the provinces surrounding Kyoto

revenue due the Imagawa.[25] Traditional *shugo* rights, particularly judicial rights, provided the basis of Imagawa power in the age of warring states.

The basic story of Imagawa rule in the *sengoku* era is revealed in documents concerning their registration of land.[26] Although the cadastres themselves are not extant, documents that refer to official inspections (*kenchi, aratame*), and to tax increases resulting from those inspections (*zōbun*), indicate that the Imagawa conducted at least sixty-six surveys of village property between 1520 and 1569. The surveys probably began earlier and were more frequent than the documents, assembled from many incomplete archives, suggest. Most inspections were small in scale and repeated examination of a single area was commonplace. They occurred both in Suruga and in neighboring Tōtōmi, a province once governed by the Imagawa but held by the Shiba for most of the fifteenth century. Upon the fall of the Shiba after 1467, the Imagawa recovered Tōtōmi—probably through confirmation of local *kokujin* rights and limited military action. The process of expansion is unclear. As governors of the only large and stable province abutting Tōtōmi, the Imagawa retained obvious advantages over native warriors who had neither formed a viable league to secure their independence nor identified a new leader outside the Shiba house.

The interesting fact about the Imagawa surveys is that at least 30 percent of them appear to have been responses to lawsuits submitted to their courts. That is, they originated in legal actions brought to the Imagawa in their traditional role as *shugo* judges.[27] Of the twenty-two documented appeals for justice that provoked land surveys, as many as seventeen were initiated by cultivators. Up to fourteen of these appeals concerned protests of increases in taxes and rents.

Given entry into the village as mediators, the Imagawa surveyed its land and tax obligations in preparation for a judgment. To a great extent, they ruled in behalf of the proprietary class. Although a few cases resulted in the award of new fiefs or other concessions to the complainants, almost all of the judgments confirmed the tax and rent increases of proprietors. This pattern of support for proprietors contributes to the conclusion that the Imagawa bound *kokujin* to themselves by guaranteeing their land and tax claims in courts of justice. The first article of the Imagawa domainal code of 1526, although it protects cultivators in some cases, provides additional evidence that certain impositions by proprietors were sanctioned by the daimyo. "The seizure without cause by the *jitō* [military proprietors or *kokujin*] of fields held for generations by a peasant family is forbidden. But when taxes and the like have not been paid, [confiscation] cannot be avoided."[28] The article prohibits arbitrary seizures and goes on to condemn conspiracy to steal, yet it also upholds the right of proprietors to raise imposts, puts the burden of resolving tax problems on the cultivator, and permits confiscation if the proprietor is dissatisfied.

The use of land surveys by the Imagawa to bind armed cultivators to themselves is revealed in the treatment of *zōbun*. *Zōbun* was an addition to the proprietary tax rolls that resulted from the inspections of villages and the subsequent recalculation of their official dues. In documents concerning thirteen of the sixty-six registrations, specific differences between the original tax owed to the proprietor and the new increments are mentioned. Increases vary between 20 and 400 percent of the original assessment.[29] Although some increases reflect the detection of reclaimed land or more productive arable, scholars conclude that most resulted from registration of the rents paid to peasant landlords that were previously excluded from proprietary tax rolls. In effect, the Imagawa appear to have used their surveys to establish proprietary rights to the incomes larger holders received from their tenants. Evidence from the Hōjō and Takeda domains indicates a broad trend toward confiscation by the daimyo of rents due peasant landlords.[30]

In some cases, the *zōbun* was seized by the Imagawa and their proprietors. In others, it was first registered as proprietary income and then reassigned as official investitures to men in the village. The enfeoffments we noted earlier in discussing Imagawa judicial actions were of this type. In their turn, these grants brought responsibilities, primarily military service. The registration and reassignment of *zōbun* occasioned more than formal change, despite the fact that the very landlords who lost their rents were frequently the recipients of the new investitures. From the perspective of the grantee, the change brought the forfeiture of some income and the imposition of official tasks. But it also brought security of tenure and an improvement in status. From the perspective of the Imagawa, the change brought new access to revenue and authority over grantees, generally armed cultivators, who posed a grave local challenge to their ascendancy.[31]

A cadastre remaining from the Takeda house of Kai, another *shugo* family that grew in power in the *sengoku* period, offers the clearest illustration of the relationship between land registration and conscription in the domain. Seventy-nine of the 108 registrants, described as cultivators (*sō-byakushō*), held lands with a tax assessment of 134,302 *kammon* (one *mon* = one copper coin; one *kan* = 1,000 *mon*). Forty-five percent of this total tax was excused for communal expenses. Seventeen registrants, described as military taxpayers (*gun'yakushu*), held lands with a tax assessment of 60,465 *kammon*, of which 60 percent was excused. Twelve registrants, described as stipendiaries (*go-onkyū*), held lands with a tax assessment of 79,789 *kammon*, all of which was excused.[32]

There is a simple correlation here between the value of holdings and the status of their holders: the tax value of the average stipendiary's land was almost four times that of the average cultivator's. Further, the stipendiary paid none of his tax, the cultivator most of his. Exemptions were systematically granted to larger holders in exchange for military service—part-time in the case of the seventeen *gun'yakushu*, regular in the case of the twelve *go-onkyū*. This cadastral survey linked absolutely the size and tax liability of lands to the martial obligations of the men who held them.

Because it is scant, the evidence linking control of *kokujin* and *jiza-murai* in the Imagawa and Takeda domains to land surveys is suggestive rather than conclusive. Why did armed men submit to judicial intervention and official registration of their lands? The divisions we observed in Kamikuze-no-shō and in the complaints submitted to Imagawa mediation reveal part of the answer. Those complaints showed village tenants at odds with their landlords and both groups at odds with their proprietors. Hence the *kokujin* proprietors who accepted Imagawa resolutions incurred debts of service while gaining confirmation of their rights over recalcitrant villagers as well as access to the *zōbun* discovered through land registration. Peasant landlords generally retained their holdings, secure both from proprietary and tenant challenges, as well as their official place in the Imagawa military hierarchy. As for smaller holders, the principal victims of judicial decisions and land surveys alike, arms were on the side of the proprietors and landlords they opposed. If justice was possible, it was available only from an outside agent. The occasional defense of the cultivator by the Imagawa, and their declared disapproval of capricious taxes, offered some hope of redress.

The local warriors who submitted to Imagawa regulations were also conceding that arms could not forever, and alone, commend their claims. Like generations of military proprietors in Suruga before them, they invoked the mediation of the Imagawa *shugo*—now a daimyo—to protect their privileges. This habit of recourse to litigation, the consent to Imagawa authority, and the mutual dependency that united the daimyo and his soldiers against lesser complainants proved the persistence of the *shugo* legacy.

Yet the legacy was put to new purposes. The land surveys that began as a pragmatic response to judicial complaints transformed both the daimyo and his domain. Unknown on any scale or with any frequency in earlier times, the surveys became the fundamental instrument of *sengoku* governance and provoked a quiet revolution in attitudes toward power.[33] As daimyo like the Imagawa registered land throughout their domains in an increasingly systematic fashion, and then allocated or confirmed rights on the basis of their cadastres, they asserted their own ultimate proprietorship in singularly clear-cut terms. No longer *shugo* who arbitrated among many private, independent proprietors at the behest of the shogunate, they became dispensers of income and administrative privileges to property now essentially their own. Entry into the village, collection of cadastres, confiscation of rents, recalculation of taxes, and apportionment of vassal claims to land—all made arbiters into lords.

The point was driven home by daimyo like the Hōjō who transferred *kokujin* vassals on occasion and went so far as to attaint the holdings of some. It was also apparent in the quid pro quo nature of land assignments: the Takeda stipendiaries were afforded large holdings and freed from taxes precisely in recompense for military duty; the landlords invested with property by the Imagawa owed their lords regular service. The most systematic use of a military tax was made by the Hōjō—daimyo of *kokujin* origin who created a vast domain in the Kantō. After a sweeping land survey conducted in 1555, they invested 556 vassals with lands bearing a tax value of 72,168 *kammon*. Each vassal was charged to support one soldier for every 6 to 8 *kan* of revenue apportioned to him.[34] No *shugo* of the high Ashikaga period had moved proprietors about at will or exacted martial levies from them in exchange for land confirmations.

The practical value of the cadastres was as great as their symbolic demonstration of the lord's primacy. The surveys yielded information on land resources and manpower that could become the basis of efficient tax and conscription systems. Although limited evidence indicates that tax rates did not change appreciably from the fifteenth to the sixteenth century, the surveys made detection of *zōbun* possible in the Imagawa and other domains.[35] Further, they gave the Imagawa and the Takeda population registries from which both daimyo families calculated the land and house surtaxes (*tansen* and *munebechisen*) that tended to become annual exactions in the *sengoku* era. These taxes had been officially levied by *shugo* before the war, but sporadically, and never on all local proprietors. The surveys also permitted the Hōjō—again the most inventive daimyo—to levy for their own use a surcharge, totaling 10 percent of the taxes registered in the cadastres, on every village in their domain. Finally, the registries assisted many daimyo—the Imagawa, Takeda, Hōjō, Uesugi, Matsudaira—to recruit corvée labor for castle construction, camp duty, transport, and supply.[36]

If cadastral surveys were the most direct expression of the daimyo's comprehensive power in his territory, the domainal codes were the most eloquent statements on his autonomy. One of eight such codes remaining from the *sengoku* era, the Imagawa formulary includes thirty-three articles issued in 1526 and twenty-one supplementary articles issued in 1553. Although the individual articles are practical observations on problems that regularly came before Imagawa tribunals, they are important as a collection for two reasons.[37]

First, the code expressed the self-consciousness of the Imagawa as independent lawmakers. The *shugo* were interpreters of Ashikaga statutes, always liable to be overruled upon appeals to the shogunate. Domainal law tended to follow Ashikaga tradition, but the compilation of local formularies that supplanted their national models completed the transfer of power from the center to the domain.

Second, the code defined the daimyo's universal and final jurisdiction in his territories. The articles addressed all classes—noble and religious proprietors, vassals, cultivators, and merchants—and pertained to all categories of land. They denied immunity to estates and declared all domainal holdings vulnerable to official entry, taxation, and regulation by the Imagawa. Further, the articles treated many disparate issues, implying that nothing lay beyond official purview: violent crimes, loans and mortgages, interest rates, inheritance practices, marine rights, doctrinal disputes in the monasteries, commerce with merchants outside the domain, the treatment of runaways, and the disposition of children from peasant families serving two landlords. The assumption of absolute jurisdiction was conveyed, finally, in articles that condemned vendettas and all forms of private justice. The law of the lord embraced all; the execution of justice was his right alone; and the lord was ultimate judge.[38]

A set of thirteen procedural laws, accompanying the main and supplementary articles of the Imagawa code, showed a keen attention to judicial conduct. Declaring that a council of daimyo representatives would meet six days a month to receive complaints, the laws set standards of rectitude and sternness: suits against parents or superiors were discouraged in all but the gravest cases; prompt action and full implementation of judgments were assured; forgery or perjury, capricious litigation, and attempts to influence jurists were condemned with harsh penalties. To permit complaints against proprietors, and so to diffuse peasant discontent, petition boxes were established throughout Imagawa holdings.[39]

The developments in domainal government we have discussed thus far were neither fully realized by 1550 nor characteristic of the majority of daimyo administrations. Only eight codes survive from the *sengoku* era, although most lords issued statutes and edicts that assume the powers expressed more clearly in the formularies. Land surveys began in the Imagawa and Hōjō domains by 1520 but spread to the holdings of the Takeda, Matsudaira, Mōri, Ōtomo, Oda, Uesugi, and Asakura only after 1550. Even so, they were comparatively rare and uniformly flawed by the use of irregular measures, varying approaches to the evaluation of fields, and dependency upon extant village records rather than direct examination of land and harvests. Few daimyo used their cadastres to conscript soldiers and to tax villages as efficiently as the Hōjō.

It is important to note, too, that registration and recruitment exacerbated two problems in the village that threatened daimyo hegemony. The enfeoffment of *kokujin* and *jizamurai* strengthened the bonds of local militias to the land. Their martial functions were legitimated, and their local power—in the form of tax and administrative privileges—confirmed. Given a secure village base, they could seek advantages elsewhere, deny their resources to the lord, and mobilize village manpower against him.[40] Further, daimyo rewards to *kokujin* and *jizamurai* accentuated both social and economic stratification in the village, and thus enhanced the potential for rebellion among the disadvantaged majority. The Imagawa code deals at length with signs of peasant distress—absconding, lapsed loans, separation of families—that needed amelioration. In general, the Imagawa and their peers manipulated the status quo in the village to their immediate gain, leaving behind conditions of instability that Hideyoshi would be the first to transform.

Despite the immaturity of domainal government and the problems posed by a landed militia, daimyo like the Imagawa were establishing patterns of local rule that would be followed by all their late *sengoku* successors. They used land surveys and law codes to establish their ultimate proprietorship; their right to survey, allocate, and tax land; their power to conscript soldiers; and their full legal jurisdiction over residents of the domain. Surveys and codes were issued primarily by larger and older daimyo houses, primarily *shugo* houses like the Imagawa, Takeda, Ōuchi, and Ōtomo. Clearly they built upon a *shugo* legacy of legal and taxation rights. Yet together with comprehensive formularies and cadastres, and the subsequent incorporation of all landholders into the daimyo's command, came a new message: the domain composed a strong and independent unit of government.

Created in response to the opportunities and exigencies of war, the domain was only as secure as its army was strong. Among the most innovative of administrators, the Imagawa proved able in defense but weak in offensive strategy. Their westward expansion ended at the Oda borders.

Oda Nobunaga

Sometime around 1400 a family named Oda entered the service of the Shiba as deputy administrators of Owari. The province was small, only eight districts, and Oda influence had grown sufficiently by the end of the fifteenth century to encourage the family's hopes for domination. We are told that Nobunaga's ancestors seized Owari from the Shiba early in the age of warring states. Yet like many upstart families, the Oda have a shallow history in documents and the trajectory of their rise is poorly charted. By the 1530s, two competing houses—both called Oda—had divided Owari into warring camps. One maintained its headquarters at Iwakura castle in the northwestern part of the province; the other held Kiyosu castle, somewhat to the south. Nobunaga's father, Nobuhide, was one of three house elders of the Kiyosu faction. The reasons for the rift in the family, even the relationship between the original Oda and their namesakes of the 1530s, are unclear. The very murkiness of his antecedents permitted Nobunaga to claim descent from the Taira clan, his major pretension to a distinguished pedigree.[41]

Oda Nobuhide never reconciled the two Oda camps, nor did he achieve command of the Kiyosu faction. Instead, he entered the annals of *sengoku* folklore as a bold and romantic leader of forays into neighboring provinces. Throughout the 1540s and early 1550s, he ate away at Mikawa villages theoretically controlled by the Matsudaira house. When the Matsudaira pledged loyalty to the Imagawa, in part to secure help against Nobuhide, they dispatched their young heir to Suruga as a hostage, only to lose him to Oda captors. Nobuhide kept the child— later known as Tokugawa Ieyasu—for several years. Nobuhide also marched north in 1544 to support the Toki family of Mino, longtime *shugo* of that province. They were under siege from another colorful, though infamous, figure of warring-states legend, Saitō Dōsan. A parvenu oil merchant turned warrior, Dōsan successfully resisted both the Toki and the Oda. The accommodating Nobuhide then concluded a treaty with the Saitō and arranged the marriage of his son, Nobunaga, to Dōsan's daughter in 1548.[42]

Upon Nobuhide's death in 1551, Nobunaga took over a family with a reputation for valor, and sheer daring, but without a firm land base. Nobuhide's jurisdiction in Owari was not well defined, and, as far as we know, he was not a lawmaker or land surveyor in the mold of the Imagawa. His hold over men like Hideyoshi's father, Yaemon, probably derived more from their pursuit of gain and adventure than from any system of conscription. His "army" may have never exceeded a few hundred soldiers. Hideyoshi's own affiliation with the Imagawa promised far more than service to the turbulent Oda.

Nobunaga advanced his family's interests in Owari by invading Kiyosu castle and establishing the dominion of his own line in the southern part of the province. Yet within a few years his links to Mikawa and Mino were broken. Saitō Dōsan's son took power in Mino and spurned the Oda alliance in 1556. The Matsudaira (or Tokugawa) of Mikawa cleared away Oda strongholds there by 1558. It was also in 1558 that Hideyoshi left the Imagawa to join Oda Nobunaga. He made the decision just as his original lord was massing a vast army to penetrate Owari and march on to the capital of Kyoto.

The ability of the Imagawa to move westward proceeded from the alliances Yoshimoto made in 1554 with the Hōjō and the Takeda, for triangular struggles between these families had preoccupied them all in earlier decades. The Hōjō of Sagami had regularly attacked Suruga, only to withdraw under counterattack from both the Imagawa and their sometime allies, the Takeda of Kai. But the Imagawa had also joined forces with the Hōjō in offensives against the Takeda. Conflicts within any one house constantly altered temporary unions. A durable Takeda-Imagawa pact was discouraged by Takeda Shingen's distrust of Imagawa Yoshimoto, who had harbored Shingen's father when the son wrested power from him. Ceaseless Hōjō appeals to Imagawa *kokujin* in eastern Suruga aggravated the enmity between those houses.

A balance was achieved in 1554 after the Hōjō again attacked Suruga while the Imagawa were engaged in Mikawa. Takeda intervention on behalf of the Imagawa broke the Hōjō campaign and moved all parties to a general truce. To ensure the peace, the three families concluded a startling number of marriage alliances. Imagawa Yoshimoto's daughter married Takeda Shingen's son. Takeda Shingen's daughter married Hōjō Ujiyasu's son. Hōjō Ujiyasu's daughter married Imagawa Yoshimoto's son. Imagawa Yoshimoto himself was already married to Takeda Shingen's sister, and his sister was the wife of Hōjō Ujiyasu. Given the ephemeral safety of alliance, the Takeda moved to secure Shinano, the Hōjō expanded into the Kantō, and the Imagawa addressed themselves again to the Oda in Owari.[43]

On two occasions, once in 1554 and once in 1558, Oda Nobunaga faced small-scale Imagawa assaults upon Owari. Imagawa Yoshimoto then began to assemble a single, vast army from Suruga, Tōtōmi, and Mikawa for a major attack. Popular war chronicles tell us that he recruited as many as 40,000 soldiers from the ranks of *kokujin* and *jizamurai*. Hideyoshi was not among them. Whatever inspired his gamble on the Oda, it was a sound one. The conclusive encounter between Oda and Imagawa troops occurred during the fifth month of 1560. On the

Owari field of Okehazama Yoshimoto's train of 40,000 was stopped by the 2,000 soldiers of Oda Nobunaga. The victory depended neither upon numbers—although these figures are doubtless exaggerated—nor upon a superior supply of muskets—still in very limited use. Nobunaga succeeded through an ambush, in a driving rain, against invaders off their guard. Imagawa Yoshimoto died on the scene, and his riddled forces began a retreat.[44]

After this astonishing rout, Nobunaga began to wage a war of consolidation in Owari. He also protected his rear through alliances with Tokugawa Ieyasu of Mikawa in 1562 and Takeda Shingen of Kai in 1565. These were the men who were completing Nobunaga's devastation of the Imagawa. Both broke their treaties with Yoshimoto's heir and recruited Imagawa vassals who were demoralized by their defeat and the loss of their lord. By 1564 the incursions of the Takeda in Suruga and the Tokugawa in Tōtōmi moved the last scion of the Imagawa house to surrender. Imagawa Ujizane, son of Yoshimoto, left Sumpu for a Kyoto monastery, although some of his troops fought desultory battles with the invaders until the end of the decade. After 230 years of primacy in Suruga, the Imagawa disappeared from the political map of Japan.

In addition to his alliances with the Takeda and Tokugawa, Nobunaga afforded himself some protection in the area near the capital by concluding a pact with Asai Nagamasa of Ōmi in 1564. Each treaty was enhanced, as was now common, by a marriage covenant. Nobunaga gave a daughter to Tokugawa Ieyasu's eldest son, a sister to Asai Nagamasa, and an adopted daughter to Takeda Shingen's son.[45] But before he used his leverage in the home provinces to try a march into Kyoto, he returned to Mino. The campaign there is interesting because Hideyoshi was at the heart of it, and because it illustrates a problem as threatening to *sengoku* daimyo as war itself—the problem of divided households.

Saitō Dōsan, the oil merchant turned daimyo, had been overpowered in Mino by his presumptive son during 1556. To observers, there was little mystery in the rebellion. This son was born in the house of Dōsan but conceived in the house of the Toki *shugo* whom Dōsan had eclipsed. His mother had been offered as a gesture of appeasement to the Saitō. Once he reached maturity, the son—Yoshitatsu—wreaked revenge upon Dōsan to repair the Toki honor. Although this story has the twists of grand opera, similarly rancorous issues concerning succession endangered daimyo families throughout the *sengoku* era. We have already observed the divisions in the Hosokawa and Oda houses. Even Imagawa Yoshimoto succeeded to power after battles with a brother who was eventually driven to suicide. Yoshimoto was seventeen at the time.

Once Saitō Yoshitatsu broke relations with the Oda, Nobunaga embarked on a series of raids upon Mino between 1559 and 1567. The final conquest of the Saitō citadel of Inabayama in 1567, most commentators report, was made possible by Hideyoshi.

Hideyoshi's relationship with Nobunaga lasted just over twenty-four years, from their meeting in 1558 until Nobunaga's death in 1582. Although we know little of Hideyoshi's career before the 1570s, his posthumous biographers bravely enter the breach to describe his apocryphal positions as a construction supervisor, during the rebuilding of Kiyosu castle, and as a supervisor of the firewood collectors. We are to understand that Hideyoshi won early favor from Nobunaga for his loyalty, provoked the animosity of Nobunaga's senior retainers for surpassing them in valor, displayed unusual tactical skill, and startled everyone with an intelligence that belied his origins. Many of these claims are based upon stories of the Mino campaign.

The Saitō stronghold at Inabayama, allegedly invincible, was best attacked from the Owari border town of Sunomata. There Hideyoshi boldly built a fortress, under the gaze of the enemy, from which to spearhead an assault. Attack was logistically impossible without a neighboring fortification and Hideyoshi's construction at Sunomata, considered foolhardy by the Oda leaders, provided the edge of victory. Subsequently, Nobunaga took Mino directly under his own control, and Hideyoshi acquired a secure place in legend. Nobunaga transferred his headquarters from Kiyosu to Inabayama, which he renamed Gifu—the place from which the Chou ruler, Wu Wang, began his military campaign to destroy his rivals and unify China in the twelfth century B.C. Lest doubt remain concerning his objectives, Nobunaga also assumed a signature motto at this time: "the realm covered with military majesty" (tenka fubu).[46]

Within twelve years of his succession to Oda headship, Nobunaga had taken over Owari, defeated the Imagawa and Saitō families, and contracted alliances with three daimyo houses. His domain was far from the largest in contemporary Japan, his ancestry was not particularly distinguished, and his holdings had seen little institutional development. Much of his success derived from his own martial ingenuity and fortuitous developments—the ambush of a huge army, the collapse of the Imagawa alliances after 1560, the splits within the Saitō house. His phoenix-like rise from the Imagawa ashes thus tends to heighten impressions that force used bravely and inventively surpassed good government in importance during the sengoku period. Yet the two were inextricably intertwined in most strong domains—those of the Hōjō,

Takeda, Mōri, and others—and were later brilliantly united by Nobu-naga as well. If he broke through to power with unexpected victories that drew young fighters to him like a magnet, he also consolidated do-mainal rule on the model of the Imagawa. Certainly he shared with them from the beginning the assumptions that power existed only within defensible borders and that bonds between a lord and his sol-diers were the essential expression of authority.

The Capital

Shortly after his defeat of the Saitō, Nobunaga received a letter from Emperor Ōgimachi, the man who succeeded Go-Nara in 1557.

> Famous general with no peer in any age, most superior in valor, and inspired by the Way of Heaven: since the provinces are now subject to your will, it is certain that you will increasingly mount in victory. With this letter we re-quest in particular, as it would be most admirable, that you issue strict orders in conformity with the emperor's wishes concerning the recovery of the imperial holdings in your two provinces of Mino and Owari as well as the other matters which were discussed.[47]

Perhaps solicited by Nobunaga, the letter refers to a meeting four days earlier between himself and the emperor's ambassador to discuss the status of imperial estates in Mino and Owari, as well as the possibil-ity of Oda assistance in repairing the palace and funding the coming-of-age ceremonies for the crown prince. Ōgimachi's financial distress was as acute as that of his predecessors. Neither hyperbolic greetings nor negotiations with a warlord were beneath his dignity when some economic advantage was in view.[48]

Around the same time, Ashikaga Yoshiaki appealed to Nobunaga for help in obtaining appointment as shogun. Brother of the shogun murdered by his vassals, and cousin to the incumbent shogun whom Matsunaga Hisahide pushed into office at the beginning of 1568, Yo-shiaki had already sought support from daimyo in Ōmi, Kōzuke, Noto, and Echizen. His overture to Nobunaga to redress the wrongs done his family by its deputies succeeded. Nobunaga summoned Yoshiaki from Echizen, where he was in hiding, and entered the capital at his side in the ninth month of 1568. The Matsunaga forces and the current shogun fled before the Oda army. Three weeks after his triumphant entry into Kyoto, Yoshiaki himself received the title of shogun from the emperor. He was the fifteenth and last of his line to secure that honor.[49]

One hundred years after war broke out in Kyoto's streets, the cycle of rebellion was beginning to close. Centripetal forces now drew the thirty-four-year-old Nobunaga to a court and a shogunate he had known only as weak, beleaguered institutions but nonetheless identified as sources of national renewal. Renewal in the most literal sense was surely in the minds of the courtiers, who envisioned restoration of their estates, and the Ashikaga, who sought a renaissance of shogunal authority. What it meant to Nobunaga was not yet clear. Many things, though, rendered the past unrecoverable. Time alone had placed the government of the high Ashikaga period beyond living memory. The now familiar role of military force in shogunal installation made a mockery of the rule of law. Land was surveyed, allocated, and governed by autonomous daimyo whose power was a function of their ability to recruit and control soldiers. And in the process of recruitment, many of these daimyo had built administrations that repudiated the spirit as well as the form of the shogunal settlement. They eliminated private proprietorships in their domains, awarded land strictly in exchange for service, made their laws and tribunals supreme, and resolved to expand their boundaries. They did not see themselves as parts of a national political whole.

Nor was the approaching integration of the warring states very apparent to anyone in 1568. A new and exciting pretender to power was on the scene. But his base was small, his alliances unsure, and his ability to reverse a century of defiance of central authorities utterly unproven. The year 1568 was a turning point marked only retrospectively as Nobunaga began to sweep all before him.

3

THE TERROR

ODA NOBUNAGA BECAME a frequent visitor to Kyoto in the years following his triumphant entry into the city with Ashikaga Yoshiaki. Although he never established a personal residence there, the capital served as the scene of his wartime diversions—his tea parties, his nō performances, his blossom-viewing outings. At mid-year in 1582 Nobunaga made his last journey to the city. He lodged on this occasion, as he had several times before, in Honnōji. A Nichiren temple surrounded by moats, watchtowers, and stout walls, Honnōji offered the protection of a fortress to a man who needed all the security he could find.[1]

On the first day of the sixth month, 1582, Nobunaga entertained a party of tea men at Honnōji. The imperial regent gathered with members of the Oda retinue to admire a distinguished collection of vessels and to drink tea with Nobunaga and his tea masters. In the early hours of the next morning, attackers surprised the last guests. Nobunaga died as the troops of Akechi Mitsuhide set fire to the temple and converged upon his guard. It is not clear whether he took his own life or fell to an enemy. His heir was quartered at Myōkakuji, another Nichiren sanctuary in the north of the city. Attempted flight ended in his death as well.[2]

The events at Honnōji might be portrayed as tragic. Nobunaga died a relatively young man, at forty-eight and the height of his powers, under attack by one of his own vassal daimyo. Further, the raid cut off one of the most remarkable careers in the history of the warring states. Within the twenty years since his conquest of Imagawa Yoshimoto, Nobunaga had brought a third of the nation under his control to demonstrate the possibility of unification.

Despite his claims upon fame and his shocking end, Nobunaga died unlamented. A man who had lived by the sword with uncommon ferocity and immersed Japan in a bloodbath it would never forget, he came, by most accounts, to a suitable reckoning. The prevailing distaste

41

for the man emerged in sympathetic expositions of Akechi Mitsuhide's motives for treachery. We are told that Mitsuhide resented his isolation from Oda councils, his peremptory transfers from domain to domain, and the forced sacrifice of his mother: one party in an exchange of hostages arranged by the Oda, she was killed in retaliation for the murder of her counterpart, a hostage in Nobunaga's custody.[3] By the eighteenth century, the popular theater reflected a consensus on Nobunaga's villainy when it allowed his assassin this speech of exoneration: "Heedless of remonstrations, Nobunaga destroyed shrines and temples, daily piling up atrocity upon atrocity. It was my calling to slay him for the sake of the Warrior's Way, for the sake of the realm. King Wu slew King Chou of the Yin; Hōjō Yoshitoki exiled the emperor. Both in our country and in China, the murder of a lord who does not know the Way has been the task of great men who thus give relief to the people."[4]

Had Nobunaga simply piled up "atrocity upon atrocity," he would scarcely bear mention in the history of a violent age. The brutal actions that served to focus criticism, however, were mere hints at Nobunaga's challenge to his society. The responses he inspired proceeded from the revelations he forced upon his peers about their own aspirations.

The first daimyo of the warring states to approach the widely shared goal of national conquest, Nobunaga exposed the consequences of that goal: accelerating violence and the certain attrition of rivals. The experiences of the Oda regime suggested that only one survivor would emerge from cataclysmic wars of unification. For all the simplicity of that discovery, and for all its clarity in the minds of the already vanquished, the point settled late upon the last and mightiest contenders for power. Nobunaga's battles illustrated what the many localized struggles of earlier years could not: the autonomous domains of the sixteenth century would all be devoured should the daimyo continue to renounce coexistence in pursuit of exclusive and conclusive victory.

Nobunaga was a lightning rod. His achievement, different in scope though not in kind from his competitors', set him above other daimyo to attract powerful reaction. Part of the reaction surely had to do with his own fierce politics. Much of it had to do with his exposure of the implications of war as the daimyo were waging it. If his death occasioned little grief, real enmity toward the man was probably rare. The death was welcome because it offered the daimyo a reprieve from a military course most had pursued but many had cause to reconsider.

Hideyoshi's career cannot be understood independently of Nobunaga's, although the two are more different than similar. Hideyoshi owed the obvious debts to his lord: promotion into the first rank of warring-states generals; a military base from which to launch the last wars of unification; a demonstration that the atomized domains of the era could be integrated under one man's control. Yet his greatest debt was a changing political climate. As Nobunaga subjugated military houses, cities, and religious institutions across the nation, he compelled reflection upon alternative approaches to pacification by both the daimyo who recoiled from Nobunaga's vision of the state and the successor who would transform it.

The Collapse of the Shogunate

When Nobunaga entered Kyoto with Ashikaga Yoshiaki in 1568, he was lord of Owari and Mino as well as parts of Ise, Iga, and southern Ōmi that he had taken on his way to the capital. He could aspire to rule over a far-flung domain as the result of shogunal and imperial support and treaties with three competitors—the Tokugawa, Takeda, and Asai. Within little more than a year, however, the dream went sour. Disillusioned by his perfunctory role in national affairs, Yoshiaki began to look for sympathetic daimyo who might rise on his behalf against Nobunaga about the start of 1570.

The misalliance between Nobunaga and Yoshiaki should have been clear from the beginning. Shortly after his investiture as shogun, Yoshiaki was compelled to issue a series of sixteen statutes prepared by Nobunaga. Ranging widely over judicial and land issues, the statutes also governed access to the shogun's person: audiences with warriors other than personal attendants, direct judicial appeals, and consultations by religious dignitaries were all forbidden. The sixth article in the series conveyed the essential message: "Once the shogun has consulted the opinion of his magistrates (*bugyōshu*), he shall not inquire into the correctness of that opinion [but shall simply adopt it]."[5] The intention to make Yoshiaki a spokesman for his subordinates was inescapable.

There were doubtless many motives behind Yoshiaki's cooperation in declaring statutes that constrained his own freedom. The dignity of his office was, after all, acknowledged in the articles concerning audiences. And the items covering land and judicature implied his ultimate authority over the nation's business. In any case, Yoshiaki's circulation of the statutes presaged no docility. Once established in Kyoto, he began to act as ruler and conciliator. He sent envoys to daimyo houses suing for peace. He tried to recover Ashikaga landholdings and demanded the restoration of imperial estates throughout the country.[6]

Yoshiaki's assertion of power was encouraged by acts of apparent homage on Nobunaga's part. In 1569, for example, Nobunaga built a Kyoto mansion for him, to replace the shogunal palaces lost earlier in the century. The new residence, Nijō *gosho*, was the first of the great urban castles of Japan, surrounded by inner and outer moats, drawbridges, stone walls, and high towers. It was also a princely home. Nobunaga himself reputedly designed its gardens, and he raided the more opulent temples for interior fittings. Waterbirds played in its moats, golden finials flew from its roofs. The residence seemed emblematic of the recovery of shogunal decorum.[7]

This mixture of patronage and bullying may have baffled Yoshiaki. He believed in restoration of the shogunate and had sought Oda assistance under the assumption that Nobunaga, too, looked forward to the rehabilitation of Ashikaga government. Nobunaga had declined Yoshiaki's offers of appointment in the new administration, but the shogun could interpret the refusal as reticence, not disdain. That sixth statute must have appeared to Yoshiaki as a touch of Nobunaga's caution that would dissipate as the shogun demonstrated a competence to rule independently.

The meaning of the statute soon came clear. In the first month of 1570, around the time that Yoshiaki began actively to oppose Oda control, Nobunaga issued the following commands:

> Item [1]: In the event that there are matters to be ordered to the provinces through [Yoshiaki's] directives (gonaisho), Nobunaga is to be informed and his own letter [of confirmation] appended.
>
> Item [4]: Insofar as the affairs of the realm have been fully entrusted to Nobunaga, all judgments shall be rendered—regardless of those concerned—in accord with his perceptions and without consultation of the shogun.[8]

Yoshiaki's resolution to acquire the substance as well as the symbols of power was at odds with Nobunaga's ambition to order the state under a single sword. The shogun was useful just so long as he remained a guarantor of the Oda mandate. Yet without moving directly against the shogun himself, Nobunaga began a campaign against the first daimyo champion to oppose the Oda, Asakura Yoshikage of Echizen.

Between the first months of 1570 and the last months of 1573 Nobunaga set the tenor of his regime. He went to war, during those years, with three major military houses (the Asakura, Asai, and Takeda) and several less formidable ones (the Rokkaku, Miyoshi, and Matsunaga). He fought the armies of two powerful religious institutions (the temples of Enryakuji on Mount Hiei and Ishiyama Honganji in Osaka), and he took the cities of Sakai and Kyoto firmly under his own jurisdiction. Not least important, he brought the Ashikaga shogunate to an end.

The campaigns of these years illustrate the critical elements of Nobunaga's period of ascendancy: the failure of alliance, the massive resistance to Oda rule, and Nobunaga's determination to annihilate opponents. As he built a domain larger than any competitor's, Nobunaga concentrated power in his own house, laying the foundation for a regime that threatened to erase the independence of the warring states.

Early in 1570 Nobunaga stormed a fortress of the Asakura in Echizen only to retreat when the armies of the Asai and the Rokkaku declared their support for the Asakura. The entry of the Asai into this conflict broke the peace treaty concluded with the Oda years earlier, an alliance that had been confirmed by the marriage of Asai Nagamasa to Nobunaga's sister in 1565. Now engaged in battle on two fronts, Nobunaga retaliated by attacking Asai Nagamasa's capital, the castle of Odani in Ōmi province.

Hideyoshi led the first of three detachments in the campaign against the Asai. In one of his earliest extant letters, he wrote to a merchant of Sakai: "We have built fortifications at three places as part of the strategy in northern Ōmi. I am ordered to man the first with three thousand troops . . . In this regard, I have urgent business for you. Send gunpowder of the highest possible quality, about thirty *kin*; also send thirty *kin* of niter."[9] Most arresting is the letter's indication of Hideyoshi's stature in the Oda army. Within twelve years of the time he joined Nobunaga, Hideyoshi had risen from the ranks of messenger and minor attendant (if we are to believe his resourceful biographers) to the position of field commander of three thousand men.

Of almost equal interest is the letter's attention to gunpowder and niter. In dispersed campaigns conducted by armies limited in numbers, Nobunaga's strength derived from a superior arsenal and the use of foot soldiers armed with muskets.[10] The decision to rely upon firearms—and to displace the mounted warrior with a historically despised infantryman—was the mark of a foresighted strategist. It transformed military organization, increased the carnage on battlefields, and shifted the martial advantage to those who held Japan's foreign ports and metal works. Nobunaga secured that advantage by taking Sakai. Both a major port and the center of arms production in the sixteenth century, the city had fallen to Nobunaga in 1569 after its citizens' council refused his demand for a huge military tribute in silver. Following a devastating raid by the Oda army, Nobunaga procured his tribute and stationed one of his deputies in Sakai as its overlord. Hideyoshi's order for gunpowder and niter was simply one of many exchanges between the Oda and the Sakai quartermasters, who were now in Nobunaga's grip.[11]

Although the Oda troops took minor citadels in the province of Ōmi, the combined forces of the Asakura and the Asai withstood assault well into 1571. Their success had much to do with Nobunaga's preoccupation elsewhere. Throughout the last months of 1570, his men fought in Kawachi province against remnants of the Miyoshi army and their occasional allies, the sectarians of the Honganji establishment. The Miyoshi, hoping to recover Kyoto now that Nobunaga had broken most ties to the Ashikaga, diverted Oda attention to yet another battle-front. They succeeded in exhausting Nobunaga's forces. Consequently unable to conclude hostilities in Ōmi to his advantage, Nobunaga arranged a truce with the Asai through the intercession of the throne.[12]

The Asai broke the truce in the fifth month of 1571, joined in battle by Honganji believers. Hideyoshi wrote of the encounter: "On the sixth [of the month] we caught the Asai as they approached Kamaba-omote where we met in battle. We cut through them and many were taken. From Minouchi to Hachiman I do not know how many were lost. We lay in wait at Hachiman for our final vengeance. Three times we met them, pursuing and crushing them. We took the heads of the dead. The others we chased into the lake."[13] This passage is a good illustration of contemporary military history. Brisk, even cryptic, it is silent in regard to numbers and arms but powerful in evoking the shifting geography of battle, the role of pursuit and ambush in lingering campaigns, and the concern with human war trophies. Hideyoshi's victory did not signal a resolution of the conflict between the Oda and the Asai. Two more major diversions in two new locales postponed Nobunaga's return to Ōmi. The first occurred on Mount Hiei, just outside the capital, the second in the eastern province of Tōtōmi.

Oda soldiers approached the monastery of Enryakuji, founded on Mount Hiei in the eighth century, toward the end of 1571. In a now familiar account, Nobunaga's first biographer described the raid: "In the dead of night his men completely encircled the broad expanse of Mount Hiei, leaving no room for escape. Then when horns were sounded as a signal for the attack, the men launched the assault from all sides with a fierce battle cry. Although the troops of the monastery contested every inch of the hill, they were not equal to the occasion. Everything, everywhere, from the central cathedral to the twenty-one shrines of the Mountain King, the bell tower, and the library, were burned to the ground."[14] As many as two thousand structures fell in the fire, and countless monks died. A monastery of immense wealth, historical distinction, and seminal religious influence was reduced to ashes.

Hiei's collusion with the Asai and the Asakura had been the immediate provocation of Nobunaga's offensive. With extensive land interests in Ōmi, the Enryakuji monks had made common cause with their neighbors to secure their boundaries against the Oda. Throughout the era of warring states, though, Hiei had epitomized the arrogance of militant churches that used religious justifications for private wars. Its monks had raided temples of both the Nichiren and Jōdo Shinshū sects, participated in far-flung daimyo campaigns, and entered the power struggles in the capital. Nobunaga's devastation of the monastery, which continues to burn in the historical imagination as the most infamous act in his career, was a symbolic attack upon armed churches across the nation.

Nobunaga redirected his attention to the Asai in 1572, but Takeda Shingen deflected it. Belatedly seizing the cause of Ashikaga Yoshiaki, Shingen reneged on his 1565 pact with the Oda and attacked Nobunaga's eastern flank. He defeated the Oda army at the battle of Mikatagahara in Tōtōmi in the twelfth month of 1572, and his conquest of that province appeared a matter of time. Only with Shingen's death in the fourth month of 1573 did the pressure on Nobunaga relax.[15]

Ashikaga Yoshiaki felt the loss of Takeda Shingen most keenly. Upon his return from Tōtōmi, Nobunaga finally confronted not only the shogun but the citizens of Kyoto as well. He demanded a large military tribute as a sign of obedience and, when the townsmen of Kyoto refused the levy, conducted fire raids throughout the upper city. The home of nobles, the shogun, and the mercantile elite, northern Kyoto was the political heart of a town that had served for eight hundred years as the nation's capital. Other military men had tried to tax it, but none had razed its buildings in a display of personal vengeance.

Nobunaga then pursued Ashikaga Yoshiaki. In the seventh month of 1573 he surrounded the shogun at his retreat near the Uji River and forced him into exile.[16] The encounter was brought on by Yoshiaki's association with antagonists on all sides of the Oda—first the Asakura and Asai, later the Miyoshi, the Honganji and Hiei communities, finally the Takeda. After the rout in Uji, the fifteenth head of the Ashikaga house took shelter on the island of Shikoku. The next month, Nobunaga turned for a last time to Ōmi.

As Nobunaga approached Odani castle in that province, Asai Nagamasa appealed to Asakura Yoshikage for reinforcements. But when Yoshikage began to lead his army south, Nobunaga intercepted him. Oda soldiers pursued the defenders to the Asakura headquarters in Echizen and captured their citadel. Yoshikage killed himself. The Oda contingent returned to Ōmi to win, without great struggle, the Asai stronghold of Odani. Nagamasa and his father took their own lives. Nagamasa's mother was finally killed after suffering the removal of her fingers. His son and heir, nephew of Nobunaga, was executed as well. His three daughters and his wife, Nobunaga's nieces and sister, were recovered and conveyed to Owari. Several days later, Nobunaga exposed the heads of Asai Nagamasa and Asakura Yoshikage in Kyoto. In time, one contemporary chronicler reports, he had those heads lacquered and gilded to display at a banquet.[17]

The most striking aspect of these four years of war is the intensity of the resistance to Nobunaga. Two allies, the Asai and Takeda, broke treaties with him; other military houses and religious establishments with holdings scattered across the large triangle formed by Echizen, Settsu, and Tōtōmi attacked his troops; and the citizens of Kyoto joined with supporters of the shogun to defy Oda commands. No daimyo of the warring-states era had faced so many challenges from such disparate opponents in so brief a time.

Although Ashikaga Yoshiaki served as standard-bearer for the challengers, the shogun's honor seems to have been little more than a pretext for battle. Nobunaga's enemies included men who had abused the shogunate themselves or ignored previous opportunities to intervene in Kyoto's politics on behalf of the Ashikaga. If they acted as shogunal loyalists now, they were responding to the threat represented by the Oda and, more important, by the unification process itself.

At the deepest level, the resistance to Nobunaga reflected the fear of consolidation that accompanied the changing goals and consequences of war in the late sixteenth century. No longer fought by many minor daimyo for independence from central authorities or for limited local ascendancy, the battles of this period engaged ever larger military houses intent upon regional, and even national, hegemony. And with these wars of expansion came the brisk annihilation of lesser contenders—great as well as humble daimyo, enemies as well as allies of the victors.

In the face of such consolidation a pattern of collective defense became conspicuous throughout Japan after 1550. We noted earlier that relations between the Imagawa, Takeda, and Hōjō altered time and again, as two of the parties aligned to restrain the growth of the third. Similar alliances, shifting constantly in membership, occurred in Kyushu, Shikoku, and western Honshu between daimyo who united to oppose neighbors capable of widespread conquest. Temporary and fragile, these pacts had a limited purpose: to prevent, or at least to stall, the local concentration of power. Rarely were they conceived as coalitions of peers in broad political accord. Stranger bedfellows than the Miyoshi and Ashikaga Yoshiaki, or the Ikkō sectarians and the monks of Mount Hiei, can hardly be imagined. The union of unnatural partners made unstable alliances all the more unstable, but it also illustrated the deepening apprehension of the time. Men took uncommon risks to preserve some balance of power.

The opposition to Oda forces appears, on a great scale, to be part of this pattern of collective defense against hegemony. The size and variety of the opposition was commensurate with the threat. The first daimyo to enter Kyoto with a large, independent land base, Nobunaga had promptly subordinated the shogun and taken Sakai. Proven in war against the Imagawa and allied with powerful men, he had also emerged as the chief danger to domainal stability, once he threw down the gauntlet before Asakura Yoshikage. At that point he became the target of joint attack, even from allies who feared for their own security. Neither truces nor marriage covenants had protected alliances before. The prospect of an unconstrained warlord in the capital was universally alarming.

The survival of the shogunate and the willingness of certain daimyo to defend it, if only as a camouflage for other purposes, is logical in this context. A symbolic authority that could sanction the causes of various lords while genuinely threatening none remained attractive. The possibilities for a resolution of the warring-states crisis remained wide open, as long as a powerless shogun held Kyoto and the home provinces. Hence a direct challenge to the shogunate from Nobunaga, a stronger man than any pretender in the Hosokawa or Miyoshi houses, provoked profound reactions from the daimyo who had much to forfeit in a new political order. Ashikaga Yoshiaki's limitations were far more convenient to them than an unpredictable Nobunaga.

Yet Nobunaga was not unpredictable. It was this fact that was frightening. His competitors could look to their own histories to chart his course. The ablest of them had steadily expanded their own domains, eliminating neighbors, taking over cities and mines, disciplining religious establishments. If there was doubt about Nobunaga's intentions, his conduct between 1570 and 1574 dispelled it. The predictable concentration of power occurred. The port of Sakai and the capital of Kyoto fell to him after violent raids; Mount Hiei was devastated; the Asai, Asakura, Rokkaku, and Miyoshi, like the Imagawa and the Saitō, were destroyed; a recalcitrant shogun was forced into an exile that would prove permanent.

The violence of these reprisals is the second striking aspect of Nobunaga's early wars. It is related, of course, to the first—the emergence of intense resistance to his regime. And as that resistance appears part of a pattern of collective defense against a potential overlord, so the reprisal appears part of a pattern too.

The defensive alliances of the late sixteenth century, such as those between the Imagawa and the Takeda against the Hōjō, seldom precluded the regional consolidation of power. The incompatibilty of most allies explains the development only in part. More important was the determination of stronger daimyo—even those embraced by treaties—to extend their dominion. Profound though the general apprehension over an overlord's ascendancy became, that fear ran no deeper than the ambition of individuals who saw themselves as victors and treated alliance as an expedient to contain others or win time. Thus the Takeda, for example, tried to maintain a balance of strength between the Imagawa and the Hōjō at the same time that they hoped to crush both parties themselves. Once Nobunaga defeated the Imagawa in Owari, the Takeda did not hesitate to take Imagawa holdings in the province of Suruga. The interest of the daimyo in local stability had yet to reconcile them to durable alliances that would survive temptations to seize the advantage.

As surely as the advantage was seized, of course, victors encountered new resistance. The expansion of the Takeda brought them into conflict with the Tokugawa as well as the Hōjō. Such resistance, the surviving hopes of numerous daimyo for greater power, the fragility of alliances, and the likelihood that one failure would precipitate disastrous consequences intensified the insecurity of conquerors. Vigilant against threats, the Takeda and their kind fortified victory with harsh policies: the annihilation of the vanquished, the purge of unreliable retainers, the subordination of monasteries and towns that might harbor opponents.

Like the Takeda and other daimyo before him, then, Nobunaga met the resistance accompanying his conquests with reprisals. He was caught in a circular pattern that threatened to become a maelstrom, consuming all who approached it. Cities, temples, military houses, and a shogunate that stood in his way encountered uncompromising responses from Nobunaga. To make concessions was to open the way for internal rebellion and hence the collapse of his regime.

It is too easy, perhaps, to portray Nobunaga as a brutal man.[18] Although the destruction of Mount Hiei and the execution of his Asai in-laws were clearly grisly, he did not depart in kind from the pattern of retaliation cut by his peers. Long before the final wars of unification, moreover, violence had become the law in his society; patricide, ruthless marriage politics, the murder of allies, and the ruin of religious institutions were common. Many families splintered, and premature death threatened all. Nobunaga himself saw seven of his ten brothers and three of his four uncles killed in battle.

Nobunaga's conduct had special dimensions, however. Kyoto was not a provincial market; Hiei was not a provincial temple; the shogunate was not a provincial institution; the Imagawa and Asakura were not new or minor houses at the periphery of power. His actions in the home provinces and their environs indicated that the consolidation of power occurring in other parts of Japan would also occur around the capital; that such consolidation would involve the extermination of opposition; and that the struggle for national hegemony would bring all contenders into final wars for survival.

The avoidance of such a resolution required breaking the pattern of conquest and resistance. Should resistance wither or a new accommodation between the daimyo emerge, the lessons of the Oda regime might lose their prophetic edge. Yet a change in unification politics seemed to demand that individual conquerors acknowledge the incompatibility between their interests in domainal stability and expansion. Given Nobunaga's mounting military advantage and his apparent contempt for the goal of balanced power among local lords, change seemed to demand a transfer of leadership as much as an alteration in political climate.

The Oda Vassals

No less than his conquests, Nobunaga's administration of his expanding domain suggested a vision of concentrated and centralized power. Nobunaga retained immediate control over the largest portion of his resources, a fief centered upon Azuchi castle in Ōmi province that spread into Mino and Owari. Although we do not know the total value of those holdings, the Ōmi property alone was appraised at 300,000 koku (one koku = approximately five bushels). Nobunaga apportioned the remaining lands taken in the early wars among his leading vassals.[19]

The major investitures went to his sons and to ten other individuals (Toyotomi Hideyoshi, Takigawa Kazumasu, Akechi Mitsuhide, Niwa Nagahide, Shibata Katsuie, Sassa Narimasa, Maeda Toshiie, Sakuma Nobumori, Ikeda Tsuneoki, and Mori Nagayoshi).[20] The most interesting feature of this group is its size. Nobunaga's high command was small. And it remained small. The ten vassals who led the first Oda campaigns and received handsome investitures in reward would continue to direct the later offensives and to divide most of the spoils; after 1574 no newcomer would enter their ranks as a general or critical fief holder. Nobunaga's circle of intimates closed with the defeat of the shogunate.

The chief Oda vassals also shared humble origins, indebted to Nobunaga for what wealth and influence they acquired. Most were minor military men of Owari whose fathers had supported the motley forces of Oda Nobuhide. A few, Takigawa Kazumasu and Hideyoshi himself, were adventurers who joined Nobunaga around the time of the Imagawa campaign. Akechi Mitsuhide was much more the outsider. A vassal of the Saitō in Mino province, he entered the Oda army after the defeat of his previous lord by Nobunaga. Mitsuhide's peculiar position

among these leading retainers may have kept him on the edge of Nobunaga's trust and, in time, influenced his treachery. The high command did include one other member, Tokugawa Ieyasu. An ally rather
than a vassal of the Oda, Ieyasu was the sole military man with an independent land base to enter, and survive in, Nobunaga's retinue. He
stood in stark contrast to his fellow commanders, throwing into relief
their exceedingly modest backgrounds.

The rise to power of the Oda vassals gives substance to portrayals
of the sixteenth century as an era of *gekokujō*—mastery of the high by
the low. If the head of the Oda house was less than a total upstart himself, his deputies were clearly new men. It was particularly from the
second layer of leadership, composed of the retainers of great daimyo,
that the lowly emerged to eclipse their betters. Hideyoshi, a farmer's
son who came to Nobunaga with nothing, left the Ōmi campaign as
castellan of Asai Nagamasa's Odani with property valued at 120,000
koku. Hideyoshi's experiences as a daimyo in Nobunaga's command
define some of the contours of the Oda government. Resembling the
experiences of most lords of the time, they indicate that Nobunaga tolerated a degree of local autonomy within the area of his conquests. As
we shall see, however, the administrations of the Oda vassals were far
from independent.

Hideyoshi brought the nucleus of his lifelong complement to the
three districts of northern Ōmi that constituted his fief. He was accompanied by his stepbrother, Hidenaga, as well as by four in-laws: Miyoshi Yoshifusa, the husband of his older sister; Sugihara Ietsugu and
Kinoshita Iesada, the uncle and brother of his wife; and Asano Nagamasa, the brother-in-law of his wife. Also among his retainers were six
or more men of Owari who had joined him during the early years of his
association with the Oda, and five vassals of the Saitō in Mino province
who had pledged loyalty to Nobunaga after the Saitō collapse. Each of
these men, leading a small contingent of his own, took up residence in
Ōmi with a fief—parceled out from Hideyoshi's own domain—ranging
in value from several hundred to several thousand *koku*. It is not certain
whether or not these retainers moved their families to Ōmi and surrendered previous holdings in Mino and Owari. At least by 1581, Nobunaga required all Oda soldiers to forfeit earlier enfeoffments upon the
occasion of a transfer.

Once in Ōmi, Hideyoshi expanded his basic force by recruiting
local retainers of the Asai house. Seven soldiers, known as the Ōmi
"Yellow Shields," formed an elite corps of warriors. Records of the
Tsukubushima shrine mention another twenty or so men of Ōmi who
became Toyotomi vassals.[21] Such recruitment may not have been widespread, however. Reports from vanquished houses suggest that the

exile or forced suicide of much of the resident military population followed Oda victories. Nobunaga did advise his vassals "to treat the samurai of the provinces with courtesy and resolve that there shall be no
negligence in this." But he also noted that "while soldiers loyal to us
should be retained, samurai who cannot be trusted should be banished
or forced to commit suicide."[22]

As lord of northern Ōmi, Hideyoshi's responsibilities extended
beyond military development to local administration. One of his first
decisions was to transfer his headquarters from the ruined stronghold
of the Asai at Odani to the town of Imahama, a port just west of that
castle on the northern shore of Lake Biwa. Imahama was milder than
Odani and commanded a fine prospect of the water. It also had less-
powerful associations with the Asai. Hideyoshi renamed the port Nagahama—the *naga* of "long and far" more felicitous than the *ima* of
"now and current"—and began reconstruction of an old fortification
there. Official summons brought members of every class into the fields
to carry rocks, move earth, and gather materials for the project. "Merchants, priests, and retainers alike: each house shall dispatch before
dawn on the ninth of this month [sixth month, 1574] a representative
with spade, hoe, and other tools. If there is any negligence, it shall be
severely punished."[23] Hideyoshi also laid out new streets and called to
his capital the merchants of prosperous Ōmi markets. A council of
three elders, assisted by a committee of ten, governed the town under
appointment from Hideyoshi.

Like daimyo elsewhere, Hideyoshi exempted the residents of his
headquarters from most standard taxes in order to encourage the immigration of merchants and hence to increase commercial activity, the
circulation of currency, and the marketing of agricultural products. He
briefly rescinded tax privileges, though, when large numbers of Ōmi
farmers deserted their fields to move to Nagahama. In his first extant
letter to his wife, One, Hideyoshi reconsidered and decided to leave the
town free of imposts, "inasmuch as you have objected [to my intention
to restore taxes]."[24] The letter is an early and interesting indication of
this woman's influence. The daughter of an Oda retainer, Sugihara Sa-
datoshi, One married Hideyoshi sometime around 1561. While she
would later compete with an expanding circle of concubines for Hideyoshi's physical attentions, she remained his most constant correspondent and a trusted political confidante throughout his life.

Hideyoshi continued his work in Ōmi by conducting local land
surveys as part of a much larger project to register the Oda domain.
The first Oda cadastres were compiled in southern Ōmi as early as
1568; surveys in Ise, the home provinces, and Echizen followed within
the decade.[25] Hideyoshi began to define the boundaries of his fief, to
sort out the tangled revenue claims of military men, and to review the

holdings of religious institutions. In an ameliorative move, he confirmed the property rights of a Jōdo Shinshū temple, Daitsūji, whose adherents had been allies of the Asai. About 1574 and 1575, in the process of the cadastral registration, Hideyoshi went on to increase the manufacture of muskets in Kunitomo, near the deserted castle of Odani. A center of arms production since the Asai and Asakura collaborated in its development during the 1550s, Kunitomo joined Sakai as a major supplier of weapons for the Oda.[26]

Little more regarding Hideyoshi's tenure in Ōmi is clear. The general objectives of his administration, though, conform to what we know of other domains in the later warring-states era: the establishment of a castle town as headquarters; the stimulation of the market through tax concessions and forced immigration; the initiation of land registration programs; the strengthening of a military base through subinfeudation and confirmation of land rights; the exploitation of resources such as metal works, mines, or forests. Some of Hideyoshi's peers in the Oda command introduced reforms that may have occurred in Ōmi as well—land reclamation and flood control projects, monopolization of local industries, and the regulation of guild rights. The most innovative policy of an Oda daimyo—Shibata Katsuie's decision to confiscate the weapons of farmers in Echizen—seems limited to one area during Nobunaga's regime but would deeply influence Hideyoshi's future government. The Echizen policy was a response to the pervasive influence of the Jōdo Shinshū sect in that province and the continuing possibility of peasant uprisings.[27]

In a sense, Hideyoshi and the other daimyo in Nobunaga's service appeared to be lords of their own domains. They governed extensive lands, where they selected their own retainers and managed their own economies. As far as we know, they rendered no land taxes to the Oda house. Nobunaga's disposition of conquered territories among vassal daimyo made administration along familiar lines possible while obviating the need to define an alternative system of rewards for the men upon whom his future offensives depended. Enfeoffment was the customary compensation for loyal service and the simplest way to recruit and retain access to large armies.

Yet in a deeper sense, Nobunaga's daimyo were not independent. They fought Oda wars, under Nobunaga's direction, with the men and resources of their fiefs. Those fiefs, moreover, were frequently rotated. Hideyoshi was moved from Ōmi to Harima; Akechi Mitsuhide was moved from Ōmi to Echizen to Tamba and anticipated a fourth change. Only Shibata Katsuie remained until 1582 in the holding he acquired in 1574. Routine reassignment transformed the Oda daimyo from domainal lords into movable agents of a superior governor.

The point became clear in a series of nine items that Nobunaga addressed to his daimyo in Echizen sometime in 1575. Similar laws for other provinces followed in later years. In these items Nobunaga defined his vassal daimyo as surrogates for himself. All decisions concerning local government were to conform to his directives: taxation, investitures, legal actions, the disposition of noble estates, and commercial policy. The items of 1575 merit a full translation, for both in tone and in content they reveal the spirit of a regime committed to centralized authority.

Item [1]: You should not require unauthorized taxes in the province. However, when there are extraordinary circumstances, you should inform us of them and, having inquired into our opinion, should conform to it.

Item [2]: Do not treat the samurai established in this province thoughtlessly. Always act with consideration, but you are not to be loose [with them]. Give great attention to the fortifications and strictly allocate land.

Item [3]: [Legal] suits should be conducted according to established law. You should render judgment strictly avoiding partiality or favoritism. However, in the event of dissatisfaction over the verdict, you are to refer the matter to us, through your agent (zasshō), and to settle [the question in this way].

Item [4]: In accordance with [my] red-seal documents, you shall restore the [estates] of the Kyoto [noble] families which were [their] active holdings (tōchigyō) before the [Shinshū] uprisings [of 1574]. This is the proper course.

Item [5]: Insofar as the barriers of the various provinces have all been abolished, you are to act accordingly in this province.

Item [6]: Inasmuch as you have taken this large province in trust, you shall be attentive in all things, and, if there is any negligence, it shall [be perceived as] a violation. Military matters are important above all. Be prudent [in providing for] weapons and provisions. It goes without saying that you will act judiciously to hold [the province] certain for the next five and ten years. You shall be resolute in administration, avoiding greed and retaining [just] what you need. [I.e., you shall not attach all lands to yourselves but shall distribute them fairly to the samurai.] Overindulgence of children [your heirs], in theatricals (sarugaku), pleasure seeking, and idle trips is forbidden.

Item [7]: You are not to indulge in hawking. However, it may be pursued in order to examine the lay of the land. It is forbidden in other cases. This does not affect children.

Item [8]: Depending on the size of your domain, you should set aside two or three areas, unattached to [specific] vassals, which you designate as lands to be specially awarded to men of [particular] loyalty. If you encourage military exploits while there are no such reward lands available, your men, seeing this, will grow weak in valor and loyalty. Bear this prudently in mind. While these [reward lands] remain uninvested in [particular] vassals, they shall be treated as part of my own [Nobunaga's] domain.

Item [9]: Needless to say, you will firmly resolve [to act], in all things, in conformity with Nobunaga's orders. However, should you consider something wrong or opposed to the law, you are not to pass over it with flattery. If you have something to say in regard [to my orders], inform me and I will comply [with the recommendation] should I judge it correct. In any event, revere me and do not feel enmity for me behind my back. It is essential that you always have concern for me. If you follow this way, you will long have good fortune as a samurai. Make prudence your exclusive concern.[28]

The last item, with its injunction to act "in all things in conformity with Nobunaga's orders," leaves no doubt that the Oda daimyo are deputies.[29] But as early as the sixth item, which describes fiefs as lands "entrusted" to the daimyo, Nobunaga's final dominion over the territory of his vassals is clear. Item eight conveys the same message: lands held in reserve to reward splendid acts shall be treated as Nobunaga's personal holdings so that special grants will come directly from him—not from his daimyo. By confirming the rights of certain nobles in vassal fiefs (item 4), Nobunaga again affirms his superior proprietary privileges. All land decisions are ultimately his.

The judicious counsel in these laws—the admonitions against frivolous pastimes and the exhortations to decorous conduct—deepens the lordly, even paternal, tone that denies any parity between Nobunaga and the men who represent him. "Revere me," Nobunaga urges in conclusion, and "you will have good fortune as a samurai." A more personal, and more fascinating, indication of his relationship with a vassal daimyo occurs in a letter Nobunaga dispatched to Hideyoshi's wife, One. Not only the most revealing document concerning Hideyoshi's married life, it is also one of the most candid items in the correspondence of the time.

Your recent journey here [to Azuchi] for the first time and your visit with me were felicitous events. I cannot exhaust my brush or my eyes [in appreciation of] the great beauty of the gifts [you brought]. Although I thought I might send something in gratitude, I have given up the idea at present as I can make no fitting return for the pleasant things I have received from you. When we meet again I shall present something. I particularly looked with admiration upon your features and your appearance which seemed doubly [beautiful] since last we met. That Tokichirō [Hideyoshi] is said to be ceaselessly dissatisfied is a great wrong, beyond words. However far he searches, this bald rat will never find again anyone like yourself. Thus from now on be steadfast, become strong as a wife, and do not give in to jealousy. It is best, in your role as a woman, to leave some things unsaid. Please show this letter to Hashiba [Hideyoshi].[30]

Together with an avuncular intimacy toward One, the letter betrays a careless presumption toward Hideyoshi. If the epithet "bald rat" is arresting in both its wit and its accuracy, the phrase is nonetheless vulgar. It recalls the spirit of comments made by the Jesuit Luis Frois about Nobunaga: "[He] despises all the other Japanese kings and princes and speaks to them over his shoulder as if they were lowly servants."[31] Never disposed to honor his men with court titles or adoptions into his own house, Nobunaga even edged toward disdain in his treatment of them.

More apparent than disdain, of course, was Nobunaga's intention to control his vassals. He replaced the vanquished with new men invested with large holdings and military responsibilities, but kept them securely bound to himself. He recruited them from minor ranks, held their numbers small, directed their campaigns, transferred them as he would, and issued the laws for their fiefs. In these respects, Nobunaga governed in the manner of his greatest warring-states peers. The nation, his conduct suggested, could be ruled as a single immense domain. Yet far more than the consolidation of regional power, the centralization of authority across the country assailed the principle of local autonomy that generations of lords had fought to preserve. While Nobunaga's administration grew out of *sengoku* practices, it was slowly shaping those practices into a disturbingly new configuration.

The Right to Rule

Ashikaga Yoshiaki's departure into exile had left Nobunaga alone at the center of government. Both the Hosokawa and the Miyoshi had known similar experiences, but in every case elevated a new Ashikaga heir to shogunal office. Nobunaga chose to let the matter rest. Neither pursued nor executed by Oda troops, Yoshiaki was left to wander about Japan, pleading until Nobunaga's death with the Shimazu, the Mōri, the Takeda, and the Hōjō for vengeance. Yet like Emperor Go-Daigo, whose goal of imperial restoration Yoshiaki's forebears had first pretended to share and then repudiated, the last Ashikaga scion nursed futile hopes for a return to the past. He and his relatives passed quietly and completely from power.

To some extent, Nobunaga drew closer to the throne in the years after 1573, apparently legitimating his position with imperial sanction. Successively promoted from *sangi* to *gondainagon* to *ukon'e no daishō* to *naidaijin*, Nobunaga became *udaijin* (minister of the right) in 1577. This was the third highest office in the court bureaucracy. Shortly thereafter he was elevated to the second rank.[32] Not surprisingly, these honors were volunteered by a court eager to absorb the current strong man and to fill the vacuum created by Yoshiaki's departure with a new, titled warlord. Nobunaga cooperated in the courtly alliance and assumed the burden conventionally associated with the throne's recognition of a military hegemon: financial support of the imperial house.

As early as 1568 and 1569, he had funded the coming-of-age ceremonies for Prince Takakura and begun reconstruction of the palace compound. He had also made efforts, though often perfunctory, to recover some traditional estates of the throne. About fifteen former holdings provided erratic revenues for the court during Nobunaga's tenure.[33] In 1571, further, he involved the townsmen of the capital in supporting the imperial house. After collecting an extraordinary levy of rice throughout Yamashiro province, he distributed the proceeds to Kyoto's neighborhood organizations as a loan and then ordered them to render a percentage of the principal to the court each year, in monthly installments.[34] This system collapsed after the Oda raid upon Kyoto in 1573, however, and Nobunaga devised a fresh scheme to support the emperor. In 1575 he assigned to the imperial family land from eleven districts in Yamashiro. Annual revenue from these holdings began to restore the throne to solvency.[35]

In serving the emperor in exchange for high title and the attendant sanction of his rule, Nobunaga appeared to conform to a pattern of legitimation long established in military circles. But in 1578 he resigned all court offices and titles and asked that they be transferred to his heir. The decision may have been made to clarify the pattern of succession. It is more likely, though, that Nobunaga had chosen to stand outside familiar governing frameworks and to remove himself from the court as he had removed himself from the shogunate. His relationship with both institutions indicates a refusal to be integrated into powerless bodies that he sought to subordinate, not to honor by acts of deference.

As he had declined appointments in Yoshiaki's administration, so he declined court promotions, despite continuing overtures from the throne. Just before the attack at Honnōji, imperial ambassadors were offering him the title of great minister of state (*daijō daijin*), imperial regent (*kampaku*), or even shogun.[36] And as he had patronized Yoshiaki and appropriated his governing rights, so Nobunaga dominated the throne with financial assistance that was as much a gesture of condescension as an act of homage. Having noted that Nobunaga established the imperial heir apparent in a Kyoto residence built by the Oda, and that he tried to advance the accession date of this malleable prince, one scholar argues that Nobunaga finally hoped to install the future emperor at Azuchi castle as his own attendant. According to a stunning report by the Jesuit Luis Frois, Azuchi was also to be the site of Nobunaga's self-proclaimed apotheosis as a living divinity.[37]

Neither a decision to master the throne nor to deify himself can be proven from the Oda records. Two points are nonetheless apparent. First, Nobunaga knew the shogunate and the court at the nadir of their influence when their heads were compelled to truckle to him for renewed, however minimal, advantages. Second, the increasing scope of his conquests and the support of his vassals provided Nobunaga with identity and authority enough. Perhaps alone among national leaders in Japan's history he appeared to believe that power legitimated itself. The role he chose to play, with a new extravagance, was daimyo—a role that generations of victorious domainal governors had exalted with their conquests, their legal and cadastral initiatives, and their demonstration of the exhaustion of older political traditions. The emblem of Nobunaga's authority was neither a princely home in Kyoto nor a suburban mansion reminiscent of the Ashikaga. It was Azuchi castle.

Nobunaga began construction of this headquarters in 1576 but did not enter it until 1579, shortly after he quit his court offices. The castle stood on a verdant crest in southern Ōmi overlooking the eastern bank of Lake Biwa. Biwa flowed into Osaka Bay via the Uji River to link Azuchi to the cities of the south. Kyoto was an easy journey by land, and three ancient highways leading to the Japan Sea and the northern provinces were close by. Rice and tea fields filled the narrow valleys that laced the hills of Ōmi.

A donjon, buildings to house the Oda family and vassals, arsenals, and warehouses occupied six walled enclosures at Azuchi castle. Hideyoshi and Takigawa Kazumasu, with thousands of their own laborers, constructed a labyrinthine stone rampart to provide the complex with its primary security. Already common in fortifications of the period, these features were more elaborate at Azuchi than at any of its prototypes. But it was the size and ornamentation of the keep that commanded attention. Rising above the stone base were six stories fitted out so graciously as to belie any martial connection. The floors were covered with tatami, the pillars finished in lacquer or gold leaf, the walls painted by Kanō Eitoku with interpretations of the Seven Sages of the Bamboo Grove, the legendary emperors of China, Shakyamuni's disciples, and hawks, dragons, plums, and tigers.[38]

Earlier donjons were elaborated watchtowers built for defense.

Azuchi changed the conventions and invited recognition of Nobunaga's eminence. Together with his mounted processions through Kyoto and his famous tea parties,[39] the castle was an accoutrement of power, a power apparently made righteous by its own assurance.

To make a real city of Azuchi, Nobunaga instituted policies already familiar to residents of Gifu, his earlier headquarters, and similar to those of Hideyoshi's Nagahama. He required all merchants using local highways to stop in Azuchi and confined the horse markets of Ōmi to its environs. He freed its citizens of taxes and abolished customs barriers and guild privileges in the city. To encourage immigration further, Nobunaga protected residents against outstanding tax claims from former landlords or military proprietors. And he enticed moneylenders with guarantees that debts would never be canceled in his capital.[40]

That Nobunaga intended to assume central authority—and to act as daimyo to the entire nation—became clear with several initiatives that signaled his ascendancy as forcefully as Azuchi castle. We have noted already that he took charge of Kyoto in 1573. He stationed his own magistrate, Murai Sadahiko, in the city to symbolize his dominion not only over local citizens but over the traditional seat of national authority as well. By 1574, Murai was the unquestioned leader of the capital. He arbitrated suits concerning noble and religious proprietors, heard complaints from townsmen over commercial transactions and guild rights, policed the streets, and supervised construction. His touch was light, however, and no fundamental transformation of the capital's economy or neighborhood political bodies occurred. Nobunaga's interests were not in the details of city management but in the acknowledgment of his right to rule Kyoto.[41]

A similar initiative was undertaken about 1580 when Nobunaga began to register the land and resources of the nation's most powerful temples. Autonomous proprietors in the high Ashikaga period, the greatest of the monasteries—like Hiei—had endured throughout the sixteenth century as independent powers with extensive lands and armies. No shogun had challenged their boundaries, disciplined their troops, or surveyed their holdings. They were the last survivors of the old order, still respected by most daimyo, and holders of historical privileges virtually as old as those of the throne.

One of the better-documented surveys took place in Nara at Kōfukuji, a monastery founded in the eighth century. In the ninth month of 1580, monks of the temple sealed, in blood, an oath of several articles. They promised to send Nobunaga a full listing of Kōfukuji's income as well as the dimensions of all lands held directly or through affiliates. Inviting him to verify their findings, in the event of doubt, through inquiries of cultivators, they agreed to the surrender of their holdings should any duplicity be proven against them.

A Kōfukuji diarist outlined the events between the delivery of the oath and the completion, thirty-eight days later, of the registry itself. He described the preparation of a registry outline, the collation of land documents, the compilation of data from both landlords and cultivators, and the conversion of income figures from cash to a rice equivalent. The total came to an impressive 34,417 *koku*.[42]

Nobunaga did not tamper either with Kōfukuji or with the other monasteries he submitted to inspection. In the eleventh month of 1580 he confirmed the holdings of all temples and shrines in Yamato province. Yet the act of registration itself—under Nobunaga's order and in the presence of his vassals Akechi Mitsuhide and Takigawa Kazumasu—effectively declared that monastery properties were held through the sufferance of a superior governor.

From the perspective of the Tokugawa period, it is easy to overlook the daring of Nobunaga's work, to see it as the natural realization of the goals of warring-states daimyo. Needless to say, that realization becomes natural only in retrospect. The ravaging of Hiei, the assaults upon Kyoto and Sakai, the registration of monastery properties—all would have seemed inconceivable to the Ashikaga shogun. Yet the mastery of Japan's many discrete and autonomous units of control was as essential to Nobunaga's vision of government as the conquest of daimyo adversaries. Indeed, the incorporation of these units into his sphere of influence lay at the center of his claim to national rule. The submission of Kyoto and monastic populations was substantively important to the consolidation of power; it was symbolically critical as an affirmation of Nobunaga's right to govern. For it was not in the often meaningless approbation of the shogunate and the court—too many times showered upon weak men—that he found legitimacy. He defined rightful rule in terms of the obeisance of the ruled—his vassals, priests and townspeople, the noble community, and Ashikaga Yoshiaki himself. If Azuchi was a physical demonstration of power, the expansion of Nobunaga's domain into Kyoto and the temples of the religious elite indicated that a daimyo, as daimyo, could command the respect that constituted authority.[43]

The Universal Front

When Nobunaga broke ground for Azuchi castle, he controlled much of the richest and strategically important land of Japan. From his base in Owari and Mino he had moved into Ise, Iga, Ōmi, Echizen, Hida, and four of the home provinces—Yamashiro, Izumi, Kawachi, and Yamato.

Alliance with the Tokugawa house afforded him influence in Mikawa and Tōtōmi as well. But by the time of his death, Nobunaga had more than doubled the size of this already remarkable domain, transforming his headquarters at Azuchi into something of a national capital.

The Oda domain expanded as the result of widely dispersed offensives that were the first and last of their kind in sixteenth-century Japan. They eclipsed the local contests of earlier decades and, with their success, provided Nobunaga's successor with a base for concentrated rather than diffuse military action. In the years following the campaign in Ōmi, Nobunaga himself turned toward consolidation of the home provinces; Shibata Katsuie assumed responsibility for the Hokuriku area; Tokugawa Ieyasu resumed the campaign against the Takeda in the east; Akechi Mitsuhide moved into the San'in provinces of western Japan; and Toyotomi Hideyoshi began his march through the San'yō circuit of the southwest.

Each of these offensives added significantly to the Oda sphere. Nobunaga finally subdued Settsu, the last of the home provinces. The Shibata armies took over Wakasa, Noto, Kaga, and part of Etchū. Tokugawa Ieyasu annexed former Takeda holdings in Suruga, Kai, Shinano, and part of Kōzuke. Akechi Mitsuhide and his men entered Tamba, Tango, Tajima, Inaba, and a portion of Hōki. Hideyoshi advanced from Harima into Bizen, Mimasaka, and Bitchū. In sum, Oda Nobunaga could lay claim to holdings in thirty-one of Japan's sixty-six provinces when he was struck down in Kyoto.

The extent of the Oda victories, however, should not distract us from their slowness and their difficulty. Settsu fell only in 1580, after a decade of war. Tokugawa Ieyasu's battles with the Takeda, which frequently progressed in favor of the enemy, concluded in 1582. Begun in 1573, they too lasted for ten years. Hideyoshi took thirty months to move from eastern to western Harima. Like the contests of earlier years, these campaigns provoked collective resistance and constant diversions. Nobunaga's generals routinely abandoned their primary marches to reinforce beleaguered confederates. And their opponents routinely received unexpected assistance from neighbors united by a common dread of the Oda. The patterns of conflict had not changed.

The battles between the Oda and the Takeda, for example, revived familiar themes. Broken off by Takeda Shingen's sudden death in 1573, they resumed the following year when a new household head, Takeda Katsuyori, entered both the Tokugawa domain of Mikawa and the Oda domain of Mino. The likelihood of an Oda defeat in the eastern provinces forced Nobunaga to summon most of his generals from other fronts for defensive action in Mino. On the battleground of Nagashino, in the fifth month of 1575, they confronted the Takeda with three thousand foot soldiers armed with muskets. Mustering the largest array of firearms yet seen in Japan, the Oda army devastated their adversaries in a bloody display of force almost as shocking to contemporaries as the wreck of Mount Hiei. It nonetheless took seven more years for the Tokugawa and Oda forces to recover their territories, enter the Takeda holdings, and force Katsuyori into surrender. Much of their opposition came from the Uesugi house, a staunch ally of the Takeda in their re-solve to break Nobunaga's grip on the east. And much of their success depended upon the assistance of the Hōjō house, briefly an ally of the Tokugawa, in their resolve to break a Takeda–Uesugi coalition that threatened Hōjō boundaries no less than those of the Oda. The de-feated Takeda Katsuyori took his own life in 1582, and Tokugawa Ieyasu occupied the Takeda domain.[44]

As expedient alliances, violent reprisals, and the annihilation of great houses increased in Nobunaga's last years, so too did the assault upon militant Buddhist temples. The target of the Oda campaign in Settsu was the Jōdo Shinshū sect. An armed and ably organized center of opposition to military rule, the sect preached individual equality in self-governing communities, shared resources, and the irrelevance of rewards for voluntary service to the congregation. Such principles pro-ceeded from the religious tenets of universal salvation, equality under Buddhist law, and the dignity of independent lay organizations. They had, moreover, a powerful political application inimical to the do-mainal order with its assumption of authoritarian government, con-tractual association between lord and enfeoffed vassal, and an unequal distribution of resources and power.

The dominant political force throughout the Hokuriku in the late fifteenth and early sixteenth centuries, Jōdo Shinshū sectarians rebelled in other areas as well, refusing to pay taxes, expropriating land, and seizing granaries. Ise, Owari, Mikawa, Kii, Yamashiro—all knew peas-ant uprisings under Shinshū direction. Nobunaga and his vassals took sectarian strongholds in Ise (1574), Echizen (1575), Owari (1575), and Kii (1577). But the headquarters of the church since 1532, the temple of Ishiyama Honganji in the Settsu city of Osaka, resisted conquest for ten years. Believers across the nation joined in its defense, aided by daimyo such as Mōri Terumoto. The indefatigable Yoshiaki raised supporters too.[45]

Despite important setbacks—principally in sea battles against the Mōri navy—Nobunaga reduced the Honganji contingents by blockad-ing Osaka Bay.[46] By the seventh month of 1580 the abbot sued for peace. His surrender, almost alone in the history of Oda wars, was ne-gotiated. The court had intervened for some time between the parties, and in the last months of confrontation one noble, Konoe Sakihisa, took up serious efforts at conciliation. When Ishiyama surrendered, Nobunaga delivered to the abbot, through Konoe, an extraordinary oath sealed in blood:

> Item: Since there is concern over the hostages [whom we have taken], they shall be turned over to you.

> Item: Those branch temples [of the Shinshū sect] which have harbored you [in the past] shall go on as before [without reprisals].

> Item: After you have withdrawn from the castle in Osaka, [your temples] in Kaga shall be returned without issue.[47]

Nobunaga gained far more than he lost from the settlement with the Honganji sectarians. Once again he had demonstrated his resolve to subordinate militant churches by forcing his opponents not only into surrender but into departure from Osaka as well. And what assurances of Nobunaga's goodwill the sectarians had received were yet to be proven. Nonetheless, it is possible to see in his concessions some break in the pattern of total reprisal against Oda enemies. There was good cause for conciliation. Unlike individual daimyo houses, the Jōdo Shinshū sect was a national organization with a history of collective defiance of military rule. It remained capable of rebellion in villages and of resumed action on a wider scale. Thus steady assault upon Shinshū communities was coupled with placation to subdue an endemic, and therefore an elusive, antagonist. The uniqueness of the Shinshū challenge provoked a unique response from Nobunaga.[48] Whether compromise might have extended to other situations is a question left open by Nobunaga's death less than two years later.

In one case, however, a new readiness in the Oda army for negotiation did appear. Toyotomi Hideyoshi advanced along the San'yō circuit by arranging truces with both the Kodera and the Ukita houses. Confirming their holdings in exchange for assistance and safe passage, he had reached the mouth of the Mōri domain by 1582. Toward the end of his life, when he commissioned an official biography, Hideyoshi chose to see his march into the San'yō as the proper beginning of his story.[49]

That biography, the *Tenshō-ki*, opens with the fall of Miki castle, held by the Bessho house, in the province of Harima. An otherwise routine event became, in the hands of a devout chronicler, the harbinger of greatness. As the new castellan of Miki, Hideyoshi "renewed the land, dredged the moat, rebuilt the houses, recalled those who had fled, summoned the townspeople, built a market in front of the temple ... This confounded with surprise the eyes and ears of all. Someone remarked, 'Hideyoshi has ten virtues: fidelity to his lord, justice to those who serve him, bravery in war, compassion for the people, righteousness in action, honesty of intention, wisdom and fortune within, authority without, astuteness in inquiry, charity in perception.' "[50] The words were carefully chosen, of course: compassion tempered justice, charity mediated authority. Subtly but inescapably the contrast was drawn with "his lord," Nobunaga.

If the capture of Miki castle and alliance with the Kodera and the Ukita was the beginning of Hideyoshi's career, the end of the Oda regime was in sight. Hideyoshi's entry into the Mōri domain brought Nobunaga and Akechi Mitsuhide together. Unable to force the Mōri into a rapid surrender in the province of Bitchū, Hideyoshi called for reinforcements. Mitsuhide was on the road to Bitchū when he made a detour for Kyoto.

A centrist and absolute governor in much of his policy, Oda Nobunaga chose a political course that many of his competitors tried to follow and that no successor would fully abandon. The right of the conqueror to control major cities and religious establishments, and to dictate the movements and administrative decisions of vassals, became a fact of life in his regime. The high costs of consolidation on Nobunaga's terms, though, led to military resistance that showed no promise of abatement. Daimyo of a third of Japan, Nobunaga still faced the Mōri, Shimazu, Uesugi, Date, Hōjō, and Chōsokabe—houses collectively more formidable than those he had already taken. The Oda advances by 1582 provided little assurance that further gains were likely.

The forcible concentration of authority was just one direction in the politics of the warring-states era, however. There was another—toward independent local government—that had provided most of the vitality of the age. The steady usurpation of independent daimyo by Nobunaga's small band of vassals seemed to close off this direction, only to reveal its centrality to sixteenth-century life. If Nobunaga was a lord who "did not know the Way," his rebuff of the throne and his attacks upon shrines, temples, cities, and the shogunate were peripheral to his basic denial of domainal rule. Once the Honnōji incident brought the terror of his regime to a close, men newly conscious of the risks of cataclysmic war would accommodate the Oda legacy to the older traditions of the warring states.

4

CONQUEST AND CONCILIATION

TOYOTOMI HIDEYOSHI had pacified all Japan by the end of 1590. The date is remarkable for its lateness if we take a broad view of the era of warring states. It marked the end of thirteen decades of fighting in a small, isolated, and homogeneous nation that had rarely known irreconcilable division and had preserved, even at the height of battle, two symbols of consolidation—the throne and the shogunate. Reunion could hardly have been deferred forever. The puzzle is that it took so long.

A narrower view of Hideyoshi's age reveals a different puzzle, of course. How could peace have been achieved so swiftly? Although Oda Nobunaga had extended his influence into a third of the country by 1582, the resistance to him was massive and unceasing. His opponents led formidable armies of their own in defense of autonomous rule. What gains Nobunaga had made, moreover, were vitiated by his assassination. Many older and better established houses had splintered under such circumstances. And who among Nobunaga's men, all new to power and accustomed to supervision, could be expected to restore order within the Oda coalition, let alone the nation?

For the authors of the formative military histories of the time, pacification depended upon Hideyoshi's martial genius and was achieved through a spectacular series of conquests. The *Tenshō-ki*, the various *Taikō-ki*, and the *Buke jiki* describe a man fiercely strong of will and inspired as a leader; a man quick to attack but patient in siege who could guide a small corps in ambush as well as a vast army in the encirclement of nine provinces. The measure of this uncommon general was victory.[1] The early accounts of Hideyoshi's career take the form of battle chronologies, tracing the inexorable progress of Toyotomi troops from central Japan to Shikoku to Kyushu to the northeast. That progress becomes the more impressive for its speed. While Nobunaga had fought the Asai for four years and the Takeda for ten, none of Hideyoshi's campaigns lasted much longer than six months and the entire nation fell to him within eight years.

In the richly textured narratives of the war tales, which illustrate the carnage of the day as surely as they describe a heroic conqueror, Oda Nobunaga and destiny emerge as important players. Nobunaga served as Hideyoshi's precursor, the man who built his successor's base, provided the necessary momentum for unification, and established a pattern of aggressive national rule. Yet neither Nobunaga nor Hideyoshi achieved success purely through personal strength. Both, according to the accounts, were agents of Heaven's Will, participants in a movement toward political consolidation and harmonious government that transcended them. Destiny accounts for the otherwise unaccountable victories of these particular individuals, and for their ultimate eclipse.[2]

The notion of destiny is useful, and even persuasive, in recounting an improbable career. Its prominence in the tales draws attention, however, to the many elements of Hideyoshi's victory that martial skill cannot explain. To concentrate upon Hideyoshi's brilliance in war and to put conquest at the center of his achievement is to miss a second Hideyoshi, one who owed less to fate for his surprising ascent than to his skill in conciliation. The conciliator is harder to discover than the conqueror. He was not the focus of contemporary attention, and his diplomacy was overshadowed by the more stunning, more tangible feats of war. Yet Hideyoshi's letters, the terms of truce and surrender he reached with his adversaries, and the catalogue of battles he never had to fight suggest that behind the story of military victory is a more important story of negotiation and alliance.

In the years after 1582 Hideyoshi came to peaceful accords with Nobunaga's staunchest enemies: the Mōri, Uesugi, Date, Ōtomo, and Satake. Such alliances precluded a number of conflicts, negotiation hastened the end of others, and generous treatment of defeated houses inclined once-obdurate opponents to arbitration. Conciliation not only narrowed the field of Hideyoshi's campaigns, it provided him, too, with the sizable armies he dispatched to Shikoku, to Kyushu, and to the northeast. Thus if he emerged after Nobunaga's death as a peerless general, it was his talent for diplomacy that made his wars manageable and his military contingents unequaled.

The extent and stability of Hideyoshi's alliances represent a fundamental break with the pattern of expansion cut by Oda Nobunaga. Indebted to his lord for the nucleus of his land and manpower, Hideyoshi extended his power by absorbing former antagonists into his settlement. Nobunaga had advanced through conquest, obliterated the vanquished, and distributed confiscated property among his own men.

Hideyoshi's departure from this example is best revealed in a registry of daimyo and their domains compiled shortly before his death in 1598.

Sixteen men listed in this document held lands, invested by Hideyoshi, valued at 200,000 *koku* or more each.[3] These were the largest and most powerful domains in the nation, collectively accounting for almost fifty percent of its wealth. Nine of the sixteen holders had either gone to war against Hideyoshi at one point in their careers or, as potential opponents, negotiated with him for peace. Five were former Oda vassals whose support Hideyoshi cultivated with handsome allocations of land. Only two men, at the bottom of the list, had been members of his retinue before 1582. By and large, Hideyoshi's intimate retainers held lands valued at under 100,000 *koku;* most received holdings ranging from 10,000 to 30,000 *koku*. Hideyoshi's personal domain was not dramatically larger than those of his most eminent daimyo.[4]

This registry draws our notice to the distinction between *fudai* and *tozama* lords. The *fudai* were those vassals who entered Toyotomi service young, voluntarily, without large holdings, and during the early phases of Hideyoshi's career. The *tozama*, daimyo with independent land bases, submitted to the Toyotomi following alliance, negotiation, or defeat.[5] The striking revelation of the registry is the importance of the latter. The investiture of sometime adversaries, and the consequent emergence of *tozama* power, is a Toyotomi phenomenon that raises two questions. Why did Hideyoshi make extraordinary concessions to outsiders? And why did the *tozama* accept Toyotomi suzerainty?

The answer to the first question lies, in part, in the military exigencies of the time. Numerous concessions to *tozama* occurred during the three years after the Honnōji incident. Several were made to avert hostilities. Others confirmed Hideyoshi's support of Oda generals capable of insurrection. The largest (to Tokugawa Ieyasu) brought an end to a campaign that was not proceeding in Hideyoshi's favor. These allocations allowed Hideyoshi to escape potentially crippling battles and to gain time for other initiatives. Of equal moment, he acquired influence over allied armies. Much of the early assistance of *tozama* soldiers was requested rather than commanded, for Hideyoshi's authority over his daimyo varied considerably and was proven only over time. Yet land concessions to the *tozama* helped neutralize their opposition at the very least, and promised to secure their military cooperation at best.

Military incentives also influenced Hideyoshi's more startling decision to award fiefs to daimyo defeated in Toyotomi wars—primarily the Chōsokabe and Shimazu. By leaving the command structure of their armies intact, Hideyoshi discouraged upheavals by displaced retainers and obviated the need to place new generals over fractious soldiers in a time of uncertainty. Thus he was able more easily to impress vanquished troops for new Toyotomi engagements. Further, leniency toward the defeated undercut resistance among still-hostile daimyo, who found reason in this demonstration of conciliation to submit without bloodshed.

If an interest in efficient mobilization of defeated forces shaped Hideyoshi's conduct toward the Chōsokabe and their peers, complementary interests were obviously at work as well. The conquered daimyo were more than able generals, they were seasoned local rulers. In a world of few constants, they represented stable rule. Strength and continuity in domainal government, no less than in military management, recommended the cause of the *tozama*. All too few of Hideyoshi's *fudai* had experience administering fiefs. Many, like Hideyoshi himself, had begun their odysseys at young ages with little education and little sense of place. A number eventually flourished as daimyo. But given the volatility and size of newly conquered domains, as well as the demands of pressing offensives, rehabilitation of the defeated made sense.

Hideyoshi's expansion of *tozama* power through the enfeoffment of former enemies was, however, something more than an act of faith. By the time he confirmed the Chōsokabe and Shimazu domains, he had seen *tozama* governments in other territories work to his advantage. As evidence of the feasibility of cooperation with *tozama* mounted, Hideyoshi had cause to extend his policy of conciliation for the most compelling of reasons: his alliances worked.

Why did they work? There can be little doubt that the first and most important of the alliances were expedient affairs not unlike Nobunaga's pacts with the Takeda and Asai. As we shall see, victory against the Akechi and Shibata in the early months after the Honnōji attack placed Hideyoshi in a strong position to negotiate. Control over the arms-producing center of Sakai, as well as the mines of Ōmi and Yamato, promised him a lasting advantage in his arsenal. By absorbing Akechi and Shibata troops into his army and establishing control over the central provinces, Hideyoshi enhanced his bargaining power. He moved with such assurance into the vacuum created by Nobunaga's death that opponents disposed to caution seized the temporary security of alliance. If conciliation afforded Hideyoshi time, it also afforded his first *tozama* time. Should treaties bring unwelcome demands for military assistance, the *tozama* could always turn against Hideyoshi at an opportune moment.

That repudiation of the alliances did not take place was the result of a variety of factors. Ieyasu's unsuccessful challenge to Hideyoshi in 1584, for example, served notice that sturdy anti-Toyotomi coalitions were unlikely to emerge. The division of interest among Hideyoshi's adversaries, and the absence of a united front against the Toyotomi when group resistance was most practical, permitted a gradual strengthening of his power that eventually made repudiation of early treaties foolhardy. The great daimyo of the 1580s, further, were conservative men. Regional hegemons who stood to lose a good deal in wars of attrition, they chose to support that leader who was familiar, disposed to confirm their claims to land, and vulnerable to the separate and collective pressure they could bring to bear on him. Of exceptional importance to the peaceable conduct of the *tozama* was the voluntary participation of several of them in Hideyoshi's first campaigns beyond the Oda borders. These men set an example of unity for their counterparts and warned reluctant members of the Toyotomi alliance that rebellion might provoke retaliation from more than Hideyoshi's *fudai* complement alone.

Indeed, to a large extent the unexampled cooperation of *tozama* such as the Mōri created the conditions for Hideyoshi's settlement. They provided the manpower for his early campaigns, demonstrated the utility of alliance through their faithfulness, and thus encouraged Hideyoshi to reach out to new allies and the defeated alike. So great were Hideyoshi's debts to those *tozama* that he continued to distribute the spoils of battle to them rather than to the *fudai*—a definitive characteristic of his administration.

But the tactical logic of war explains their fidelity only in part. It is inadequate, too, for understanding Hideyoshi's lasting commitment to *tozama* when the opportunities to strengthen his own house were great. Like the preoccupation of the *Taikō-ki* authors with the explanatory device of destiny, a retrospective discovery of the rationality of alliance lends an air of inevitability to events of immense surprise. The lessons of the *sengoku* era had amply shown that the military solution to a century of civil war did not have to take the shape it did. The contrast between Nobunaga's tortuous expansion by conquest and Hideyoshi's experience of conciliation merits further reflection here, for there appears to be a causal relation between the terror of the first regime and the readiness for political integration in the second. Nobunaga moved from destruction of the shogunate to threaten all the lords of his day with extinction. His legacy to Hideyoshi, then, was one of fear. Without it, how many daimyo would have taken the risks of alliance? To a large extent, the search for security replaced the desire for conquest during Hideyoshi's tenure. And that shift in goal, and consequently in thought, remains inexplicable without a climate of dread.

We must return, though, to our starting point. If there was a climate of dread, the conqueror of the *Taikō-ki* knew how to intensify it, and the conciliator of Hideyoshi's correspondence knew how to turn it to advantage. The tension between Hideyoshi's various roles never relaxed. The outcome of his efforts became clear only in time. Chance, unpredictable exercises of personality, Hideyoshi's esteem as a parvenu for Japan's martial houses, and the caution of adversaries figured importantly in the equation of unification. Of greatest significance was an emerging decision, made gradually by both Hideyoshi and the daimyo, that the domains must survive. The crucial choice of the 1580s was in favor of land division and the participation of *tozama* in a national settlement.

Early Initiatives: Yamazaki, Kiyosu, and Kyoto

Nothing was certain in the weeks following Mitsuhide's strike against Nobunaga and his heir. Courtiers and military men alike responded to news of the attack on Honnōji with apprehension.[6] Few would have predicted Hideyoshi's rapid rise to primacy. In retrospect, it was the daring of his conduct that afforded him an advantage. There was little unique about his army, and neither pedigree nor status in the Oda coalition made him a natural choice for leadership.

Mitsuhide's raid was shrewd in its timing. Nobunaga's meager guard perished with him, and most Oda daimyo, involved in distant campaigns, were incapable of swift retaliation. Thus Mitsuhide's army went on to plunder Azuchi without challenge and tried to bring the province of Ōmi under Akechi control. On the seventh of the sixth month, five days after the Honnōji affair, an intimidated court sent congratulations to Mitsuhide. He made overtures to Kyoto's citizens by declaring tax exemptions, by donating five hundred units of silver to the emperor, and by distributing gifts to leading temples and shrines. Soon he began seeking friends among enemies of the Oda house.[7]

Mitsuhide acted with considerable poise in the early days after his vengeance. It is possible that he envisioned succeeding the Oda. More likely than Akechi hegemony, however, was a shift in power that assured Mitsuhide a place of new importance. He had allies in the Chōsokabe and could look for support from vassals and relatives among the Oda daimyo (the Hosokawa, the Takayama, the Nakagawa, and the Tsutsui).

For eleven days Mitsuhide went untouched. Tokugawa Ieyasu, conducting an inspection tour of Sakai when he learned the news of Honnōji, returned to Mikawa to gather troops. Niwa Nagahide and Nobunaga's second son might have led an army massed in Osaka against the assassin, but they hesitated. Other contingents, assembling near Kyoto to join Hideyoshi's campaign against the Mōri, held back as well. Their leaders were inclined neither to reinforce nor to attack a confederate in such troubled circumstances.

Hideyoshi's course was not so complicated. On the day after Nobunaga's death, an emissary dispatched by Akechi Mitsuhide to the Mōri fell into his hands. Given intelligence about events in Kyoto, Hideyoshi prepared for an attack on the Akechi army by taking immediate steps to conclude his current campaign, a march through the provinces of the San'in and the San'yō that had led him to the stronghold of the Mōri house in Bitchū. Hideyoshi's systematic flooding of Takamatsu castle with the waters of the Ashimori River had already brought his opponents close to surrender. Summoning the Mōri negotiator, Ankokuji Ekei, to arrange a truce, Hideyoshi agreed to cease hostilities upon recognition by the Mōri of Oda supremacy in Hōki, Mimasaka, and Bitchū. Ignorant of the Honnōji story, Ankokuji welcomed the reprieve. Bitchū had been all but reduced; Mimasaka was largely in enemy hands; Toyotomi control of the unoccupied portion of Hōki appeared a matter of time. Thus he allowed Hideyoshi to enter Takamatsu castle on the fourth day of the sixth month. On the sixth day, Hideyoshi left Takamatsu to march to the capital.[8]

The seventh saw him at Himeji, already eighty kilometers from the Bitchū camp. By the ninth he was on the road to Kyoto with fresh troops. On the thirteenth he faced Akechi Mitsuhide in the neighborhood of Yamazaki in Yamashiro province, not far from the capital. Mitsuhide's army was decimated. Stragglers fled to Kyoto, and Mitsuhide retreated north, beyond Fushimi, but was cut down in the village of Ogurusu by a group of peasants. Hideyoshi collected Mitsuhide's head and body and carried them back to Honnōji for the approval of Nobunaga's spirit. Imperial felicitations followed on the next day.[9]

Many things defeated Mitsuhide. His original army, estimated at just over 10,000, was exhausted after its recent marches. Nearby friends turned on him to support Hideyoshi. Niwa Nagahide and Oda Nobukatsu too joined Hideyoshi near Osaka, thus swelling his forces to about 20,000. The surprise of the Toyotomi arrival and the numerical supremacy of the Toyotomi command brought the encounter with Mitsuhide to a close within two hours. Yamazaki was a rout.

Perhaps the Mōri themselves gave this victory to Hideyoshi. They finally had news of Honnōji on the fourth of the month, two days before Hideyoshi's departure from Bitchū. Safe from the threat of Oda reinforcements, the Mōri might have resumed the struggle at Takamatsu. Popular wisdom has it that two men, Ankokuji Ekei and Kobayakawa Takakage, pressed restraint upon their peers in the Mōri house.[10] Both men would enjoy close and rewarding relations with Hideyoshi in the future. Ekei was eventually enfeoffed in Shikoku with 60,000 koku. Takakage, later appointed as a Toyotomi elder, acquired a domain in Kyushu worth 300,000 koku. If these two men were responsible for the temperate response of the Mōri to the announcement from Honnōji, why did they allow their challenger a safe departure from Bitchū in 1582?

Both men had some knowledge of Hideyoshi. The Zen priest Ekei, long an intermediary for the Mōri with the Oda, first met with Hideyoshi in 1573.[11] Hideyoshi made his initial contact with Takakage in a letter of 1569: "The monk from Eikōji, envoy from Motonari to Nobunaga, has arrived ... Apart from Oda Nobunaga I express my friendship; it is necessary for us hereafter to discuss [all things] without reserve. While we are young there should be no differences between us and it is proper that we set an example [to others]. Thus, even though we have not met, I send you a horse by the name of Tobikasuge."[12] Neither Mōri Motonari, Takakage's natural father, nor his successor, Mōri Terumoto, ever came to terms with Nobunaga. But Hideyoshi continued his overtures with regular letters that broadcast the victories of the Oda and sought an accommodation with Takakage.[13]

Separated by only three years in age, and professionally respectful of each other, Hideyoshi and Takakage may have laid the foundation for alliance in their letters. The remarkable cordiality of their association after 1582 cannot be explained fully in terms of a correspondence that doubtless proceeded as much from opportunism as from concern with the peace. Nonetheless, that correspondence alone illuminates the early Kobayakawa-Toyotomi relationship and suggests that some of Hideyoshi's treaties may have been rooted in such early exchanges of regard.

The fidelity of the Mōri to the Takamatsu truce guaranteed Hideyoshi a strike against Mitsuhide. And the success of that strike gave Hideyoshi unusual influence at the Kiyosu conference. Within a month of Nobunaga's death, on the twenty-seventh day of the sixth month, 1582, his vassals gathered at Kiyosu castle in Owari to select an heir and to divide recently conquered domains.[14] Most of Nobunaga's men were present. Sassa Narimasa and Tokugawa Ieyasu alone failed to appear; Narimasa stood guard in Etchū against attack, Ieyasu chose to protect his interests in Mikawa. The meeting reflected, if not a common purpose among the Oda generals, at least a temporary commitment to a common front. Open dissent among them might have canceled their collective gains by inviting retaliation from new coalitions. But the Kiyosu conference affirmed their alliance even as it betokened their weakness. The absence of an obvious successor to Nobunaga and the forced fraternity of his daimyo revealed a divided group.

The death of Nobunaga's eldest son and heir, Nobutada, after the Honnōji raid left three contenders for family headship. Shibata Katsuie, at the age of sixty the senior conferee and leader of the deliberations, championed Nobunaga's third son, Nobutaka. As a participant in the battle of Yamazaki, Nobutaka shared the credit for avenging his father that was denied to Nobukatsu, Nobunaga's second son and another claimant to the privileges of succession.

Hideyoshi disregarded both men to support Nobunaga's grandson, Nobutada's son—Sambōshi. He was, arguably, the logical choice. Sambōshi's election would ensure lineal passage of inheritance rights while avoiding promotion of either of his uncles, now in their mid-twenties, who lacked the strength to prevail at Kiyosu. The very existence of a conference governed not by Oda sons but by Oda vassals illustrated the vulnerability of these brothers. They had not been at the vanguard of Nobunaga's offensives, nor did they hold his largest fiefs. Under the shadow of the Oda heir, they were never raised to leadership in the family. Indeed, both had been adopted into other houses—Nobutaka into the Kambe, Nobukatsu into the Kitabatake.

Certainly Hideyoshi used his influence as the hero of Yamazaki to press Sambōshi's suit. And that influence itself might have been decisive.[15] The Ikeda, Niwa, Nakagawa, and Takayama—once Hideyoshi's peers in the Oda hierarchy—all took his lead during the campaign against Mitsuhide and showed support for his favorite at Kiyosu. Yet Hideyoshi used his influence to general advantage by advancing a contender who relieved the unease of Nobunaga's daimyo. Sambōshi, three years old at the time of the conference and without defensible concerns of his own, did not present the immediate threat to the Oda vassals that Nobutaka or Nobukatsu posed. Hence the Oda generals agreed to take an oath of loyalty to Sambōshi during the Kiyosu meeting. Nobutaka became the child's guardian. The balance of power among Nobunaga's survivors was thus left unaffected in the short run.

The division of domains at Kiyosu also reflected the preoccupation of the conference's participants with equal authority. No general emerged with a commanding land advantage; most holdings were simply confirmed. Hideyoshi did receive Yamashiro, Kawachi, and Tamba (Mitsuhide's former fief) in recognition of his march against the Akechi army. But Shibata Katsuie took over Toyotomi holdings in Ōmi while retaining control of Echizen. Nobunaga's lands rotated within the family. There were no surprises here. Predictable too was the decision to assign joint authority over Kyoto to four of Nobunaga's most powerful vassals: Hideyoshi, Niwa Nagahide, Ikeda Tsuneoki, and Shibata Katsuie. Once more the Kiyosu conferees had avoided real resolution of the problem of succession.

After the Kiyosu gathering, as other daimyo returned to their headquarters, Hideyoshi set off for the capital. He began the construction of a fortification at Yamazaki and installed his deputies as governors of Kyoto. They did not share control with representatives of Niwa, Ikeda, or Shibata. The first two men never stationed, and perhaps never intended to station, their own lieutenants in Kyoto. Deferential toward Hideyoshi at the daimyo conference, they yielded again to him in the administration of the capital. We do not know what happened to Katsuie's deputy in Kyoto. The intention of the Kiyosu elders may have been to exercise authority in Kyoto sequentially rather than jointly. Yet if Hideyoshi legitimately enjoyed an exclusive first tenure in the capital, his actions there gave no hint that he would relinquish power or that he sought to enforce the collective will of the four Oda elders. Not only did Yamazaki castle cast a long shadow over its environs, Hideyoshi's aggressive efforts to settle the land claims of the aristocracy, his deepening interests in the commercial life of the city, and his unilateral decision to close the capital toll barriers called attention to a strong and personal rule.[16]

Hideyoshi's presence in Kyoto exacerbated his already uneasy relations with Shibata Katsuie, the grey eminence of Nobunaga's circle who refused to be subordinate to a man fourteen years his junior. Katsuie's wariness was not ill founded. Within two months of the Kiyosu conference, Hideyoshi wrote a young mistress in his own hand: "I am [now] in Sakamoto. I will have the investitures in Ōmi reviewed and its castles destroyed. When there is time I shall recover Osaka and shall station my men there. I shall order them to level the castles of the whole land to prevent further rebellions and to preserve the nation in peace for fifty years."[17] In this letter Hideyoshi begins to assume the tone of authority. The Oda loyalist who rushed to meet Mitsuhide, the decorous patron of Sambōshi, and the Kiyosu elder attending to the affairs of the capital begins to declare himself as a national peacemaker. Already the balance of power among Nobunaga's vassals had tilted, and the deeper succession problems raised by the Honnōji incident had been exposed. But for all the bravado of his letter, Hideyoshi's place in the Oda coalition was a delicate one. Two challenges—one from Shibata Katsuie, another from Tokugawa Ieyasu—soon emerged to test his pretentions to power.

War within the Oda Camp

By the autumn of 1582, Katsuie's opposition to Hideyoshi had begun to harden. His major support came from Oda Nobutaka. Still nursing hopes of succeeding his father, Nobutaka looked to the Shibata house to assert his claims against Sambōshi. As a sign of alliance, after the Honnōji incident Nobutaka wed his aunt Oichi to Katsuie. Already the survivor of one political union—as widow of Nobunaga's sometime ally, Asai Nagamasa, who lost his sons and his own life in war with the Oda—Oichi accompanied Katsuie to Echizen at the request of her nephew.

Hideyoshi was well aware of the Shibata-Nobutaka alliance. In the tenth month of 1582 he dispatched a long, carefully crafted letter to two of Nobutaka's retainers. It opens in a friendly fashion: "You have heard something [of the difficulties] between Shibata and myself and have offered to use your good offices [on my behalf]. For this I am very grateful. However, since the agreement made . . . in the [Kiyosu] oaths which were sealed in blood has been violated, there may be no need for you to enter into this matter." The letter proceeds with a cunning mixture of warning and recapitulation of past events, making clear just what Hideyoshi's difficulty with Nobutaka, and his defender Shibata Katsuie, was: "Although not many days have passed [since the Kiyosu conference], Nobutaka says that he will not move the young lord [Sambōshi] to Azuchi; until now, indeed, he has not done so." This was the basic message: Hideyoshi has noted Nobutaka's disrespect for the legitimate heir and is not prepared to countenance the treachery implied by failure to install Sambōshi in Azuchi castle.

The letter continues with autobiography. A discursive narrative reviews Hideyoshi's contributions to the success of the Oda with an unavoidable point: if Nobutaka cannot be persuaded of Hideyoshi's goodwill, sheer comprehension of his military ability should reveal the recklessness of a challenge.

> As you know, during his lifetime our lord [Nobunaga] bestowed upon me the provinces of Harima and Tajima, in addition to the northern districts [of Ōmi] . . . As our lord ordered me to serve as the vanguard in the western provinces, I was campaigning in Harima when Bessho of Miki [castle] plotted rebellion and caused me great trouble. Just at that time, Araki also rebelled at Itami in Settsu and cut the highways. But finally I took Bessho's head. Thereupon our lord repeatedly sent me rewards and letters of gratitude, granting me gold mines in Tajima and utensils for the tea ceremony.[18]

Hideyoshi goes on at length, chronicling his always triumphant progress. Sometimes maudlin, sometimes self-deprecatory in a disarming way, Hideyoshi is bullying Nobutaka into compliance.

This long letter is typical of Hideyoshi. He used his correspondence, almost compulsively, to recite his history, to edify his reader, and perhaps to reassure himself. The communication to Nobutaka's retainers is particularly interesting as it discloses something of Hideyoshi's negotiating style while it confirms what little we know of his attitude toward Nobunaga. Hideyoshi was faithful to his lord; his lord rewarded him handsomely. Then Hideyoshi remained fastidious after Honnōji. He avenged his lord, presented Mitsuhide's head before Nobunaga's dead body, and honored his heir. Hideyoshi later adopted

Nobunaga's fourth son, and he presided over Nobunaga's funeral rites at Daitokuji. In keeping with this conduct, Hideyoshi's letter to Nobutaka is punctilious in acknowledging Nobunaga's greatness and his own gratitude to him.

Hence Hideyoshi's biographers represent him as a loyal retainer to Nobunaga. Abler perhaps than Nobunaga, the Hideyoshi of the *Tenshō-ki* and *Taikō-ki* is a true vassal. Nor can we alter that picture. We can impugn Hideyoshi's motives, and we can distrust allegations of friendship between the two men. We can wonder about the extent to which Hideyoshi admired his lord. But Hideyoshi's care in correspondence and deportment conceals the shading of his feelings toward Nobunaga. By carrying himself as a loyalist, he was able to use his own history of Oda support to chastise an Oda rival. In the letter he links an implicit rebuke of Nobutaka to an allegation of disloyalty and establishes himself as the defender of the legitimate heir. It is a nice turn.

Yet the letter did not relieve the tension between Hideyoshi and Shibata Katsuie. Indeed, it had a provocative effect. By the last months of 1582 Katsuie stood at the head of a league of generals ready to advance against Hideyoshi on behalf of Oda Nobutaka. Takigawa Kazumasu, Katsuie's most valuable supporter, took the initiative by raising troops in Ise. Hideyoshi entered that province in the second month of 1583, only to be diverted by news that Katsuie himself, released by an early spring thaw from the snowbound hills of Echizen, had set up camp in Ōmi. Hideyoshi left Ise, built a string of fortifications before the Shibata army in Ōmi, and began to broadcast plans for the conquest of his new opponents to the Uesugi, the Mōri, and the Kobayakawa. Temporarily abandoning his command in Ōmi, Hideyoshi proceeded to the province of Mino where he prepared an attack upon Shibata Katsuie's mascot, Oda Nobutaka. In Mino, however, Hideyoshi learned toward the end of the fourth month that his troops in Ōmi had fallen to the armies of Shibata Katsuie.[19]

All of Hideyoshi's military historians describe the ensuing events as the most important in his career. Once informed of the defeat of his men in Ōmi, Hideyoshi immediately set off for vengeance. Said to have covered the fifty-two kilometers from Mino to Shibata Katsuie's camp in an implausible five hours, he had nine of his most trusted lieutenants lead a contingent of horsemen against the unprepared Shibata army, estimated at 30,000, in the field of Shizugatake. The enemy scattered. Hideyoshi pursued Katsuie to Echizen where, on the twenty-fourth day of the fourth month, Katsuie took his own life.[20] In a letter to Kobayakawa Takakage, Hideyoshi described the events at the lofty nine-story castle of the Shibata in Kita-no-shō: "Katsuie was a warrior who drilled daily in military affairs. But when we had pressed with up to seven thrusts, he was no longer able to resist. Katsuie climbed to the ninth floor of his keep, addressed some words to those assembled and declared his intention to kill himself to serve [as an example] to later generations. His men, deeply moved, shed tears which soaked the sleeves of their armor. When all was quiet to the east and the west, Katsuie stabbed his wife, children, and other members of his family, and then cut his stomach, together with over eighty retainers."[21] That wife was Oichi. Hideyoshi collected her three adolescent daughters, children of Asai Nagamasa, and conducted them from Echizen to Osaka.

With Katsuie's death, Nobutaka lost the pillar of his campaign. Shortly thereafter his brother Oda Nobukatsu, now aligned with Hideyoshi, attacked the citadel of Gifu and precipitated Nobutaka's suicide. Takigawa Kazumasu surrendered to Hideyoshi in the early part of the eighth month, 1583.

The battle of Shizugatake, most critical to Hideyoshi's conquest of the Shibata and their allies, became a memorable illustration of Toyotomi speed and daring. It was won by a small group of proven *fudai* without *tozama* assistance. The victory was spectacular enough to elicit congratulations from the Tokugawa, the Uesugi, and the Hōjō. The author of the *Tenshō-ki* saw it as the beginning of a new era: "There were three talents [essential to] Minamoto no Yoritomo's pacification of Japan. Yoshitsune excelled in battle skill; Kajiwara Kagetoki concentrated upon worldly affairs; Hōjō Tokimasa pursued the way of government . . . But now Hideyoshi, with a single heart, advanced his plans, laid in provisions, and then fought his wars. Truly he is a great leader, unknown to previous ages."[22]

His triumph over Katsuie did not discourage one further challenge from the Oda camp. For eight months in 1584 Hideyoshi was involved in a sporadic war with Tokugawa Ieyasu. He too represented a Nobunaga son, Hideyoshi's former ally Oda Nobukatsu. The troops of Hideyoshi and Ieyasu engaged in only two major confrontations, the battles of Komaki and Nagakute. Komaki tapered off without resolution in the third month of 1584. Early in the fourth month, an army under the direction of Hideyoshi's nephew Hidetsugu was routed at Nagakute. The Toyotomi lost three generals. Despite the Nagakute victory, Ieyasu made peace with Hideyoshi in the twelfth month of 1584 after desultory negotiations and occasional fighting.[23]

Both the Shibata and the Tokugawa offensives had promised success. Katsuie had mustered allies on three sides of Hideyoshi and counted upon the neutrality, possibly the assistance, of three major houses: the Uesugi, the Mōri, the Tokugawa.[24] Further, Katsuie had faced an untested Toyotomi coalition. Hideyoshi's supporters at Kiyosu had not yet faced internecine conflict and might well have retreated from the armies of the Shibata. Tokugawa Ieyasu had operated from a position of even greater strength than Katsuie. By 1584 he controlled most of Mikawa, Tōtōmi, Suruga, Kai, and Shinano. His personal holdings and the size of his army made him at least the equal of Hideyoshi. He had allies as well as in-laws in the Hōjō of Odawara—two of his daughters had married into that family. The Sassa in Echigo, the Chōsokabe in Shikoku, and the great temple of Negoro on the Kii peninsula had also offered support of the offensive.

To an extent, Hideyoshi's survival of these encounters depended upon the strength of his forces. Although the battle of Shizugatake was won by a comparatively small contingent, Hideyoshi's letters, the *Tenshō-ki*, and the *Buke jiki* suggest that the Toyotomi were able to raise 50,000 or more soldiers in 1583 and 1584. We have little hard evidence concerning either this number or the recruitment practices that may make it plausible. Most of the unit commanders who routinely led his armies were *fudai* assembled in Owari and Mino and augmented during Hideyoshi's campaigns for Nobunaga in Ōmi and the Chūgoku.[25] To their experience and their numbers Hideyoshi gradually added the strength of others. (Takayama Ukon, Tsutsui Junkei, and their subordinates abandoned Akechi Mitsuhide to join the Toyotomi. Oda Nobukatsu was active on Hideyoshi's behalf in 1583. The Kanamori and Maeda left Shibata Katsuie for Hideyoshi at Shizugatake. The Ikeda and Nakagawa, formerly Oda daimyo, also came to serve the Toyotomi.[26]) Their effectiveness was enhanced by what most historians judge to be a superior supply of muskets. As many as 4,850 Toyotomi troops were equipped with firearms at the battle of Komaki.[27] By holding Sakai and Kunitomo in Ōmi, Hideyoshi governed not only the leading forging centers in the nation but the only large-scale armament producers outside of northern Kyushu and the Kii peninsula.

Hideyoshi's military power alone did not bring the Shibata and Tokugawa confrontations to a close, however. Critical to Hideyoshi's success was the conduct of potentially hostile families. The Mōri failed to assist Shibata Katsuie. Uesugi Kagekatsu exchanged pledges of loyalty with Hideyoshi and even raided the Shibata rear guard before the battle of Shizugatake.[28] The Hōjō as well as the Chōsokabe kept a careful distance from Ieyasu's contest with Toyotomi troops.

The Mōri and the Uesugi probably kept their distance from Ieyasu for the same reasons that Ieyasu made his peace with Hideyoshi. That is, both the *tozama* and the Tokugawa stood to gain from alliance with the Toyotomi and to lose from war. Because they confronted Hideyoshi from positions of strength, the major daimyo were able to bargain for security of tenure. Ieyasu, for example, won recognition of his rights to the five provinces he held.[29] Additional concessions—freedom from military exactions until 1590—confirmed Ieyasu's powerful position in the daimyo assembly. Although there could be no guarantees of security in *sengoku* society, Ieyasu's victory at Nagakute, his association with the principal Oda vassals, and his pact with the Hōjō made him a virtual peer of Hideyoshi and assured his power in negotiation. Continued war, on the other hand, promised no welcome result. Ieyasu's patron, Oda Nobukatsu, had surrendered to Hideyoshi late in 1584 and hence undermined the Tokugawa cause. The studied neutrality of the Hōjō and the Chōsokabe doubtless alarmed Ieyasu as well.

No less crucial in Ieyasu's decision to make peace were the very conditions of the late warring-states world. By 1580 regional consolidation of land holdings was far advanced; competition had narrowed to no more than twelve great houses with exceedingly large domains.[30] A decade earlier the stakes had been different. The Imagawa had reached for the capital from a base of only two provinces. The Asai had been lords of a single portion of Ōmi. The risks of battle in the 1580s had increased substantially. Ieyasu had already seen Shibata Katsuie lose everything in his challenge to the Toyotomi. Given Hideyoshi's control of the central provinces and the likelihood of protracted conflict, Ieyasu could not have been sanguine about a lingering confrontation and the possible forfeiture of five provinces.

Since Hideyoshi already had an advantage, and had displayed a disposition for conciliation, it may have appeared sensible to let him entertain the dangers of pacification while his allies enjoyed a privileged association. That association was protected by two facts. First, the opportunity of the *tozama* to negotiate with Hideyoshi was predicated upon their ability to challenge him militarily. Second, the *tozama* numbers were growing. The *tozama* were increasingly valuable to each other, both as separate and collective restraints upon the growth of a despotic Toyotomi government.

Land and Lordship

Hideyoshi was not a reluctant leader who had authority thrust upon him. Confident after Nobunaga's death that he could "preserve the nation in peace for fifty years," he was prepared to make a far bolder prediction by the end of 1584: "The government of Japan will be superior to anything since Yoritomo."[31] On the basis of only two major victories and one military stalemate, Hideyoshi displayed that assurance in power which can inspire submission.

His disposition of land following the Shibata and Tokugawa campaigns became the measure of power. If he had acted as an Oda defender in his vengeance against Mitsuhide, his conduct at Kiyosu, and his response to Katsuie's challenge, Hideyoshi soon dropped the pretense of good stewardship to focus attention upon the transfer of authority to himself. Late in 1584, the *Tenshō-ki* tells us, he exercised the definitive privilege of lordship by investing fiefs in thirty-six men.[32] One recipient was a family member, nineteen were *fudai*, one was an ally attracted during the San'yō campaign, and three cannot be identified conclusively.[33] The most noteworthy grants went to twelve former peers, daimyo who had served Oda Nobunaga at Hideyoshi's side. The form of extant enfeoffment documents leaves no doubt that Hideyoshi had independently assumed the right to confirm or redistribute holdings throughout the Oda sphere:

> Because of your assistance to me, I bestow upon you all rights to the district of Shisō in the province of Harima.
> This area shall be your domain in full.
> Tenshō 12 [1584], seventh month, eighteenth day
> [Hideyoshi's monogram]
> To: Kuroda Kambei Dono [Yoshitaka][34]

Among the many grantees of 1584, two names stand out. One was Oda Nobukatsu, Nobunaga's second son and a supporter of Tokugawa Ieyasu in his attack upon the Toyotomi. The other was Sambōshi, Nobunaga's grandson and the successor whom Hideyoshi had so artfully championed. Now lord rather than vassal or peer of these men, Hideyoshi mounted a quiet coup by bestowing land upon them. The shift in roles was sufficiently subtle, perhaps sufficiently unremarkable by this point, to escape notice in either the military tales or contemporary letters. Both Oda heirs entered Toyotomi service, though Nobukatsu eventually broke ranks with his nephew to support the forces of the Tokugawa in 1600. A certain romantic pathos continued to surround Sambōshi. He became a Christian and died at the age of twenty-five.

The enfeoffments of 1584 do not tell the full story of Hideyoshi's achievement in the two years following the Honnōji incident. Although the fact could hardly have been clear at the time, Hideyoshi had absorbed thirty-seven provinces into his sphere: ten provinces in the San'in and San'yō that he had taken with Akechi Mitsuhide in their last campaigns for Nobunaga; nine provinces, stretching from Tamba in the west to Owari in the east, which were held by Oda vassals who had either allied with him or been defeated; and the five home provinces and neighboring Iga that he claimed by dint of his hold on the capital. Truce or alliance afforded him influence in five provinces held by the Tokugawa, six held by the Mōri, and one held by the Uesugi.[35]

Hideyoshi made land grants in only a fraction of these provinces in 1584. Not until the completion of his cadastral surveys and the subse-

quent investiture of daimyo across the country would his claims to ultimate control be defined.[36] For most practical purposes, nonetheless,
Toyotomi dominion had been established. The Mōri, Kobayakawa,
Uesugi, Oda, and Tokugawa sent hostages to Hideyoshi. Within a year,
these and other daimyo from the thirty-seven provinces would take
formal oaths of loyalty to him.[37] By the end of the decade, all would
fight under his command. A brief and abortive rebellion would occur
only once within the boundaries of the domain Hideyoshi had formed
by 1584.

The support of former Oda daimyo may not be so surprising.
Trained to obedience, most surrendered the initiative to Hideyoshi immediately following Nobunaga's death and permitted him to retain it as
long as he achieved success. Nobunaga's rotation of their fiefs and the
demands of long campaigns had, in any case, left them without invincible land bases from which to launch a challenge. It seems small wonder
that Hideyoshi's chief threat within the Oda league was Shibata Katsuie—the sole vassal whom Nobunaga had not transferred from holding to holding. Further, the Oda men were isolated. Survivors of a lord
who had made all outsiders his enemies, they had little choice but to
look within their ranks for a leader.

And in Hideyoshi they discovered an accommodating lord. With
the exception of unrepentant Shibata and Akechi supporters, the Oda
vassals received confirmations of their fiefs. Even those daimyo who
had fought for Hideyoshi's enemies (such as the Sassa), who had
switched allegiance from the Shibata to the Toyotomi mid-campaign
(such as the Maeda), or who had remained aloof from the fray (such as
the Niwa) retained their lands. The chameleon Oda Nobukatsu served
as the best symbol of a Toyotomi readiness for reconciliation. By and
large, these men remained in their original holdings. The Niwa, the
Oda, and the Ikeda did receive transfers out of the Biwa and Settsu
areas to make room for a secure buffer of Hideyoshi's intimates around
Kyoto and Osaka. Gratuitous or general transfers of Nobunaga's former generals, however, did not take place.

Surely it made sense for Hideyoshi to treat these daimyo, many of
whom had already rendered him military support, with care. Yet recognition of the prudence of his conduct does not detract from its symbolic
importance. Tempering his assertion of authority with endorsement of
current landholding practices, Hideyoshi retreated from the reign of
terror. He began to adopt the sons of rival daimyo; he did not instigate a
purge.[38] He assimilated the Oda scions into his command rather than
exile or murder them. He abandoned his march against Tokugawa
Ieyasu without pursuing a resolution of the contest. To assume that Hideyoshi had no choice in these matters is to forget Nobunaga's conduct.

Such actions may help explain his alliances with the Mōri, Kobayakawa, and Uesugi, for it is these pacts—not those with the Oda men—that defy easy analysis. Those alliances were yet to be proven, of course. The clearest lesson of Hideyoshi's first two years in power was a home truth: power tends to accrue to the man who behaves as if power were already his.

Beyond the Oda Boundaries: Shikoku, Etchū, and Kii

Hideyoshi's campaign in Shikoku, which followed closely upon his negotiations with Tokugawa Ieyasu, is noteworthy for several reasons. It was won quickly as a result of the largest offensive yet launched in warring-states history, and it was the first expedition by the Toyotomi well outside the sphere of Oda Nobunaga's influence. In effect, it became proof of Hideyoshi's power to extend his dominion beyond central Japan. It is more important as a successful test of the *tozama* and as a demonstration of Hideyoshi's resolve to form new alliances.

The offensive began in the sixth month of 1585 when Hideyoshi's generals moved against Chōsokabe Motochika. Long an adversary of Nobunaga and briefly an ally of Ieyasu, Motochika commanded Shikoku's four provinces by the time of the Toyotomi campaign. He had used the three years of grace after Nobunaga's death to bring the island fully under his sway, even as Ieyasu waited in vain for him to join the resistance to Hideyoshi. The encounter between Chōsokabe and Toyotomi forces, when it did come, was brief.

Hideyoshi's stepbrother and nephew—Hidenaga and Hidetsugu— led 60,000 troops against Shikoku's eastern province of Awa; 30,000 soldiers of the Mōri under the lead of Kobayakawa Takakage and Kikkawa Motoharu attacked the northwest province of Iyo; the combined armies of the Hachisuka, Ukita, Kuroda, and others landed in Sanuki. Within a month, Chōsokabe Motochika sued for peace. The terms of surrender, arranged on the twenty-fifth day of the seventh month, permitted the Chōsokabe to retain the province of Tosa. Motochika's third son entered Hideyoshi's retinue as a hostage. The remainder of the island was divided, in the eighth month, among Hideyoshi's daimyo. Kobayakawa Takakage received most of Iyo; the Sengoku acquired a large domain in Sanuki; Hachisuka Iemasa took control of a substantial part of Awa. Smaller grants in these provinces went to the Ankokuji, Akamatsu, Kuroshima, Tokui, and Sogo. Of the leading grantees, only Hachisuka and Sengoku were *fudai*. Sogo was a local general who joined Hideyoshi after having been displaced from Awa by the Chōsokabe.[39]

The investiture of a defeated house was unprecedented. While the Chōsokabe did not survive as lords of all Shikoku, they were awarded one of the largest holdings on the island, later valued at 228,000 *koku*.

Motochika acknowledged the princeliness of the concession by traveling to Kyoto at the end of the year to pledge a formal oath of loyalty and to present Hideyoshi with gold bullion and a sword. Thereafter he assumed one of Hideyoshi's surnames, Hashiba, and joined the Toyotomi campaigns in Kyushu and the eastern provinces.[40]

Anticipation of future help from Chōsokabe soldiers doubtless influenced Hideyoshi's decision to enfeoff these enemies. Equally important was the history of the family. *Jitō* in Shikoku under the Kamakura administration, the Chōsokabe acted as deputies of the Hosokawa during the Ashikaga tenure. They were an important presence on the island throughout the *sengoku* years; by 1574 they controlled all of Tosa. Reconciliation with the house promised orderly rule in that province and became a straightforward endorsement of domainal government by seasoned lords.[41]

The endorsement became all the firmer with subsequent enfeoffments in Shikoku. Hideyoshi neither retained the island for himself nor gave it into the charge of *fudai*. He parceled it out, primarily to the *tozama* who had both ensured victory and proven the power of his alliances. Reliance on the Mōri and their collaterals in the Kobayakawa and Kikkawa houses had elicited a stunning show of support, reminiscent of their help after the Honnōji incident. By turning Iyo over to his old correspondent Kobayakawa Takakage, Hideyoshi made a return on at least two debts. The Mōri negotiator Ankokuji Ekei also received a Shikoku fief.

It was such cooperation by the *tozama*, of course, that gave Hideyoshi an incentive to sustain the Chōsokabe. If he had reason to anticipate difficulties from them, the location of firm allies throughout the island and along the Inland Sea routes would constrain rebellion. Yet by electing to enfeoff the Chōsokabe and the *tozama*, Hideyoshi denied land to long-time vassals.

Hideyoshi treated yet another enemy with restraint in 1585. After the Shikoku campaign, he turned with a separate army to Etchū. There Sassa Narimasa, an old and wily Nobunaga hand who had supported first the Shibata and later the Tokugawa, attempted to take the Hokuriku from Toyotomi control. Maeda forces contained him but could not reduce him. On the sixth day of the eighth month Hideyoshi entered Etchū. The Maeda stood to the west; the Uesugi posted troops along the eastern boundary. Narimasa watched his fortifications fall effortlessly. On the twenty-ninth day of the month, having launched no single offensive himself, he journeyed to Hideyoshi's base, with a shaven head and dressed in monk's clothing, to surrender. Hideyoshi stripped him of all but a small holding in Etchū, then dispatched his wife and children to Osaka as hostages. "As Kuranosuke [Narimasa] is in a state of regret over many things," Hideyoshi wrote his own wife, "I confiscated his province but saved his life."[42]

The province of Etchū was entrusted to Maeda Toshiie and his son. They now held Noto, Kaga, and Narimasa's former domain. At the time of Hideyoshi's death, their fiefs would be valued at 445,000 koku. But the award of Etchū was only the first of many indications of Hideyoshi's esteem for the Maeda. Grateful for their earlier assistance against Shibata Katsuie, he was clearly moved by their continuing resistance to the Sassa. For months the Sassa had attempted to win Maeda Toshiie as an ally. Had they succeeded, the Niwa of Echizen—always a disturbing element in the north—might have spurned the Toyotomi as well. Such a triple alliance would have tempted the Uesugi in new directions. Thus Hideyoshi came to see in Toshiie a most valuable supporter.[43]

Maeda assistance to the Toyotomi in the Hokuriku was very much like Kobayakawa assistance to the Toyotomi on Shikoku: prompt and critical. Hideyoshi's grant to Toshiie in Etchū, furthermore, was very much like his grant to Takakage in Iyo: handsome, and made at a sacrifice to the *fudai*. Two complementary patterns of conduct, the voluntary consent of several important *tozama* to advance Hideyoshi's cause, and Hideyoshi's resolution to build his settlement upon such men, began to emerge from these decisions. The compromises on both sides were clear. In acknowledging Hideyoshi's lordship, the *tozama* forfeited their autonomy and personal hopes for dominion over the nation. In ceding land to the *tozama*, Hideyoshi circumscribed the wealth of his own house.

Shortly before the Shikoku and Etchū offensives, Hideyoshi was involved in a somewhat different confrontation that sheds additional light on his attitude toward pacification. In the third month of 1585 he met two Buddhist communities in battle. His marches against the Shingon monks of Negoro and the Jōdo Shinshū sectarians of Saiga on the Kii peninsula were the only military incidents involving the Toyotomi and the church after Nobunaga's death.

The complicity of Negoro and Saiga with Tokugawa Ieyasu, following their stout resistance to Oda Nobunaga, provoked Hideyoshi's raids. Negoro was a leading arms producer and had supplied the monks of Ishiyama Honganji. Saiga had survived a meeting with Oda forces in 1577 to preserve its independence as a Jōdo Shinshū bastion. Yet both centers of opposition fell to Hideyoshi within three days early in the third month of 1585. In an attack that recalled Nobunaga's strike against Mount Hiei, 40,000 Toyotomi soldiers leveled scores of

Negoro buildings and claimed its arms cache. Virtually the peer of Hiei in physical grandeur and resources, Negoro was the last great monastery to fall in the wars of unification. Hideyoshi's troops proceeded to the Saiga area where twenty-six villages had rallied under the Shinshū banner as an autonomous political community. With their surrender, the last armed enclave of Shinshū sectarians disappeared from Japan.[44]

To guarantee an end to religious rebellion on the Kii peninsula, Hideyoshi sent the following warning to the monks of Mount Kōya, headquarters of the Shingon sect, in the same year.

> Item [3]: The [contemplative] monks, the priests in the world (gyōnin), and others have not been prudent in their religious studies. The manufacture or retention of senseless weapons, muskets, and the like is treacherous and wicked.

> Item [6]: Inasmuch as you saw with your own eyes that Mount Hiei and Negoro temple were finally destroyed for acting with enmity against the realm, you should be discerning in this matter.[45]

The Kōya authorities were not slow to grasp the point. Although they had supported the opposition of other religious communities to Nobunaga and Hideyoshi, the monks sent an obsequious reply and surrendered all arms during the first systematic seizure of weapons in the Toyotomi tenure.[46]

Like Nobunaga before him, Hideyoshi was no friend of a militant church. Indeed, he completed Nobunaga's work by disciplining the last armed monks, eradicating their armories, reducing their properties, cutting their ties to guilds and commercial establishments, and relocating popular temples away from their congregations. Hideyoshi even kept a close watch on temple administration, particularly in the area of the capital. Some of his most curious edicts enjoin monks to observe their prayer schedules and their rules of abstinence.[47]

But Hideyoshi also extended to the religious community a policy of reconciliation similar to that extended to the Chōsokabe. He issued permission to the priests of Mount Hiei to rebuild their sanctuary and then contributed 1,500 koku to the effort. A number of his daimyo—the Tokugawa, Ukita, Uesugi, and Mōri—followed suit. He awarded the Honganji establishment land for a new temple in Osaka, and with a resplendent retinue of courtiers and vassals attended the consecration ceremonies for the completed enclave. Negoro was rebuilt by Hideyoshi's brother-in-law ten years after its destruction, and Kōya received donations for two new sub-monasteries and the reconstruction of its main hall.[48]

As the Chōsokabe was a venerable daimyo house, so Hiei, Negoro, and Kōya were the most sacred Buddhist institutions in the nation.

Honganji was among the most popular of sixteenth-century sects. In rebuilding their temples—when there were no compelling reasons to do so—Hideyoshi played the benevolent and forgiving patron. It was a role he played throughout his life with mounting ostentation, and it was designed to win adulation. The source of Hideyoshi's vanity was a confidence that his acts were healing and thus deserving of commendation. This is the interesting point. In his pursuit of approval, Hideyoshi made a show of generosity that displayed his self-consciousness as a unifier, in more than military terms, and his concern with laudable government.

The Kyushu Campaign

War in Kyushu confronted Hideyoshi with all the anomalies of that island's past. Located at the periphery of the Japanese realm, Kyushu was often isolated from the concerns of Honshū, slow to resonate with change in the capital. The turmoil of the warring-states era intruded upon the island, but it never entirely recast the roles of local leadership. In Kyushu alone a large military elite with Kamakura and Muromachi origins survived the *sengoku* era to meet the upstart Hideyoshi in battle. The Ōtomo and the Shimazu, major adversaries in Kyushu, had served as *shugo* there since the Kamakura period. The Ryūzōji, Arima, and Itō ancestors were *jitō* on the island under the Kamakura regime. The Akitsuki settled in Chikuzen at the end of the twelfth century. Four great *shugo* houses had disappeared during the *sengoku* struggles (the Shibukawa and Kikuchi fell to neighbors early in the warring-states age; the Shōni and Ōuchi fell to vassals at mid-century). Yet no Honshū family had broken the hold of natives on their land.

The political insularity of Kyushu contrasted with its strong cosmopolitan character. If the island was at the edge of Kyoto's jurisdiction, it was also the nation's link to the outside world. Hakata, Hirado, Nagasaki, and other Kyushu cities served as ports of call during the warring-states period for Korean, Chinese, Southeast Asian, and Portuguese vessels. Several daimyo—Arima, Ōmura, Ōtomo, Ōuchi—were actively involved in overseas trade. They became enmeshed as well in the troublesome network of Christian missionaries. Particularly after China severed relations with Japan because of the depredations of pirate-traders, the Portuguese carracks emerged as carriers of continental silk to Kyushu. And the daimyo who harbored these European Black Ships bound themselves to the Jesuits who attempted to manipulate docking decisions to evangelical advantage. Arima, Ōmura, and Ōtomo were baptized. Not accidentally, their chaplains summoned Portuguese captains to their ports.[49]

However deeply trade considerations influenced conversions after the arrival of the missionaries in 1549, Kyushu was shaken in the following decades by genuine Christian fervor. With the reduction of the number of Portuguese voyages and the identification of Nagasaki as the great ships' regular harbor, the Jesuits could less and less count upon commercial incentives to spread their mission. They had never been able, in any case, to regulate the ships' movements absolutely. Despite Nagasaki's monopoly on the carrack trade, mass conversions continued in Christian domains; the desecration of Buddhist and Shintō sanctuaries proceeded as well. Much of this zeal was born of confusion, resentment of Buddhist tyranny, and lingering hopes of economic advantage. Some of it reflected piety. Jesuit reports of the sincerity of converts aside, the nature of the propaganda effort mustered in the early seventeenth century to destroy Christian belief suggests that faith occasionally flourished. Once the anti-Christian movement began in earnest in Japan, the Tokugawa government circulated printed copies, in simple language, of rebuttals to the foreign priests' message. The philosophical sophistication of some of these tracts, the effort to frame elegant arguments to refute Christian theology, indicates a need to attack Christianity at the level of doctrine.[50] The Christian community in Kyushu survived crucifixions and interrogations. Part of it eventually went underground.

Christianity in Kyushu was divisive. There was widespread resentment of rampages that resulted in the leveling of shrines and temples.[51] Forced conversions within the ranks of Christian daimyo were unsavory to many retainers. Wars between Christian and non-Christian domains on the island began to take on a crusade-like quality. And the delivery by Ōmura of the port of Nagasaki to Jesuit administrators enraged his own generals and daimyo competitors for foreign trade.

In 1587, then, Kyushu was a region of experienced rulers, a region linked to foreign trade routes, a region singularly engaged by the problem of Christianity. After the home provinces, it had the most fully developed cities in the country. Numerous ports and castle towns that had grown with generations of stable governors provided an urban flavor unknown to the far eastern or far western provinces of Honshū. Its troops were well-equipped with both foreign and domestically produced muskets. Its tea men used Korean ceramics unfamiliar to most of their colleagues elsewhere. The patterns of Kyushu textiles were inspired by the weavers of the southern islands. And if these factors alone failed to announce Kyushu's distinction, the tropical foliage and the warm air served decidedly to separate it from neighboring Honshū.

Hideyoshi's active intervention in the affairs of the island began with an embassy by Ōtomo Sōrin to Osaka castle in the fourth month of 1586. It was the first major request for help from a daimyo outside

the Toyotomi coalition. At the time, Sōrin begged Hideyoshi's help in
the prolonged Ōtomo struggle against Shimazu Yoshihisa. When Yoshihisa rejected Toyotomi overtures concerning a truce, preparations
for the Kyushu campaign were initiated. The campaign lasted half a
year, from the eleventh month of 1586 until the fifth month of 1587. It
was massive and conclusive. It also led Hideyoshi to new encounters—
with the Christians and with the Chinese continent.[52]

The Toyotomi invasion of Kyushu began with two advance expe-
ditions by Kobayakawa Takakage and Chōsokabe Motochika in the
eleventh month of 1586. While Takakage acquired a hold in Buzen,
Motochika was routed upon confronting the Shimazu in Bungo. Toyotomi Hidenaga and Ukita Naoie led the main Toyotomi army into the
island late in the first month of 1587, and Hideyoshi followed with a
huge contingent in the last days of the third month.

The collective campaign was by far the largest yet in Hideyoshi's
martial history. Several lists of troop levies for the Kyushu offensive
remain—none, however, with Hideyoshi's seal. After greeting his assembled daimyo in Osaka castle on New Year's Day in 1587, Hideyoshi
apparently announced assignments for the forthcoming initiative. Sev-
enty-seven daimyo were required to raise between 100 and 15,000 soldiers each, for a total of approximately 250,000 troops.[53] More reliable
records for the later Kantō and Korean wars involve equally remarkable figures and suggest that the Kyushu force may indeed have been
mammoth. Since the Toyotomi army was joined on the island by local
opponents of the Shimazu, its size alone, even allowing for a considerable margin of error in the list of troop levies, seemed to assure victory.

The Kyushu battle plan was simply conceived. While Toyotomi
Hidenaga led his army down the eastern coast of the island, Hideyo-
shi's own arrival in Kyushu was followed by battles in the north and a
slow march along the western outreaches into the Shimazu heartland.
The Akitsuki of Chikuzen joined Hideyoshi after a brisk defeat; the
Ryūzōji turned to him when the Toyotomi entered Chikugo. The
Ōtomo were already allied with Hideyoshi, and other opponents of the
Shimazu soon followed—the Arima, Nabeshima, Itō, Matsuura, and
Ōmura. As if this force were insufficient, Hideyoshi mobilized local
Honganji believers. The abbot Kennyo had been dispatched to Kyushu
specifically to prepare his lay congregations there for war.[54]

Toyotomi soldiers encountered stiff Shimazu opposition only at
Takashiro in Hyūga. When Hidenaga took that fortress, the Shimazu
delivered a hostage, and the way to surrender was cleared. Persuaded
that continued defiance was futile, Shimazu Yoshihisa himself traveled
with a small party to Hideyoshi's headquarters at Taheiji—a camp only
fifty kilometers from the Shimazu capital of Kagoshima. On the eighth

day of the fifth month, 1587, he surrendered. Two days earlier Yoshi-hisa had taken the tonsure and adopted a priestly name.

The terms of surrender are clear from a letter sent from Kyushu to Hideyoshi's wife later that month:

Item: The hostage of Shimazu Yoshihisa [is to be] one daughter about fifteen [years old].

Item: Yoshihisa will reside in Kyoto.

Item: The hostages of the elders [are to be] about ten men.

Item: As for the hostages of Shimazu Hyōgo no kami [Yoshihiro, younger brother of Yoshihisa], he shall have in attendance in Osaka his fifteen[-year-old] heir (sōryō no ko). Further, he shall send his eight[-year-old] child out as a hostage.[55]

After the conquest of Kyushu, Hideyoshi had before him a vast new territory for disposal, and again he turned to the practices we observed in Shikoku—enfeoffment of the defeated and the tozama, with modest concessions to the fudai. Shimazu Yoshihiro retained Satsuma, most of Ōsumi, and southern Hyūga. Although the family forfeited its northern acquisitions, an area governed by the Shimazu since the late twelfth century remained in the family's control. Given a holding later valued at 559,530 koku, the Shimazu was the wealthiest house on Kyushu and the sixth largest power in the nation.

The province of Bungo stayed in the hands of the Ōtomo, the family whose request for help had brought Hideyoshi to Kyushu. The holdings of the Ryūzōji in six districts of Hizen were confirmed, as were those of the Arima, Ōmura, Matsuura, and Gotō in the same province. All of these houses had supported Hideyoshi after his arrival on the island. The Akitsuki were enfeoffed in Hyūga, and several minor daimyo of Kyushu recovered former holdings in Higo and Chikuzen.

The largest new investiture went to Kobayakawa Takakage, who left his fief on Shikoku to govern most of Chikuzen, two districts of Chikugo, and part of Hizen. His brother, Kobayakawa Hidekane, also received a substantial holding in Chikugo. Sassa Narimasa was awarded virtually all of Higo, despite his defeat two years earlier in Etchū. Kuroda Yoshitaka, a daimyo of Harima who joined Hideyoshi during his San'yō campaign, took over much of Buzen. While the fudai acquired several smaller fiefs in Kyushu, their major gains occurred as Hideyoshi redistributed the lands of Iyo vacated by the Kobayakawa. At least five Toyotomi vassals divided a fief valued at over 300,000 koku. The Ikoma also acquired part of Sanuki.[56]

If Hideyoshi's disposition of Shikoku left any doubt about his resolve to build a tozama base, the pattern of enfeoffment in Kyushu confirmed his commitment to outsiders. Each of the major new allotments underlined his support of a particular constituency. Significant improvement of the Kobayakawa domain rewarded the unfaltering help of a leading house that had first resisted Hideyoshi and then negotiated for peace. The Kuroda, representative of many smaller daimyo who joined Hideyoshi in the face of attack, served as an example to other opportunists who continued to support the Toyotomi loyally. The most puzzling grant, to Sassa Narimasa, addressed the former Oda coalition. Several of its members—primarily Niwa Nagahide and Tokugawa Ieyasu—were reluctant allies. By restoring a fief to an important but defiant peer in the Oda army, Hideyoshi attempted to heal wounds left open by the campaigns of 1582–1585.

The confirmation of the claims of local landholders, including the Shimazu, had the merits associated with the Chōsokabe case. The insularity of Kyushu and the longevity in rule of the island elite recommended continuity in leadership. Indeed, it was in a domain acquired by a newcomer that rebellion against the Toyotomi would later occur. Because the Chōsokabe had emerged as trustworthy vassals, Hideyoshi had reason to expect similar obedience from the Shimazu.

Local enfeoffment of the Kyushu *tozama* had two final advantages. It saved time—the time required to introduce a new system of control—just when new campaigns loomed and new pacification strategies needed attention. Further, local investiture gave a base to the daimyo and vassal bands whom Hideyoshi would summon for later wars. This purpose seems puzzling at first glance. The army already under Hideyoshi's control was ample to launch an offensive against the last stronghold of Toyotomi opposition, the eastern provinces. In fact, Kyushu troops were not extensively used in that offensive. They were essential, however, to a campaign Hideyoshi discussed in closing the letter to his wife last quoted: "By fast ships I have dispatched [orders] to Korea to serve the throne of Japan. Should [Korea] fail to serve [our throne], I have dispatched [the message] by fast ships that I will punish [that country] next year. Even China will enter my grip; I will command it during my lifetime."[57] The invasion of Korea did not take place until 1592. Yet it was with the submission of Kyushu that the thought of continental conquest first actively engaged Hideyoshi.

Hideyoshi's entry into the island ended not only with a plan for overseas conquest but also with the following announcement:

Item [1]: Japan is the Land of the Gods. Diffusion here from the Kirishitan Country of a pernicious doctrine is most undesirable.

Item [2]: To approach the people of our provinces and districts and, making them into [Kirishitan] sectarians, cause them to destroy the shrines of the gods and the temples of the Buddhas is a thing unheard of in previous ages . . .

Item [3]: It is the judgment [of the Lord of the *Tenka*] that since the Bateren [padres] by means of their clever doctrine amass parishioners as they please, the aforementioned violation of the Buddhist law . . . has resulted. That being outrageous, the Bateren can hardly be allowed to remain on Japanese soil.[58]

Hideyoshi found in Kyushu a Christian church reminiscent of the Honganji establishment, and he responded predictably.[59] There is no reason to conclude that by 1587 he detected a philosophical threat in Christianity and so determined to destroy the gospel. Certainly there is no evidence that he wished to exclude Europeans from Japanese soil. He specifically exempted traders from any form of discipline in the fourth item of the announcement. Nor is there evidence that Hideyoshi feared native believers and intended to persecute them. Gamō, Konishi, Kuroda, and Ōtomo were all Christian daimyo who rose successfully in his ranks. The target of this edict was an evangelical band of priests who sowed disorder, maintained an independent base in Nagasaki, acted as gold and silver brokers for Kyushu generals, trafficked in shares of the Portuguese carracks, and inspired raids on native sanctuaries.

Such accusations were true. The economic stability of the mission was based on shareholding in the great ship. The brokerage business afforded the Jesuits a measure of security beyond the insufficient support supplied by the Vatican. Nagasaki was a safe haven in an island otherwise rent by warfare.[60] And as for the desecration of heathen temples and the divisiveness of forced conversions—the Jesuits were, after all, soldiers of Christ who had come out of a Counter-Reformation world prepared for spiritual battle. There were at least two perspectives on Jesuit activities in Kyushu. But Hideyoshi, fresh from war with a Buddhist church bent on independence, was ill-disposed to adopt the indulgent one.[61]

Hideyoshi's expulsion order was not enforced. As he was prepared to tolerate, even to patronize, a submissive Buddhist establishment, he was prepared to threaten but leave undisturbed an acquiescent Christian church. His continuing deference to the Jesuits and his offer of land in Kyoto to the Franciscans when they arrived in 1593 make sense only if the 1587 edict is seen as a stiff warning to a company of militant evangelists. After Hideyoshi took Nagasaki in hand, proselytizing efforts in northern Kyushu gradually quieted. And fervor having subsided, Hideyoshi received the priests cordially. So handsome was his treatment of the Franciscans that their leader offered a remarkable paean: "While this king lives we can enjoy much security for he is like a father to us: he has given food to us as to the poor and also permission to build a monastery and a church."[62]

The Kantō and the Eastern Provinces

Hideyoshi went to war in Japan for a final time in 1590. The campaign might have been avoided. At least twice after returning from Kyushu, in 1588 and 1589, Hideyoshi sent envoys to Hōjō Ujimasa requesting his presence in the capital and offering implicit promises of confirmation of Hōjō holdings in the Kantō.[63] Ujimasa's intimacy with Tokugawa Ieyasu and the relative remoteness of his domain from the Toyotomi heartland presaged polite relations between the Hōjō and Hideyoshi. But while Ujimasa's brother traveled to Kyoto, Ujimasa himself declined the opportunity.

Hideyoshi waited three years for a reconciliation with the Hōjō, but Ujimasa could not have been deceived about the inevitability of armed encounter in the absence of some mark of submission. It is possible that he looked for Tokugawa assistance and a break in the Toyotomi coalition to protect his independence. Ieyasu had yet to participate in one of Hideyoshi's campaigns, and he had made peace and exchanged relatives with the Hōjō in 1584. But Ieyasu had also urged Ujimasa to submit, and very early in the eventual Hōjō-Toyotomi confrontation Ieyasu arrayed his troops against Ujimasa. Even then the Kantō army refused to surrender. Perhaps Ujimasa saw in the survival of the Shimazu and Chōsokabe evidence that he had little to lose by defying Hideyoshi. But neither house had retained all its former territories; both suffered human losses and devastation of their holdings.

Obdurate Hōjō resistance to Hideyoshi in the face of almost certain defeat is a reminder that alliance was painful. If it brought security of tenure to the daimyo and hastened the peace, it nevertheless signaled the end of autonomy. Hideyoshi's success in alliance tends to disguise unification as a peaceful confirmation of the status quo. The defiance of the Hōjō recalls the upheaval of the process and throws into relief the real sacrifices of Hideyoshi's allies. Hōjō defiance need not have been fed by false hopes to survive, merely by desperation and by pride.

The Toyotomi waged war on Ujimasa between the fourth and the eighth months of 1590. At stake were nine provinces (Izu, Sagami, Musashi, Kazusa, Awa, Shimōsa, Kōzuke, Shimotsuke, and Hitachi). Hideyoshi began his march eastward from Kyoto on the first day of the third month.[64] Two armies preceded him: Tokugawa Ieyasu and Oda Nobukatsu advanced along the Tōkai highway; Maeda Toshiie and

Uesugi Kagekatsu took the Tōsan route. A substantial navy led by Chōsokabe Motochika and others sailed to the port of Shimizu in Suruga. The size of the collective force is estimated at well over 200,000 soldiers. Because one of the surviving plans for the siege of Odawara castle calls for approximately 125,000 troops, the figure may be accurate.[65] That plan did not include all the vassal bands called to the east. Natsuka Masaie was apparently in charge of the commissariat and was able to deliver 200,000 *koku* of rice to feed the extraordinary army. How many men were involved in supply, transport, and other logistical operations is unclear.

Hōjō Ujimasa adopted a policy of passive resistance in the face of this onslaught. He withdrew with most of his command to Odawara castle in Sagami. Similar tactics had protected him in past confrontations. Thus in the fourth month of 1590 Hideyoshi encircled that fortification and threw up a rampart at nearby Ishigamayama. Like many of the great castles of its day, Odawara's security lay in its walls. This mass of stonework controlled the approach of the enemy who would fall prey, once within its compass, to entrapment and constant attack from the towers lining the way. Hideyoshi determined, then, to exhaust Odawara's defenders through siege. He wrote his wife in the middle of the fourth month: "We have encircled Odawara at a two to three *chō* [distance], attached a double thickness of moats and walls, and will not release a single enemy. Above all, as men from the eight provinces of the Kantō are confined [in Odawara], if I proceed to dry Odawara to death, the way is open to Ōshū. Thus I am, needless to say, satisfied." He is more succinct later in the letter: "I have swiftly placed the enemy in a birdcage."[66]

In the long weeks thereafter, the Odawara environs took on the atmosphere of a carnival. If Ujimasa had hoped that confusion, fatigue, dwindling supplies, and the sheer misery of inaction would reduce Hideyoshi's forces, he hoped in vain. Hideyoshi gathered his concubines and his tea men about him. His generals summoned their women and their entertainers as well. Merchants hawked their wares, burlesque players were abundant, musicians and dancers relieved the tedium of summer evenings. Hideyoshi found ample time to compose the letters to his spouse that chronicled his days. "People as far as Dewa and Ōshū are already in attendance. You should be at peace as I have quickly taken over many castles."[67]

Most of Hideyoshi's extant personal letters are to his wife, a confidante and companion of some importance. He never spared her the details of his political and military life. But then, he never really spared any of his correspondents similar information. These letters, which tell us so much of his affairs while conveying little of his interior life, seem to reflect an insatiable need to track and announce his progress. Hideyoshi may have wished to address posterity—the official biography and the nō plays he commissioned to celebrate his work suggest as much—yet he spoke with some urgency to his contemporaries and, one suspects, to himself.

While Hideyoshi lay crouched before Odawara, the Sanada, Uesugi, and Maeda moved through Kōzuke and Musashi. Asano and Kimura seized castles in Awa, Kazusa, and Shimōsa. Most of the Kantō was essentially abandoned to the Toyotomi as Hōjō Ujimasa centered his resistance in Sagami. But that resistance faltered toward the end of the sixth month. Hideyoshi sent another messenger to the castle urging surrender; even one of Ujimasa's brothers, Ujimori, entered the fortification to urge submission. Three days after the Toyotomi opened an attack with muskets, Ujimasa began negotiations. And early in the seventh month Ujimasa's son, Ujinao, surrendered Odawara to Hideyoshi. A week later Ujimasa committed suicide under order. Ujinao and Ujimori were permitted to go into exile at Mount Kōya. The entire Hōjō domain was confiscated.

These were extraordinary developments. There were some indications of the old indulgence—Ujinao and Ujimori received allowances, and Ujimori was eventually enfeoffed in Kawachi. But the elimination of Ujimasa overshadowed the two pardons.

The blow was not struck to frighten Ujimasa's northern neighbors into compliance. Even as the siege of Odawara progressed, the most formidable of those neighbors, Date Masamune, appeared in Hideyoshi's camp to secure a truce. Early in the sixth month of 1590, Masamune pledged loyalty to the Toyotomi and received confirmation of a fief valued at almost 700,000 koku. Somewhat earlier, in the fifth month, the Satake and Utsunomiya aligned with Hideyoshi and joined his Kantō campaign. The Sanada of Kōzuke were already Toyotomi allies. Thus northern Honshū, though not subdued entirely, promised to fall with some ease.[68]

The most important thing about the Hōjō confiscation is that it happened at all. It demonstrated that Hideyoshi could and would seize land. He had a range of choices, and he was conscious of them. Yet his intention in this instance was not to display a new ruthlessness; nor was it to enlarge vastly his personal holdings and thus commit himself to different forms of rule. The meaning of the confiscation must be found in its results and in its timing.

Shortly after the fall of Hōjō Ujimasa, Ieyasu was awarded eight Kantō provinces and ordered to make his headquarters in the town of Edo in Musashi. The change dramatically increased the value of his holdings—to 2,402,000 koku—and left him the wealthiest of Toyotomi daimyo, with land revenue greater than that of Hideyoshi himself. It also removed him considerably further east of the capital. The familiar explanation of the transfer is persuasive. Ieyasu's help in the Odawara offensive demonstrated his commitment to the Toyotomi coalition while it failed fully to relieve Hideyoshi's distrust. Given Ieyasu's cooperation in the Kantō despite temptation to honor his Hōjō alliance, a reward was in order. By moving the Tokugawa into a richer but distant domain, Hideyoshi was able both to promote Ieyasu and to isolate his forces from the sensitive central provinces.

Insofar as Hideyoshi's domestic campaigns came largely to an end with the surrender of Odawara, the Kantō was the last large reserve of land to which the Tokugawa could be moved without disturbance elsewhere. The timely conjunction of the Hōjō conquest, the need to reward Ieyasu, and the opportunity to effect an easy transfer moved Hideyoshi to attaint Ujimasa's domain. Hideyoshi then offered Ieyasu's former holdings to Oda Nobukatsu, another important general in the Kantō offensive. But Nobukatsu was unwilling to remove himself from the Oda base and face the disruption of the transfer. When he refused Hideyoshi's offer, he was exiled to Kōzuke, where he took the tonsure. Hideyoshi's nephew and future heir, Hidetsugu, took over Nobukatsu's lands in Owari.[69]

The former Tokugawa domain was divided among numerous daimyo. The largest grants went to Mōri Hideyori and Ikeda Terumasa, former vassals of Oda Nobunaga; Hashiba Hidekatsu, Nobunaga's fourth son; Ishikawa Kazumasa, a former retainer of Tokugawa Ieyasu; and Horio Yoshiharu and Nakamura Kazuuji, both *fudai* of Hideyoshi. Again Hideyoshi distributed land he might have kept himself, and again he included outsiders.[70] In the midst of these transfers, Hideyoshi moved north with Date Masamune to complete the work of pacification. By the ninth month of 1590 he was satisfied that the outreaches of northeastern Honshū were submissive, and he returned to Kyoto.

Conclusion

It is little wonder that Hideyoshi's conquests, as varied as they were decisive, shaped so much of his legend. The emergency marches against the Akechi and the Shibata, the encirclement of the two islands of Shikoku and Kyushu with massive land and sea forces, the siege of Odawara—such adventures caught the imagination of Hideyoshi's early historians and drew deeply upon their literary resources. Enriching their tales were the remarkable personalities of the time: the weary yet determined Shibata Katsuie, who bristled before the upstart and went to his death a victim not so much of ambition as of offended

vanity; the crafty Tokugawa Ieyasu, who was submissive when it satisfied him to be submissive; the defiant Hōjō Ujimasa, who valued his
independence more than his security. Accident and good fortune, no
less than these human players, also gave color to the story of Toyotomi
conquest: the restraint of the Mōri after the siege of Takamatsu castle,
the enmity between Nobunaga's sons, the abduction of critical messengers.

Yet even the most single-minded accounts of Hideyoshi's battles
suggest the importance of the theme of alliance. If his campaigns were
few, loyal allies kept them so. If his armies were as able as they were
immense, they were led by gallant daimyo who had entered the Toyotomi coalition. The Kobayakawa fought for Hideyoshi in Shikoku, the
Maeda in Etchū, the Chōsokabe in Kyushu, the Uesugi and Tokugawa
in the Kantō. Hideyoshi's generals were not common soldiers from the
farms of Owari and Mino. They formed an assembly of the warring-
states elite—long divided but now allied under one banner.

Hideyoshi's *tozama* were well rewarded for their services. The Tokugawa, Mōri, Maeda, and Uesugi emerged as the wealthiest daimyo
houses of the period. Not far behind were the Date and Satake, despite
their exceedingly late entry into the Toyotomi alliance. Also high on
the list were the Chōsokabe and the Shimazu, those vanquished outsiders whom Hideyoshi had chosen to leave in power. Many and diverse
military motives moved both the *tozama* to alliance and Hideyoshi to
generous land concessions. Their accommodation is sensible in retrospect, the more so since Nobunaga's frightening regime had exposed
the consequences of intractability for aggressor and opponent alike. But
wartime accommodation gave no assurance of future stability. What
would happen when the emergency was over, when the rewards ran
out, when a political settlement placed unwelcome constraints upon the
allies and their leader?

There were worrisome signs that a transition to peacetime accord
might not occur without rebellion and new coups. Obdurate Hōjō resistance to the Toyotomi, when the family had little hope of survival,
threatened the very spirit of unification. Severe imbalances in land distribution between the greatest *tozama* and the overwhelming majority of
remaining daimyo might provoke reaction. And whatever the course
pursued by the daimyo, their ability to lead their retainers, the armed
peasantry, and a militant Buddhist church into a new political settlement was far from clear.

There were also signs, however, that a peaceful accord might be
reached. The *tozama* had actually taken Hideyoshi's lead in battle and
marshaled their troops against his enemies. Alliance had meant more

than passive withdrawal from hostility. In collective obedience to a single hegemon, the daimyo had managed to find both common cause and security.

Hideyoshi, too, had shown a taste for compromise. Through apprehension, gratitude, and esteem for his fellow daimyo, he had confirmed *tozama* fiefs and neglected to concentrate land in his own house. He had been willing, as well, to absorb the defeated into his coalition. Neither ruthless in victory nor arrogant in alliance, neither dependent upon insiders nor greedy for land control, he offered promise of that departure from Nobunaga's pattern which might make political cohesion possible.

5

TOYOTOMI POLICY: SHAPING
THE NEW ORDER

BY THE MIDDLE of the seventeenth century, war was a distant memory in Japan. The occasional vendetta, rarely involving as many as a hundred men, was the last reminder of the cataclysmic struggles of the era of warring states. Few military men knew how to fire a musket after 1650, armor served as a decoration of great halls, and samurai learned to wield their swords in gymnasia in pursuit of personal cultivation or recreation. While philosophers reconceived the warrior as a gentleman and moral exemplar to justify the privileges of a large, anachronistic military class, its members turned to government service, to scholarship, and sometimes to medicine to occupy themselves usefully. They wrote labored treatises on the Way of the Warrior and retold the tales of their ancestors, for the heroic feats of yesterday remained one source of the peacetime soldier's prestige. Yet reflections upon the ever more romanticized past were exercises in nostalgia. Within a generation of Hideyoshi's death, armed conflict had all but disappeared from his country.

This extraordinary development in a society that had customarily resorted to battle to decide significant issues was not apparent in 1590, though the transformation surely began in that year. Even after Hideyoshi's conquest of the Kantō and the northern domains, historical enemies continued to share borders. Defeated leaders such as Ashikaga Yoshiaki still looked for vengeance. Garrisons surrounded all vital resources while men of every station—priests, peasants, pirates, townsmen—stood ready to defend local interests. Many daimyo, moreover, might have found in assassination or new coups an opportunity to replace their peasant lord with a more suitable leader. In all respects, Japanese society remained volatile following the pacification of the northeast.

Hideyoshi himself did not regard his most recent conquests as an occasion for jubilation when he returned to Kyoto from the Tōhoku campaign on the first day of the ninth month, 1590. Although he presided over a tea party in the capital three weeks later, he mounted no parades, received neither the daimyo nor the nobility in his residence, and began no round of thanksgiving prayers at Kyoto's temples and shrines to mark the end of fighting. The *Taikō-ki* describes a mood of apprehension and fatigue: "[Hideyoshi's] honored senior vassals and retainers were uneasily composed, hoping finally that they might return their shields and spears to boxes, their bows to bow cases, and take comfort from the exertions of recent years."[1]

Yet for all the likelihood of resumed hostilities, Hideyoshi's peace held. The new scale and technology of combat doubtless deterred some warriors from a challenge. Kyushu had been torn apart for six months in 1586–87 by more than a quarter of a million soldiers; there and elsewhere long lines of musketeers had mowed down their adversaries with no pretense of chivalry. Such developments made continued resistance either reckless or costly in the extreme.

Incidents more telling than battle may also have discouraged challengers after 1590: the surrender of the Shimazu domain to Hideyoshi by the head of that house, dressed as a monk, at a campsite in southern Kyushu; the abandonment of Odawara castle by two generations of Hōjō leaders; the journey of Date Masamune to ask for clemency at the Toyotomi stronghold in Sagami. These moments distilled for potential rivals the experience of complex campaigns, imparting finality to Hideyoshi's conquests and an image of invincibility to the conqueror himself.

To some extent, the distractions of individual daimyo helped keep the peace of 1590. Tokugawa Ieyasu was preoccupied with his move to the Kantō. Other Toyotomi generals, released from the punishing inertia of the Odawara siege, returned home to cope again with the problems of governing. Kyushu leaders had only begun the reconstruction of their administrations, and winter snows immobilized troops from Echizen to Mutsu. The ensuing armistice, fortified by the definitive victories of recent months, developed a momentum of its own.

The principal constraint upon hostility, however, was a political and social settlement, both intricate and broadly conceived, that created the conditions for lasting order. Although it had begun to emerge in wartime, Hideyoshi's settlement took shape in the 1590s. His sober return from the east was an acknowledgment that the trying tasks of pacification remained unfinished. Odawara was a milestone not a destination.

The policy Hideyoshi unfolded had a dual character. Some of his edicts, unprecedented and revolutionary in effect, asserted the right of a single leader to direct the nation's course and were greater in scope than any statutes promulgated since the emergence of the imperial state in the eighth century. They indicated that Hideyoshi understood the power attending national conquest and was prepared to use it, radically centralizing authority in the Toyotomi administration. Other elements of Hideyoshi's policy, deeply rooted in warring-states tradition, restricted the growth of central power by reinforcing the position of the daimyo. As a whole, the Toyotomi polity was Hideyoshi's greatest legacy to his successors. Made possible by his military achievement, the social and political settlement proved to be a far more important, and lasting, victory. Although leadership would pass to a new house, generations of Tokugawa shogun and their daimyo would alter very little the Toyotomi framework of government. The quiet of 1650 owed something to the general who first unified the warring states, much more to the governor who created a sound context for union.

We know Hideyoshi's policy primarily through his red-seal papers, or *shuinjō*—documents issued with a vermilion chop containing the characters *hide* and *yoshi*. The first dates from 1583, the last was dispatched not long before his death. Although most of Hideyoshi's correspondence before 1585 concludes with either a monogram (*kaō*) or the more familiar black chop—less formal styles he used occasionally throughout his life—his later preference for *shuinjō* has led historians to describe Hideyoshi's government as the Red-Seal System. Nobunaga, other warring-states lords, and even the Ashikaga had used *shuin* from time to time, yet Hideyoshi was the first routinely to conduct national business with missives bearing his red stamp.[2]

The red-seal papers have a remarkable scope. They include vesting documents for fiefs, edicts, letters, troop and manpower levies, statutes for certain cities. But for all their variety and their bulk—there are thousands of *shuinjō* surviving—these papers are not a compendium of Toyotomi policy. Hideyoshi did not use them to provide a systematic exposition of governing practices nor, as far as we know, did he retain an archivist to keep and organize his pronouncements after they were delivered. Thus we must look for details concerning the cadastral survey, for example, in the many communications between Toyotomi magistrates and the daimyo. In the end, the completed cadastres themselves tell us most about the character of this complex undertaking.

If the red-seal papers do not constitute a full statement of Toyotomi policy, they are also something less than public statutes issued by a faceless authority to his deputies. Most of the documents are personal letters from Hideyoshi to individual daimyo. They trace day-to-day decisions about a settlement that evolved from many separate actions. Even in matters of general concern, when numerous officials required information, Hideyoshi normally turned to private correspondence rather than to universal proclamations.³ On occasion, when he used representatives to announce his orders, Hideyoshi subsequently sent his own statement of intentions to the daimyo affected. He specified, further, that copies of those letters be returned with the correspondent's chop to indicate compliance.⁴ This direct, particular approach to lawmaking reaffirmed the bonds between lord and vassal and gave the red-seal papers the tone of timely advice.

The word "law" must be used with hesitation, then, in describing the *shuinjō*. Many of the papers involve enfeoffments and other land matters. The remainder, direct or indirect commands, are seldom prefaced, like later Tokugawa documents, by headings such as *sadame* (law), *oboe* (memorandum), or *kinsei* (prohibition). The choice of heading, when a heading is used, seems arbitrary. But, of course, the nomenclature of formal legal procedure is barely relevant to documents usually conceived as personal instructions.⁵ In most cases, Hideyoshi simply declared his interests and, by using the language of command, communicated a sense of obligation to his correspondent. Thus the red-seal papers not only reveal much of what we know of Hideyoshi's policy, they also disclose the temperament of the author—a man who, committed to formidable change, trusted in a voluminous, direct, and unsystematic correspondence to achieve it.

The Sword Hunt

Roughly a year after the conquest of Kyushu, and while his inconclusive negotiations with the Hōjō dragged on, Hideyoshi issued one of his most extraordinary red-seal papers. It signaled the beginning of his political settlement.

> Item [1]: The farmers of the various provinces are strictly forbidden to possess long swords, short swords, bows, spears, muskets, or any other form of weapon. If there are persons who maintain unnecessary implements (*irazaru dōgu*), cause hardship in the collection of annual taxes, and [thus] foment uprisings, or commit wrong acts toward the retainers, they shall, needless to say, be brought to judgment. Since [in such cases] the paddies and dry fields of the places concerned will not be cultivated and the fiefs will be wasted, the lords of the provinces, the retainers, and the representatives shall therefore strictly collect all these weapons mentioned and deliver them [to us].

> Item [2]: So that the long and short swords collected shall not be wasted, they shall be [melted down and] used as rivets and clamps in the forthcoming construction of the Great Buddha. This will be an act by which the farmers will be saved in this life, needless to say, and in the life to come.

Item [3]: If farmers possess agricultural tools alone and engage [themselves] completely in cultivation, they shall [prosper] unto eternity, even to [the generations of] their children and grandchildren. [Thus] it is with compassion for the farmers that we rule in this manner. Truly [these orders] will be the foundation of the safety of the country and the happiness of all people. In another country the ruler Yao of China pacified the realm and [then] used precious swords and sharp blades as farming tools. There has been no [such] attempt in our country. Observing the meaning [of our orders], and understanding their various purposes, the farmers shall invest their energies in agriculture and [the cultivation] of mulberry trees [for silkworms].

Collect the above-mentioned implements without fail and deliver them [to us].

Tenshō 16 [1588], seventh month, eighth day [Hideyoshi's red seal][6]

The style and tone of this edict are as significant as its content. In addition to bearing Hideyoshi's vermilion chop, the edict appeared, in the most distinguished form of the age, on *tategami*—large sheets of paper carrying their message in long, uninterrupted, and continuous vertical lines. Of greater interest, the edict was not addressed to an individual correspondent.[7]

The three items address the nation. They do so, moreover, in a stern and magisterial tone. Contrasting the experience of China with that of "our country" (*honchō*), Hideyoshi obliterates domainal boundaries to invoke an image of the whole. One year earlier, when he ordered the missionaries to depart, he used similar language. "Japan," he said, "is the land of the gods"; the evangelists would "not be permitted to remain in the territory of Japan."[8] While national references would increasingly lace Hideyoshi's red-seal papers, so too would projections concerning the "children and grandchildren" of his people. In the present edict, he makes sanguine predictions about "eternity." Notions of both time and place began to expand for Hideyoshi as the disarray of the warring states gave way to greater stability.

Accompanying this wider perspective was a lofty portrayal of his objectives. Not only did Hideyoshi act "with compassion for the farmers," he characterized his edict as "the foundation of the safety of the country and the happiness of all people." Implicit in the third item, further, was the organic view of society elaborated by his Tokugawa successors. The farmers were to "engage completely" in their calling to ensure the prosperity of all. They were members of the social body who undermined its health when "the paddies and dry fields . . . [were] wasted." With a flourish reminiscent of the earliest imperial legislation, Hideyoshi also advised farmers that their weapons would be used in the construction of the Great Buddha, a national monument. Already the material providers of the country, the peasants would nourish the state spiritually.

Underlying the arch prose of the edict was an obvious purpose. Hideyoshi sought to disarm all cultivators, to eliminate local caches of weapons, and to break the habit of armed response to disturbances. As early as 1585 he had begun seizing weapons from religious establishments such as Mount Kōya, and, in expanding in other documents upon the present edict, he ordered that all townsmen be disarmed as well.[9] There had been previous attempts to collect the tools of war in Japan. We are told that Emperor Tenchi beat swords into plowshares in 645; the Kamakura administration confiscated some weapons in the thirteenth century; and Shibata Katsuie eradicated Jōdo Shinshū arsenals in 1576.[10] Nonetheless, Hideyoshi's reference to the novelty of his edict, and his use of Emperor Yao as a model, are appropriate: no Japanese leader had ever attempted a nationwide purge of arms.

A month after the edict appeared, Hideyoshi began receiving huge deliveries from the Toyotomi magistrates and daimyo representatives who shared the responsibility for collecting arms.

Receipt for the arms of the farmers of the Enuma district of Kaga

Item: 1,073 long swords (*katana*)

Item: 1,540 short swords (*wakizashi*)

Item: 160 spearheads (*yarimi*)

Item: 500 bodkins [?] (*kōgai*)

Item: 700 daggers (*kogatana*)

The above—five items.
Tenshō 16 [1588], eighth month, eighteenth day.[11]

An author of the *Tamon'in nikki* described the confusion attending such pillage in uncharacteristically sharp remarks: "Because they are thoroughly collecting swords and spears and all such implements in the provinces, all of Nara is in an uproar. It is said that they will be used as rivets in the Great Buddha, but from now on the people will only be put to increasing hardship."[12]

The mounted magistrates who rounded up everything from muskets to daggers changed men's thoughts about themselves. Farmers had borne arms for centuries and taken part in the contests that helped fix the rights of lordship. Their military role brought political influence and obscured class boundaries. A pivotal member of his community by the warring-states era, the armed peasant symbolized opportunity. The confiscation of his weapons, far more than a "hardship," altered a condition of life. An anonymous graffito that appeared in Kyoto sometime

after the edict on arms reflected the mood of helpless anger brought on
by this and other incursions into daily life:

> In my dreams at night
> I am tormented by
> The government's orders.
> I do not know if there will be a tomorrow
> In my life of dew.[13]

The apparent absence of widespread resistance to the edict is consequently surprising. Although it was not enforced immediately across
the country, documents from Kaga, Izumo, and the home provinces indicate compliance while making no suggestion of peasant defiance of
the "sword-collecting magistrates" (katana gari bugyō). A letter from
Shimazu Yoshihiro to domainal officials in Satsuma, written just five
months after the proclamation of the edict, supports the Tamon'in nikki
observations concerning the sometimes prompt response to the order.
Yoshihiro observed that because weapons from the various provinces
had been delivered to Kyoto, he was worried over the delay in dispatching the arms of Satsuma. Given the fame of the long blades from
that province, he added, any failure on the part of the Shimazu to comply with the edict would be particularly conspicuous.[14]

The unequivocal assertion of authority in Hideyoshi's edict may
itself have helped stifle dissent. Like his sweeping invasions, the items
left no margin for misunderstanding: violators would, "needless to say,
be brought to judgment." Once the first deliveries of arms were in, men
like Yoshihiro may have acted in fearful obedience. Yoshihiro's desire
to see Satsuma in conformity with national statutes shows the subordination of the domain to a central power that the edict both assumed and
promoted.

The edict also engaged the collective interest of the daimyo and
their high retainers in a cunning fashion. If peasant recruits were useful
in large campaigns, they were also able to "cause hardship in the collection of annual taxes," to "foment uprisings," to "commit wrong acts
toward the retainers," and to ignore cultivation for other pursuits.
Armed farmers impeded local rule as gravely as they threatened a national settlement. A universal order to seize their weapons, much as it
preempted domainal authority, achieved several salutary results from
the perspective of the daimyo: it enabled them to disarm cultivators
without sacrificing a military advantage to neighboring lords who might
maintain peasant conscripts; and it transferred responsibility for a desirable but unpopular policy from local officials deeply involved in
agrarian politics to a national leader. The edict had the pleasing, and

paradoxical, effect of increasing central power while suggesting the usefulness of concerted action instigated from above.

Perhaps the most brilliant effect of the edict was the distinction accorded the bearing of arms. Now forbidden to farmers, to townsmen, and to priests, the sword became a badge of privilege reserved for the warrior class. By dignifying the full-time soldier at the same moment that he restricted the power of peasants, Hideyoshi deepened rifts in status and separated the cultivator from his chief prospective allies in opposing the new regime.

Freezing the Social Order

In the eighth month of 1591, one year after his conquest of the northern domains and three years after his edict on arms, Hideyoshi addressed the nation with a new edict:

Item [1]: Should there be any [upper- or lower-ranking military] men, including *hōkōnin, samurai, chūgen, komono,* and *arashiko,* who have newly become townsmen or farmers since the campaign in Ōshū [northern Japan] of the previous seventh month [1590], the villagers and the townsmen shall conduct an examination and shall absolutely not harbor [them]. If there is any concealment, all in that neighborhood (*sono itchō*) and that place shall be brought to judgment.

Item [2]: Should any farmer, abandoning his fields, go into trade or wage labor, that person, needless to say, and all in his village (*jige-chū*) shall be brought to judgment. Moreover, the officials shall strictly examine and shall not harbor anyone who neither performs military service nor engages in [the cultivation of] fields. If there is no [compliance] with these orders, the retainers [shall be found] negligent and their investitures confiscated. If there is any concealment by the townsmen or farmers, the whole village, or likewise the whole neighborhood, shall be in offense.

Item [3]: You shall absolutely not employ any [military] man—whether samurai or *komono*—who has left his master without asking leave. Conduct a thorough examination [of a military man who seeks employ] and establish a guarantor [for him]. If the [military] man in question has a lord and this is reported, you shall accordingly arrest him and hand him over to his previous master. If you violate these laws and permit such a person to go free, three heads shall be cut off and dispatched [to the previous master] in place of that one man. Should you fail to order restitution with those three men's [heads], the new master shall be brought to judgment without inquiries into the merits [of the case].[15]

Absolutely without precedent in Japan, these items identify three professional orders and forbid movement between them. The man who converted himself from peasant to lord of the realm—and who depended upon *fudai* of comparable enterprise—fixed the boundaries of occupation in this edict with the language of a police state. Hideyoshi requires mutual surveillance by the residents of towns and villages, rigorous examination of strangers, and corporate punishment. The penalties he mentions are draconian: attainder and the execution of innocent men; those he hints at—"all in that neighborhood shall be brought to judgment"—are ominous in their vagueness. Disobedience, he promises, will be handled "without inquiries into the merits [of the case]."

In this edict Hideyoshi was not much concerned with townsmen, a group he simply calls *chōnin*, without distinguishing between artisan and merchant. The commercial community was still small, politically unthreatening, and concentrated in easily monitored centers. Like the daimyo of the time, Hideyoshi encouraged urban development by easing both taxes and political control within the city. Migration into towns was not strenuously checked.[16] The edict sought, rather, an irreversible separation of peasants and warriors. The first item forbids military men in active service late in 1590—from porters and handlers of the dead to foot soldiers and mounted retainers—to reenter village society. The second prohibits farmers from leaving full-time cultivation. This tightening of control on the agrarian community, in the wake of the arms seizures, was certainly important. Yet the edict's impact upon military men was far more profound.

By establishing military service (*hōkō*) and farming as exclusive pursuits, and by ordering farmers to expel warriors from their midst, Hideyoshi denied samurai, in principle, an independent land base. He attempted to remove them, too, from family members, tenants, and military subordinates in the village. They were to become wards of their daimyo in barracks towns, shedding attachments to place. Implicit in the edict is the assumption that a man's function is his most important attribute and that the warrior must define himself solely in terms of the command structure of his lord. Both the physical separation of the soldier from the land and the necessary shift in his self-perception presaged seminal change in Japanese society.

The change was eased, certainly, by the conditions of *sengoku* warfare and the policy of the daimyo toward their retainers. Prolonged campaigns as well as the need to maintain standing armies of defense had already removed many soldiers from the land to the castles of their lords. The refinement of internal military organizations and the transfer of fiefs following new conquests also weakened the soldier's ties to his

holdings. Indeed, to encourage this development Oda Nobunaga frequently rotated his men and forbade them to retain former holdings;
the Hōjō and the Tokugawa not only reassigned retainers but scattered
their fiefs. At the deepest level, moreover, the cadastral surveys of the
warring-states era had made landholding conditional upon investiture
by the daimyo.[17]

The change required by Hideyoshi's edict was eased, too, by gradual implementation. No statements of alarm give evidence of an overnight revolution. Case studies of class composition in villages of the late
sixteenth and seventeenth century suggest that samurai withdrew from
the land very slowly.[18] The clearest evidence of a transition appears in
the division of some domains, by the daimyo, into kurairi-chi (lands for
the support of the lord himself) and kyūnin-chi (lands for the support of
retainers). Although military men might reside on kyūnin-chi, those
holdings had a general association with the entire military community
and were governed by the daimyo.[19] But not until the Tokugawa ordered in 1615 that the daimyo retain only one castle each and assemble
there all domainal retainers were the implications of Hideyoshi's edict
drawn out and the appropriate residence of military men defined. Even
then, landed vassals stayed on in certain parts of the country and the
complete transfer of the rest proceeded at an uneven pace.[20]

Neither the stirrings of change in the sengoku era nor the slowness
of the transition to a landless army, however, diminishes the importance of Hideyoshi's edict. Land rewards and martial service had been
inextricably linked throughout Japan's medieval history and remained
associated, beyond imaginable alteration, in 1590. Like the armed peasant and the presumption of social mobility, the fief was a constant in
the warring-states world. Yet in a few words Hideyoshi eliminated
those three constants, undertaking a drastic solution to the problems
that underlay much of the upheaval of his age: the emergence of the
village as an armed unit of resistance to authority, as a source of recruitment for competing warrior leagues, and as a base of independence for the fief holder.

Hideyoshi could not have foreseen some of the most significant
results of his edicts: the development of large, commercially lively
cities as merchants, artisans, bankers, and laborers moved to castle
towns in the wake of military retainers; the growth of a complex bureaucracy to replace former fief holders; or the official propagation of
Confucianism to rationalize the new social order. The purposes that
Confucianism would serve, however, he understood. In symbolic matters Hideyoshi was careful to heighten the dignity of warriors now cut
off from the village and in need of reorientation. Not only did military
men alone retain the right to bear arms, their robes were to be richer

than the commoners': "*Kosode* (narrow-sleeved kimono), formal clothing, and the like shall have silk linings." Distinctions between the military ranks, further, were to be preserved: "*Chūgen* and *komono* should
not wear leather *tabi*."[21] While later sumptuary legislation would condemn ostentation, Hideyoshi's early edicts enjoined military men to
dress up to their status. The attention to ritual and protocol in military
society of the late sixteenth century reflected the need for sources of
honor to substitute for the fief. Seating arrangements, the location of
homes in castle towns, hair styles, the privilege of eating white rice all
became indexes of social distinction.

Individual daimyo also tried to enlarge the vision, and the identity,
of their uprooted subordinates with uplifting advice. Chōsokabe Motochika urged his men to practice humanity and righteousness, reminded
them that "it should be the primary concern of everyone to train himself unceasingly in military accomplishment," and then went on:
"Strive to develop accomplishments appropriate to your status. Furthermore, you must always keep in your mind the study of books and
pursuit of arts insofar as these are consistent with your duties." He also
exhorted them to "live up to the teachings of the various [Buddhist]
sects."[22] Familiar to much military counsel and often trite in expression,
these sentiments remain intriguing in their concern with self-cultivation, a universal moral order, and dedication to calling. Anticipating the
Confucian tutors to the Tokugawa, Motochika was leading his retainers
into a society in which status (*bungen*) and its requirements replaced
material rewards in importance.

The dispensation of new privileges and moralistic disquisitions
could not, of course, ameliorate all distress in the martial ranks. De-
sertion from daimyo armies and decisions to surrender arms in order to
resume farming became commonplace.[23] Despite this disruption in
their domains, the daimyo complied with Hideyoshi's edict. First displayed in the substitution of general retainer lands for the individual
fief, compliance was best demonstrated in their unfaltering, if gradual,
progress toward class separation. None of Hideyoshi's successors
would renounce the terms or the assumptions of the edict of 1591.

The motives behind compliance surely involved the same self-interest that encourged acceptance of the law on arms. By removing soldiers
from the land, Hideyoshi's daimyo gained direct access to village resources and close control over the military men who were now entirely
dependent upon them. While no daimyo of the *sengoku* era had cut off
soldiers from their fiefs, many had pursued the advantages of such a
decision through domain-wide taxation, cadastral surveys, and controls
on the independence of their vassals. Hideyoshi's edict, daring as it
was, simply pressed these initiatives to a logical conclusion. The readi-

ness of Chōsokabe Motochika to define a moral context for the order is a revealing comment on the receptivity of some daimyo to the change. Once again, because the order came from the victor of the *sengoku* campaigns, the daimyo escaped personal responsibility for another desirable but unsettling policy. As the law on arms had closed the grip of local lords on the agrarian community, so the more recent law gave them greater power over their entire domains.

The oppressive effect of the edict, for all but the daimyo elite, is nonetheless indisputable. Under threat of the gravest penalties, Hideyoshi denied men the right to change estate. He denied them, too, the right to move freely about the country. The final item of the edict of 1591 required military men to remain in the employ of their current masters, unless permission to leave was granted. In numerous other statutes, farmers were also forbidden to change residence: "No farmer—resisting his taxes and avoiding his corvée responsibilities—shall flee to neighboring or other villages. If anyone conceal such a runaway, the individual, needless to say, and all residents of that place shall be judged in offense."[24]

The prohibition against movement is clearest in another major law issued by Hideyoshi, probably in 1592. While the original edict does not survive, this domainal version states its purpose.

Item [1]: [The compiling of] a census has been ordered by the Regent to the sixty-six provinces . . .

Item [2]: You are to register, by village, the number of houses and the number of persons—men and women, old and young.

Addendum: Register, in each place, the military men as military men, the farmers as farmers, and the townsmen as townsmen . . .

Item [3]: People from other provinces or districts shall not be permitted [to reside or register in other places].

Addendum: If [he] has a guarantor, that person shall entrust [to us] a written vow to the gods, sealed in blood, that there will not be any disturbance . . . Requests for change of residence since the seventh month of the previous year will not be permitted.[25]

Although the third item sanctions the occasional transfer, these directives prohibit nearly all movement. Hideyoshi thus tried to hold rein over the more expansive daimyo who were no longer free to recruit from rival camps and to prevent those large-scale migrations that aided aggression. He also kept farmers in their fields. Uncultivated property and absconding peasants were an intolerable drain on resources.

Needless to say, Hideyoshi's edicts raised enormous questions. How was the distinction between warrior and farmer to be made in a judicious fashion? How were ownership and cultivating claims to land in the village to be resolved upon the withdrawal of military proprietors? And how were armies to be supported? Hideyoshi would have appeared foolish had his major orders prompted nothing more than chaos; as an unproven national leader, he could not afford to let these questions go unanswered. The Toyotomi cadastres, produced by the most extensive land surveys in Japan's history, provided solutions to the harder problems raised by Hideyoshi's edicts. His registration project was as broad in conception as his laws, yet immensely more detailed. It demonstrated his ability to administer a nationwide program with both rigor and consistency and became the foundation not only of his social policy but of his settlement with the daimyo as well.

The Land Survey

Hideyoshi's cadastral surveys (*kenchi*) owed much to the work of warring-states daimyo. Not only had they fostered the habit of registration throughout much of Japan, they had used their cadastres to establish ultimate proprietorship over their domains and to improve their access to local resources. Limited in extent and flawed in procedure, however, the wartime surveys did not provide Hideyoshi with a model of efficiency. Some cadastres failed to indicate the size, type, and specific location of fields; others omitted mention of the value of those fields; very few listed tenant cultivators; and all used different standards of measurement.[26] Statements on value, when they did appear, almost invariably recorded the assessed tax rather than the estimated product of landholdings. Further, value was sometimes expressed in cash and sometimes in rice within the same domain.[27]

Although we know little about how warring-states cadastres were assembled, many of their discrepancies were surely a result of simple differences in the time and place of compilation and the absence of uniform directives to registrars. But many more discrepancies derived from the modest nature of the registration efforts themselves. Nearly all registers completed before the late 1580s were *sashidashi*—reports on local resources, in response to official orders, involving neither the direct inspection of land nor the active intervention of outside agents. Oda Nobunaga's survey of Kōfukuji's holdings is a case in point. While Akechi Mitsuhide and Takigawa Kazumasu remained at the temple during the survey period and finally received the registry prepared there for Nobunaga's benefit, religious officials did their own accounting, on the basis of available documentation, within a month's time.[28] Similar collations of older records by proprietors, and sometimes by villagers, produced most *sengoku* cadastres and account for the disparities among them.[29]

There were, of course, certain checks on the honesty of the *sashi-dashi* surveyors: serial demands for new assessments, the offer of rewards to farmers or officials who revealed deceit in the cadastres, and the annual spring estimates of the harvest. Yet such checks could not eliminate the fundamental problem of the *sashidashi* surveys with their emphasis upon submitting often imprecise records rather than on inspecting land. Nor could they resolve the technical difficulties posed by the registration of property long held by independent proprietors with different accounting systems. Many *sengoku* daimyo were new to power over large domains; most governed potentially rebellious peasants and vassals; all were preoccupied with the continuing demands of battle. It is small wonder that the *kenchi* were conducted by stable and experienced houses, and that progress toward standardized surveys was gradual.

With the unification of the warring states, the cadastral work improved significantly. The first measure of Hideyoshi's success is the geographical spread of his surveys. By 1598 his magistrates had assessed the land of twenty to thirty provinces. Most remaining provinces, largely held by *tozama*, were examined by representatives of local daimyo who, in general, employed Hideyoshi's guidelines. Although part of the Tōhoku as well as several islands may not have been inspected before 1600, most of the territory of Japan was surveyed during the Toyotomi tenure.[30]

Far more important than the scale of this labor was the creation of firm principles of registration. Certainly no scheme sprang full-born from the mind of Hideyoshi or any of his deputies immediately following Nobunaga's death. Between 1582 and the early 1590s they employed different surveying approaches inspired by local custom and the precedents of other examiners. But by 1594 they had developed a routine, more exact and consistent than the prototypes, that required fresh surveys of much of Japan. *Kenchi* officials crossed and recrossed many areas. Parts of Yamashiro were surveyed by eight different teams.[31]

A clear statement of mature Toyotomi policy concerning land registration is contained in the instructions issued to surveyors in the home provinces during the eighth month of 1594.

Item [1]: You shall measure wet and dry fields and residence [plots] using a rod of 6 *shaku*, 3 *sun* [to equal 1 *ken*], and [calculating] the *tan* at 5 by 60 *ken* or 300 *bu*.

Item [2]: Superior paddies [are to be registered with a value of] 1 *koku*, 5 *to* [per *tan*]; medium paddies [with a value of] 1 *koku*, 3 *to*; inferior paddy [with a value of] 1 *koku*, 1 *to*; and very inferior paddy [with a value] to be determined upon examination [by the magistrate].

Item [3]: Register residence [plots] at 1 *koku*, 2 *to*.

Item [4]: Determine the value of mountain, wild, and riverbed fields after inquiries into previous evaluations and direct examinations.

Item [7]: Determine the value of all superior, medium, and inferior [fields], as well as wetland, barley fields, and sites damaged by drought or flood, after examination and consideration.

Item [9]: The *masu* [a measure of volume] shall be the *Kyō-masu*. The magistrates of the cadastral survey are to provide themselves with the current *Kyō-masu*, and to distribute them everywhere. They are to gather up all previous *masu* [in the villages] and to confiscate them.

Item [10]: The cadastral registry is to be copied by the farmers and a receipt [for it] required. You shall order that there be no discrepancies in measurement or evaluation henceforth. The cadastral magistrates shall place their seals on the registries of the various [villages] and turn them [the copies] over [to the residents].[32]

Like similar orders issued to other Toyotomi surveyors, these instructions require the measurement of all land parcels and their classification as paddy, dry field, or residential lot (which included kitchen gardens). They also provide a basis for calculating the value of land, a point to which we shall return. The following portion of one *kenchi* register from 1594 suggests the style of registration (Table 1). This document comes from the village of Tenkawa in the Kaigawa district of Settsu province and describes almost two thousand parcels of land.[33]

The name of the magistrate responsible for the Tenkawa survey, Ishikawa Kyūgo, appears on the cover sheet of this cadastre and again, with his seal, at its conclusion. In Hideyoshi's period the *sashidashi kenchi* undertaken by local proprietors came to an end. Deputies of the Toyotomi or the *tozama* daimyo who completed their own registries supervised the cadastral work.[34]

Another improvement in the Toyotomi surveys, indicated by items

Table 1. Part of a *kenchi* register from 1594.

Location within the village	Type and quality of the field	Size, in *bu*	Value in *koku, to, shō, gō*	Cultivator
Ōgawara	superior paddy	240	1.1.2.0	Shirōbei
Same	superior dry field	96	0.3.8.4	Same
Same	superior paddy	385	1.7.9.7	Magobei
Same	superior paddy	325	1.5.1.7	Yagorō
Same	superior paddy	300	1.4.0.0	Hikozaemon
Same	superior paddy	415	1.9.3.8	Gorōbei

one and nine of the 1594 instructions, was the establishment of universal standards of line, area, and volume measures.[35] Ordering his surveyors to discard local measuring tools and to leave their *ken* rods and *masu* containers in the villages, Hideyoshi attempted to train the population in the use of nationwide standards.[36] The introduction of new units served a further purpose as well. Because determining the size of a field was essential to the task of evaluation, and because available data was both limited and inconsistent, the definition of Toyotomi measures demanded active examination of land. Simple recalculation of area was largely impossible, the paperwork *kenchi* a thing of the past.

The shift in the Toyotomi years to personal inspection of holdings was encouraged by the need to classify plots not only according to their type (paddy or dry field) but also according to their fertility. Item two of the 1594 instructions establishes four categories of irrigated fields and assigns a standard yield to each category. Virtually all similar instructions establish four categories for dry fields as well, and, again, assign standard yields to each. These standard assessments varied by province, and often by district. Once a field was measured and categorized, its value was calculated by multiplying the size by the standard yield assigned each *tan* of land in that field's category. Thus even when cadastres survive independently of the instructions that governed their compilation, elementary arithmetic will uncover the formulas by which value was determined.[37]

How the Toyotomi established standard yield in the first place is not clear. Historians conclude that test plots of superior paddy were harvested and measured under the inspection of magistrates. These magistrates then averaged the total yield of hulled rice from the sample fields (approximately half of the unhulled harvest) to determine a value for all superior paddies in the area concerned. Valuation of medium and inferior paddy seems to have been made by reducing the first figure in steps of 2 *to*. If superior paddy yielded 1.5 *koku* of hulled rice, medium was appraised at 1.3 *koku*, inferior at 1.1 *koku*. Superior dry field, in an equally mechanical fashion, was valued at, or slightly above, the level of inferior paddy. Simple deductions, again in steps of 2 *to*, rendered appraisals for medium and inferior dry field.[38]

A fair amount of physical inspection, at least of the better rice harvests, probably did take place. Cadastres from Ōmi and Echizen, for example, indicate that Hideyoshi's surveyors did not rely upon a single set of field valuations, such as those defined for the home provinces in 1594, but appraised the classes of paddy and dry field differently in different locales. The magistrates assigned to Ōmi in 1591 judged superior paddy between 1.8 and 1.5 *koku*, depending upon the village. The relation between paddy and dry field values also escapes formulaic description. In one village, superior dry field was worth approximately as much as medium paddy, in another it was worth 2 *to* less than inferior paddy. The Echizen records show analogous variations.[39] The freedom of these surveyors to make valuations above those officially assigned to the rich lands in the area of the capital discourages the conclusion that their figures were concessions to peasants or reflections of inaccurate local records.

In instructions to the surveyors of the Shimazu fief, Hideyoshi abandoned the simple, province-wide guidelines of earlier years. The Shimazu orders call for the classification of villages (as superior, medium, inferior, and very inferior) as well as the classification of the fields within them. A superior paddy in a superior village was to be valued at 1.6 *koku*, a superior paddy in a very inferior village at 1 *koku*.[40] Thus the guidelines and the cadastres themselves tended toward greater specificity as the *kenchi* magistrates grew more familiar with land conditions through actual investigation.

As the previous discussion suggests, Hideyoshi's cadastral program improved upon its predecessors in its fundamental approach to land valuation. Value was a statement of total productivity made uniformly in terms of a rice equivalence (*kokudaka*). Tax rates and the consequent levies on individual villages were established each year, in separate documents. Again, the inconsistencies of *sengoku* registers—which normally recorded the tax assessment and used varying units of value such as cash or rice—were eliminated in theory.[41]

In view of the earlier trend in many areas of Japan to appraise and to tax land in cash, speculation has emerged concerning Hideyoshi's decision to appraise land in rice. Some historians observe that daimyo required enormous amounts of rice to provision armies, could not depend upon underdeveloped markets to obtain supplies, and consequently exacted taxes in food rations. Others argue that Hideyoshi sought to exclude peasants from commercial transactions by demanding taxes in produce that he and his vassals could then exchange in a market they hoped to dominate. Both arguments, however, avoid the simpler observation that contemporary currencies were deeply confused; there was nothing resembling a national monetary system to rationalize the registration of land in terms of cash. Rice, on the other hand, was a measurable and marketable quantity against which taxes could be fixed in accord with its fluctuating value.[42]

The establishment of the *kokudaka* system did not mean that all or most taxes were collected in rice. Even as Nobunaga began to evaluate land in terms of rice, he deplored the tendency to collect imposts in kind because of the uncertain monetary situation. One of Hideyoshi's commands to the men who administered his own property, moreover, indicates that he was receiving payments in gold and silver: "With regard to the market price [of rice], in conjunction with the [tax] deliveries to be made in gold and silver: every month we shall examine the [exchange rates for rice and these metals] in Kyoto, Fushimi, Sakai, and Osaka. Then we shall determine the amount of gold and silver due as tax payments on the basis of these market considerations."[43] Descriptions of land dimensions and productivity, the cadastres did not dictate tax policy to daimyo either. A rice statement of value was a steady base against which they were free to assign annual dues in rice, cash, or other forms.

The difficulties posed by the rice standard—particularly those of computing a rice-equivalent value for dry grains—raise the issue of error in all of Hideyoshi's cadastral work. We do not know how much and what sort of study went into the decision to evaluate the product of good dry fields at the level of inferior paddy.[44] The derivation of the worth of a dry field from paddy figures, by formula, seems arbitrary. The predilection to judge domestic plots in the class of superior dry fields presents problems as well. There can be no doubt that Hideyoshi's deputies exercised their own discretion throughout the registration process. Items four through eight of the 1594 instructions, which recommend both great and small matters to the judgment of the inspectors, draw attention to the complexity of their task. With responsibility for entire provinces, those magistrates could not linger in any particular village to reinforce a first analysis with extensive reexamination. They were, moreover, dependent upon local assistance and information for many of their decisions.

Local assistance was especially significant since the surveying team was not large. For the 1594 registration of the Shimazu holdings, for example, Hideyoshi appointed Ishida Mitsunari and only twenty-five other magistrates. The domainal representative of Shimazu Yoshihisa became an associate magistrate who deputized samurai and village officials to assist Mitsunari. These officials, as well as whole communities on occasion, took oaths promising fair reporting.[45] In these instructions to *kenchi* assistants in his own domain, Chōsokabe Motochika describes the concern of Hideyoshi and other daimyo over the responsibility—and the temptations—of large groups of fledgling surveyors:

Item [3]: *Sake* is strictly forbidden while [you are] surveying.

Item [4]: You shall go out in the morning at the Hour of the Rabbit [about 5 A.M.] and return in the evening at the Hour of the Monkey, last third [about 6:30 P.M.]. Do your calculations at your lodging [during the evening].

Item [6]: If there are disputes over land or fields which are not resolved on the basis of our various instructions, report [the matter to us].

Item [7]: You may not accept any gift, whether large or small.

Item [8]: Entertainment by the *jitō*, the farmers, or the village officials is strictly forbidden.

Item [9]: Should there be any inappropriate act by yourselves, needless to say, or by your underlings, you shall be brought to judgment as soon as we hear [of the act].

Item [11]: If you pass even one day unjustifiably, you will be in offense.[46]

Whether or not the *kenchi bugyō* met with full cooperation from villagers and samurai recruits, significant improvements in the registries over short time spans as resurveying took place indicate that Hideyoshi's early records were as tentative and imperfect as might be expected. Accuracy came, and was apparently meant to come, with repeated inspection. The assignment of a regular and increasingly experienced corps of magistrates introduced an additional degree of accuracy and consistency into the Toyotomi cadastres. There was, then, a certain alleviation of the intractable problem of error and faulty advice.

There was, however, no full alleviation in Hideyoshi's time—or in the Tokugawa period either—of the problem of regional measures. Local variants in the linear unit (*ken*) remained common in the Tōhoku, throughout Kyushu, and in parts of Shinano, Hitachi, Awa, and Settsu. Traditional methods of defining one unit of area (the *tan*) survived along the Tōsandō, in the Chūgoku, and in most other circuits.[47] The measure for volume (*Kyō-masu*) met with acceptance very slowly and continued to vary somewhat in size. In 1596, Ishida Mitsunari included the following article in instructions to residents of his fief: "After the coming autumn, you are not to use the old *masu*, currently in circulation, which [bear] our seal and have been distributed. Since there are both wider and more narrow *masu* among those passed out by the cadastral officials last year, we shall collect them all, select the medium [size] among them, and then distribute that [size]."[48]

There is also doubt about the extent to which domains adopted the *kokudaka* system. Hideyoshi himself had the northern provinces registered in cash, not in rice equivalences. Although the cadastres of the other provinces do state land value in rice, it is possible that measurement of the harvest in *masu* and careful calculation of the yield in *koku* occurred only in lands surveyed directly by Toyotomi magistrates (the domains held by Hideyoshi and his *fudai*, domains in which recent transfers had taken place, or domains held by suspicious *tozama*—the Shimazu and the Date, for example). In the remaining provinces, registries were compiled by *tozama*—the Maeda, Uesugi, Chōsokabe, Toku-gawa, Ōtomo, Ukita, and others. In these domains, current statements of value—usually computed in cash—were probably converted, according to local formulas, into rice statements. Active surveys were taking place in some of these areas, and they tended to conform to Hideyoshi's own guidelines for inspection and measurement. Nonetheless, the historical preference for monetary evaluations persisted. Hideyoshi's demands for statements in terms of rice may consequently have provoked recalculations on paper that did not render accurate *kokudaka* figures.[49]

Acknowledgment of the limits of Hideyoshi's success in establishing national measures or in producing correct *kokudaka* figures need not detract from the magnitude of his effort. Nor should a consideration of the imperfect judgment of his magistrates—working quickly and with the help of biased informants—conceal the extent of his reach. Hideyoshi improved upon the most advanced registration techniques of his age to achieve exceptional results. He oversaw the registration of much of the country's land; he demanded that Toyotomi deputies or daimyo officials, not local landholders, supervise that registration; he defined universal standards of measurement that were employed widely; he required the direct inspection of land and its yield; he established the principle that land be uniformly evaluated in terms of its total product and that value be uniformly expressed in a rice equivalence.

The Surveys and the Class Laws

One of the most important features of Hideyoshi's cadastres was the registration of an individual cultivator for each plot surveyed. Because more and more names appeared on the successive registers of certain villages as resurveying took place, and because large holdings in some areas diminished over time, it appears that *kenchi* magistrates attempted to identify lands with the persons actively working them. Further, the cadastres made no distinction between owners, tenants, and other subordinate help, thus erasing, on paper at least, those hierarchical relationships that had characterized the warring-states holding. All registrants apparently shared equal status and enjoyed exclusive claims to their property.[50]

Some historians consequently find in the cadastres evidence of an egalitarian commitment to free the tenant from his landlord and break the bonds of dependency. They note, in support of this radical contention, the alarm felt by large holders over the *kenchi*. In Ōmi, for example, one landlord had twenty-three tenants sign an oath—prior to the local survey—that the *kenchi* would cause no difference in their relations. Even if they were listed as cultivators in the cadastre, the twenty-three promised, they would continue to regard their lands as possessions of the landlord, would never sell them, and would not complain should the landlord reclaim them directly.[51] An order by Hideyoshi's deputy, Ishida Mitsunari, strengthens the impression that cadastral registrants were to enjoy sole claim to their holdings: "At the time of the recent land survey, it was decided to register in the cadastres [the holder] of cultivating rights to every paddy and dry field. The seizure [of these rights] by any individual, or the displacement [of a registrant] by one [who claims that] cultivating rights were previously his, is forbidden."[52] The exaction of rents, corvée labor, and miscellaneous taxes by villagers, and the sale of laborers, were proscribed as well.[53] It is interesting, too, that Hideyoshi counseled his daimyo against immoderate intrusions in village affairs: "The retainers of the various provinces and places shall order that the annual taxes and the gold be collected, using discretion in all things so as to avoid disturbance (meiwaku) to the farmers. Do not entrust [matters] to deputies, but be attentive [to affairs yourselves]. Should there be an individual who makes an impossible demand of the farmers, that retainer shall be in offense."[54]

Surely simple prudence recommended such conduct. Prudence may also have recommended the occasional amelioration of village conflicts through some leveling of inequalities in wealth. It is not at all clear, however, that Hideyoshi undertook a social revolution. All Toyotomi cadastres continued to register extensive parcels of land — those too large for a single family to farm—under one name, suggesting that efforts to detect and promote the actual cultivator were not made consistently. Twenty-eight of the Tenkawa registrants, for example, retained holdings over ten *tan* each; sixty-three registrants held less than one *tan* each. Further, taxes were levied on the village, not the individual, and in accord with separate lists kept by the headmen who apportioned them. Those lists tended to recognize traditional large holders, not the newer cadastral registrants, as the landowners responsible for collecting dues and managing local affairs. The official cadastre for a certain Imazaike village, for example, registered eighty cultivators; the village tax list mentioned only forty.[55] Customary governing arrangements, and customary claims by landlords, seem to have prevailed in the village.

Interest in registering cultivators as fully as possible is compatible with toleration of the privileges of local elites if we understand the *kenchi* in the context of Hideyoshi's class laws.[56] Registries of full-time cultivators and permanent village residents, the cadastres served as a census of the agrarian community. Registrants were disarmed and forbidden to change either occupation or place of work; nonregistrants, primarily military vassals, were prohibited from renewing their claims to village holdings.

The cadastres also laid the basis for dividing the rights to property held by previously enfeoffed soldiers who were withdrawing from the village. As reasonably close records of how land was apportioned and who actually worked it, the registries helped prevent violent competition over former military holdings as the class composition in farming areas changed.

Some toleration of the claims of large holders, on the other hand, deflected the resentment of powerful men who were useful to the authorities as village managers. As long as they were denied arms and mobility, these individuals might become valuable agents of daimyo interested not in the redistribution of property but in the restoration of local order. A fair number of these large holders were doubtless military men who were permitted to resume cultivator status and to retain extensive properties lest their discontent over the loss of land fester. It was not the inequalities in local wealth and power that concerned Hideyoshi. It was the centrality of armed warriors to village life and the ambiguity between farming and military occupations that he sought to eliminate. Thus by using his cadastres to identify full-time farmers and to sort out viable claims to cultivating privileges, he established the groundwork for class separation but did not necessarily destroy the landholding and governing practices of those who remained in the village.

The *kenchi* also served the purposes of Hideyoshi's edicts by providing the daimyo with fairly accurate assessments of domainal land, computed according to universal standards. For example, surveys of the domain of Satake Yoshinobu reported a total product of 545,800 *koku.* Given this figure, the daimyo could establish a rational salary scale for his retainers. Once he had developed procedures for collecting taxes across his domain, the income could be distributed systematically to city-based vassals whose allowances in *koku* would replace their fiefs. Neither an equitable and reliable plan for compensating military men nor the elimination of the fief was possible without the information produced by the Toyotomi surveys.

The effect of the *kenchi* and the class laws, of course, was to make peasants the supporters of an urban military, dividing the population into a group of providers and a group of consumers. No such clear distinction had existed since the beginning of military rule. The economic strain of these policies on the peasantry was considerable and makes most sanguine views of the social effects of the cadastral surveys somewhat suspect. Not only did Hideyoshi's surveys make concealment of resources difficult, tax rates were high: "After the crops have been inspected, the lord should take two-thirds and the farmer one-third." Even in the event of calamity, the daimyo were to have their due: "Should there be a [tax] exemption because of damage [to the harvest], one-third of what is yielded shall go to the farmers and two-thirds to the retainers."[57] The redefinition of certain measures, furthermore, served to increase those supplementary imposts that were adjusted to the unit of land rather than to the total product.

Rigorous cadastral surveys, high taxes, and controls on movement took their toll on the village. Despite the ferocious language of Hideyoshi's laws, farmers continued to risk punishment by absconding. Yet the basic constraints upon them did not change. Hideyoshi was prepared to endure turmoil in both domainal armies and peasant communities in order to transfer power from the armed local proprietor to himself and his daimyo.

The Cadastres and the Daimyo

The cadastral surveys of the Toyotomi era had implications far beyond the separation of classes and the efficient administration of the domains. They went to the quick of Hideyoshi's relationship with the daimyo. Although most *tozama* registered their own lands, delivery of all cadastres to Hideyoshi confirmed his lordship unequivocally. The registries also gave him a record of the country's resources better than any his predecessors had commanded. He could use that information to control the expenditures of the daimyo, to tax them systematically, and to reapportion the nation's holdings. In effect, he could use the cadastres to transform the role of the daimyo.

The radicalism of Hideyoshi's edicts on arms and class was absent, however, from his policy toward domainal lords. Despite the potential for structural political change implicit in his land surveys—change as sweeping as any we have seen thus far—Hideyoshi continued to act on the assumption underlying his wartime alliances: that he would preserve the domains in exchange for national hegemony. The most immediate and complex of all his relations, those with his daimyo, elicited from Hideyoshi a response profoundly different from the attitude he displayed toward commoners and common soldiers. That response lies at the heart of his settlement and gives to what may otherwise seem an absolutist regime another dimension.

The vesting documents issued by Hideyoshi in the 1580s were brief and general, much like the announcement delivered to Kuroda Yoshitaka in 1584: "Because of your assistance to me, I bestow upon you all rights (*isshiki*) to the district of Shisō in the province of Harima."[58] With the completion of the sophisticated cadastres of the 1590s, he was able to dispatch documents with considerably more detail. The vesting order sent to the Satake is typical of Hideyoshi's later land grants:

Item: 150,000 *koku*	(of this, 50,000 *koku* in additions)	Yoshinobu
Item: 100,000 *koku*	(without tax; of this, 90,000 *koku* in additions)	Yoshinobu *kurairi* [personal allowance]
Item: 50,000 *koku*	(without tax; of this, 40,000 *koku* in additions)	Yoshishige [Yoshinobu's father]
Item: 60,000 *koku*	(of this, 10,000 *koku* without tax; 50,000 *koku* in additions)	Satake Nakatsukasa Tayū
Item: 168,800 *koku*	(of this, 40,000 *koku* in additions)	*yoriki kerai* [direct retainers]
Item: 10,000 *koku*		*taikō-sama go-kurairi* [Hideyoshi's allowance]
Item: 1,000 *koku*		to the administrator of Satake Nakatsukasa's land
Item: 3,000 *koku*		Ishida Jibu Shōyū
Item: 3,000 *koku*		Mashita Uemon no Jō

For a total of 545,800 *koku*.
The above, [determined] on the basis of the recent cadastral survey, is to be under your control.
Bunroku 4 [1595], sixth month, nineteenth day
[Hideyoshi's red seal]
To: Hashiba Hitachi Jijū Dono[59]

The figures that appear in such documents became the essential descriptions of daimyo status. If Satake Yoshinobu was a *tozama* and lord of Hitachi province, he was also—and more important—daimyo of a domain with a yield of 545,800 *koku*. Hideyoshi's only full roster of daimyo identifies his men in terms, and generally in order, of the value of their holdings. Neither this roster nor the investiture decrees makes detailed references to domainal geography. Place was not as important to status as income.[60]

As the Satake document suggests, Hideyoshi's later vesting orders indicated, in large numbers, the basic division of daimyo revenues: amounts to be reserved for collaterals, for maintenance of the daimyo's personal establishment, for administrative expenses, for the support of temples and shrines, and for the upkeep of his army. While these allotments were not highly specific, their very existence signaled a close knowledge of domainal holdings and some intent to control them. By designating the sums to be assigned to family members, Hideyoshi also retained authority over decisions that his successors would entrust to the heads of daimyo households.[61]

Hideyoshi's direct claims to revenue were more significant than these internal allotments. The Satake grant included two small awards for Mashita Nagamori and Ishida Mitsunari, the Toyotomi magistrates who registered the Satake domain. Similar awards to cadastral supervisors occurred elsewhere as well, though all such awards were probably made only once and not renewed. That was not the case with Hideyoshi's personal allowance (taikō-sama go-kurairi). Hideyoshi set aside 10,-000 koku of the Satake grant to generate an annual income for himself.

Far and away the major exaction Hideyoshi made of his men, however, was the military tax (gun'yaku). Excluding the three appropriations just mentioned, other sums specifically exempted from taxation, and the direct grants to Yoshinobu and Satake Nakatsukasa Tayū's representative, the Satake document mentions three taxable items: 150,000 koku of Yoshinobu's allotment, 50,000 koku of Satake Nakatsukasa Tayū's allotment, and 168,000 koku reserved for the ranking household retainers. The total is 368,000 koku. To understand the meaning of the tax, we must turn to another vesting document, one of the most explicit Hideyoshi ever issued:

> We have assigned all the rights (isshiki) to a fief in Tango valued at 110,700 koku to [Hosokawa] father and son. Of this, the military tax is 3,000 men for the Shōshō [Hosokawa junior] and 1,000 men for Yūsai [Hosokawa senior], for a total of 4,000 men in tax. The remainder [of the fief] is untaxed: 24,700 koku to be vested in the Shōshō; 6,000 koku in [Yūsai]. In its entirety, this shall be your domain.
>
> Tenshō 17 [1589], ninth month, twenty-seventh day
> [Hideyoshi's monogram]
> To: Hashiba Tango Shōshō Dono [Hosokawa Tadaoki]
> Yūsai Dono[62]

Deducting the 30,700 koku of untaxed allowance, the remaining 80,000 koku of the domain's yield was to sustain 4,000 soldiers for Hideyoshi's use. Thus the military tax imposed upon the Hosokawa was five men for every hundred *koku* of taxable land. Although Hideyoshi rarely specified the number of men he expected the daimyo to maintain with their taxable holdings, comparing the size of daimyo investitures with the size of the armies they contributed to certain campaigns suggests a ratio. Examination of the battle rosters for the Korean invasion of 1592, for example, indicates that daimyo from Kyushu mustered about five soldiers for every hundred *koku* of their investitures, daimyo from Shikoku and the Chūgoku about four soldiers, and daimyo charged with naval maneuvers about five soldiers. The Mōri case seems particularly clear. An investiture decree of 1591 assigned Mōri Terumoto 734,000 *koku* of taxable holdings. Inasmuch as he recruited 30,000 soldiers for the Korean campaign, his military tax for that offensive was just about four men per hundred *koku*.[63] The apparent adjustment of the *gun'yaku* to geographical considerations is reflected, too, in documents concerning the Kantō offensive of 1590. Hideyoshi required four men per hundred *koku* from daimyo of the Chūgoku, six and one-half men per hundred *koku* from daimyo in the northeast (essentially, from Tokugawa Ieyasu).[64]

The limitations of such evidence, and the unknown factors affecting it, caution against firm conclusions. Nonetheless, it is apparent that by 1590 Hideyoshi had tied military obligations to domainal grants and that he drew in an orderly form upon those obligations. Most vesting documents may fail to dictate troop figures for two reasons. First, the manpower liability of *gun'yaku* land was probably understood by the daimyo. With the exception of the heavy Tokugawa contribution to the Odawara campaign—influenced not only by geographical factors but by Ieyasu's exemption from earlier Toyotomi levies and his ambiguous relationship with the Hōjō—Hideyoshi's expectations ranged from four to five men per hundred *koku*. Second, Hideyoshi may have failed to announce a strict ratio between men and land to leave his own hand free.

To return to the Satake document, then, Hideyoshi placed no ceiling upon the number of men he could recruit from this daimyo house but probably expected Yoshinobu to support four or five soldiers for every one hundred *koku* of taxable land; that is, between 15,000 and 18,-500 troops. By the standards of the seventeenth century, when *gun'yaku* figures are better known, a five-man tax was high—double the average rate of the Tokugawa. Although cadastral surveys were not a precondition of large-scale recruitment, they rationalized the process, enabled Hideyoshi to balance the levies on different domains, and established martial duty as a specific tax assessed against a specific investiture.[65]

*   *   *

Hideyoshi's investiture documents make clear his assertion of authority over the daimyo. The new specificity of the allotments, Hideyoshi's personal claims to resources, and the steep military tax clarified the lines of command. Remarkable improvements upon their *sengoku* antecedents, those documents seem, upon first reflection, part of the same authoritarian pattern of rule revealed in Hideyoshi's edicts on arms and class.

While the edicts renounced the social order of the warring-states era, however, the investiture decrees reaffirmed the relationship between master and man at the highest level. The Satake document confirmed the holdings of Lord Hashiba, the Lord of Hitachi (Satake Yoshinobu), and recognized them "to be under [Yoshinobu's] *control*" (*go-shihai narare sōrō nari*). Yoshinobu was not the temporary representative of a national governor, but the lord of his own domain. In return for the fief, and Hideyoshi's implicit promise to protect it, Yoshinobu was to render the revenue from 10,000 *koku* to the Toyotomi and to maintain an army for Toyotomi campaigns. For all the refinement of the document, its nomenclature, assumptions, and demands belong to a familiar universe. Hideyoshi was putting into place the most advanced practices of *sengoku* daimyo and asserting the now conventional rights of lordship to survey, vest, and tax land. As warring-states lords had governed their retainers, so Hideyoshi governed his daimyo.

The analogy would be facetious had Hideyoshi pressed his demands to new extremes by concentrating wealth and military power in his own house. His attachments on daimyo resources, though, remained largely symbolic. Ten thousand *koku*, the figure he claimed in most extant vesting decrees, was less than 2 percent of the Satake and Shimazu domains, roughly 1 percent of the Maeda and Uesugi domains. Such attachments were most common on the holdings of *tozama*, moreover, and did not involve all members of that group. The Mōri and Kobayakawa, for example, did not contribute to the *taikō-sama go-kurairi*.[66]

The military tax, of course, was formidable. Yet its size obscures a more important point. While he demanded access to domainal soldiers, Hideyoshi never nationalized local armies, dictated their organization or stipends, or enforced reductions in their numbers. The management of troops remained the exclusive responsibility of the daimyo who mustered them, led them in battle, rewarded them, and disciplined them. Hideyoshi held no monopoly on military power.

The point would hardly deserve notice were it not for the scope and ambition of his edicts as well as his cadastral survey. The *kenchi* bound the nation by common practices and indicated that Hideyoshi thought of his country as a unit to be registered according to a single system of standards. The edicts assumed that the nation shared both collective problems and a collective destiny that one man might manage through his agents. Hideyoshi's vision of the whole, after more than a century of atomization, was sure. His sense of his own supremacy was startling. Even Nobunaga—who was born to military life and commanded a far lesser territory—never attempted legislation across his territories to change the very conditions of vassalage. Hideyoshi had the imagination to break with precedent and the apparent resolve to draw power to himself.

Implicit in his vesting documents, however, was the assumption that the domain was a fixture of national life. Hideyoshi resolved to eliminate subinfeudation, only to channel his demands for manpower and revenue through vassal lords who rendered him his due in exchange for land and local control. At the very moment that he was changing the lives of farmers and military retainers, Hideyoshi preserved a constant of the warring-states world: the daimyo domain.

Attainder, Transfer, and the Toyotomi Holdings

The link between the daimyo and his domain could be assailed, in ways well known to survivors of the warring states, through the rotation or confiscation of holdings. The importance of the domain to national politics could also be denied by significantly reducing the land apportioned to vassal lords and by transferring most property to the direct control of the Toyotomi. The survival of the fief would have meant little in the face of sustained assault of this kind. Any understanding of Hideyoshi's commitment to the domain must rely, consequently, upon a review of his major land transactions. The following list omits those wartime investitures and attainders, already noted in chapter 4, that succeeded Hideyoshi's victories.

Prior to 1593 Hideyoshi made six major attainders unrelated to conquest. He reclaimed the Bitō fief in Sanuki when the Bitō head displayed cowardice and incompetence in the Kyushu campaign; he seized the Harima holdings of Takayama Ukon, whom he distrusted as a powerful Christian advocate; and he removed the Kimura and the Kunohe from the Tōhoku after they raised local rebellions following the Toyotomi pacification of the north. We have noted already that Oda Nobukatsu was forced into exile when he defied orders to leave his domain in Owari for the former Tokugawa territories; Hideyoshi attainted the domain. The most interesting attainder before 1593 involved Sassa Narimasa, the Oda daimyo who had resisted Hideyoshi in Etchū but was later enfeoffed in Higo as a reward for his participation in the Kyushu offensive. Although directed to postpone a land survey of Higo and to confirm the claims to land of local warriors, Narimasa defied orders, precipitated local uprisings, and was condemned to death. As far as we know, Hideyoshi redistributed nearly all the attainted lands, and *tozama* and *fudai* shared in the gains in roughly equal parts.[67]

The greater number and precision of cadastres and vesting documents for the later years of Hideyoshi's rule make analysis of the last series of confiscations somewhat easier. A close study of Hideyoshi's land transactions between 1593 and 1598 reveals six incidents of fief attainder or major reduction of holdings.[68] Three of them resulted from death. After Mōri Hideyori died in 1593, his child-heir was left with a fief in Shinano of 10,000 *koku* and the remainder was awarded to a Toyotomi *fudai*, Kyōgoku Takatomo. Following the death of Hashiba Hideyasu, Hideyoshi promoted the *fudai* Mashita Nagamori to a domain of 200,000 *koku* in Yamato Kōriyama. The forced suicide of Hideyoshi's nephew, Toyotomi Hidetsugu, in 1595 resulted in the move of another *fudai*, Fukushima Masanori, to Hidetsugu's holdings in Owari. (The Hidetsugu episode will concern us again in chapter 8.)

Each of the other three incidents involved a number of daimyo. First, in 1593 Hideyoshi confiscated the domains of Ōtomo Yoshimune, Shimazu Tadatatsu, and Hata Nobutoki. All had deserted their posts during the Korean campaign and left other Japanese troops exposed. Hideyoshi transferred four *fudai* to the Ōtomo holding in Bungo, but retained a large portion of that fief himself. Tadatatsu's holding in Satsuma seems to have been absorbed by the main Shimazu line. The disposition of the Hata fief in Hizen, about 80,000 *koku*, is unclear. That holding, too, was probably distributed among local daimyo.

A second group attainder took place in 1595 when Hideyoshi seized the domains of five vassals in Tajima who had been intimate with Toyotomi Hidetsugu. All five—Maeno Nagayasu, Maeno Nagashige, Watarase Shigeaki, Hattori Kazutada, and Hitotsuyanagi Kayū—were put in the custody of Toyotomi daimyo and compelled to take their own lives. The greater part of their collective holdings, over 53,000 *koku*, was transferred to Koide Yoshimasa, another *fudai* lord.

The last series of attainders and transfers occurred in 1597 and 1598. Although it includes three separate cases, the interrelations of the resulting land transactions make it convenient to discuss the sequence as a whole. Late in 1597 Hideyoshi relieved Utsunomiya Kunioka of a fief in Shimotsuke worth 180,000 *koku*. The cause is undocumented. Several months later, Gamō Hideyuki left a vast domain in Aizu of Mutsu province to replace the Utsunomiya. Hideyoshi subsequently enfeoffed Uesugi Kagekatsu in Aizu with a holding valued at nearly 1,000,000 *koku*.[69] Until 1598 Kagekatsu had held a fief valued at 550,000 *koku* in Echigo.

The reason for the Gamō transfer is not known, but a number of points should be noted. Most important, Hideyuki was a young boy. His father, Ujisato, had died prematurely in 1595, leaving the child with by far the most powerful domain in the northern provinces. By transferring the Uesugi to Mutsu, Hideyoshi removed the vulnerable successor of the Gamō house from a strategic fief and advanced one of his future deputies (*tairō*) to a suitably distinguished position. In the process, he also took the edge off Tokugawa Ieyasu's awesome land advantage in the area.

Following Uesugi Kagekatsu's move, five *fudai* were advanced from Echizen to new and larger domains in Echigo. Hideyoshi proceeded to set aside a holding in Echizen for himself and to locate Kobayakawa Hideaki at Kita-no-shō, in the same province, with a fief of 120,000 *koku*. Hideaki's is the last case of fief reduction or transfer in this sequence. Shortly before his transfer in 1597, Hideaki had lost a domain of 336,000 *koku* in Chikuzen, Chikugo, and Hizen. The consensus of historical opinion is that he was being punished for failure as leader of the second Korean campaign by the move to Echizen. Hideaki's domain in Chikuzen and Chikugo Hideyoshi retained for himself.

In addition to the twenty confiscations and reductions mentioned, the most reliable account of domainal changes between 1593 and 1598 lists twenty-four transfers of vassals to larger fiefs, twenty-four additions to current holdings, and eleven new enfeoffments. Although most improvements were small, some were spectacular. Uesugi Kagekatsu had gained over 400,000 *koku* in the move to Mutsu; Mashita Nagamori gained 150,000 *koku* in the move to Yamato Kōriyama; Fukushima Masanori gained 90,000 *koku* in the move to Owari; the four *fudai* who moved to Bungo divided 170,000 *koku*; the five who moved to Echigo divided 540,000 *koku*. These transfers and additions were responses not only to attainders but to those important vacancies created, for example, by Tokugawa Ieyasu's departure for the Kantō or by the death of Hideyoshi's childless stepbrother, Hidenaga.[70]

This list of attainders, transfers, and subsequent investitures may not be complete. And what information we do have contains lacunae. The disposition of Hidetsugu's holdings beyond Owari, for example, is not fully documented. Yet the catalogue we have just reviewed does note the important reversals in daimyo fortunes and invites several general comments. First, these transactions left no doubt that Hideyoshi was the ultimate proprietor of the nation's land, that he felt free to distribute and redistribute holdings, and that all investitures were conditional. Necessarily disruptive to all involved, his land decisions also weakened even the beneficiaries during the time of resettlement.

A total of seventeen attainders and three reductions in fief is not, however, large in a group of over two hundred daimyo, particularly during a transition from civil war to peacetime rule. Further, a good reason can be adduced for most of the changes. Inasmuch as Hideyoshi served no indictments and held no hearings before he disciplined his men, the explanation for his attainders and fief reductions must remain speculative.[71] Nonetheless, it appears that two of these actions were provoked by rebellion, five by poor performance in battle, and six—those against Hidetsugu and his sympathizers—by alleged treachery. One man was punished for refusing a transfer, one for unseemly evangelism, and one—Sassa Narimasa—for malfeasance in administering his domain. Three fiefs rotated when children succeeded deceased fathers, and one, the Utsunomiya, for unknown reasons.

The most interesting thing about the list of confiscations is that only one daimyo, a man whom Hideyoshi had cause to suspect in any case, was punished for local mismanagement. Although blameless administrators were doubtless as rare in the Toyotomi regime as in any other, Hideyoshi did not seek out domainal problems as pretexts for widespread attainder. Clearly the succession of young and untried heirs concerned him. Yet the reapportionment of fiefs upon a daimyo's death was minimal. By and large, land changes resulted from military failure and disloyalty.

The link between these basic offenses and subsequent attainder suggests that the daimyo were not threatened by arbitrary or capricious denial of tenure, and that they held their fiefs securely for as long as they displayed fealty and rendered satisfactory military service. Similarly, most nondisciplinary transfers occurred to improve vassal holdings and not simply to wreak havoc. It is difficult to discern in twenty-four rotations, all beneficial, a plan to enfeeble the daimyo through general, routine redistributions of domains.

A final point, implicit in the disposition of attainted land, bears reflection: Hideyoshi himself did not profit inordinately from confiscation and fief reduction. He made his principal gains in Bungo (roughly 170,000 *koku*), Echizen (roughly 132,000 *koku*), and Chikuzen (roughly 185,000 *koku*). The first resulted from the confiscation of the Ōtomo fief, the second from the transfers following the Gamō ouster from Mutsu, the last from Kobayakawa Hideaki's disgrace. Inasmuch as land valued at over 2,000,000 *koku* changed hands after 1593 alone, he had stood to acquire much more. Hideyoshi originally designated the attainted holdings of Owari, Tajima, and Shimotsuke as his own domain (*kurairi*), only to release them promptly to various *fudai*. Most confiscated lands passed directly to Toyotomi daimyo without a passing registration as *kurairi*.

Hideyoshi left no accounting of his own properties, but tentative lists compiled on the basis of the red-seal papers and daimyo records estimate their value in the range of 2,000,000 *koku*.[72] This figure includes his various attachments on daimyo resources and the revenue he gained through attainder. Thus even after the improvement to his fortune, he merely moved within respectable distance of Tokugawa Ieyasu—whose domain was valued at 2,402,000 *koku*. Before the improvement, his holdings were comparable to those of the Mōri, Uesugi, and Maeda. The nearly 500,000 *koku* acquired by Hideyoshi through attainder, though a large fraction of his total holdings, did not increase his domain to the point at which it either dwarfed the largest *tozama* fiefs or dominated the national landscape.

It is true that the *fudai* tended to profit from Hideyoshi's later land actions, as they had not profited from his conquests, and that the balance of power between insiders and outsiders tilted somewhat. Yet the tilt was hardly precipitous. At the time of Hideyoshi's death, thirty-six daimyo held domains valued at or above 100,000 *koku* each. Not only were these the richest and militarily strongest fiefs, they produced 64 percent of the country's wealth. Twenty-two of the holders were *tozama*, controlling lands worth 9,463,730 *koku*; and fourteen were *fudai*, controlling lands worth 2,249,000 *koku*. Given a national base of 18,-280,880 *koku*, the greatest *tozama* held 52 percent of the total, the greatest *fudai* 12 percent, and Hideyoshi himself 11 percent.[73]

To identify the *fudai* fully with Hideyoshi's interests, however, is to overlook the independence and new territorial concerns that their domains represented. Although some union of purpose and natural sympathy between Hideyoshi and his insiders might be assumed, the superior claim of the fief upon the loyalty of the *fudai* gradually revealed itself. Two years after Hideyoshi's death, when his young successor was challenged by Tokugawa Ieyasu, only four of the fourteen most powerful *fudai* daimyo sided unequivocally with the Toyotomi heir. Six supported the Tokugawa; one joined the Toyotomi, only to change sides; and three took no action, though two sons of the three turned to Ieyasu. While these observations need not impugn the fidelity of the *fudai* to Hideyoshi during his lifetime, they suggest that any axiomatic association between the Toyotomi cause and Hideyoshi's more intimate vassals is suspicious, at the very least. Like all daimyo, the *fudai* were both vassals of their lord and domainal governors with local cares.[74]

Whether we assume an affinity between Hideyoshi and the insiders or not, two patterns of conduct emerge in Hideyoshi's peacetime land transactions that conform to his conduct during war. As Hideyoshi had distributed battle spoils either to the vanquished or to Toyotomi supporters, so he continued to distribute attainted holdings among the daimyo. As he had used wartime transfers either to reward his men or to protect his own interests in the home provinces, so he continued to refrain from arbitrary attainders or rotations. Hideyoshi's actions affirmed again that land was to be held, in the main, by daimyo members of his alliance and that the concentration of property in his own house was not a critical goal of unification.

Central and Local Spheres of Influence

If the daimyo remained the principal landholders in the nation, and reasonably secure ones, did they also survive as local governors with a fair amount of latitude for independent action? We have noted already their fiscal and military obligations to Hideyoshi, as well as their submission to his direction in matters of arms control and the separation of classes. Were they, then, puppets—appeased with land and immediate authority over their armies but otherwise reduced to Toyotomi manipulation? The evidence is mixed and inconclusive, but suggestive.

Hideyoshi's impositions upon the daimyo did not stop with the edicts or the tax demands appearing in his vesting decrees. In addition to military support, he exacted extraordinary manpower levies for his construction projects. The *Taikō-ki* describes the building of Osaka castle in extravagant terms: "The people from over thirty provinces who brought great and smaller stones by land and sea from neighboring and distant parts resembled ants scurrying into ant hills. All were confounded by it. Castle holders from the provinces—great and small alike—all gathered in Osaka. They erected the walls, raised the eaves, built the gates, bestowed upon everything a great beauty and splendor."[75] Equally breathless narratives describe the contributions of the daimyo to Jurakutei, Hideyoshi's Kyoto residence, and to Fushimi castle, his retirement villa just south of the capital. Popular sources recount, however unscrupulously, that as many as 250,000 laborers participated in the Fushimi project.[76]

The accounts acquire a measure of credibility from Hideyoshi's red-seal order for assistance in erecting the Great Buddha in Kyoto in 1591. He claimed at least 62,120 men from twenty-eight daimyo for that work.[77] Later, in a letter to Kikkawa Hiroie, he remarked upon the construction at Fushimi: "I have ordered the lords from the Kantō, from Dewa, the north country, and the central provinces—all without exception—to attend to the construction effort near Kyoto. Thus even those gathered in camp [for the Korean invasion] do not outnumber all these."[78] Although we cannot reconstruct Hideyoshi's levies of manpower in detail, such evidence suggests that on occasion they approached the size of his levies of soldiers and generated enormous activity in the cities concerned. The evidence also suggests that Hideyoshi appealed to his men individually, and unpredictably, for assistance, instead of recruiting laborers from his own holdings or taxing the daimyo systematically to provide a fund for public works. His requests for manpower drew repeated attention to his personal authority over domainal lords as well as his decision to channel his demands through them.

Just as valuable to the daimyo as their laborers were their mining revenues. The introduction from China of cupellation processes for refining gold and silver, and the combination of placer excavation with deep tunneling for ore, had transformed the mining industry in Japan by the middle of the *sengoku* period. Those daimyo who exploited the major deposits acquired an important advantage over their peers: they were able to use these precious metals to attract the quartermasters who provided muskets and other essential supplies. Hideyoshi seized the advantage, however, by identifying gold and silver as national resources that he put under his own authority. By the time of his death he drew annual tribute from mines in as many as thirty provinces. Although he left some mining rights to his daimyo, by 1598 Hideyoshi was drawing approximately 3,400 *mai* of gold and 80,000 *mai* of silver from regions as scattered as Sado, Mutsu, Hitachi, Tajima, Etchū, and Hōki. (One *mai* = approximately 165 grams.) While we do not know enough of the total yield of gold and silver in the late sixteenth century to evaluate this sum comparatively, the absolute amounts are impressive.[79]

By draining daimyo resources Hideyoshi not only enriched himself, he diverted both energy and revenue from local military development. But his clearest control over martial activity, other than his laws on arms and class, involved castles. As early as 1573 he had leveled nine fortifications in Harima. After succeeding Nobunaga, Hideyoshi sent "castle-smashing commissioners" (*shiro wari bugyō*) to Ōmi, Ise, Owari, Etchū, Bungo, Higo, Chikuzen, Chikugo, Buzen, Tamba, and most of the Kantō and the north. They were supplied with peremptory, far-ranging orders: "Dispatch the hostages from this province [Ise] by the twenty-seventh of the month and then proceed promptly and thoroughly to complete destruction of the castles."[80] As a result of such directions, Hideyoshi began to realize the prophecy he had made in 1582: "I shall order them to level the castles of the whole land to prevent further rebellions and to preserve the nation in peace for over fifty years."[81] Almost inexorably, fortresses began to disappear from the landscape. Nambu Nobunao lost thirty-six of his forty-eight citadels in Mutsu; Kobayakawa Takakage left only three castles standing in Chikuzen; Hosokawa Yūsai destroyed all but six castles in Tamba.[82]

Such "castles" were often little more than rough fortifications protected by walls or natural barriers. They crowded the landscape, nonetheless, serving as crucial supply and defense posts for armies engaged in the far-flung campaigns of the warring-states era. With the elimination of such strategic command posts, war between daimyo became foolhardy. Although Hideyoshi did not reduce his daimyo to one castle each, as would the Tokugawa in 1615, his purge carried a persuasive symbolic message. It introduced, particularly into areas once hostile to Hideyoshi, proof of his will to hold the peace.

It may seem ironic that this destruction of fortifications took place just as the largest and richest enceintes in Japan began to rise. While Hideyoshi eliminated minor forts and the great headquarters of adversaries such as Shibata Katsuie, he and his daimyo erected castles that represented their exalted views of themselves. Replacing the multiple, businesslike posts of wartime armies were the elegant compounds of peacetime lords. These castles were safer and stronger than earlier compounds. Their complex moats, gun stations, iron-cleated doors, mazelike approaches, and fireproofed walls prepared the residents for battle. Yet few of the structures saw armed confrontation, and most survived as the refined headquarters they were built to be. They were showcase castles, modeled upon Hideyoshi's own buildings, whose military function was defense. Their predecessors, rough battle stations used to spearhead offensive campaigns, were what Hideyoshi resolved to level.

Hideyoshi's claims on labor, his extension of his *kurairi* to include gold and silver, and his elimination of castles affected most daimyo directly. This was not the case with three other policies, all concerning international affairs, that took a toll upon the lords of northern Kyushu and the home provinces, where Christianity and foreign trade had greatest impact. The first policy we have already encountered: Hideyoshi's ban, issued in 1587, on Christian proselytism and forced baptism. Although he did not prohibit conversion and did not, in the end, expel Catholic missionaries, Hideyoshi served notice that disruptive foreign creeds were a matter for national regulation. We shall return to this problem in chapter 8.

The second policy involved piracy. Following the pacification of Kyushu, Hideyoshi attempted to clear away seafaring predators:

Item [1]: Inasmuch as pirate ships on the seas of our provinces are strictly forbidden, you are to inform us if there are now individuals running thieving ships at Itsukushima between the provinces of Bingo and Iyo. [Such piracy] shall be judged an offense.

Item [2]: Order that all who use ships along the coast of our provinces—whether sailors or fishermen—be immediately investigated by the retainers and deputies (jitō daikan) of the [appropriate] places. Order them to take oaths to the effect that they will not hereafter engage in the least in piracy, require their joint seals [on the oaths], and have the lords of the [various] provinces collect them.

Item [3]: Hereafter, if vassals and proprietors are negligent and pirates are discovered, [the vassals] shall be brought to justice, they shall be found guilty of wrongdoing, their fiefs and their possessions shall be permanently confiscated.

Strictly order [the enforcement] of these articles. If there is a violator, he shall immediately be declared in offense.[83]

We know little about the Toyotomi campaign against pirate-traders, but Hideyoshi is credited with eliminating the leagues of Japanese, Korean, Chinese, and European sailors who preyed upon their competitors, destroyed official trade relations between the Japanese and Chinese governments, and made every form of sea travel hazardous. It is likely that Hideyoshi brought an end to illegal profiteering less through active policing of the Japanese waterways than through the conquest of northern Kyushu. By incorporating Kyushu daimyo into the Toyotomi federation, and by locating fudai throughout the northern provinces of the island, he eliminated the secret harbors and local cooperation that were preconditions of successful piracy.

The third of Hideyoshi's international policies was the encouragement, and possibly the control, of foreign commerce. Hideyoshi went out of his way to reassure Portuguese merchants that any restrictions upon the missionaries would not include them: "Since the Black Ships engage in trade, this matter is separate. They shall pursue trade in the various items over the [coming] years and months."[84] In letters to the Viceroy of the Indies and Spanish officials in Manila, Hideyoshi sought ever wider contact between the colonial empires and Japan. He also hoped to resume official trade with his Far Eastern neighbors.

There is some evidence, further, that foreign commerce was to be centrally managed:

From the first year of Bunroku [1592], individuals from Nagasaki, Kyoto, and Sakai received red-seal documents and were authorized to sail to these countries for purposes of trade: Kōnan [south Vietnam], Tonkin [north Vietnam], Champa [Vietnam south of Kōnan], Kamboja [Cambodia], Rokukan [southern Thailand], Patani [Thailand], Shiyamu [Siam], Taiwan, Roson [the Philippines], and Amakō [Macao]. Five ships from Nagasaki [were authorized]: two ships to Suetsugu Heizō; one ship to Funamoto Yaheiji; one ship to Araki Sōtarō; and one ship to Itoya Zuiemon. Three ships from

Kyoto [were authorized]: one ship to Chaya Shirōjirō; one ship to the Suminokura; one ship to the Fushimiya. One ship from Sakai [was authorized]
to the Iyoya.[85]

This record claims that eight shippers received formal permits for foreign trade ventures and implies that such permission was exclusive.
The consequent assumption has been that Hideyoshi took control of
international commerce in 1592 by licensing official traders and rele-
gating to their houses shipping that originated in Japan.

The difficulty with this account is its very late publication and the
absence of contemporary corroboration. The source, the *Nagasaki ji-
tsuroku taisei*, was begun in 1760 and completed some years later. Its
general reliability as well as the specificity of this entry increases the
credibility of the report. Private ventures doubtless continued to dominate Japanese trade with foreign nations during Hideyoshi's period, but
official voyages may have commenced as well. Hideyoshi's correspondence with foreign powers, his overtures to the Portuguese, his attack
upon outlaws, and his hopes of restoring trade with Korea—one puta-
tive cause of his war with that country—indicate that he claimed ultimate authority over Japanese commerce as one of the prerogatives of
national rule.

Each of the actions surveyed here falls into one or more of three
categories: regulation of the domestic aspects of international relations,
supplementary taxation, and pacification. By containing piracy, for example, Hideyoshi improved conditions for official traders, diverted
commerce and its profits to ports he controlled himself, and eased the
sometimes explosive tensions between illegal shippers and their protectors. The edict on Christianity had grave implications for Japan's association with the West, but Hideyoshi's concern with internal order
and sectarian conflict was most apparent at the time.

Nearly all of these initiatives, much as they impinged upon domainal administration, involved matters of national, not uniquely local,
interest. The pacification policies, moreover, were mild indeed when
compared with the edicts on arms and class. Hideyoshi's taxes served
only himself, of course, yet they belonged to an old pattern of lordly
imposition: the daimyo of the warring-states era had recruited corvée
labor throughout their holdings, and Nobunaga's vassals had erected
Azuchi. Nobunaga had also appropriated metals mined in the fiefs of
his vassals, just as *sengoku* daimyo exploited local mines regardless of
the territorial rights of their own feudatories. Thus the claims of precedent established a context for Hideyoshi's added constraints upon the
daimyo.

We have not noted, nor is there evidence of, intrusions in specifically domainal concerns. The absence of evidence is itself suggestive. Apparently, Hideyoshi was prepared to leave to his daimyo not only the management of their armies but the management of other significant matters as well, such as justice, domestic commerce, Buddhism and Shintō, education, and urban and village policy. "The Hundred Article Code" compiled by the Chōsokabe in 1597, the only daimyo code to survive from the 1590s, offers a concrete indication of a domainal lord's jurisdiction over such affairs. This refined document, which approximates a local constitution and surpasses all of Hideyoshi's legislation in detail, deals with crimes, lawsuits, litigation, and punishment; merchants, sea traffic, loans, mortgages, and property sales; the regulation and support of shrines and temples; taxes on land, labor, and special products as well as the time and method of payment; reclamation, land development, irrigation, and boundaries; tenantry, wages, and contracts; and the administrative structure governing retainers and villagers.[86] Statutes issued by other daimyo, though not assembled into comprehensive formularies, cover the same terrain.

Hideyoshi's implicit assignment of internal domainal matters to daimyo supervision creates the impression that he began to set a boundary between the realms of central and local jurisdiction. The boundary was not yet well defined: Christianity remained a national problem, religions already established in Japan a domainal one; foreign commerce, whether it involved pirates or peaceable traders, became an issue for the central administration despite the intricate role such commerce played in certain daimyo economies; the limits of Hideyoshi's access to labor and other forms of tribute, if limits existed, seem dictated by his own appetite and sense of propriety. If the apportionment of responsibility was tentative, however, Hideyoshi displayed no intention of administering the domains himself or through deputies dispatched from his own house.

The Enforcers of the Law

Who *were* the men who carried out Hideyoshi's direct orders and oversaw his personal interests? Had the domains been overrun with Toyotomi supervisors or ultimately dominated by a bureaucracy inimical to the interests of the daimyo, local freedom of action would have been deeply in jeopardy. The forms of Toyotomi administration were as significant to the daimyo as the content of Hideyoshi's policy.

Some of Hideyoshi's administrative arrangements we have already noted. Most leading *tozama*—the Maeda, Uesugi, Chōsokabe, Tokugawa, Ōtomo, and Ukita, for instance—carried out their own land surveys. The Mōri domain was registered by a fellow daimyo, Ankokuji Ekei, but inasmuch as Ekei had originally been a vassal of the Mōri, the *kenchi* effectively took place under Mōri auspices. While Hideyoshi's magistrates led other survey teams, they relied—as we saw in the Shimazu case—upon local assistance.[87]

Most of the "sword-collecting magistrates" (*katana-gari bugyō*) whom we can identify received special appointments from Hideyoshi, although some were local men. Both Shimazu Yoshihiro's letter and Hideyoshi's demand that temple officials collect the weapons of Mount Kōya suggest a fair amount of self-enforcement.[88] The same seems true of the laws concerning changes of residence and occupation. The gradual implementation of the laws, as well as the absence of any documented scheme to enforce compliance, suggests that action was left to the daimyo. We know of Hideyoshi's decision to conduct a census only from the subsequent directives issued by the Date and the Kikkawa in their domains. The Chōsokabe code required travelers to possess permits, again implying the importance of local initiative.[89] Hideyoshi attacked piracy, much as he had disarmed Kōya, by compelling military men stationed near the sea to investigate sailors and fishermen and to administer oaths—bearing the seals of the retainers—foreswearing illegal activity.

Hideyoshi's exactions of labor, military service, and domainal revenue all went through the daimyo. The men responsible for mines and Toyotomi agricultural holdings are more difficult to identify. In rare cases, we know the names of the mining officials: Hayashi Narinaga and Yanagisawa Motomasa in the Mōri domain, or Ōhashi Hachizō in the Date domain. Because the appointment and organization of these officials is so poorly documented, it is possible that they were drawn—perhaps in rotation—from the circle of daimyo retainers within the geographical area concerned. There is no evidence that Hideyoshi identified a regular cadre of representatives (*daikan*) similar to the career officials who later administered Tokugawa properties. Most of the agricultural *daikan* who appear in the record were *fudai* daimyo: Asano Nagamasa, Ishida Mitsunari, Katō Kiyomasa, Katō Yoshiaki, Miyabe Keijun. They supervised Hideyoshi's holdings, often adjoining their own lands, while maintaining their separate domains. Historians presume, though evidence is limited, that *tozama* also took charge of Toyotomi landholdings within and abutting their own fiefs. Other *daikan*, particularly in Ōmi, were drawn into service from large temples and shrines such as Kannonji and Shōmyōji.[90]

As we have seen it thus far, Hideyoshi's administration had a loose structure that accorded the daimyo a prominent part. The roles and character of the Toyotomi deputies, however, provide a sharper insight into the organization of Hideyoshi's regime. The men who served Hideyoshi directly received the title of *bugyō*, "magistrate," or "commissioner." Widely used in the Ashikaga and warring-states periods, it was borne in Hideyoshi's era by land surveyors, collectors of weapons, construction supervisors, city managers, quartermasters, directors of social events, destroyers of castles—almost anyone with an official assignment. Yet Hideyoshi left no list of magistrates, no administrative charts, and no statements on procedure to draw into relief the contours of his governing establishment. The man who systematically registered the property of the nation provided us no clue that administrative organization absorbed him. To identify his assistants and their tasks, and to determine the order of precedence among them, we must turn to the occasional revelations of the red-seal papers.

Hideyoshi drew his deputies from a broad pool. The *kenchi* magistrates, the officials we know best because of the comparative wealth of documentation, numbered over fifty men and had varying backgrounds. Most were *fudai* but many—in the Maeda, Uesugi, Hosokawa, Ankokuji, Kyōgoku, Takigawa, and Gamō houses—were *tozama*. In every case, these commissioners registered land outside their own domains.[91] Although Hideyoshi normally turned to military men for assistance, merchants served him as quartermasters, city officials, and advisors. The traders Kamiya Sōtan, Shimai Sōshitsu, Suminokura Ryōi, Imai Sōkyū, and Sen no Rikyū were all at one time within Hideyoshi's inner circle.[92]

With the exception of the city magistrates, whose tenures tended to be long and whose tasks were wide-ranging, the assignments of the *bugyō* appear specific and their appointments limited in duration. Iki Nagahama, for instance, leveled castles in Owari, and Yamaguchi Munenaga collected arms in Kaga, but neither they nor most of their peers survive in the record as regular members of Hideyoshi's entourage. The fleeting appearance of most magistrates suggests that Hideyoshi favored ad hoc nominations.

Only toward the close of Hideyoshi's life did a body of representatives rise surely to leadership from the larger corps of counselors who had moved close to power in the middle years of the Toyotomi regime. After 1595, a cabinet form of rule began to emerge. In the eighth month of that year, six *tozama* issued, on Hideyoshi's behalf, a code of regulations for all of Japan's social classes. Kobayakawa Takakage, Mōri Terumoto, Maeda Toshiie, Ukita Hideie, and Tokugawa Ieyasu signed the five main articles; Uesugi Kagekatsu added his monogram to those of the others at the conclusion of the nine supplementary articles. Though less than a lucid synthesis of Toyotomi policy, the code received wide circulation—among courtiers, military and religious men—as a general statement on conduct and, of greater moment, as a demonstration of the signatories' authority in Hideyoshi's circle.[93]

The timing of this development reveals its purpose. The code of 1595 appeared within a month of Toyotomi Hidetsugu's death and the elevation of Toyotomi Hideyori as Hideyoshi's successor. Hideyoshi's condemnation of Hidetsugu, his nephew and designated heir, to advance his son will concern us later. Here it is sufficient to note that the more powerful *tozama* were assembled as a group of spokesmen just when a two-year-old child had been named to succeed his now aged father. The spokesmen's principal function became clear, three years later, when Hideyoshi named them as elders (*tairō*) and guardians of the heir and compelled them to take elaborate oaths of loyalty to the child. Drawn together to ease the transition from Hideyoshi's administration to Hideyori's, the major *tozama* were meant to ensure Toyotomi primacy.[94]

While the *tairō* issued few corporate documents after 1595, and none unrelated to Hideyori, a second body of Toyotomi representatives emerged to oversee more routine affairs.[95] Alluded to in the code of 1595, this additional group of governors included Ishida Mitsunari, Mashita Nagamori, Natsuka Masaie, Maeda Gen'i, and Asano Nagamasa.[96] All of these individuals had served Hideyoshi as land surveyors, city commissioners, or military commanders. Indeed, their names appeared with sufficient prominence in the Toyotomi papers to draw the attention of Hideyoshi's early biographer, Oze Hoan. As early as 1585, Hoan wrote in his *Taikō-ki*, they had been appointed as the *go-bugyō*, a five-man council concerned with national affairs subordinate only to Hideyoshi.[97] Although biographical study of these officials tends to disprove Hoan's assertion (Natsuka Masaie was not even a vassal of Hideyoshi in 1585), neither Hideyoshi's pronounced, and unusual, favor for them nor their eventual promotion is disputable.[98]

About 1595 these five commissioners, acting together, took on many tasks of government. They carried out the interrogation of Hidetsugu and then presided over the dismantling of his Kyoto establishment. They superintended the inspection and transfer of the vast Gamō fief in Mutsu. They reiterated tax policy, published laws concerning mutual surveillance and responsibility among the Toyotomi retainers, and took final charge of Hideyoshi's *kurairi*. It was they who received the loyalty oaths of the *tozama* to Hideyori and it was they, officially named in Hideyoshi's last correspondence as the "five *bugyō*," who were entrusted with the basic business of the realm.[99] While the elders ensured the passage of power, these magistrates were to govern in Hideyoshi's stead.

Thus, as Hideyoshi prepared for death, he learned to delegate authority to carefully chosen representatives. But his late and perhaps reluctant appointment of a vassal elite suggests no history of tight organization throughout his tenure. Indeed, not until Hideyoshi's end did an observer report on his administrative arrangements. Hideyoshi's protégé Gien, abbot of Sambōin monastery, wrote on the seventh day of the eighth month, 1598: "They say that the Taikō is sick and in discomfort at his residence. We can do nothing but pray for a miracle. Asano Danjō [Nagamasa], Mashita Uemon no Jō [Nagamori], Ishida Jibu Shōyū [Mitsunari], Tokuzen'in [Maeda Gen'i], and Natsuka Ōkura Tayū [Masaie] have been appointed as the five men and shall order the affairs of Japan. I understand that [the Taikō] called the five men variously to his side yesterday and [made known] this intention."[100]

Hideyoshi's personal and somewhat informal approach to administration, his preference for ad hoc appointments, and the late formation of a hierarchy that was neither large nor complex are not, in the end, as interesting as the most basic feature of his government. With the exception of the merchants and priests who served as quartermasters and city officials, all of the Toyotomi magistrates were daimyo. Hideyoshi did not form a professional cadre of officials, supported by salaries rather than fiefs, whose financial rewards depended upon their employment in a central bureaucracy and whose loyalties belonged exclusively to the state. He entrusted government to lords with domainal interests and domainal problems who derived their incomes—except for the occasional grant to a cadastral magistrate—from their fiefs. His more important officials, moreover, were large holders with weighty local concerns.

The five elders maintained enormous domains. Tokugawa Ieyasu had the largest holding in the nation, valued at 2,402,000 koku; Mōri Terumoto ranked second, with 1,125,000 koku; Uesugi Kagekatsu third, with 919,000 koku; Maeda Toshiie fourth, with 765,000 koku, if we include the grants of his two sons; and Ukita Hideie ninth, with 474,000 koku. Suggestions that Hideyoshi appointed these men as regents for his heir because he feared their power overlook the fact that he granted them their vast domains in the first place. The Tokugawa fief was more than doubled by Hideyoshi and the Uesugi fief improved by 400,000 koku.

The five magistrates, three of whom were *fudai*, began with much smaller holdings. Yet during his final years, Hideyoshi promoted all of them to fiefs significantly larger than those they had held before 1595. He awarded lands valued at 200,000 koku to both Mashita Nagamori and Ishida Mitsunari, placing them among the wealthiest daimyo in the nation. Asano Nagamasa advanced to a fief of 120,000 koku, and Maeda Gen'i and Natsuka Masaie acquired domains valued at 50,000 koku each. Although the last grants were less than princely, the collective holdings of the *bugyō* were large and deliberately increased as they moved into power. *Fudai* or not, these men were fief holders absorbed both by local concerns and the future stability of the system in which they had acquired so large a stake.

Hideyoshi's appointments reveal the assumption that officials should hold substantial fiefs, that they should share the preoccupations of domainal lords, and that the problems of central and local administration were linked inextricably. There is no presumption in these appointments that the center of government and the fief were dichotomous entities that should be ruled by hostile parties. Indeed, Hideyoshi identified the national interest with the interests of the daimyo by choosing his deputies from the pool of large landholders. Regarding the fief as the essential source of power and prestige, he promoted valued subordinates to consequential domains and then to national administrative authority.

Hostages and Oaths

In entrusting government to individual men well known to him, rather than to permanent organs of administration, Hideyoshi displayed the preference for particular, noninstitutional forms of rule that runs throughout his regime. The preference is singularly clear in his policy on taking hostages. To secure the obedience of his daimyo in times of crisis, Hideyoshi did not simply rely upon the general threat of military reprisal or attainder. In many respects a medieval man who thought in concrete terms, he clung to the conventions of the past to assure himself of control. He took bodies as sureties of the peace.

Though not surprising in itself, the policy deserves consideration as a measure of Hideyoshi's habits of mind. Lost to us in a brisk survey of ten years of decisions is the deliberate pace of events and the many small choices that slowly, almost imperceptibly, reveal a pattern. The rare dramatic choice—to surrender much of Mutsu to the Uesugi, for example, or to elevate five powerful *tozama* as guardians of the heir—illuminates the pattern beyond mistake for a moment and reminds us, because alternative courses were at hand, that resolve existed where caprice might otherwise be discovered. Yet what appears, after sorting the recalcitrant evidence, as a "system" with a certain abstract quality was surely something rather different to Hideyoshi himself. An ambitious, sometimes enlightened man who looked with remarkable detachment at his society (for his vision of a landless soldiery required a new eye), he was also a man of his age who responded to unfamiliar challenges with little time for reflection and the past as his principal guide. Hideyoshi's concern with hostages is a useful indication of the power of that past, of a mentality more attuned to momentary emergencies than to building a "system," and of the ascendancy of the particular over the theoretical in his administration.

To some extent, Hideyoshi took hostages from individual *tozama* as he formed alliances or concluded campaigns. We know that he demanded guarantors of peace from the Mōri, Uesugi, Tokugawa, Chōsokabe, Shimazu, and Satake. How many hostages he required, how long and where he kept them, is not always clear. An order to Date Masamune, however, is unusually explicit.

> As we have saved your life on two or three occasions, you will excel in your efforts on behalf of the Taikō, needless to say, and in establishing O-Hiroi [Hideyori, Hideyoshi's son] and will inform the retainers of your house regarding your obligations [to us]. Since it will be difficult to attend to your duty if men are not available [to us], you will summon all the wives and children of your house elders and have them reside in Kyoto. A thousand persons shall always be in attendance and they shall serve us. They may [remain at] Masamune's residence in Fushimi or you may give [other] homes to these people of your house [in Fushimi]. The area [there] will be called Date-chō. Order this to the appropriate families.[101]

On three occasions, Hideyoshi also called for a general delivery of hostages. He summoned the wives and children of the "various" daimyo to Kyoto in the ninth month of 1589, just before opening the Odawara offensive. Again, in the first month of 1592, he ordered that hostages be dispatched to Osaka in conjunction with the invasion of Korea. Finally, days before his death, he left his elders with this demand: "Once Hideyori has been installed in Osaka castle, the wives and children of the 'various' generals are also to proceed to Osaka."[102] A difficulty with the orders involves the meaning of "various"—the word *sho* may indicate either "all" or "many" vassals. The sources also omit mention of the duration of the summons. The sequential appearance of new demands suggests that hostages were held in times of crisis or mass mobilization of the military. Hideyoshi probably did not keep permanent hostages from all vassal houses, and he probably did not require them from *fudai*.

Hideyoshi also created military enclaves near his castles in Kyoto and Fushimi where important vassals were expected to keep homes. In a sense, the assembly of his men close to him anticipated the alternate attendance system (*sankin kōtai*) of his Tokugawa successors. The Tokugawa compelled their daimyo to locate residences in the shogunal capital for their wives and heirs and to spend one year out of every two in that capital themselves.

In at least two respects, however, the Toyotomi practice differed from *sankin kōtai*: residence near Hideyoshi's castles was not scheduled nor was it expected of all daimyo. The more generous estimates of the number of daimyo mansions in Kyoto do not exceed thirty, and most accounts of Fushimi number the homes of retainers at not more than twenty. A regular guard was posted at Osaka castle, where large groups of retainers occasionally assembled, but no substantial daimyo neighborhood was formed there during Hideyoshi's tenure. The men who did live close to Hideyoshi on occasion were either political confidants or potentially dangerous *tozama*. Members of the first group included the elders, the *bugyō*, Ankokuji Ekei, Sen no Rikyū, Hosokawa Yūsai, and relatives; members of the second group included Shimazu Yoshihiro and Date Masamune. The great majority of *fudai*, as well as most *tozama*, never resided near Hideyoshi's castles.[103]

For some, then, residence in Hideyoshi's capitals was a burden of unsure alliance; for others, it may have been a symbol of influence, a practice Hideyoshi employed to develop unity within the emerging Toyotomi hierarchy.[104] In both cases, Hideyoshi's concern with physical proximity is arresting. Regardless of the small size of his country and the formidable opposition he could bring to bear against dissenters, Hideyoshi reinforced his power by surrounding himself—from day to day—with representatives of the men upon whom his peace depended.

His preoccupation with oaths reflects a similar attention to personal expressions of loyalty. Hideyoshi's era was really one of oath taking as much as it was one of lawmaking. He demanded oaths when *tozama* joined his alliance, when his various heirs were named to succeed to Toyotomi headship, when he gave orders to his cadastral magistrates or to the officials charged to contain piracy.[105] But the most dramatic oath was read and signed in Kyoto in 1588. During the fourth month of that year Hideyoshi entertained the emperor with lavish festivities in his own capital residence. In the course of the imperial visit, the Toyotomi vassals swore an oath of three articles.

Item: We shed heartfelt tears, sincerely grateful that this imperial progress to Jurakutei has been proclaimed.

Item: Each of us will strictly remonstrate should there be any lawless person who [impinges upon] the lands of the throne or the various investitures of the nobility and princely abbots (*monzeki*). We assert this for the present, needless to say, and unto [the generations of our] children and grandchildren, without exception.

Item: In all things, we will not violate in the least the orders of the Kampaku [Hideyoshi].[106]

The crucial article is the last, of course. Twenty-nine men put their signatures to the document, most of them *tozama*. The Tokugawa, Maeda, Oda, Ukita, Niwa, and others all pledged, under the most elaborate circumstances, to submit to Hideyoshi's will.

The interesting point here is that Hideyoshi could not forgo individual assurances of fealty from his daimyo. While he could abstract the general population into groups of "townsmen" or "farmers" or "retainers" whom he addressed in magisterial edicts, he kept his relations with domainal lords immediate, almost private. The bifurcation in his radical policies toward commoners and common soldiers and his conservative policies toward the daimyo finds a parallel in his approaches toward these groups. Thus generalizations about Hideyoshi's treatment of his great vassals, however clear the pattern may appear, must acknowledge its personal character. Many encounters between Hideyoshi and his men—each, perhaps, conceived by Hideyoshi as discrete—formed a collective settlement imperfectly described as a polity or a system.

Conclusion

The tenor of Hideyoshi's administration is well conveyed in a document he did not write. It is a reasonably long document of its kind, at least for the late sixteenth century, though rather short for what it may be construed to be—a sort of Toyotomi constitution. Startling in its randomness, its jolting shifts of interest, and its attention to colorful detail, the document is the code of fourteen articles issued in 1595 by six *tozama* daimyo, five of whom later became guardians of Hideyoshi's son. The code is popularly called "The Wall Writings of Osaka Castle" ("Ōsaka jōchū kabegaki").

Item [1]: In marriage relationships, the daimyo should obtain the approval of the ruler before settling the matter.

Item [2]: Greater and lesser lords are strictly prohibited from entering deliberately into contracts and from signing oaths and the like.

Item [3]: If there is a fight or quarrel, the one who exercises forbearance will be favored.

Item [4]: If someone makes a false accusation, both parties will be summoned and an investigation vigorously conducted.

Item [5]: Those who have permission to ride in palanquins are [Tokugawa] Ieyasu, [Maeda] Toshiie, [Uesugi] Kagekatsu, [Mōri] Terumoto, [Kobayakawa] Takakage, elderly court nobles, venerable and high-ranking monks. As for others, even daimyo—if young—should ride on horseback. Those fifty years of age or more have permission to ride in simple palanquins if the journey is at least one *ri*. Those who are ill also have permission to ride in simple palanquins.

Anyone who violates the preceding articles will be severely punished at once.
Bunroku 4 [1595], eighth month, third day
[signed] Takakage, Terumoto, Toshiie, Hideie, Ieyasu

Supplementary Articles

Item [1]: Court nobles and noble abbots should be prepared in their family callings and should devote themselves to serving the imperial government.

Item [2]: Those of the temples and shrines should observe the temple laws and shrine laws of the past and should devote themselves to maintaining repairs. They should not be negligent in learning and religious practices.

Item [3]: Concerning the management of fiefs throughout the country: after the crops have been inspected, the lord should take two-thirds and the farmer one-third. In any case, orders should be issued which will ensure that the fields do not become devastated.

Item [4]: One of lesser status may keep, in addition to his principal wife, one handmaid, but he should not maintain a separate house. Even one of greater status should not exceed one or two concubines.

Item [5]: Conform to the limitations of your fief; in all things your actions should be [consistent with your standing].

Item [6]: In a direct appeal, if a complaint is made, it should first be addressed to the ten men and the ten men will take steps to summon both parties and they will definitely hear what the parties have to say. If it is a petition of direct appeal, since that is a special matter, it should be reported to the undersigned. Upon discussion, if it is a matter which should reach the ruler's ears, it will be reported to him.

Item [7]: The chrysanthemum and the paulownia may not be used as crests on clothing without permission. Those given robes by the ruler may wear them. But their crests may not be transferred or redyed onto other robes.

Item [8]: *Sake* should be consumed according to one's ability to hold it. However, heavy drinking is prohibited.

Item [9]: It is strictly prohibited to go about wearing a kerchief which conceals the face.

Anyone who violates the preceding articles will be severely punished.

Bunroku 4 [1595], eighth month, third day

[signed] Takakage, Terumoto, Toshiie, Kagekatsu, Hideie, Ieyasu[107]

Implicitly speaking for Hideyoshi, the six *tozama* represent the Toyotomi administration as a universal authority. It governs all groups (the military, the nobility, the religious community, the general populace) with a broad responsibility to keep the peace, execute justice, and oversee local rule. At once great in range and specific in detail, the articles assume that national jurisdiction is now centered on one man and his agents. Although the code lacks the grandiloquence of Hideyoshi's edicts on arms, class, Christianity, and piracy, it shares their perception of central government.

But the code also takes the domains for granted and recognizes the daimyo as local governors. Indeed, the issuance of the code by six *tozama* indicates that national administration is founded upon daimyo participation. And to a large extent, that national administration is portrayed as a moderator that regulates daimyo marriages (to prevent unions concluded for military reasons), prohibits treasonous alliances, adjudicates quarrels, equalizes tax rates, and upholds decorum. The last point is striking as a reminder of the growing emphasis on status and its requirements in the late sixteenth-century world. As soldiers lost their fiefs and daimyo became peacetime administrators, order was increasingly associated with the clarification of roles and their symbols. Thus palanquins and crests became measures of power no less than of dignity.

Most peculiar in this code, especially since it came from the daimyo, is the absence of tension and qualification. The items imply an apparently happy accommodation of central to domainal authority without defining the limits of jurisdiction. The brevity of the code, its lack of concern with theoretical matters, and its place in a legal tradition that relied as much upon custom as upon statute help conceal conflict, of course. Its matter-of-fact tone conceals, as well, the dimensions of the social and political change that made such a document possible. Yet in submerging conflict and treading lightly over change, the code raises again the major questions posed by Hideyoshi's regime. How did Hideyoshi and the daimyo perceive each other? What was the nature of the settlement they reached? And why did they sacrifice certain advantages to reach it?

6

FEDERATION AND ITS MOTIVES

THE GOVERNMENT THAT took shape in Hideyoshi's hands has not gone without labels. Most often, with rich diversity of meaning, it is called feudal. For Japanese scholars the word usually refers to the system of closed classes: a population of cultivators, bound irrevocably to their fields and denied political power, paid high taxes in kind to a ruling group of military men who exercised exclusive control over the state. Scholars disagree over the extent to which social and economic stratification survived in the village. They also maintain divergent perspectives on Hideyoshi's agrarian policy. Some find it a reactionary response to the increased freedom and mobility of the era of warring states; others argue that registration in the official cadastres gave the majority of peasants a security and independence of tenure that they had not enjoyed as tenants or servant laborers in the late medieval period. Transcending these differences, however, is a consensus that Hideyoshi's regime instituted stern controls based upon class division. There is general recognition, too, of several, perhaps ironic, developments: villagers increasingly came to govern their internal affairs in the stead of absentee overlords, and de facto rights of land ownership (the right to alienate property, for example) devolved upon farmers rather than feudal proprietors. This combination of social and political suppression with village self-regulation constitutes, for many historians, the unique variant of late Japanese feudalism.[1]

The term feudal can also refer, of course, to the broader configuration of power in the Toyotomi years. Two hundred daimyo, invested with most of the land of Japan, maintained armies for the service of their lord and, insofar as they exercised most rights of domainal governance, preserved a condition of "parcellized sovereignty" in the nation.[2] A feudal strain can also be discovered in the personal and particular forms of rule preferred by Hideyoshi—in his demands for oaths of fealty and for hostages, his substitution of private correspondence for universal laws, and his reliance upon random summonings to obtain labor in lieu of a routine tax for public works. Shunning the development of national institutions of judicature, defense, finance, and administration, Hideyoshi governed as lord to his vassals.

But where some have found feudalism, others have found absolutism. Less concerned with class relations or the survival of the domain, they focus attention upon the remarkable emergence of a strong central power. Not unlike a Renaissance monarch, Hideyoshi concentrated authority in himself, reasserting control over once fractious and independent feudatories. All land and military resources were ultimately at his disposal; final judicial authority rested in his person; and the gravest matters of domestic and foreign policy fell within his purview. He alone granted freedom to evangelists, for instance, or the right to bear arms. No administration since the Heian era had exerted so broad or so unchallenged a command of Japan. That command, moreover, was restrained neither by charters nor by independent organs of government. To all apparent purposes Hideyoshi was an autocrat whose power stopped where he chose—in his wisdom or lack of interest or fatigue—to stop it.

Although the terms feudalism and absolutism have been borrowed from analyses of European development, neither is altogether inappropriate to Japan. The terms are used with more subtlety than our synopsis reveals, yet even a brief reflection indicates their utility in drawing out patterns of political decision and in establishing a perspective on an often confusing scene. As the very possibility of using such opposite characterizations suggests, however, each focuses upon a different dimension of the Toyotomi regime, and neither is satisfactory to embrace the whole. These words become particularly troublesome when we concentrate upon the structure of national and local government and the distribution of political authority within the ruling elite. "Feudalism" obscures the breadth and complexity of a central power that had far more than a military relationship with the domainal administrators and ignores the gradual disappearance of subinfeudation. "Absolutism" fails to describe a government in which, to use Perry Anderson's hyperbolic but telling phrase, "army, fiscality, bureaucracy, legality and diplomacy—all the key institutional complexes of Absolutism in Europe were defective or missing."[3] Unless one overlooks contradictory evidence, or chooses to read it as somehow unrepresentative of the true drift of unification politics, Hideyoshi's regime—like all regimes—resists inclusion in any abstract scheme of development.

The terms feudalism and absolutism are most helpful in discussing late sixteenth-century Japan when they are juxtaposed to illuminate the dichotomous features of rule of the time. Disparities are clearest in the matters of military control, taxation, land apportionment, and administration. Hideyoshi pursued a bold and inventive pacification policy by disarming peasants and withdrawing soldiers from their fiefs, but he neither reduced nor nationalized the standing armies of his daimyo. He laid claim to manpower and metal resources but imposed no heavy, universal tax on agriculture and none at all on local commerce. He amply demonstrated his proprietorship over the nation's land but left almost all holdings under control of the daimyo and thus improved his own domain modestly. While steadily enlarging the sphere of central jurisdiction, he entrusted the enforcement of his policies either to local lords or to ad hoc appointees drawn primarily from the pool of daimyo. The interests and income of his officials centered upon their domains.

Because such dichotomous features appear consistently and in critical areas of government, it seems necessary to treat them as fundamental aspects of Hideyoshi's political settlement. The challenge, of course, is to account for those features and to characterize the settlement itself in terms consistent with its disparate parts. Some historians embrace the anomalies, though generally in descriptions of Tokugawa rather than Toyotomi rule, with the phrase "centralized feudalism."[4] The phrase acknowledges the political dichotomies as fundamental, but it also implies an arrested political development or a schizophrenic approach to rule. Those who use the phrase tend to see the settlement shaped by Hideyoshi as an aberration produced by wartime compromises, a failure of vision, or the short-sighted decision to incorporate daimyo administrators into the central government.

Hideyoshi's rule comes into view as a more finely crafted phenomenon when we sort out the functions of center and domain and so place the apparent contradictions of the time in context. We must be guided by Hideyoshi's actual conduct of affairs, as it is imperfectly known to us, for the settlement evolved in many discrete decisions and never achieved the form of a constitution. Hideyoshi's peacetime rule was also brief; the satisfaction of seeing time refine its contours and a second or third generation of successors explore its meaning is denied to us. Government soon lost the direct imprint of Hideyoshi's hand, and there can be no assurance that patterns of rule emerged as he might have shaped them. In delineating the roles of the center and of the domain, then, we cannot hallow as "rights" those practices that custom alone assigned to different parties, nor can we regard as mature a still tentative polity.

In practice, Hideyoshi had the land of Japan surveyed and made investitures on the basis of his cadastres; he also retained the prerogative of transferring and attainting holdings. In exchange for investitures, he demanded fealty, military and labor services, precious metals mined in the domains, and some land revenues from his daimyo. Hideyoshi also assumed responsibility to hold the peace. For peasants, townsmen, and priests this meant the seizure of weapons, fixed occupations, and fixed residences. For military men it meant separation from the land. And for daimyo it meant reduction of castles, the delivery of hostages, and controls on marriages and other alliances. Attainder and land transfers can be regarded as pacification policies as well. Finally, Hideyoshi took charge of what we might call matters of public, or common, concern. In the arena of international relations he regulated missionary activity, contained piracy, and may have supervised foreign commerce. As we shall see, he also waged a foreign war.

On the domestic scene, Hideyoshi exercised final judicial power, rectified weights and measures and advised the daimyo on a standard rate of taxation, played a custodial role toward the imperial court, and, as the fourteen-article code of 1595 suggests, remained a general counselor on public conduct. To introduce a subject we shall pursue only briefly here, he also placed important cities under his jurisdiction: Kyoto, Osaka, Sakai, Hakata, and Nagasaki were governed by Toyotomi magistrates; Ōtsu, Sakamoto, Ōmi Hachiman, Kōriyama, and Hirado were governed by Toyotomi family members or important *fudai*. Denying the rights of traditional proprietors in these towns, Hideyoshi unified control under his representatives. Their agents policed the streets, punished criminals, and presided over urban judiciaries; they eliminated customs barriers, market fees, and guilds; they set city tax policy, oversaw public works, and regulated temples and shrines. In effect, Hideyoshi assumed sole authority over the national nodes of commerce, population growth, and political activity through his men and, in the process, identified the city as a unique resource and unit of government. His control over leading towns became one of the clearest expressions of national integration.

As for the daimyo, they held almost ninety percent of the nation's land, and insofar as they refrained from rebellion and rendered satisfactory military service, they held their domains securely, without threat of capricious confiscation. They retained control over local armies and administered justice, commerce, agrarian affairs, religion, and towns on the domainal level. The daimyo collected and expended all local taxes, except for the occasional allowance claimed as *kurairi* by Hideyoshi. They enforced his laws within their boundaries and were sometimes called upon as magistrates to undertake tasks—the registration of land, for example—in other domains. Ten daimyo were appointed to serve as interim administrators and regents during the minority of Hideyoshi's heir.

*　　*　　*

This sketch of functions brings into profile two separate developments, developments that can be seen as inimical, certainly, but that might also be seen as complementary. On one hand, domainal rule—a *sengoku* legacy that Hideyoshi had respected in wartime—survived unification. And it survived in far more than a perfunctory sense: land and armies belonged to the daimyo. On the other hand, Hideyoshi defined a place for central authority: as a warring-states lord writ large he exercised proprietary privileges across the country; as pacifier and guardian of the public province he spread his control from missionary activity to cities. Insofar as center and domain are perceived as hostile entities with fully divergent goals, the Toyotomi settlement must appear a stalemate—part feudal, part absolutist—formed by parties sufficiently strong to stall each other's growth. Yet it is possible, pursuing the conclusion implicit in the last two chapters, that the Toyotomi settlement was a purposeful alignment between two entities with certain common interests and a commitment to the separation of powers. If we regard the settlement as federal—as the union of semi-autonomous domains under an integral authority—Hideyoshi's actions appear neither as arbitrary extensions or abridgments of control nor as studies in political paradox. They emerge, rather, as markers of the boundaries between two fields of power dominated by different poles but drawn into a balanced relationship.

We cannot, of course, demonstrate beyond doubt either the existence of complementary objectives among Hideyoshi and his daimyo or their intentional formation of a federation. Yet we can reflect upon two questions that lie at the heart of a judgment. Were the daimyo prepared for union and accepting of the transcendent role of a central authority? Did Hideyoshi see the domains as an essential part of his settlement and conceive of his own role as preserver of those domains?

The Daimyo and Hideyoshi

The first question is both more stubborn and more important, for conciliation could not have occurred and peace prevailed without the support of the daimyo. Certainly the military considerations behind alliance continued to matter: Hideyoshi's control of the home provinces, his superior arsenal and greater momentum, and the divisions between his adversaries. Ankokuji Ekei's perception of the Toyotomi, formed as early as 1583, probably needed little revision in 1590: "[Hideyoshi's] forces are great in number, abundantly mobile, advanced in battle strategy, and rich in rice and money. The Mōri forces, in contrast, are few in number, phlegmatic, unskilled in maneuvers, and lacking in rice and money. Should these parties meet in combat, seven or eight in ten of the Mōri force will fall."[5]

Despite the military exigencies, though, the interests of the daimyo could not have remained long divided nor their conservative inclinations dominant had they stood to lose their domains. Alliance survived because the daimyo emerged in healthy shape from confrontation with the Toyotomi. In peace as in war, Hideyoshi limited attainder and transfer, improved a number of fiefs, and left local governance to domainal lords. Further, the burdens he imposed were familiar. In registering, vesting, and placing a military tax on land, Hideyoshi worked within a framework the daimyo themselves had defined. He was careful to preserve the etiquette of lordship—his vesting documents addressed the recipients with time-honored titles and acknowledged the integrity of the domain—and the forms of rule, from the taking of hostages to the use of red-seal papers, derived from *sengoku* conventions as well. In effect, the drama of reunion was tempered by customary patterns of association.

Can we, however, move beyond considerations of Hideyoshi's martial advantage and the inducements to union represented by the fief? The exceptional behavior of the daimyo invites speculation. Not only did they accept an overlord, they paid him homage: twenty-nine of the most important daimyo, twenty-six of whom used the Toyotomi surname, pledged loyalty to Hideyoshi in the presence of the emperor; as many as thirty built homes in Kyoto, under the shadow of the Toyotomi mansion, as a practical sign of allegiance; most sent laborers to erect monuments to Hideyoshi's glory; and all referred to Hideyoshi in correspondence in terms—*uesama, denka, kampaku-sama*—that affirmed his lordship.[6] Equally significant, the daimyo considerably enlarged Hideyoshi's jurisdiction by surrendering major governing prerogatives to him: control over leading cities, for example, rights to mine revenue, authority over foreign affairs, and the power to discipline local lords.

Both the marks of homage and the surrender of the public province became, in themselves, basic signs of assent to authority. Such actions, because they could not be consistently coerced, took the form of decision. Ambitious men used to considerable freedom and supported by personal armies, the daimyo participated in potentially degrading displays of fealty to a general of peasant origin and, in the process, helped make Hideyoshi what he was. The question, of course, is why did they conspire in his transformation?

Easily overlooked, when we conceive of unification as a struggle between Hideyoshi and the daimyo, is the vulnerability of the daimyo themselves. For all their progress in military and administrative consolidation, they neither led monolithic forces nor maintained secure boundaries. All had seen great peers—the Ōuchi, the Yamana, the

Amako, the Hosokawa—fall to subordinates or rival lords. The immediate threat to the daimyo came not from a Hideyoshi but from their vassals and their neighbors. The situation was unchanged in the 1580s. The Shimazu and the Ōtomo, the Uesugi and the Maeda, the Ukita and the Mōri shared hostile borders; challenges from collaterals, sons, and brothers disturbed the Mōri, Shimazu, Tokugawa, and Uesugi. If the Oda could be undone by assassination, what was to protect other houses?

Given such volatility, Hideyoshi was useful as a formidable military support to allies in trouble—the Ōtomo, for example. He served, in this respect, a familiar warring-states role. Yet it was not just daimyo in imminent danger who opted for the security of Toyotomi alliance. The Mōri, Kobayakawa, Maeda, Uesugi, Niwa, Ikeda, Satake, and others chose to submit to Hideyoshi's leadership. And collective submission necessarily changed Hideyoshi's function. As daimyo throughout the nation were subsumed under a common alliance, that alliance increasingly took strength not from the martial resources of its leader but from its inclusiveness, from the constraints placed upon the daimyo by each other. Insofar as the daimyo formed complex peer relationships by binding themselves to Hideyoshi, the center became at once the lord and guarantor of individual vassals and an entity—more abstract than personal—around which the daimyo could unite to lay down arms. The widespread decision to renounce the risks of war in favor of alliance suggests that the daimyo were prepared to use Hideyoshi to achieve stability among themselves.

If we view Hideyoshi as a link between his vassals, the acts of fealty by the daimyo acquire a new meaning. Surely these acts, at least for some, displayed genuine homage. Yet two other purposes bear mention. First, by pledging loyalty or delivering hostages to Hideyoshi the daimyo were effectively making peace with each other. Those hostages—as well as the destruction of castles, the abandonment of old allegiances, the controls on marriage alliances—were as important to their mutual security as they were to Toyotomi ascendancy. What might have seemed unthinkable to the Uesugi or the Tokugawa individually as a sign of subservience to an arriviste, served, when an action engaged the body of daimyo, as a joint surety against belligerence.

Certain acts of fealty, such as the construction of Toyotomi castles, served the further purpose of dignifying the central authority and, in turn, the men who submitted to it. If the daimyo were going to use a strong man as a symbol of corporate alliance, it was fitting that he convey majesty sufficient to command obedience. There were clearly risks in cooperating to ennoble a potential dictator. There were graver risks, however, in maintaining a weak head over war-seasoned vassals.

Checks on his power—preeminently the local land bases and armies of the daimyo—helped reduce fears of outrageous aggression against themselves. The submersion of Hideyoshi's personality in titles such as *uesama* (Our Superior) or in residences too grand to admit of an individual character had the effect, too, of changing a challenging man into an idea.

The fourteen-article code issued by six *tozama* in 1595 gives substance to the notion that the daimyo envisioned the central authority as a stabilizer. Though firmly associated with Hideyoshi, the code bore daimyo signatures and survives as the clearest indication of daimyo thought about the role of authority. The emphasis throughout the articles is on easing tension. Private alliances, resourceful marriages that betokened military union, quarrels, and false accusations—all manner of discord from treason to brawls—were proscribed. Further, the code urged correct procedure in law and domainal management to sustain order. Given the opportunity to address the nation, the framers of the code represented the central authority as rectifier of relations between the daimyo.

A more interesting, though oblique, indication of the daimyo mentality is their acceptance of the laws on arms and separation of the classes. Such acceptance could be coerced no more than acts of fealty. We have noted already that the edicts furthered domainal consolidation. Hideyoshi was useful to his vassals not only because general alliance served as an occasion to cease fire, but because his legislation reduced the power of internal adversaries in the domains. Yet insofar as daimyo were willing to disarm farmers who were potential recruits and to weaken the ties of vassals to their fiefs—thus courting dissent and reducing their own military resources—they were also preparing for an era in which administrative control was more important than an ambitious army motivated by rewards of land. Disarmament and challenges to the fief were inconceivable if the daimyo contemplated endless struggles. Hence compliance with Hideyoshi's edicts helped keep the peace even while it signaled a shift to a peacetime perspective. More than the shows of homage, it suggested a readiness for coexistence.

Surrender of the public province to Hideyoshi presents somewhat different problems. The decision assumes a view of central authority broader than that of arbiter. To approach an understanding of it, we must plumb again the *sengoku* foundation of Hideyoshi's settlement, for the peace rested upon more than the immediate military and political interests of its shapers. In recovering a center and defining its prerogatives, the daimyo could draw upon a long and varied experience.

Perhaps because it is deceptively simple, a basic observation may elude us: the antagonists of the warring states shared a common language, a common religion, and a common cultural and political tradition. Though mountains impeded communication, Japan was not an Italy—internally divided but linked by equivalents of the Mediterranean, the Adriatic, and the Tyrrhenian seas to other worlds. The country was small, isolated, and poor in seafarers. Until the *sengoku* era, moreover, it had been essentially unified. Hideyoshi's references in his documents to "our country" or to "Japan" may hardly have been noted by daimyo who, for all their battles, reflexively shared his sense of the whole. The similarities between them—in their rites of passage, their artistic pursuits, their architecture, their sports and clothing and diet—were more apparent than their differences.

The various links of the daimyo to the traditional capital, for example, were particularly important in tying them to an entity larger than their domains. Some daimyo, like the Mōri, preserved their association with the imperial court through occasional gifts and donations. Others built small monasteries around Kyoto's Zen temples where they buried their dead and sought retreat. Most continued to use the titles of the court or the Ashikaga shogunate in their signatures. Although very few may have aped the nobility by blackening their teeth like Imagawa Yoshimoto, several called in noble tutors to lecture on the *Tale of Genji* and other classics. It was a sorry daimyo indeed who could not compose an artful poem with ancient allusions, and at least one, Hosokawa Yūsai, was a master of the poetic tradition. When Oda Nobunaga wanted to bestow a princely gift upon Uesugi Kenshin, his choice fell upon two screens depicting the capital. Other daimyo imported fans with scenes of Kyoto. When prominent provincials wanted portraits painted, they appealed to the Kanō masters of Kyoto. And whoever the painter, those portraits borrowed the poses, the dress, and the style of a four-hundred-year-old convention derived from the court. The Shimazu, Mōri, Maeda, Hosokawa, Chōsokabe, Katō, Gamō, Fukushima, and others look disconcertingly similar in their court noble's robes and headgear.[7]

The daily reminders of interdependency were no less compelling than the bonds of a common culture. All daimyo who used firearms relied upon Kyoto, Sakai, and the Kyushu ports for muskets or gunpowder. All, consequently, worried about the security of those cities as well as currency standards and the exchange rates for precious metals. Furthermore, in refining those metals, the daimyo employed cupellation procedures that were first introduced into the Iwami area around 1530 but that, like muskets, quickly became part of a national technology. The shared technology was only the most visible aspect of a common course of development. From land surveys to the abolition of guilds and market fees, from conscription strategies to taxation systems, the daimyo traveled parallel paths as governors. If we speak of the Mōri or Hōjō domains as large, the measure is comparative in a nation of less than 380,000 square kilometers divided among as many as two hundred lords: the geographical centers of both domains were about a day's journey from their boundaries, and few people were isolated, except by choice or coercion, from the news and influence of neighbors. The refrain in the Imagawa code that merchants, peasants, and military men were not to traffic with outsiders simply draws attention to the fact that borders rarely blocked passage or ideas.[8] Men like Hideyoshi crossed domainal lines to change lords or build armies from the martial families of several provinces. The consolidated campaigns against common enemies, the fief transfers that followed victory or alliance, and the steady traffic of spies, quartermasters, and wanderers lifted many inhabitants of the warring states into a larger society. The daimyo fraternity was also bound, however quarrelsomely, by ancestry and by marriage.

Sengoku society was not, then, without centripetal forces that could be marshaled to support the Toyotomi settlement. Equally important, war had brought about an empirical discovery of the need for consolidated rule on the domainal level, a discovery with implications for the state macrocosm. Both to secure and to expand their holdings, the daimyo had assumed vast powers. Taking over domainal markets and ports, they encouraged wide and free trade to improve their own access to supplies, to stimulate production by providing an outlet for agricultural goods, and to allow farmers to convert produce into the cash many daimyo wanted as taxes. They seized and exploited mines to generate revenue for quartermasters. They eliminated the sanctuary of noble estates, disciplined martial religious communities, and centered judicial power in themselves. In sum, the daimyo expanded their jurisdiction far beyond the surveying, vesting, and military taxation of land. They began to evolve, in the process, a working definition of the "public province" as those matters that, because of their vital relation either to the war effort or domainal stability, the daimyo could not entrust to others. If it remained tentatively conceived and was never framed in explicit statements, this notion could, nonetheless be translated to the national level.

The notion of public province had a long history prior to the era of warring states, and it is probable that daimyo saw their *sengoku* experiences in the light of that history. Those daimyo with *shugo* or deputy-*shugo* pedigrees, those who applied for the title during wartime, and those who rallied under the banner of Ashikaga Yoshiaki or his shogunal forebears could all locate themselves within a tradition of legitimate public authority. While the daimyo rebelled against the control of the shogunate and greatly surpassed their *shugo* predecessors in power, few escaped the shadow of the old order: their judicial and taxation initiatives mimicked those of the *shugo*; their law codes borrowed the language of Ashikaga statutes; and their continuing problems—from the suits of estate proprietors to the military challenges of former authorities—kept the idea of the shogunate alive. And insofar as the idea survived, so too did two inextricable concepts associated with the Ashikaga: that local officials enjoyed certain rights of governance, to be sure, but that those rights were delegated by a central authority that retained unique prerogatives—final judicial power, for example, control over foreign affairs, custodianship of the court and its capital. Oda Nobunaga's manipulation of the shogun revived the memory of older assumptions of rule and suggested that a postwar settlement could be built upon the Ashikaga legacy as well as upon the *sengoku* experience.

The daimyo did not really have to go back to the Ashikaga period, however, for a model of hierarchical distribution of authority. Few lacked a personal history of subordination, the experience of defining their own governing spheres in relation (or opposition) to superiors. It is instructive to consider the ten largest daimyo houses of Hideyoshi's regime. The Maeda and the Hori had been *fudai* of Oda Nobunaga; the Tokugawa, originally within the Imagawa sphere of influence, had served Nobunaga as well; the Uesugi and the Mōri had been vassals of *shugo* daimyo until they achieved independence in the 1550s; the Ukita had remained vassals of the Uragami until the 1570s, while the Nabeshima had only broken away from the Ryūzōji in the 1580s; the Shimazu and the Satake came from *shugo* houses that professed allegiance to the shogunate well into the sixteenth century; only the Date, of *kokujin* origin, had not been vassal or nominal ally of a greater house in the middle years of the *sengoku* period.

Thus even the greatest members of the Toyotomi alliance were accustomed to overlords. As surely as they fought against submission, they lived by the rules of a command structure. Hideyoshi was the unifier not of autonomous kingdoms but of domains created and recreated by the vicissitudes of war and governed by men used to changing fortunes. The political landscape of Suruga and Tōtōmi, for example, altered with generations of warriors: these provinces fell sequentially under the Imagawa, Takeda, Tokugawa, and Toyotomi.

The daimyo experience of interdependency, their evolving definition of the lord's authority, and their adjustment to superior powers may have been brought to bear in the rehabilitation of an old Japanese word, though not one in frequent use during wartime, that appeared in a new guise at the end of the sixteenth century. Later a staple in Tokugawa documents, the word occurs rarely enough in Hideyoshi's time to raise doubts about its importance, even while its occasional prominence draws attention to what may be a new attitude toward the state. The word, *kōgi*, combines two characters meaning "public" or "official," and "affair" or "matter." In the Ashikaga period, the term referred to the shogun himself, the embodiment of public authority. Hideyoshi's biographer used it in a similar sense in the *Tenshō-ki: kōgi* was Hideyoshi.[9]

Yet the word also found a more literal application. The domainal code of the Chōsokabe observes that: "As soon as an order affecting public affairs (*kōgi*) is issued it must be carried out conscientiously." The oaths of loyalty to Hideyoshi's heir, taken by the elders, state: "Inasmuch as we understand it to be for the sake of public affairs (*kōgi*), we will discard personal enmities toward our peers and will not act on our own interests." Maeda Gen'i sternly warned residents of Kyoto against violations when orders concerning "the business of public affairs (*kōgi goyō*) and administration" were issued.[10]

Grafted together in this usage of *kōgi*, perhaps, are the concepts we have reflected upon as the foundation of Hideyoshi's settlement. First, especially in the loyalty oath, the term assumes that individuals and individual units of governance are part of a whole—a public. Further, the term reflects the notion that certain nameless, transcendent matters take precedence over private interests. Implicit in the idea, too, is the need for an overseer or a body of overseers. It was the identification of the public interest with the person of the shogun that inspired the original usage of *kōgi*, and though the term acquired a more abstract dimension in Hideyoshi's day, it still carried the sense of a political center.

The immediate acquaintance of the daimyo with the public province, of course, was pragmatic and Hobbesian. They seized mines, battled Ikkō sectarians, and ran stern courts to fight Leviathans at home and on their borders. The pragmatic ground of Hideyoshi's claims to the public province was also clear. Let us take the case of cities. Hideyoshi could assume jurisdiction over important towns by dint of conquest, the example set by Oda Nobunaga and the daimyo in their various domains, and, to an extent, the example of the Ashikaga, who had generally supervised Kyoto. But his claims were also fortified by daimyo distrust of one another. Kyoto, Hakata, and Sakai, for example—with their ties to markets throughout Japan, their bankers and national warehouses, their port facilities and links to vital communications arteries—were better left to a central authority subject to the collective pressure of the daimyo than to local lords. The *sengoku* experience had provided ample warning against independent daimyo administrators: the Ōmura had ceded Nagasaki to the Jesuits, the Hosokawa had closed off access to the port of Hyōgo, and battles between the

Hosokawa, Miyoshi, and Matsunaga had threatened to destroy Sakai. Similar observations can be made of international commerce and the propagation of Christianity. Rivalries to attract the Portuguese Black Ships had both pitched the daimyo of Kyushu into struggle and given the foreigners a bargaining advantage. Zealous evangelism had intensified sectarian conflict in Kyushu. The sensitivity of international affairs thus recommended central control. Even Hideyoshi's power to discipline the daimyo made sense. If treason met no reaction, alliance afforded no protection against lawlessness and continued war.

In effect, the "public affairs" under Hideyoshi's jurisdiction tended to be practical matters—much like those the daimyo governed in their own domains—that could not be entrusted to a single lord or that were essential, like the pacification policies, to securing alliance. And such concern with mutual political advantage doubtless remained embedded in the late sixteenth-century formulation of *kōgi*. But the genius of that formulation was its linkage of a self-interest to a new and broad philosophy of rule. While serving as a powerful and necessary justification for pragmatic action, *kōgi* signaled the shift in consciousness required for federation and institutional change. *Kōgi* united self-interest to ideology: the definition of government as protector of the public good.

The surrender of the public province to Hideyoshi was made easier by his often moderate use of power. Many important towns—Nara, Kamakura, Kagoshima, Niigata, Shizuoka, and Gifu—were left alone. Administrative malfeasance became grounds for attainder only once, and Christian evangelism was tolerated. The revenues from mines must surely have been a sore point. Hideyoshi was clearly not, in all things, a moderate lord, and his rule displayed more than one inconsistency. For the daimyo, perhaps, gold and silver served as unavoidable tribute that they rendered to protect other interests.

The subject of moderation introduces a new series of issues. We have suggested that the daimyo participated in the creation of a national authority by electing alliance, by paying homage to Hideyoshi, and by consenting to his authority over certain public affairs. The irreducible element in their compromises was the domain itself—a unit all had fought to defend and allied to stabilize. The domain was the crucial reality of sixteenth-century life, and had its integrity been severely undermined, by the demobilization of armies for example, alliance could probably not have been sustained without a yet more sweeping transformation of consciousness. The daimyo were only one party to the settlement that emerged, however, and the conduct of its architect now requires attention. Whatever the military power at Hideyoshi's disposal, however ready the daimyo for a cease-fire, and however strong the forces drawing the domains toward union, compromise demanded some community of interest.

Hideyoshi and the Daimyo

In many respects Hideyoshi was cast in the mold of an absolute governor. Quite apart from his edicts or his cadastral surveys, his language was the language of supremacy. "I have made justice correct," Hideyoshi informed the Viceroy of the Indies; "I have established security." He reminded other correspondents of the soothsayer's prediction at the time of his birth: "When he reaches the prime of life . . . his authority will emanate to the myriad peoples." He foresaw that his government would "be superior to anything since Yoritomo" and appeared sure that even China would enter his grip. Most telling of all, he sometimes closed private letters with the signature "Tenka"—The Realm. Not only did he govern his nation, he embodied it. Such rhetorical flourishes were not embedded in the tradition of leadership in Japan and announced a style of rule as new as its scope.[11]

Combined with Hideyoshi's sense of destiny was a remarkable imagination. He conceived of soldiers without fiefs, of peasants without arms, and of vanquished enemies restored to power. He looked forward to building an empire. He had a genius for the unpredictable but effective act—the rebuilding of Hiei, the conversion of swords into hardware for an icon, the construction of a castle on the former site of the Honganji headquarters. Perhaps because he came from nowhere and repeatedly defied the odds against him, Hideyoshi maintained the mental freedom of a new man. He looked at the world in fresh terms, for the conventional pieties could hardly make his own experience intelligible.

There was every likelihood, then, that Hideyoshi would enter upon a collision course with the daimyo. Why should a man who envisioned an end to subinfeudation support the domain? Why should a man of immense and often well-founded pride endure the presence of local lords? And why should a victor leave the balance of military power with others? Again, we cannot forget the exigencies of war. Hideyoshi was indebted to daimyo whose alliances and military assistance made conquest possible. Even after the surrender of the Hōjō, he governed an explosive society that might revert to battle in the face of total change. The changes he did undertake, moreover, depended upon the cooperation of the daimyo who implemented them. Lacking a national bureaucratic structure, Hideyoshi and his band of *fudai* could not have registered land, collected weapons, exploited mines, or transformed the conditions of vassalage by themselves.

Emphasis upon the conservative motives for sustaining the domainal order nonetheless obscures the fact that Hideyoshi was not inherently a conservative man. Throughout his campaigns he was a risk taker who abandoned the Mōri offensive to attack Akechi Mitsuhide, who pressed his candidate for Oda succession upon the participants in the Kiyosu conference, and who ventured to Shikoku before his alliances were proven. Arrogance, ambition, and daring—not prudence—led Hideyoshi to leadership. Are we to conclude that he suppressed the traits that made him a great general as he turned toward peacetime rule, that he was a man of two temperaments fitted to very different tasks? The boldness of his language, let alone his legislation or his reach for empire, strains the plausibility of that judgment.

Such a judgment also fails to explain the extent of Hideyoshi's concessions. Even the most conservative ruler might have built a larger land base for himself and shared administrative authority only with long-time associates. Indeed, conservatism might have recommended that course. Hideyoshi's grants to the Shimazu and the Tokugawa, as well as his choice of five *tozama* as guardians for his heir, seem riskier than cautious. It is possible that such actions showed a want of will or political inspiration, though not in any ordinary sense, for Hideyoshi had both will and inspiration enough when it came to the challenge of pacification. He may have been unable to see, however, beyond the domainal order, too firm a fixture of sixteenth-century life to imagine changing.

Let us turn this proposition on its head, though, to speculate that Hideyoshi conspired not just in the protection but in the enhancement of daimyo power, much in the way the daimyo conspired in the creation of a central authority. From this perspective, Hideyoshi's actions display not lack of resolve but an intention to promote the daimyo.

His large and consistent land concessions to the *tozama*, made at a cost to himself and the *fudai*, serve as the first indication of commitment to local lords. Yet Hideyoshi went further than guaranteeing the integrity of some domains and quantitatively improving others; his policies on class, castles, and administration qualitatively altered the status of all daimyo. As soldiers withdrew from their fiefs, the daimyo emerged as the only landed powers in the nation. Because domainal resources fell under their direct control, the military position of the daimyo was strengthened as well: with the end of subinfeudation, vassals could no longer support their own militias. Moreover, the destruction of minor castles, held by subordinates of the daimyo, left the greatest trappings of power to domainal lords alone. The castles of the late sixteenth century were the more awe inspiring for their singular association with the daimyo fraternity. Finally, when he assigned administrative tasks outside their own domains to certain daimyo, and when he entrusted his government to ten lords before he died, Hideyoshi gave local governors power and prestige to be sure, but also a greater stake in the affairs of the nation.

Through such innovations, Hideyoshi dramatically elevated the daimyo above their immediate family members and collaterals, their chief commanders, and their vassals. They were peers only of one another. In ceremonial matters, too, Hideyoshi singled the daimyo out. He oversaw their promotions at court and greeted them together with the emperor and the nobility at his Kyoto residence. On this most solemn occasion of Hideyoshi's life, he did not isolate himself with his family in disdain of his confederates. On other occasions as well Hideyoshi reaffirmed the relationships of the daimyo to each other and himself, traveling together with them to visit his mother's mortuary temple, entertaining them at elaborate theatricals and tea parties, distributing precious coins among them, and assembling them around his deathbed. In happier times he assembled the greater daimyo in homes surrounding his castles.[12]

These actions had a double edge, needless to say. Yet the irritation they caused to daimyo enticed into acts of homage was surely tempered by several considerations. Hideyoshi's festivities were the most glamorous of a glamorous age and shed luster upon the men who joined them. Indeed, they defined the elect. Attendance upon Hideyoshi also kept the daimyo in proximity to national power. And Hideyoshi's almost insatiable desire for their company offered them some hope against autocracy: imperious isolation was more dangerous than social patronage.

Patronage may not have been the major part of Hideyoshi's design, however. He must have taken a parvenu's pride in seeing great lords use his surname or in making love to their daughters, for his concubines came from the Maeda, Gamō, Kyōgoku, and Asai houses.[13] But the satisfaction of such coups is proportional to one's esteem for one's counterparts. For some new rulers of humble birth, esteem may be linked to jealousy or fear and thus inspire attempts to humiliate the old guard. A newcomer can measure his success in the abasement of wellborn rivals. Hideyoshi's course seems to have been different. Rather than glorify himself by diminishing others, he measured his success by the acclaim of already distinguished men whose power and dignity he enhanced. As the daimyo grew in stature, so too did the man who led them.

Friendship may have colored Hideyoshi's relationships with some of his men. He conducted a confidential correspondence with Kobayakawa Takakage until Takakage's death, for example, and used personal postscripts in more official letters to the Tokugawa and the Maeda to acknowledge gifts and to ask about the health of family members. He worried about the illness of Maeda Toshiie's wife, even sent her a strengthening carp to speed recovery, and grieved over the deaths of his generals. After Ikeda Tsuneoki and his son, Motosuke, fell at Naga-kute, Hideyoshi wrote Tsuneoki's wife that: "There is simply nothing I can say about the recent [deaths of your husband] Shōnyū and your son. I share your sorrow and your grief . . . Numberless times I convey my anguish."[14]

More apparent than Hideyoshi's friendly regard for the daimyo is an admiration for the military tradition that led him to compare himself to Yoritomo, to emulate the behavior of Ashikaga Yoshimitsu, to build castles on the model of Azuchi, and to conform to the etiquette of lord-ship in everything from his vesting documents to his adoption of dai-myo sons. Such conduct has little to do with political conservatism. It signifies in formal and even emotional terms the parvenu's concern with customary sources of prestige. A wanderer who changed status as well as place and who matured in the army of an iconoclastic Nobu-naga, Hideyoshi might have dispensed with tradition. Instead, he found his place within it. And the men who had proven themselves in war and in domainal governance functioned, at once, as his mentors, his peers, and his vassals. He had grown up with them, administered his fiefs as they had administered theirs, fought and negotiated with them, and learned their manners and their culture—from poetry to nō drama to tea to garden design.

We need not assign to Hideyoshi two temperaments, one appro-priate to conquest and the other to peacetime consolidation, to account both for his daring as a general and for his postwar concessions to the daimyo. Throughout his career pursuit of personal glory was me-diated by a respect for, and a need for the approbation of, his daimyo. The man who conquered Kyushu also wanted to conquer China. The skillful conciliator who drew the Tokugawa and the Shimazu into his settlement continued to dispense land and administrative prerogatives to the daimyo until his death. This is not to say that no tension existed between personal ambition and regard for the group of daimyo. It is simply to acknowledge that Hideyoshi's esteem for men who were once his models and then his peers served as a major influence upon his conduct once those men became his vassals. While sheer apprehension over the military power of local lords cannot explain Hideyoshi's grant to the Uesugi, for example, or his pleasure in performing nō before daimyo audiences, his admiration for daimyo society helps illuminate his motives.

Conviction, as well as personality, may have shaped Hideyoshi's decisions. Two arresting points deserve consideration. First, Hideyoshi generally confined his political actions to making and keeping the peace—limiting arms, regulating ports and markets, disciplining treasonous daimyo. He acted as a controller of daimyo and their domains. And implicit in a policy that focuses upon control is both an acceptance of (or resignation to) the underlying political order and an accommodation by the regulator to the powerful parties who need regulation. In effect, a policy of control tends to assume the legitimacy of the controlled. Second, and more important, Hideyoshi placed structural constraints upon the emergence of an absolutist central authority by permitting daimyo to hold almost all of the nation's land, to maintain their own armies, and to assume national administrative responsibility. The decisions concerning land and administration are particularly significant, for in them Hideyoshi had a fair latitude to introduce change. Instead, he built a system that put the survival of the central government in graver jeopardy than the survival of the domains.

Conclusion

Hideyoshi's tenure in power was a remarkable moment in Japan's history, a rare turning point when many courses seemed open and the selection of one eludes full comprehension. It is comparable to the years around 700, when clan leaders submitted to the throne to create a Chinese-style polity, or to the years after 1868, when the daimyo surrendered their domains to the Meiji administration to begin the conversion to a Western-style constitutional monarchy. Although the Toyotomi settlement did not involve the sweeping and fundamental transformation that followed the establishment of the Ritsu-Ryō and Meiji states, it shared characteristics with those counterparts. It followed a long period of violence when political values as well as political structures were challenged. It brought about immediate and demonstrable change, primarily the alignment of divided local powers under a new central authority. Despite accompanying upheaval, the settlement was made and maintained by members of the governing elite, not by outsiders or rebels in lower social strata. The resolution of conflict, and the basic redirection of the polity, required sacrifices that cannot be explained purely in terms of military expedients or personal advantage. The resolution seems to have been built, therefore, upon the surprising accord among leaders that sometimes emerges in times of crisis as a result of a collective lift in imagination and a resolve to survive.

Like the coups and political assassinations of the seventh century or the encroachments of the West in the nineteenth, there was a catalyst in the creation of the Toyotomi settlement: Oda Nobunaga. His regime resembled a reign of terror that drew out the full, frightening implications of warring-states history and threatened all familiar institutions with destruction. Nobunaga brought the shogunate to a humiliating end; he eliminated the Imagawa, the Takeda, and the Asakura—*shugo* houses that had made the transition to wartime rule and that had set an example, with their law codes and cadastral surveys, of both political continuity and orderly domainal rule; he leveled the ancient monasteries of Mount Hiei and waged a relentless ten-year war against the Honganji establishment; he submitted the sturdy citizens of Sakai and Kyoto to his authority after fire raids and huge demands for tribute; he replaced the mounted knight with the musketeer, turning military organization on its head and further brutalizing warfare; he resigned his courtly titles to stand outside the venerable traditions of political legitimacy in Japan; and he relied upon an army of new men whom he denied secure and independent tenures and treated with aloofness. The ultimate *sengoku* man, who seemed to revere nothing but power and who placed all constants at risk, Oda Nobunaga shocked his contemporaries into reflection.

Nobunaga thus left a dual legacy to his successor. Hideyoshi inherited a land base as well as a model for governing cities, disciplining the church, and registering property. These were practical advantages in the task of unification. But Nobunaga also left a psychological imprint: a legacy of fear that made the daimyo feel the urgency of some resolution short of disaster and the loss of all domains. Without Nobunaga it is doubtful that so many critical lords would have entered into early alliance with Hideyoshi and then granted him both homage and significant governing concessions. And without faithful allies, it is inconceivable that Hideyoshi would have made domainal rule and power sharing the foundation of his settlement. That settlement emerged reciprocally in Nobunaga's shadow: the daimyo elected the security of alliance, and Hideyoshi found in their allegiance a strong motive for federation.

The matter of federation brings us full circle. We observed earlier that Hideyoshi and his daimyo appeared to enter into a purposeful alignment in the service of a common interest and with a commitment to some separation of powers. The common interest was the survival of the domain—the center of five generations of struggle and administrative development. For the daimyo, the primacy of the domain is indisputable. For Hideyoshi, it apparently represented not only a basis for sound rule and a precondition of peace, but an indispensable platform for men he valued. His exceptional actions on behalf of his vassals suggest that, in conviction as in disposition, Hideyoshi shared the daimyo's perception of the importance of the domain.

The separation of powers remained crudely defined and untested by crisis. In practice, local lords retained control over domainal management and armies. Their prerogatives were singularly well protected. As long as land, wealth, and military power remained concentrated in their hands, it was the survival of a strong central authority that was most in jeopardy. Hideyoshi, in practice, functioned first as overlord—with conventional privileges to invest land and exact a military tax. Further, and more important, he functioned as pacifier, as guarantor of a peace founded upon the domain. None of his policies—from the takeover of Kyoto to the separation of classes—indicates an intention to obliterate local rule and so to reconceive the center as either adversary of the daimyo or dictatorial governor of domainal matters.

In many respects, perhaps paradoxically, Hideyoshi exceeded Nobunaga in power. He controlled more cities, extended his jurisdiction to foreign affairs, disarmed peasants, and began the removal of soldiers from the land. Yet these actions took place within an essentially conservative context. *Tozama* as well as *fudai* survived, they participated in national administration, and the most intrusive of Hideyoshi's initiatives addressed their collective concern with the consolidation of domainal power and the reduction of external threats. His most forceful policies had the curious effect of enhancing the stature and the security of the daimyo as a group, if not always as individuals.

To define Hideyoshi's settlement as federal—as the union of semi-autonomous domains under an overseer of the common interest—is not to minimize conflict or the dimensions of the change. Conflict and change were tightly linked. As clearly as Hideyoshi was transformed from general into national governor, so were the daimyo transformed from regional lords dependent upon their vassals into confederates dependent upon each other and the central authority. With peace and an end to subinfeudation, domains could only be improved through gifts, the allegiance of soldiers secured only through salaries limited to current resources, and political initiatives pursued only with the tacit consent of peers and superiors.

These changes, in addition to the extradomainal responsibilities of some lords and the ceremonial ties to Hideyoshi of all, subtly but surely altered the perspective of the daimyo. They could no longer pretend to freedom or to rely fully upon their own men. The assault differed from war merely in form. Moreover, the daimyo were not really equal. In conceding land and power, Hideyoshi favored the great *tozama*. These were the men he esteemed, wanted to trust, and looked to for affirmations of his own greatness. Even during Hideyoshi's lifetime, the Maeda, the Mōri, the Tokugawa, the Uesugi, and a few others formed a sort of oligarchy. Though the Toyotomi federation embraced all lords, it was primarily a handsome accommodation among the men at the very top of *sengoku* society.

Postwar conflict also centered on the prerogatives of the ruler, of course. Hideyoshi himself, however much a joint creation of the daimyo, wanted their gold and silver, threatened their ports and markets, and remained unpredictable. There were losers in more than military terms in political reunion; there were few tidy edges in federation; and there were no assurances of peaceable adjustment in the future.

The major theme of late sixteenth-century Japanese history is nonetheless one of reconciliation. It overshadows the story of war and continued political uncertainty. It is a theme limited, of course, to the powerful men who survived the *sengoku* era to choose a new direction for the national polity. The history of the Buddhist sects, of commoners and common soldiers, of shogunal loyalists and former estate holders is very different. Hideyoshi and his daimyo alike were tyrants from many viewpoints who allied to protect themselves. But this is the point. The ties between them were stronger than their ties to other groups. The terms feudalism and absolutism deal badly with a settlement made collectively within an elite to save its members from each other and their lesser adversaries. Federation resolved one set of problems only to lay bare the separation between the confederates and the people they governed.

7

THE PURSUIT OF LEGITIMACY

MOST BIOGRAPHIES OF Hideyoshi, especially the works ·written during the Tokugawa period that center on his military career, refer to him as *taikō*—the retired imperial regent. Many men occupied this court position, but only one is invariably associated with it. No other individual in Japanese history has ever been so successfully, or so exclusively, linked with the official title he held.[1] These same biographies, both scholarly and popular, include on their covers or within their pages the portrait that serves as the frontispiece. It is the most famous of Hideyoshi's likenesses. Actors playing his role bend themselves to this image; textbooks and all manner of memorabilia show Hideyoshi as a stern, slight man wrapped in courtly robes. His hat, coat, and trousers are the formal garments of a high-ranking noble. The clothing and the pose of the body deliberately invite confusion with similar paintings of emperors and princes.[2] Yet the unmistakable features, more familiar perhaps than those of any other premodern Japanese figure, reveal Hideyoshi.

He survives in the public mind as a courtier, no less than as a general, because he cultivated the role with exuberance. After climbing to the pinnacle of the imperial bureaucracy, he revived the ceremonies of state and brought a new pageantry to official life. With the same determination that characterized his conquests, he fitted himself to a princely post and legitimated his rule by becoming the throne's ranking minister. His behavior is startling, particularly in view of Nobunaga's example, and raises two questions. What moved Hideyoshi to seek justification for his power beyond the covenants he made with his men? And why did he go to the court for that justification?

The changes wrought by daimyo of the warring-states era went to the heart of the problem of legitimacy. These men defined the right to rule not as a function of offices and titles awarded by a central administration but as a function of military power and the allegiance of a corps of vassals. Nobunaga acted upon these assumptions single-mindedly, declining places within traditional frameworks of national government. Even after he extended his authority to great monasteries and cities, he justified his rule in terms of the obeisance of the ruled. Hideyoshi too observed *sengoku* conventions. He founded his settlement upon daimyo alliances that presumed a shared commitment to the domainal order. His men acknowledged his lordship by acts of homage, compliance with his laws, and service in his wars. Hideyoshi fulfilled his part of the implicit contract underlying alliance by preserving and protecting their fiefs.

Increasingly, however, pressure was put on the particular and conditional bonds that joined Hideyoshi and his daimyo. His appropriation of prerogatives to govern that had no foundation in covenants between lord and vassal—including diplomacy and, later, waging a foreign war—subtly altered his role in national affairs. Further, the very size of his federation brought a new formality and objectivity to Hideyoshi's relations with his men. He controlled not twenty but two hundred daimyo, not six but sixty-six provinces. He began to have the daimyo take oaths in groups and to standardize military taxes; he addressed his statutes on arms and the separation of classes to all men impersonally; he used intermediaries to register the country's land according to uniform specifications. As he bound the nation by common practices and guided it to a common destiny, the immediacy of alliance could not be maintained.

Alliance was also strained by peace. The military expedients that had encouraged federation diminished, relieving Hideyoshi of his critical role in the state. Thus the bonds of war that had given him power had to be transmuted into a mandate for normal rule. To ensure continuity in administration and the stability of the Toyotomi settlement, they also had to be made durable. The transfer of authority in *sengoku* society was always traumatic, and Hideyoshi's age, the absence of a strong heir, and the brevity of his time in power combined to make succession an unusually volatile issue. All of these factors contributed to Hideyoshi's decision to broaden the base of his legitimacy, to enhance his alliances by grounding them in larger traditions of law and institutional authority. But pragmatic motives alone did not shape his conduct.

Legitimacy is a matter of conviction and assent—the conviction of the ruler that his power is righteous and the assent of the ruled to that righteousness. Because it is a phenomenon that exists in the minds of men, legitimacy is difficult both to define and to test, particularly as it engages the governed. The obedience of Hideyoshi's daimyo, strong men capable of insurrection whose support of the Toyotomi federation was voluntary in the final instance, is the surest measure of their assent. But whether it was rooted in more than Hideyoshi's respect for their domains is problematic. They did fight the Korean war—one possible affirmation of an unconditional allegiance; they did not all transfer fealty to his heir, a child unable to protect the federation. Their relationship with Hideyoshi, the universal governor, was ambiguous and may never have transcended the requirements of feudal contracts.

That Hideyoshi sought to transcend those contracts is apparent in his studied and systematic pursuit of a noble role to overlay his identity as conqueror. If the attitude of the ruled toward legitimacy is elusive, the perception of the ruler is traced in the forms he borrows or creates to rationalize power. Hideyoshi borrowed the forms of the court, asserting that alliance was insufficient to make his rule righteous. He associated national power with the throne. The uses to which he put his aristocratic promotions—immoderate self-promotion and reaffirmation of medieval values—reveal something more than a pragmatic interest in succession or new political privileges.

Hideyoshi's position in the court was novel and even astonishing for a military man. He was promoted to the offices of great minister of state and imperial regent, not shogun. For Tokugawa commentators, who lived under a shogunate and assumed that shogunal title was the ultimate encomium, these appointments reflected Hideyoshi's poor pedigree and his ineligibility for a post that members of the Minamoto clan alone had held. The observation was self-serving, needless to say, and ignored both the superior lineages of all regents other than Hideyoshi and the purely circumstantial association between the rank of shogun and Minamoto descent. It also failed to recognize the crucial element of Hideyoshi's choice of title: a resolution, like Nobunaga's, to dissociate himself from a shogunal institution that he knew in a debilitated state. Nor was the earlier history of the Kamakura or Ashikaga administrations necessarily edifying to Hideyoshi. Both had, essentially, a police function, and neither, despite a steady accretion of powers, had ever achieved the jurisdiction over private estates, religious institutions, cities, and local armies so essential to Nobunaga and Hideyoshi. Shogunal power was partial power, and shogunal title would diminish a man who held greater military and political authority than any of his martial predecessors.

Why, then, did Hideyoshi seek sanction from a court that had not only been embarrassed by decades of war and poverty but that had been unable to exercise active power to govern since the thirteenth century? Why did he fail to put himself—free of traditional entanglements and glorified only by his own conduct—at the center of a new regime in the manner of Nobunaga? If he required a transformation of wartime contracts into the basis of a universal authority, Hideyoshi had alternatives at hand. He could have created a new title, usurped the throne, invoked a sacred commission, either from the nation's priests or heaven itself (on the evidence, perhaps, of his miraculous birth), or declared a Toyotomi dictatorship.

Hideyoshi's decision to turn to the court proceeded, in part, from the history of that institution and, in part, from his need to unite himself to the deepest source of honor in the country. Humbler by birth than any of his daimyo confederates, Hideyoshi's ambition was equaled only by his desire for conventional approbation.

Court and Shogunate before 1467

To an extent, Hideyoshi's relations with the throne followed a course defined by generations of military men before him. So correctly did Hideyoshi pursue the typical legitimation procedure—delivery of services to the imperial house in exchange for high title—that his imitation of past practices seems to throw into relief the classic court-camp relationship. The relationship was not classic, however, and the differences reflect the changing world view produced by a century of civil war.

Yoritomo and all later shogun legitimated their rule by receiving appointment from the emperor. They acquired not only military commissions but also aristocratic rank and title as well. Yoritomo, for example, rose to the senior second rank and held the titles of *gondainagon* and *ukon'e no daishō*.[3] Like many of his successors, he preferred to use the nomenclature of the nobility. Ashikaga Takauji was named *gondainagon* at the second rank. Most of his shogunal descendants held the same court title, but five achieved the first rank, junior grade, and one—Ashikaga Yoshimitsu—became great minister of state (*daijō daijin*). Six Ashikaga rulers received that title posthumously. Hence these men were absorbed into the hierarchies of ranks and titles adopted from China and refined to the purposes of the Japanese imperial state. The shogun became representatives of the throne as bearers primarily of military but also of courtly appointments.

In exchange for recognition, the shogun and their men assumed a filial posture toward the emperor. They presented themselves as loyal deputies and ministered to the needs of the court. They attempted, with uneven success, to keep the peace; they protected the imperial estates and secured the emperor's revenue; they maintained public buildings. It was this exercise, imperial sanction repaid by devotion, that came ideally to convey legitimacy and that so influenced Hideyoshi's behavior.

Clearly there was much of the charade about this business. Patronage of the emperor by the shogun illustrated the growing debility of the throne while it became itself a form of abuse. Military power grew at the expense of the court. Those unfortunate emperors who fought to contain shogunal usurpation only reduced their own influence in the process. Even the most chastened monarchs suffered periodic indignities as their shogun failed to perform the services upon which the court increasingly depended. Why, then, did the throne legitimate military authority?

The easiest and truest answer is that it had no choice. By the time the Taira and Minamoto went to war in 1180, the withering of public institutions and the expansion of the estate system had given prominence to private armies used by the official and proprietary classes alike to preserve order. The Taira and Minamoto became a kind of national guard as early as the tenth century. Thus as Yoritomo emerged from conquest of the Taira in 1185 to formalize command over vassals throughout the country, the court looked to him to regulate a now significant military population and to recover the peace. Indeed, evidence exists that the court pressed upon Yoritomo judicial responsibilities that he was not eager to accept.[4] The throne had fair use of the Minamoto. And once an acceleration of military advances into the civil domain provoked resistance, the aristocracy had been too long out of armed politics to mount a successful challenge. Two abortive "restorations" of imperial power—the first attempted as early as 1221, the second led by Go-Daigo in 1333—showed the court unable to elicit wide support for its political causes.

Perhaps the most telling note of their failure is the judgment of historians of the time. The need to resolve intellectually a contradiction between imperial primacy and shogunal ascendance moved historical writing from anecdote to analysis and exposed an unbecoming verdict on the emperor's place.[5] In dealing with the failed restorations, commentators condemned the court for violating its sacerdotal privilege to traffic ineptly in practical affairs. They separated symbolic and actual power: they justified military rule because it was necessary and relegated the throne to a position of superior, but ritualistic, authority. The interesting point, of course, is that these writers viewed themselves as imperial loyalists.

Unable to eliminate military rule, the court attempted to turn it to advantage. By entitling the shogun and his men, the emperor reaffirmed his ultimate right to do so. Promotions were volunteered by, seldom coerced from, a throne eager to preside at least over the passage of power. Further, an interest in creating a stable and mutually advantageous relationship between court and camp prompted the emperor to offer honors that might dispose military men to conscientious behavior. His revenue was secured, his palace maintained, his ceremonial life financed by the shogun he courted with promotions. The imperial house was locked into cordial association with the military to sustain itself.

One of the more interesting problems in Japanese history concerns the survival of the throne once military men had appropriated most prerogatives to govern. Why did the throne retain symbolic power and the right to legitimate successive shogun? In good measure, the answer lies in the longevity of imperial rule prior to the development of the shogunate and in the successful concentration within the imperial house of both political and religious authority. By the fourth century the emperor's clan had established in the Yamato plain a hegemony based on martial superiority and buttressed by assertions of sacred ancestry. Representing himself as a descendant of the heavens' principal divinity, the head of the clan emerged as godlike himself and chief priest before the national altar. His essential claim to primacy was numinous. The penetration of Chinese monarchical ideas in the seventh century helped both to confirm and to broaden the political privileges of the imperial family while the efforts made shortly thereafter to compose a native history, which traced the divine descent, helped effect its spiritual ascendance. Wedding domestic religious beliefs to a continental view of kingship, the throne monopolized divergent sources of power.

With time, the emperor's role became increasingly complex. More than monarch or priest, he emerged as a symbol of historical continuity and political cohesion. His spiritual authority as son of the gods bound heaven and earth together, embodying the principle of eternal regeneration. In effect, he survived as an indispensable part of the nation's definition of itself.

For Yoritomo and his successors the formal political authority of the throne and its varied symbolic authority remained strong. To look elsewhere for justification of their position was as unlikely an effort as it was unnecessary. The effort was unlikely because no vaguely similar source of legitimacy existed. The throne held religious power not only as head of the native cult but as the main patron and protector of the Buddhist church. In addition to its influence as the legal seat of political authority, it retained a sort of tribal dominion over the Minamoto and Ashikaga. Both families were descended from emperors. Hence time and the habit of allegiance to the throne combined with recognition of its multifaceted power to encourage military obeisance.

The effort to abjure justification altogether was unnecessary because the court was, in the end, a malleable establishment. The throne retained primacy by permitting actual responsibility for governing to flow to abler contenders. Never did the imperial institution depend for its influence upon the personality of the king. The restoration incidents in 1221 and 1333 are exceptions to a pattern of imperial deference to deputies. Long before the rise of the Minamoto, the court had known two prolonged intervals of proxy rule by the Soga and the Fujiwara houses. The judgment of those historians who chronicled the "restorations," then, was not really novel. Rather early on, the imperial family had consented to a division between real and symbolic authority.

In a sense, it was the very ease of takeover by deputies that discouraged the military from pursuing alternative sources of legitimacy and discouraged them, too, from any real inquiry into the reasons or need for a superior confirmation of power. For the medieval military elite, the officers of the Kamakura and Ashikaga regimes, two additional factors ensured the close affiliation of the shogun with the court, factors absent in Hideyoshi's period. First, the Minamoto and the Ashikaga needed all the leverage the throne offered. They did not come to power as the result of total conquest. They had a limited military hold on the country and an imperfect command through their vassals over even the martial population of Japan. Support from aristocratic proprietors and court officials was as important to the shogun as the symbolic endorsement of the throne. They were, and largely intended to be, sharers of power with the traditional holders. Never, as we have noted, did shogun assume absolute control over the nobility and the religious establishment. Their legal codes alone are an admission of partial jurisdiction.[6]

For many members of the medieval warrior elite, moreover, a true dichotomy between court and camp did not exist. The growth of an independent shogunal administration, the emergence of a distinct military culture, the tension between civil and martial governors—these and other developments drew attention to divisions between groups. Yet military houses first appeared as accepted adjuncts to an estate system created within the law.[7] And the most distinguished of them came from cadet branches of the imperial family that served as semiofficial police forces. Yoritomo, himself the descendant of an emperor, regarded his shogunate as the legal outgrowth of a now frayed imperial system. His early biographers depict him as a loyal subordinate of the throne less because it was advantageous to do so than because it was obviously correct. It remained to later historians—really to Tokugawa-period historians—to identify Minamoto government as a turning point in the affairs of the nation.[8]

The strains between shogun and emperor did come clearer in 1221 and 1333. The warriors who resisted restoration forces and thus acquired a temporary renegade status could not continue to view their institutions as fully complementary to those of the imperial state. But those conflicts had an almost internecine quality about them. Aristocrats and ranking military men had become part of a common governing community. Though the court bureaucracy functioned ineffectively, the nobility remained an important proprietary class and shared responsibility for land administration with officers of the shogun. Some blurring of distinctions between titles also blurred distinctions between groups: not only did warriors hold court offices, Fujiwara scions and imperial princes sat in Kamakura after 1226 as titular shogun when Yoritomo's line failed, and courtiers were appointed as *shugo* during the brief restoration of 1333. Marriages between military men and noblewomen—not strictly intermarriages, because elite warriors had both aristocratic pedigrees and titles themselves—continued to merge bloodlines that had never been, in any case, quite separate. At least five Hōjō regents, the effective rulers of the Kamakura regime after 1200, took Fujiwara brides. Eight Ashikaga shogun found spouses in the same clan.[9] And military men constantly reaffirmed their membership in noble society by conforming to a courtly definition of gentility. The confusion engendered by the two restorations is perhaps the most interesting indication of the absence of absolute divisions of class and interest between court and camp. Prominent military families supported the emperors who attempted to throw off the shogun, while prominent courtiers cautioned against the uprisings. No unified aristocracy confronted a unified military in either 1221 or 1333.[10]

A sound argument can be made that aristocratic and military societies *were* deeply divided by class and interest in medieval Japan. Certainly only the upper crust of the martial community ever blended with the nobility. But rarely is there a perfect congruence between political reality and social assumptions about the political order. Enough mutual needs and clear bonds did exist before 1500 to create a semblance of union between court and camp and to conceal deepening rifts. Linked by ancestry and by culture, courtiers and officials of the shogunate also lived by the same ideas: that government existed to distribute rights to property that were to be exercised privately, and that government functioned within a system of law and formal appointment, not armed strength. No shogun did without imperial confirmation; none repudiated estate law.

Indeed, even in matters of style—often the sharpest indicators of identity—highly placed military men used the conventions of the court.

They wrote their documents in a form of Chinese that departed only gradually, and never entirely, from the official language of imperial correspondence; they dated events according to imperial era names; they used courtly ranks and titles, not a new system of honors of their own, to dignify their subordinates as well as themselves; and they adopted court ceremonial—from the rites of initiation to the rites of mourning—in their private households. Whether in their coinage or their carriages, their clothing or their cosmetics, the noble and military elites were nearly indistinguishable.

Despite the deepening rifts, then, many factors contributed to the persistence of an idea of unity. Military integration into the court was simply taken for granted, and no contemporary chronicler made moment of the homage warriors paid to the throne. Even critical interpreters of the restorations perceived military men as deputies of flawed monarchs who remained irrevocably at the head of a unified government: "It is desirable to have an Emperor whose behavior as an Emperor is good, but Japan is a country that has had the tradition . . . that no person should become Emperor who is not in the imperial line of descent . . . But since it has necessarily become difficult for an Emperor to govern the state well by himself, it was established that a Great Imperial Chieftain would be appointed and used as an Imperial Guardian."[11] History was a continuum to medieval writers. They made no significant break between imperial and military eras of rule and assumed that imperial ascendancy was eternal: "It has therefore become established that a man becomes Emperor in China because he has fought and defeated [the ruling house of the previous dynasty]. But in this country of Japan there has never been . . . an Emperor who has not been of the imperial line of descent . . . there certainly will never be the slightest departure from [this custom]."[12] Thus Yoritomo and his successors sought the sanction of the throne not only because it was an eminent, adaptable, and politically useful institution, but also because they shared with their contemporaries an unconscious world view which admitted of a single locus of ultimate authority.

Hideyoshi and the Court

The separation between the military and the nobility was more pronounced after 1500, and, of greater significance, it was better perceived. A century of civil war had disturbed the medieval world view. The cataclysm of 1467 was not over in several weeks—the duration of the 1221 incident—nor in three years—the length of the rebellion begun in 1333. The court's place in Japanese society was slowly altered as prolonged anarchy forced recognition of divisions of power that had long existed unacknowledged. The emperor's weakness became all too clear as he was forced to turn to occasional patrons for the simple necessities. His palace fell into ruin, and his estates were confiscated by distinguished families, such as the Imagawa, that wrote into their domainal codes an end to noble privileges.[13] The supremacy of an autonomous military was no longer in dispute. The throne's deputies in the Ashikaga house lost national influence, and new pretenders to power kept their distance from court. Oda Nobunaga's destruction of northern Kyoto was an act of lese majesty, his refusal of noble appointment a repudiation of all medieval precedents. Warlords as well as the sectarians of popular churches demolished the family temples of aristocrats. They also permitted the ancestral shrine of the imperial house in Ise to waste. The violence of *sengoku* society suggested that harmony must always be an illusion.

The introduction by the Tokugawa of a new Confucian orthodoxy to bind and regulate postwar society finally announced the death of the medieval order. In a self-conscious Tokugawa world, the need for new moral and political constraints to protect the power of the shogun, to control class relations, and to justify military law became obvious. Its scholars and rulers were troubled by the interplay of past and present, the nature of authority, and a remarkable range of other problems that revealed, with their lack of ready solutions, the absence of constants. The intellectual turmoil of the Tokugawa period was the legacy of thirteen decades of upheaval.

So traditional was Hideyoshi's conduct toward the throne, however, that such upheaval might never have taken place. Overlooking Nobunaga's estrangement from the court and a century of insolent disregard of the imperial pleasure, Hideyoshi behaved not unlike Yoritomo. He was not a medieval man, he did not require whatever immediate leverage the throne could afford, and he was not linked to the nobility by culture or birth. His rule was neither a natural outgrowth of the imperial state nor even of the Ashikaga system. Nonetheless, he followed the example of his Minamoto and Ashikaga predecessors in obtaining the emperor's sanction for his authority. He honored the emperor and returned his house to a place of dignity in the nation.

Hideyoshi's Promotions

Like Nobunaga, Hideyoshi found himself showered with unsolicited honors from the court. Promotions were pressed upon him at turning points in his career and became convenient markers of his growing importance. After his arrival in Kyoto following the Kiyosu conference, the emperor cited him for "extraordinary bravery" in the assault on Akechi Mitsuhide and awarded him the junior fifth rank, lower grade. An advance to junior fourth rank, lower grade, with the office of *sangi*, attended his conquest of Shibata Katsuie. When he came to terms with Tokugawa Ieyasu, Hideyoshi acquired the title of *gondainagon* at the junior third rank. These were rapid promotions volunteered by a court eager to win the sympathy of the current strong man.[14]

In the third month of 1585 a more substantial promotion was awarded Hideyoshi for his restoration of the retired emperor's palace. The *Tenshō-ki* records his receipt of *naidaijin* title at the second rank:

> The retired emperor's palace had wasted away from of old. Herewith, Asō [Hideyoshi] presented himself at the previous residence of the retired emperor and expressed his wish to reconstruct [the quarters] so that enthronement ceremonies might be carried out and the retired emperor installed in his own palace. [Maeda] Gen'i was appointed Mimbu-kyō Hōin, entrusted with the responsibility, an auspicious day was chosen, and work begun. At the same time, Taira no Ason Hideyoshi-kyō was promoted and, as the chief support of the various offices, was an assistant to the Imperial Way. He was appointed *naidaijin* by the following imperial proclamation: "To Taira no Ason Hideyoshi, Gondainagon Fujiwara Ason: Tsunemotosen presents the imperial decree; the above mentioned is graciously appointed to the position of *naidaijin*, Tenshō 13, third month, tenth day . . ." On that day, Hideyoshi visited the court and presented gifts of one thousand *ryō* of silver and a large sword.[15]

During the next year Emperor Ōgimachi did indeed resign, at the age of seventy, and his son, Go-Yōzei, was enthroned. The custom of imperial retirement had earlier been abandoned by an indigent aristocracy unable to afford either accession ceremonies for the heir or appropriate quarters for the retired monarch.

Hideyoshi's restoration of the palace and his gifts relieved the court of chronic financial embarrassment and may amply have justified his promotion. But the *Tenshō-ki's* representation of Hideyoshi as the "chief support of the various offices" and "an assistant to the Imperial Way" is also telling. The hope not merely of a courteous association but of a real cordiality between Hideyoshi and the court may have prompted the appointment. Nobunaga had been awarded the same office for similar kindnesses—repair of the palace and financial donations to the throne.[16] We still see an almost mercenary court struggling for alliance with a warlord who is invited into its membership with a high, but not lofty, title. The court was even willing to impute to Hideyoshi a Taira and Fujiwara lineage—perhaps as much to excuse itself of affiliating with a peasant as to flatter Hideyoshi.

Hideyoshi's promotion to *naidaijin* was soon overshadowed by his elevation to the position of *kampaku* in the seventh month of 1585—shortly before his conquest of the Chōsokabe. He was the first military leader to receive the title. He also received the junior first rank, the highest rank available to a living official. This was an unprecedented promotion and one that caused some opposition in aristocratic circles.[17] *Kampaku* was the title used from the mid-Heian period to designate the regent of an adult emperor. Together with the older title of *sesshō*, regent of a child emperor, the Fujiwara family had used it to contain governing power within their own company for over two hundred years. Although the office of *kampaku* began to decline in importance in the eleventh century and eventually lost all association with administrative power, it remained one of the two most prestigious positions at court. It also retained some panache in wider society, since its holders were all members of the *go-sekke*, five branch lines of the Fujiwara (the Nijō, Kujō, Konoe, Ichijō, and Takatsukasa) that were descended from Michinaga—the most eminent Fujiwara—and represented the cream of the nobility.

With help from an ally in the aristocratic Imadegawa family, Hideyoshi was named *kampaku* in the face of competing claims from the Nijō and Konoe houses. Thus he became the first regent in Japan's history to rule without benefit of a blood tie to Michinaga. Konoe Sakihisa adopted him in order to provide a link to the Fujiwara. Even in a country notoriously adept at redesigning offices to conform with the exigencies of power, the decision was a radical one.

Hideyoshi's investiture as regent was accompanied by a presentation of nō drama at the palace. The emperor presided, flanked by the crown prince and Hideyoshi. Three former regents were present, and courtiers mingled with military guests.[18] Months after these ceremonies, Hideyoshi adopted the surname Toyotomi. Discarding the name Hashiba, which he had used since his early days in Nobunaga's service, Hideyoshi chose this auspicious combination of characters, "bountiful minister," to suggest a filial posture toward the throne. The name was probably selected in consultation with courtiers and then granted by the emperor.[19]

Finally, in the twelfth month of 1586, Hideyoshi climbed to the top of the court bureaucracy. Like Ashikaga Yoshimitsu, he was named great minister of state. Bereft of specific responsibility, the title remained the highest of court honors. Combined with the title of *kampaku*, it afforded Hideyoshi a distinction enjoyed by no military predecessor or successor. He became known as *taikō*, the retired regent, after his heir rose to the position of *kampaku* in 1591.

As interesting as Hideyoshi's own rise at court was the rise of his family members. His mother and wife were entitled personally by the emperor as *ōmandokoro* and *kita no mandokoro*. Once used by the womenfolk of all senior aristocrats, these titles had become conventional honors for the mothers and wives of *kampaku* but did remain exclusively in the throne's gift. Hideyoshi's stepbrother became Yamato *dainagon*. His nephew and original heir served as *naidaijin* before his own promotion to *kampaku*. Hideyori, the son born of Hideyoshi's old age in 1593, eventually assumed the title of *naidaijin*.[20]

What is striking in Hideyoshi's career at court is the readiness of the throne and its advisors to advance him. By making Hideyoshi one of them—not just as a military deputy but as their ranking minister—the nobles stood to benefit materially and to bring themselves once more, if not to the center of power, at least in pleasing proximity to it. Their overtures to Nobunaga suggest the same interest in absorbing the leading warlord into the court and so recovering a degree of influence in government.[21] In offering the sacrosanct office of regent to an upstart, the emperor also abandoned the assumption that military men occupied the subordinate place in the official hierarchy conveyed by the title of shogun. Once Hideyoshi was named regent and great minister of state, he could reunite the nation under the direct aegis of the throne.

Almost equally striking is Hideyoshi's enthusiastic response to the court. He accepted his titles, certainly participated in the lobbying efforts behind the *kampaku* promotion, took a surname illustrating devotion to the throne, and welcomed adoption into the Fujiwara clan. More interesting was his addition of a *kampaku* or *taikō* signature to virtually all of his public and personal correspondence—even to letters addressed to his children and his wife. His oaths invoked the household deity of the Fujiwara, and he called upon his family and his vassals to pledge loyalty to the emperor.

He also arranged for the aristocratic promotion of those vassals. Tokugawa Ieyasu held the title of *dainagon* and, later, Edo *daidaijin;* Maeda Toshiie rose from the position of *sakon'e no gon shōshō* to *dainagon;* Ukita Hideie was *sangi ukon'e no chūjō.* Indeed, only twenty of the 200 daimyo listed in Hideyoshi's final roster of vassals were without court posts.[22] Further, Hideyoshi referred to his men in terms of their noble titles in most of his communications to them. This had been the custom of the Ashikaga, but not, of course, of Nobunaga.

Hideyoshi strengthened his links to the nobility by adopting both Emperor Go-Yōzei's younger brother, Hachijō no Miya Toshihito, and Konoe Sakihisa's daughter. This woman later became the consort of Go-Yōzei. Lest he embarrass himself in noble company, Hideyoshi took lessons in court etiquette from Hosokawa Yūsai.[23] He fostered his association with the throne in many ways—building his residence on the site of the original imperial palace, contributing to the reconstruction of the Ise shrine and then excusing it from cadastral registration—yet from the court's vantage point, Hideyoshi's fealty was best measured in his financial services.

Hideyoshi's Service to the Throne

Hideyoshi fulfilled his part of the legitimation pact by rendering traditional services to the emperor. He returned the imperial family to solvency, restored the palace, and publicly displayed homage to the throne. Each of these tasks had been performed by major military leaders in earlier times. Hideyoshi's care in discharging time-honored obligations clarifies their scope while it reveals his concern for the proprieties.

After 1575, as we have noted, the primary source of imperial income was land in eleven districts in Yamashiro that Nobunaga had allocated for the throne's use. References to revenue from this land all but disappear from court records by 1581, however, and no evidence exists that two of the districts ever delivered tribute at all, although the return may have been more routine than the documents suggest. Payments normally arrived in the form of rice; some were made in gold and silver.[24] The rather random character of payments to the throne suggests Nobunaga's preoccupation elsewhere. Yet the fact that very modest funds returned the emperor to a degree of comfort unknown for some time and provoked his inordinate gratitude is itself an interesting commentary upon the ravages of the *sengoku* period. The imperial family was no longer in a desperate financial position when Nobunaga died. It was Hideyoshi, though, who set the throne on a firm economic base.

During the course of at least four separate years—1585, 1588, 1590, and 1591—Hideyoshi presented to courtiers and religious institutions substantial properties around Kyoto, primarily in the province of Yamashiro. Shortly after his elevation as *kampaku*, he awarded lands worth 1,000 *koku* to his adoptive house of Konoe. Parcels worth approximately 500 *koku* each went to the other *go-sekke* (the Nijō, Kujō, Ichijō, and Takatsukasa). Several temples, including Shōren'in and Kyokurakuji, also received small holdings at that time. Ōmi property valued at 8,000 *koku* was distributed among courtiers and *monzeki* (princely abbots) when the emperor paid an official visit to Hideyoshi's mansion in 1588. Go-Yōzei, the reigning monarch, received a gift of 553 *mai* of silver and 500 *koku* of rice during the ceremonies; the retired emperor Ōgimachi was given 300 *koku* of rice. Two years later, in 1590, Prince Toshihito—Hideyoshi's adopted son—received lands worth 3,000 *koku* to add to an earlier allocation, and the empress dowager received a property of 200 *koku*. Again in 1591 Hideyoshi made grants to courtiers and religious establishments.[25]

Although there is no specific mention of gifts of land to the imperial family during these years, it was apparently the beneficiary of grants of some size. A record of the late Tokugawa period, the *Kinri gosho oyobi miyake kuge go-ryōchi ki*, suggests that the revenue of the emperor approached 10,000 *koku* during the tenure of Hideyoshi.[26] A part of this income came from the properties in Yamashiro presented to the throne by Nobunaga. Other offerings arrived from traditional imperial holdings where Hideyoshi exerted pressure on behalf of the court. Yamakuni in Tamba and Yokota in Izumo, for example, delivered rice to the palace. A mine in Niwa periodically sent one hundred *mai* of silver.[27] By and large, however, the greatly increased revenue of the imperial family came from lands in Yamashiro province newly assigned to the throne by Hideyoshi.

These allocations probably accompanied Hideyoshi's cadastral surveys of Yamashiro, a complex registration that began in 1582. Embracing the capital itself and traditionally a preserve of the court, Yamashiro had contained no fewer than fifty-eight separate estates in the Ashikaga period and continued to be strongly identified with aristocratic interests.[28] Hideyoshi was consequently careful in his directions to the surveyors: "The current land survey [is being conducted] in order to ascertain distinctions [between domains] inasmuch as the various domains are [now] confused. Certainly there shall not be the slightest violation or disturbance in the proper tenure of any noble or religious holding."[29] This respect for the court was not unusual; later Hideyoshi would dismiss a Kyoto administrator for neglect of the throne.[30] As a result of the survey, Hideyoshi determined the extent of the standing claims to land in the province and established a basis for awards.

If the imperial house did receive as much as 10,000 *koku* through Hideyoshi's efforts, it was far better off than it had been earlier in the century but still considerably below the level of opulence enjoyed by emperors in the Muromachi period. Hideyoshi wanted a comfortable court, apparently, not an affluent one. (The Tokugawa would eventually increase imperial revenues to 20,000 *koku*.[31]) Yet Hideyoshi also contributed to imperial coffers in other important ways. We have seen that he made periodic gifts—1,000 *ryō* of silver when he was appointed *naidaijin*, larger amounts when the emperor visited Jurakutei. He funded the accession ceremonies of Go-Yōzei; he built a retirement palace for Ōgimachi.[32] He also reconstructed the imperial compound itself. Between 1589 and 1591, Hideyoshi had eleven structures rebuilt, from the *shishinden* (official ceremonial hall) to the bath. Some years earlier, in 1570, Nobunaga had begun repairs on three of the buildings in the complex.[33]

Hideyoshi extended the palace boundaries somewhat and returned its buildings to grandeur; there was no question, though, of restoring the throne to the state it had enjoyed in palmier days. Until the late Heian period the palace, the great chambers of state, and the imperial granaries and stables occupied eight square blocks in the north-central part of Kyoto. Not included within those walls were vast imperial gardens, aristocratic residences, retired emperors' quarters, and detached palaces. Even in the thirteenth century the Kan'in palace, closely modeled on the emperor's personal complex in the Heian compound, contained roughly the same number of buildings as its predecessor—about thirty—and was otherwise in accord with Heian standards of luxury.[34] It was the smaller Tsuchimikado palace, well but moderately maintained by the Ashikaga until 1500, that Hideyoshi reconstructed.[35] The labor was not on a vast scale, yet the result was a beautiful and graceful complex, surrounded by gardens and gravel terraces, that dominated the eastern part of the capital. For the first time in a century, the emperor lived in a residence befitting his stature.

Courtly Pageantry

Correct rather than munificent toward the court in financial matters, Hideyoshi was far more expansive in ceremonial matters. He exploited the full symbolic power of the throne to demonstrate his political primacy. The disparity between his generous but not extravagant allocations to the emperor and his flamboyant use of courtly festivity begins to reveal the objectives Hideyoshi sought as the emperor's Bountiful Minister.

Hideyoshi mixed with the aristocrats on many occasions. The formal exchange of greetings at New Year's, the congratulatory toasts on festive days, the ceremonies upon the completion of palace buildings, the tea parties, the visits to mark important births and betrothals—all were opportunities seized to demonstrate Toyotomi intimacy with the throne. Frequently after 1592, when Hideyoshi began to study nō drama, he met with courtiers for afternoons or evenings of plays. To celebrate the birth of his son in 1593, for example, Hideyoshi hosted three days of nō performances at the palace. Hideyoshi was, in fact, as punctilious in his public shows of closeness to the emperor as he was in his affirmations of gratitude to Nobunaga. He regularly enjoined his vassals to respect for the throne and elicited from his nephew, at that time his heir, an oath that included this article: "I will act faithfully toward the court and render service to it."[36] Far and away the most ambitious, as well as the most memorable, of Hideyoshi's own displays of homage took place during the Juraku *gyōkō*—the imperial progress to Jurakutei. The event became legendary even as it was drawing to a close.

The Juraku *gyōkō*, the official visit by Emperor Go-Yōzei and ex-Emperor Ōgimachi to Hideyoshi's Kyoto mansion, Jurakutei, took place from the fourteenth to the eighteenth of the fourth month, 1588.[37] Preparations for the occasion were under way a year in advance. Maeda Gen'i, Hideyoshi's Kyoto administrator, was charged to examine materials concerning two similar visits made during the Ashikaga period. In 1408 Emperor Go-Komatsu had proceeded in state to Ashikaga Yoshi-mitsu's residence in Kitayama; in 1467 Emperor Go-Tsuchimikado and ex-Emperor Go-Komatsu had journeyed to Ashikaga Yoshimasa's quarters on Muromachi. Gen'i studied diary accounts of the two proto-types to judge the etiquette appropriate to such events.

On the first day of the Juraku *gyōkō*, Hideyoshi traveled to the palace to attend the departure of the imperial party. Although Yoshimitsu and Yoshimasa had simply awaited the emperor at their own gates, Hideyoshi escorted Go-Yōzei from the palace and stooped to carry his train as he entered the royal ox cart. The procession stretched along the fourteen blocks separating the emperor's residence from Jurakutei. As its first members arrived at Hideyoshi's garden, the last were yet to begin the walk. Six thousand guards lined the streets while the parties of the emperor and ex-emperor, the empress and the dowager, the leading courtier families, and the imperial musicians, servants, and ladies-in-waiting advanced to Jurakutei. The participants were festooned with Chinese silks of five colors, depicting seasonal birds and flowers, the spring cherries of Yoshino, the autumn maples of Takidagawa. When this assembly reached its destination, a banquet was laid and the first musical recital began. Courtiers entertained the company on the flute, the lute, and the reed pipes.

The activities of the second day were by far the most significant. It was at this time that Hideyoshi presented his major gifts to his guests. As we noted earlier, 553 *mai* of silver and 800 *koku* of rice went to the emperor alone. Later in the day, Hideyoshi's vassals swore the oath of three articles to the imperial family discussed in chapter 5.

Item: We shed heartfelt tears, sincerely grateful that this imperial progress to Jurakutei has been proclaimed.

Item: Each of us will strictly remonstrate should there be any lawless person who [impinges upon] the lands of the throne or the various investitures of the nobility and princely abbots (*monzeki*). We assert this for the present, needless to say, and unto [the generations of our] children and grandchildren without exception.

Item: In all things, we will not violate in the least the orders of the Kampaku [Hideyoshi].[38]

The myriad deities, including the Fujiwara household god—now Hideyoshi's household god—were invoked to bear witness to the pledge.

The third day of festivities was given over to a poetry party that proceeded far into the night accompanied by generous amounts of wine. Courtiers and warriors freely capped each other's verses with only occasional grace.

Go-Yōzei:
  Today is the day
  We achieve what we awaited.
  In the branches of the pine
  I see the promise of our relations
  Extending for ages.

Hideyoshi:
  As my lord of myriad ages
  Has proceeded here in state,
  We may henceforth come close together
  Like the green pine
  Standing tall by the eaves.

This was the first round in a hundred-verse sequence on pine trees.[39] As a long spring rain broke against the mansion roof, Fujiwara Nobufusa suggested:

  From this day on,
  Under the shade of the pine
  In the garden,
  We can count that the future of our lord
  Will continue for a thousand ages.

Tokugawa Ieyasu continued:

  In every needle
  Of the green-standing pine,
  I see the promise of
  Our lord's
  Thousand years [of rule].

The guests from the palace were entertained on the following day by ten presentations of court music and dance (*bugaku*). After the dancing, Hideyoshi's wife and mother continued what had become a daily habit of gift-giving by offering presents to their guests. Robes, coins, incense, and precious papers were lavishly distributed. The courtiers returned to their own homes on the fifth day, thus drawing to a close this bountiful entertainment.

As interesting as the *gyōkō* itself is Hideyoshi's decision to engrave it in the public memory. The *Tenshō-ki* includes a lengthy chapter on the *gyōkō*, originally composed and copied for distribution to court and military families. The Date, Kajūji, and Asano copies of this account, among others, still survive.[40] Numerous additional versions have been lost. Painfully detailed, the *Tenshō-ki* chapter lists *all* the pine poems, the seating charts for major banquets and entertainments, the order of the procession from the palace, the gifts exchanged, the costumes worn, the plays performed. It is more than a simple memoir. It is an official record, widely circulated, of an event designed simultaneously to display homage to the throne and to cast distinction upon the Toyotomi house. The record was as important as the event itself. It helped fix in the national mind Hideyoshi's place in society and his ability to conduct—very well indeed—the ceremonies of state.

Hence the sober tone of the *Tenshō-ki* narrative. It is full of the glory and pomp of the affair, and altogether humorless. The ironies of a farmer's son reading labored though proper poetry before the one hundred seventh emperor of Japan settle nicely below the surface. In the *Tenshō-ki* account we have the fully noble Hideyoshi in a position presumably natural to him.

It is well to remember that the throne had not occupied a crucial position in the lives of most warriors in the *sengoku* period. For many it represented what Max Weber calls the "authority of the eternal yesterday."[41] Yet if Hideyoshi was going to legitimate his power by invoking that authority, he had to convert a vague acceptance of the emperor's transcendent position into a more pronounced respect. To give weight to the imperial offices he held, Hideyoshi affirmed the court's significance before his vassals. Thus the *gyōkō* in particular, and other ceremonies to a lesser extent, were important not only because they expressed Toyotomi devotion to the throne, but also because they enhanced in the military mind an image of the emperor's historical supremacy. Elaborate exercises in fealty had a dual purpose: they confirmed Hideyoshi's place as the emperor's ranking minister, and they reminded his retainers of the imperial dignity that made the ministerial role so lofty. Hideyoshi cultivated respect for his rule by reviving stately ceremonies and drawing attention to the majesty of the throne that honored him. The *gyōkō*, and the record of it, were designed for

Hideyoshi's benefit. The emperor—who, it should be noted, traveled from the palace to Jurakutei as a *visitor*—honored Hideyoshi by the event more, perhaps, than he himself was honored.

The Motives of the Bountiful Minister

In receiving sanction for his rule from the emperor and then reviving the decorum of palace life, Hideyoshi was clearly making gestures of healing and renewal. His actions affirmed traditional values before the nobility itself, needless to say, and also before the religious community, the residents of the capital, those daimyo who had preserved some contact with the throne through gifts or emergency services, and all who could be reminded by Hideyoshi's ostentatious homage of the court's age-old authority. Like his Minamoto and Ashikaga predecessors, Hideyoshi used the throne as a symbol of continuity and cohesion; unlike his predecessors, he saw the court not as the center of a national union that men took for granted but as a binding element between groups dissociated by war. The extravagance of his ceremonial, the merging of warriors and courtiers and priests at his festivities, the sponsorship of courtly processions so long and elaborate that they must impress all who saw or heard of them—such things fostered a harmony long lost. Hideyoshi's acts of amelioration were many and diverse; they ranged from rehabilitation of defeated daimyo houses to restoration of temples destroyed in battle, from the rebuilding of cities to the containment of pirates. In honoring the throne, he called upon yet another source of regeneration.

He looked to the court, furthermore, to provide a framework of tradition, history, and law for his regime. By enhancing feudal contracts with imperial sanction, he linked new and old principles of legitimacy. He became regent as well as lord, sedulously using his aristocratic title and a surname having noble associations. He fitted his daimyo, too, into the structure of court and gave weight to decisions concerning his successor by asking for imperial ratification. In effect, Hideyoshi began to lift his alliances out of a particularistic setting. At the Juraku *gyōkō* his men pledged loyalty to the throne and its first minister rather than to a military hegemon. Because he was regent and not shogun, Hideyoshi drew upon the ancient and unconditional power of the emperor himself and so converted a martial into a universal rule. His interest in the broadest possible mandate is suggested not only by his deliberate identification with the throne despite Nobunaga's example, but by his failure to seek the apparently appropriate title of shogun. He went to the heart of traditional authority, avoiding the lesser promotions befitting lesser rulers.

Finally, Hideyoshi affiliated himself with the imperial court because it dignified but did not threaten him. The most literate, civilized, and eminently pedigreed society in the nation, the court instantly provided Hideyoshi with a culture and a link to the esteemed men of the past that he could never supply for himself. It also provided a ready vehicle for the pageantry, the patronage, and the self-glorification that drew attention to his power while satisfying a voracious appetite for display. As we shall increasingly note, he drew pleasure from ritual, and he needed adulation. He found his pleasures and elicited approval in many ways. Yet his behavior toward the throne illustrates Hideyoshi's concern for conventional approbation and his determination to make the court a major stage for his ceremony. His differences from Nobunaga in these respects have various sources. Hideyoshi's lineage was far humbler, his temperament more suited to princely acts, and his disposition for reconciliation—whether with the *tozama*, the monasteries, or the court—pronounced. Such aspects of his character combined to make him value tradition and seek his place within time-hallowed frameworks of rule.

It was the very weakness of the courtly framework, however, that attracted him. Historically limited to a symbolic authority, much reduced in influence by the upheaval of the warring-states era, and forced to appeal to Hideyoshi for favor, the court could be used to Hideyoshi's purposes. Although he rebuilt the palace and restored the imperial house to solvency, Hideyoshi gave the throne neither wealth nor a sufficiently majestic presence to overshadow himself. He did not revive an active imperial bureaucracy or govern through courtly organs. Indeed, he denied the nobility any practical power in the capital by eliminating its toll barriers, guilds, and land taxes. In the kindliest fashion, Hideyoshi cannibalized the throne. Able to borrow its luster without submitting to its direction, he needed no other source of legitimacy. Any new form of rule—outright usurpation, dictatorship, divine covenant—was unnecessary, hazardous, and lacking in the rectitude Hideyoshi could claim for his relationship with the emperor. He was the good patron and loyal minister of the court, the healer and ritualist, unquestionably the man of power and grace.

While Hideyoshi's conduct surely reveals reverence for the imperial history, it suggests little religious or superstitious attachment to the throne. There are curious bits of evidence that raise the possibility of such attachment: his talk of a miraculous conception involving the sun, the imperial progenitrix; his inveterate descriptions of Japan as the "Land of the Gods"; his self-effacing decision at the *gyōkō* to lift the imperial train. Yet these things admit of many interpretations, and few further marks of sacral devotion appear. The calculation of Hideyoshi's overtures to the court, as well as his containment of the throne's privileges, leaves the political character of his life as a noble most apparent.

Public Display and the Projection of Authority

Hideyoshi's ceremonial concerns extended beyond courtly circles. Two particularly lustrous entertainments of military men and commoners, as grand in their way as the *gyōkō*, we shall consider in a moment. While much of their grandeur proceeded from Hideyoshi's taste for show, there was always a political dimension to his display, both within and outside the court. Again to use Weber's terms, Hideyoshi legitimated his rule in part by exercising a "charismatic" authority. He clearly felt an inner calling to lead and may well have inspired obedience in his vassals "because they believed in him." That force of personality was bolstered by Hideyoshi's invocation of a "legal" authority as well. He occupied two legally constituted offices, the highest in the state, into which he was inducted by the emperor himself. Yet in a country where major titles were often held by the impotent and where appointment did not fix power and responsibility, ambitious rulers went beyond the acquisition of high but often symbolic positions to invest those positions, through their behavior, with importance. In addition to the legal sanction of rule, Japan's greatest leaders finally appealed to the authority of "tradition."

For Hideyoshi this meant adopting a conventional posture toward the throne, but it also meant conforming to a pattern of ostentation established by the Soga, Fujiwara, Taira, Minamoto, and Ashikaga. It was the imperial family itself that set a lasting example for these proxies. Patrons and practitioners of the arts, protectors of the church, architects of peerless palaces and temples—the high nobility of Kyoto bequeathed to the military elite a history of grand behavior. Indeed, the claim to cultural leadership came to be intimately associated with the mandate to rule.[42] That claim had rather little to do, before the Tokugawa period, with Confucian concepts of goodness and righteousness. Elegance and grace were the mark of the Japanese courtier, more than classical learning and moral cultivation. He might better be discovered in the pages of Castiglione than in the pages of the *Analects*. Yet the assumption of princely habits conveyed a political message. A general preference for the splashier manifestations of taste—large buildings, theatricals, religious processions—indicates that civil and military pretenders to power used symbolic behavior to affirm their authority.

Clearly in Hideyoshi's case, display—massive, untrammeled, even vulgar as it was—became an additional component of the process of legitimation. To complement his behavior at court and to project himself before those with little exposure to, or interest in, noble society, Hideyoshi launched other ceremonies. Merchants, townspeople, tea men, and entertainers all became part of his audience. He played the universal ruler by appealing to a universal community, leaving no opportunity for acclamation unexplored. His approach to legitimation was multifaceted and unparalleled. Among Japanese rulers, he alone feted the common man.

The Kitano tea party was the most unusual of Hideyoshi's festivities and his boldest effort to impress the general public. Held several months before the imperial visit, this party took place on the grounds of the Kitano shrine in Kyoto during the autumn of 1587, immediately after the submission of Kyushu and shortly after Hideyoshi's appointment as the great minister of state. Late in the seventh month, this announcement was posted.

Item: We order that a grand tea party [be held] in the woods of Kitano from the first to the tenth of the tenth month, depending upon the weather; in conjunction with [this party], the famous [tea] vessels, without exception, will be assembled. This [event] is being held so that [the vessels] can be displayed to serious persons.

Item: [Persons] serious about the tea ceremony, whether they are [military] attendants, townsmen, or farmers, should bring along one kettle, one ladle, one drinking vessel, and either tea or barley.

Item: In regard to seating mats, two *tatami* [per person] should be sufficient as [the event] will be in a pine grove. Practitioners of *wabi-cha* [a simplified style], may bring either *tojitsuke* or *inabaki* [roughly sewn mats or rice straw].

Item: The Japanese, needless to say, even the Chinese, anyone with a connoisseur's interest, should join in. As for dress, it should be at one's pleasure and diverse.

Item: So that even persons from distant places can be shown [the vessels], the festivities will extend from the first of the tenth month until [the tenth].

Item: Insofar as what has been ordered above has been arranged in consideration for practitioners of *wabi*, those who fail to come for this occasion shall be regarded in offense should they hereafter prepare even barley tea. Even those who go to the places [or attend the tea services] of persons who fail to attend [this tea party at Kitano] shall similarly be regarded [in offense].

Item: We order that practitioners of *wabi*, whoever they are and from whatever distant place, shall be served tea from the hand [of Hideyoshi].[43]

Although there is no record of Chinese participation in this purportedly international event, fifteen hundred or so small enclosures filled the Kitano wood as men from all stations and many locations gathered in response to Hideyoshi's invitation. His own prize vessels, as well as his golden tea house, were displayed in a twelve-mat area near the main shrine. There Hideyoshi joined three of his tea masters to serve just over eight hundred guests personally on the morning of the first day. Later that afternoon he made his way about the grounds, visiting other tea people, viewing their utensils, and receiving refreshment.[44]

The size of this party gave the event the quality of a "bash"—of little concern, perhaps, to Hideyoshi, who obviously reached for a spectacular effect. And indeed, this party has no counterpart in Japanese history. While Ashikaga Yoshimochi invited "all interested viewers" to a day of nō performance at Kitano in 1413, this is as close as any of Hideyoshi's predecessors or successors came to so large and personal an entertainment of the public.[45]

On other occasions Hideyoshi mixed in less flamboyant ways with commoners. He often shared tea with merchant connoisseurs, he conspicuously participated in the Gion festival, he joined Kyoto's exuberant neighborhood dances (furyū), and he invited the public to nō performances in Osaka and Fushimi. Most of his entertainments, however, were reserved for the military elite. The last and most famous of these took place not long before Hideyoshi's death, in the third month of 1598. His final party was a blossom viewing at the ninth-century temple of Daigo, just southeast of the capital.

Daigo was a battlefield during the sengoku era. Even in the late sixteenth century, little of a once beautiful compound that stretched from the valley into the reaches of Mount Yari had been restored. Only its extraordinary sweep of weeping cherry trees survived intact. The abbot Gien, a member of the Nijō family, prevailed upon Hideyoshi to visit the temple in the hope of persuading the taikō to help in repair.[46] Sometime before his journey to Daigo in the second month of 1598, Hideyoshi sent the young priest a grove of Fushimi cherries as a gesture of interest. Well impressed with his subsequent journey to the Daigo site, he promised to return with his wife and son in the blooming season. Hideyoshi ordered, therefore, the repair of the main gate and the construction of a tea house for flower viewing.

A scant week later he was back. Clearly making preparations for a large-scale party, he again examined the existing structures and commissioned a full complex of new residential and entertainment buildings. Within days of that visit Hideyoshi undertook a third trip to draw plans for a garden. He fixed the basic design of a pond, islands, and moss-covered banks. He set positions for waterfalls and bridges and an offertory hall (goma-dō), which was to serve as the focus of the garden landscape. He also planned numerous groupings of over eight hundred rocks with distinctive shapes and colors.[47]

The party took place on the fifteenth day of the third month, just a month after Hideyoshi's first visit to Daigo.[48] Neither the building complex nor the new garden had been completed—construction would continue for years—but the cherry blossoms were at their height. Hundreds of Hideyoshi's retainers and their wives wandered along a long route from a point midway up Mount Yari to the gates of Sambōin, the residence Hideyoshi was building for the abbot Gien. They rested at the many tea pavilions along the way while they enjoyed the flowers and the entertainment of musicians. Just before the Sambōin entrance, they stopped in a freshly planted grove of over five hundred mature trees moved from Yamashiro, Yamato, Kawachi, Settsu, and Izumi for the event. The festivities concluded with a poetry party in Sambōin's first finished rooms, which overlooked the beginnings of Hideyoshi's garden.

The Daigo entertainment was only the last in a long series of similar entertainments. In 1594 Hideyoshi had arranged an elaborate journey with his major retainers to the hills of Yoshino for a viewing of cherry blossoms. Then he proceeded with them to Mount Kōya to conduct memorial ceremonies for his dead parents.[49] In 1589 Hideyoshi had called nobles and senior vassals to Jurakutei, where he distributed almost 5,000 pieces of gold and over 20,000 pieces of silver as gifts and then celebrated the affair with a huge banquet.[50] Few years went by without full-scale presentations of nō, usually lasting three days, at Fushimi or Osaka, Nagoya or Kyoto. Tea parties involving large displays of vessels and services by Hideyoshi's eight tea masters took place at Daitokuji, Myōrenji, Nanzenji, and Shōkokuji. He routinely staged hawking parties, boating trips, religious pilgrimages. And always he brought musicians, actors, and tea men to lift the proceedings above the commonplace.

Nor did Hideyoshi overlook the opportunity to commemorate these affairs. The Yoshino and Kōya trips became the subjects of separate nō plays written by his secretary. The Daigo and Yoshino blossom viewings were remembered in colorful screens.[51] These plays and paintings, like the gyōkō record, became testimonials to events not allowed to pass from memory. Far from incidental amusements, these too were political affairs construed and chronicled to buttress Hideyoshi's military success.

Monuments to Power: Hideyoshi Rebuilds the Capital

For both commoners and military men, these festivities were surpassed in their impact by Hideyoshi's building projects. As he did not entertain in quiet salons removed from public view, so he did not erect residences or chapels for private pleasure alone. The most prolific builder in Japanese history, he converted Nagahama, Ōmi Hachiman, Himeji, Fushimi, and Osaka into important military and commercial cities. He had a significant influence upon Nagasaki and Hakata.[52] His major project, however, was the reconstruction of Kyoto.

Recently the Ashikaga headquarters, for eight centuries the imperial center, Kyoto was the traditional capital of Japan. It was also the national religious center, and the hub of trade and production. The concentration of the aristocracy as well as the clerical and military elites there had attracted craftsmen who developed the city into the largest producer of silk, metalware, lacquer products, paper, fine pottery, and other luxuries in the nation. Indeed, until the end of the *sengoku* era, Kyoto was virtually the only significant urban center in Japan; no more than four or five other cities could claim populations near 10,000.[53]

Kyoto's multifaceted importance in Japan made the city a major tourist attraction. By the sixteenth century, pilgrimages to its shrines and temples had increased sufficiently to generate prosperous settlements of shops, inns, and places of entertainment before the gates of leading religious establishments. Gion, Kitano, Tōji, Kiyomizu, Tōfukuji, and Chionji were all approached through busy neighborhoods grown to serve the streams of visitors. Travelers came too for the incense, fans, medicines, silks, sandals, and pottery that made Kyoto's artisans famous. Itinerant merchants carried the capital's goods into the provinces. Fans, cloth, and swords reached the more affluent warriors; tea whisks, fine umbrellas, and hair ornaments had a wider appeal.[54]

Merchants and returning visitors took home not only souvenirs but tales of a fine city. The farmers of Niigata, unlikely to undertake journeys to the distant capital, learned enough of Kyoto to sing its praises in folk songs:

The Capital of delightful flowers!
The brush not supple enough to write of it!
In the East—Gion, Kiyomizu,
And in the tempest of Otowa's crashing falls,
The cherry blossoms of Jishu scatter.[55]

Emigrants and travelers brought to Tsuwano and to Takayama—far west and north of the capital—the inspiration for annual processions modeled on Kyoto's Gion festival. Seven provincial towns, bounded by hills reminiscent of Kyoto's Higashiyama and washed by rivers resembling the Kamo, styled themselves "small Kyoto."[56]

The nation's religious community was also closely bound to Kyoto. Most provincial temples were branches of Kyoto monasteries, and many priests had trained or spent lengthy visits in the capital. As for ranking military men, they not only consumed Kyoto's goods and depended upon its banking facilities, they buried their dead in the capital's temples and endowed sub-monasteries at major Zen headquarters as retreats for family members.[57] They commissioned paintings of Kyoto on fans and on screens and summoned its aristocrats to lecture on the classics and instruct them in poetry.

The city was, therefore, an attractive showcase for Hideyoshi's buildings. Blended with Kyoto's historic appeal was its continuing centrality to the lives of many Japanese. Any construction in the capital was a public act. Hideyoshi's efforts ranged from repair of the palace to the rebuilding of major bridges, from the erection of the largest Buddha in the nation to the introduction of new streets, from the restoration of important temples to the completion of a stone rampart around the city. His first project coincided with his promotion to the position of great minister of state in 1586. A courtier required a courtly residence; hence Hideyoshi ordered the construction of Jurakutei, the "Residence of Gathered Pleasures," to serve as his official Kyoto headquarters.

Completed in 1587 in time for the *gyōkō*, it occupied part of the plot originally used for the Heian imperial compound. One hundred thousand laborers provided by Hideyoshi's vassals reputedly worked on the building. Materials were brought from the far north, from Shikoku, and from areas closer by. Decorative stones for its gardens were gathered from temples throughout Kyoto, and hundreds of pine trees to line its arcades were transplanted from the precincts of Yoshida shrine.[58] Contained by the inner moat, four separate walled compounds enclosed Jurakutei's keep, Hideyoshi's residence, separate quarters for his intimates, stables, storehouses, and kitchens. Several major vassals constructed homes within the outer moat in a ring around the central complex.

A screen depicting Jurakutei soon after its completion is the most reliable indication of its original appearance.[59] Its focus is the three-story keep with gilded dolphin finials and end tiles (fig. 2). The tower, suitable for tea parties or moon gazing, has large latticed windows facing every prospect and an open veranda. The walls are whitewashed and the roofs gabled. Watchtowers and a corridor of barracks rise above the stone rampart in the screen, but these too, with their fresh white paint and golden tiles, seem more decorative than defensive. One watchtower appears to be a recreational penthouse. A few residential

Fig. 2. Jurakutei, a detail from *Jurakutei-zu*, a screen in the collection of the Mitsui Bunko, Tokyo

buildings skirt out from the gold-leaf clouds of the screen with cypress-bark roofs and ornate beams. An early version of the *Taikō-ki* provides additional description of the buildings:

> The stone wall [stretched] for 3,000 *bu* on four sides like a mountain. As for the look of the *sakura mon* [residential entry gate], its pillars were iron and its doors copper; the tower was decorated with stars. [Along] the joints of the tiles, jeweled tigers roared in the wind, golden dragons sang in the clouds . . . The residential palace was thatched with cypress bark. By the entrance stairs there was a carriage porch. A stage stood in the garden . . . Even to the rear palaces, [the work] taxed the skills of the artisans and exhausted the hands of the painters. The splendor was exceedingly great.[60]

Jurakutei was heir to Nobunaga's Azuchi castle. Like the proto-type, it retained the conventions of the fortress—moats, walls, donjon, protective outer circles. Like the prototype, it introduced so many deco-rative elements as to convert a martial compound into a princely resi-dence—gilded fixtures, airy towers, gabled roofs, distinguished homes and reception areas. It was heir as well to the castle on Nijō that No-bunaga had erected for Ashikaga Yoshiaki. Jurakutei, too, was sur-rounded by the streets of the city and took on the quality of the en-claves of earlier aristocrats and the Ashikaga shogun.

We know rather little of Jurakutei beyond what we are told by the screen and the descriptions of it in the various biographies of Hideyo-shi. Its life was short; its end painful. Hideyoshi transferred the castle to his nephew when the younger man succeeded as *kampaku*. And when Hideyoshi ordered the suicide of this heir in 1594, he also leveled Jura-kutei, a baneful reminder of his nephew's history. "Not a single roof remains. Everything—even to the foundations—has been demol-ished."[61]

Several beautiful buildings from Jurakutei that were dismantled and reconstructed elsewhere serve as refreshing reminders that refine-ment could temper ostentation in Hideyoshi's projects. Jurakutei was, after all, a setting for his courtly life—a palace as well as a castle, an af-firmation of dignity as well as a show of power. Here the *gyōkō* took place and here Hideyoshi entertained his vassals at tea parties and nō performances. It was the gleaming center of a new Kyoto, and the cen-ter too of a daimyo enclave in the city. Hideyoshi's family members and several intimate vassals were housed within Jurakutei's outer ram-part. But others, as many as thirty, were allotted spaces for homes to the north, south, and west of the castle. The settlement grew up actively after 1591, when Hideyoshi moved three large communities of com-moners to other neighborhoods to allow sufficient plots for military mansions. These homes were not simple affairs. Many included gar-dens with tea houses and nō stages. Most included buildings for a sub-stantial retinue, such as that of the Date, which approached a thousand persons.[62]

While Jurakutei was being built, Hideyoshi began plans for his next major project in Kyoto (map 2). On another site with aristocratic associations—a plot in the eastern hills within south Rokuhara, where Emperor Go-Shirakawa had built a villa in the twelfth century—Hi-deyoshi erected a massive statue of the Buddha as a national monu-ment. Size and drama were the guiding criteria. Planned in 1586 and completed in 1595, the building housing the great Vairocana Buddha was a two-story, tile-roofed wonder, forty-five meters high, eighty-one

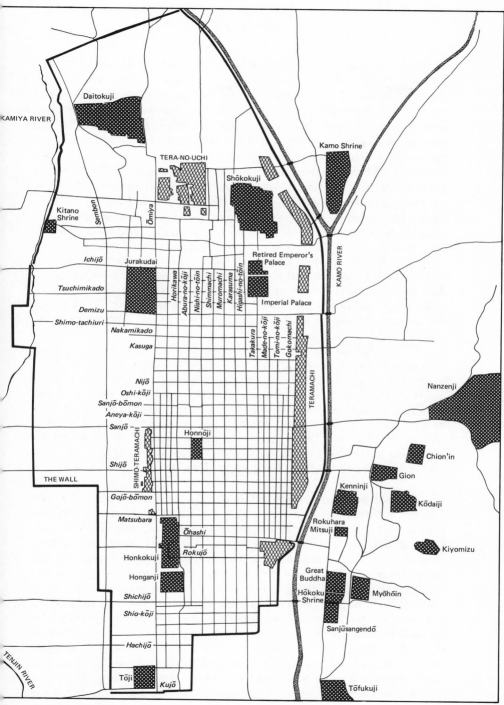

Map 2. Hideyoshi's Kyoto

meters long, fifty meters wide. It was the largest building ever constructed in premodern Japan. The labor involved at least 62,000 men recruited by the daimyo. Special carpenters were called from Nara, and the building materials were brought from Shikoku, Kyushu, Kumano, and numerous other locales. Imai Sōkyū, a wealthy Sakai merchant and tea man, was appointed to collect the lacquer that eventually covered the wooden Vairocana.[63]

Ground-breaking and consecration ceremonies included public nō performances by the Kanze and Komparu schools of actors and dances by commoners at specified centers throughout the capital. A new bridge across the Kamo River was constructed to ease the flow of pilgrimage traffic and to provide a full view of the temple as one approached it. The public nature of the undertaking was most clearly conveyed by one of the articles in Hideyoshi's sword-hunt edict of 1588: "So that the long and short swords collected shall not be wasted, they shall be [melted down and] used as rivets and clamps in the forthcoming construction of the Great Buddha. This will be an act by which the farmers will be saved in this life, needless to say, and in the life to come."[64]

No matter that the sword hunt was an undisguised effort to disarm commoners. Here, however obvious the propaganda, the confiscation of weapons is given the function of a public work. Clearly piety did not motivate the Hōkōji construction. Had he been interested in good deeds, Hideyoshi might have repaired damage done to the Nara Daibutsu during a battle between the Miyoshi and the Matsunaga in 1567. Not until Tokugawa Tsunayoshi took up that project in 1708 was the enclosure of the Nara image replaced. Hideyoshi was apparently content to let it waste while he built a grander version in Kyoto.

The third enormous project undertaken by Hideyoshi in Kyoto was the construction of a wall about the city. During five months in 1591 a huge labor force, conscripted from vassal armies, noble households, and Kyoto's temples and shrines, erected a stone and earthen rampart, the odoi. Enclosed on the east and west by the Kamo and Kamiya rivers, Kujō became its southern boundary, Takagamine its northern boundary. Where rivers did not provide natural moats, deep trenches were dug. A grove of bamboo, visible from any position in the city, was planted atop the wall to prevent erosion. Approximately 22.5 kilometers long, the odoi rose to a height of 3 meters. It was about 9 meters in width. These last two measurements are average calculations, for the wall varied considerably in shape from location to location. The waters flowing around it spread from 3.6 to 18 meters in width.

A contemporary diary by Konoe Nobutada indicates the great

speed with which the project proceeded. "From the first month of Ten-shō nineteen [1591], they have been made to dig a moat outside the city and bamboo has been planted [atop the earth dug out for the moat]. By the second month the work was more than half completed . . . There are ten openings in this wall. As for the nature of the enterprise—when a malefactor appears, a bell can quickly be sounded, the ten gates will be closed at this signal, and [the criminal] will be encircled."[65] The motive for construction cited by Nobutada is not altogether unconvincing. Certainly the *odoi* provided a barrier between this frequently belea-guered city and potential adversaries. It further sealed internal antago-nists against easy escape. It was, in this sense, an extension of the con-cept of neighborhood gates and enclosures that protected smaller areas of the city from brigands and arsonists. Nonetheless, it seems a cum-bersome and inefficient defense against the lone adventurer who might seek refuge in the streets and easily avoid detection.

If it was meant to contain or deter larger groups, even armies, the wall was little more than a weak line of resistance. It need only be compared to the higher, deeper, and labyrinthine rampart of Hideyo-shi's Osaka castle to be discounted as a major defense. The Kyoto *odoi* was sparsely reinforced by stone and could easily be scaled. Moreover, at many points the mound was quite low and guarded merely by a nar-row stream. As far as we know, no watchtowers rose from the rampart, no arsenals stood nearby, no stations were conveniently positioned to accommodate troops. The *odoi* was not, in effect, a castle wall.

There were no precedents for the *odoi* in the history of feudal for-tress towns. While the castle itself stood braced by walls, the sur-rounding town was undefended. Thus Jurakutei found conventional protection in its own stone rampart. The *odoi* was an anomalous addi-tion, unfamiliar to the medieval or *sengoku* Japanese city. It was not, however, utterly unfamiliar to Kyoto. A single prototype for the *odoi* exists: the *rajō*, an earthen wall built during the eighth century that was meant to enclose the capital in the manner of Ch'ang-an, the T'ang model for the city. Although the *rajō* may never have extended much beyond the great southern gate of Kyoto, the plan was to circle the city in emulation of leading Chinese capitals.[66] Hideyoshi's work is close in spirit to the *rajō*. He consulted Hosokawa Yūsai—a daimyo, poet, and historian of the city—regarding the original enclosure before beginning construction and apparently sought to recover something of the flavor of the old capital with his wall.[67] He was also pressing plans for the conquest of China at the time and may have wished to create monu-ments suitably impressive for the expected ambassadors from the Ming court.

* * *

One more of Hideyoshi's schemes in the capital evokes comparison with the planning of the early city. In the decade prior to 1592, most of Kyoto's downtown temples were relocated to three areas along the outskirts of town. The longest and most significant grouping occurred at the city's eastern boundary along the former Higashi Kyōgoku, newly renamed Teramachi. A 1637 map lists approximately 120 temples stretching along this avenue from Kuramaguchi in the north to an area just south of Rokujō. Records involving the move are incomplete and scattered, but most, if not all, of these temples must have been transferred under Hideyoshi's direction. Many were Nichiren sanctuaries, but certain Jishū, Jōdo, Zen, and Tendai monasteries were also moved. The Jesuit Luis Frois was on hand to describe the event: "During this year [1592] the Kampaku has accomplished a deed completely without precedent in the capital . . . He has caused all the Buddhist priests to move from their temples, and these have been relocated in a designated place within the enclosure of the wall . . . The suffering of the believers as well as the priests is great."[68]

In the north-central part of the capital Hideyoshi created a second temple complex. A number of temples had occupied the area before the *sengoku* era, leaving behind the name Tera-no-uchi. The same 1637 map indicates sixteen sanctuaries within this neighborhood, most, again, relocated by Hideyoshi. A third temple area, Shimo-teramachi, rose west of Ōmiya between Aneya-kōji and Matsubara. During the Tokugawa period about forty monastic compounds stood here. Each of these groupings was located beyond the settled parts of the city in largely unoccupied and uncultivated areas. The financial burden of the move was apparently borne entirely by the religious establishment itself.

Several reasons suggest themselves for this massive relocation. Perhaps most important, it separated churches intimately related to the communal life of the city from close contact with their congregations and consequently defused lingering aspirations among sectarians to rebel. The relocation plan was also consistent with the zoning patterns of emerging castle towns. Temples were frequently arranged along the boundaries of military settlements, partially to serve as an outer rampart against attack, partially to demonstrate control by the daimyo over local populations. Both at Osaka and Fushimi, Hideyoshi relegated temples to well-defined areas at the edges of town.[69] Finally, Hideyoshi's exclusion of religious sanctuaries from the central city was an unmistakable throwback to Heian-kyō. The wariness and antipathy to Buddhist power that had led Heian's builders to prohibit the erection of temples within its boundaries also guided Hideyoshi. With the exceptions of Tōji and Saiji, official temple compounds had been unknown in the early capital. Hideyoshi's policy of relocation was then, another gesture of return to the past.

Some further interest in zoning was apparent in Hideyoshi's treatment of the Jurakutei neighborhood. In 1591 Hideyoshi ordered the removal of commoners' homes from the area between Jurakutei and the palace in order to create a residential district for the military and the aristocracy. Most townspeople went to unsettled quarters in the Nishijin neighborhood around Sembon and Ichijō. Kajūji Harutoyo recorded the progress of the move in his diary: "Tenshō 19, first month, twenty-ninth day: [Due to] the relocation of residences within Kyoto, the townspeople are scrambling to break down their homes ... Second month, third day: In the evening, I went out to view the transfer of the houses within Kyoto. The people throughout [the area] are miserable. It is as if the streets have been burned out with the progress of an uprising."[70] The move may well have occasioned some chaos. Involved were the homes of Juraku-machi, part of the Rokuchō-machi, which had traditionally provided daily services for the court, and nine of the sixty-nine blocks constituting Tachiuri-gumi.

The removal of the commoners from the Jurakutei area and the addition of new roads that chopped up certain parts of the city has led to speculation that Hideyoshi intended to disrupt and enfeeble the neighborhood organizations that had acquired political influence in the capital. Certainly the move from Jurakutei was disruptive. Yet relatively few blocks were touched, and no attempt was made to alter the configuration of mercantile complexes north and south of Hideyoshi's castle. The move was initiated to convenience Hideyoshi and the daimyo, not to punish the townspeople.

The new street plan, far from abusing Kyoto's commoners, invited commercial development. Hideyoshi added a number of streets running north and south between Teramachi and Takakura in the east, and between Horikawa and Ōmiya in the west. Oshi-kōji was their northern terminus.[71] These additions are notable principally in their conservativeness. They did not substantially alter the grid pattern of the original city, for they replaced small alleys that had always existed between the major thoroughfares. Moreover, the new roads were built in the eastern and western margins of the city, deliberately avoiding disruption of the well-settled central area where the block associations were strongest. They appeared in thinly populated districts to break large spaces into commercially viable lots. Indeed, development proceeded rapidly. By the early years of the Tokugawa period, paintings of the capital show these areas well settled, two- and even three-story houses rising along their streets. Hideyoshi's reconstruction of the principal bridges across the Kamo River encouraged development. He replaced the simple wooden crossings at Sanjō, Gojō, and Shichijō with large and broad bridges on stone pilings, the first of their kind in the capital.[72]

A final aspect of Hideyoshi's activity in the city we have considered before. He endowed and helped to reconstruct major monasteries, principally those with aristocratic and shogunal connections. Located away from downtown Kyoto, these temples were not involved in the move to Teramachi and its counterparts. The Zen temples in the city received the most substantial help. Supplements to existing lands valued at 800 *koku* went to Nanzenji; 1,800 *koku* to Tōfukuji; 1,320 *koku* to Shōkokuji; 820 *koku* to Kenninji, for example. In addition to the sub-monasteries built by Hideyoshi and his vassals at most of these temples, basic reconstruction of the main lecture hall of Nanzenji and the Buddha hall and abbot's quarters of Kenninji proceeded with Toyotomi assistance.[73]

The Shingon temples of Tōji, Daigoji, and Rokuhara Mitsuji received lands and funds for building; 2,300 *koku* went to Tōji alone. Myōhōin and Sanjūsangendō, both Tendai temples, acquired similar help.[74] Rather curiously, the most expansive treatment was accorded the Shinshū sectarians—Nobunaga's implacable enemies at Ishiyama and adversaries of Hideyoshi on the Kii peninsula. We have already noted Hideyoshi's offer of land in Osaka to compensate for the loss of Ishiyama. Hideyoshi even attended the dedication of the new monastery in the Temma district of that city. In 1591, however, he invited the head of the Shinshū sect, Kennyo, to select a Kyoto site for his headquarters, known as Honganji. With the sole stipulation that he choose land upstream of the point where the Yodo River joins Toba, Kennyo was free to determine the location. He settled upon a southern property of three square blocks that cut substantially into the compound of Honkokuji, the chief Nichiren temple in the capital.[75] The land was an extravagant gift, more so in that it occupied a prominent position. But it also carried a cost: very close proximity to Hideyoshi and the certainty of his surveillance.

It is difficult to subsume the changes wrought in Kyoto by Hideyoshi under any single heading. His projects were so many, his interests so diverse, his impact upon the city so strong. Indeed, the Kyoto we know today is Hideyoshi's town. Three patterns of development do emerge, nonetheless, to suggest the varying intentions behind his transformation of the capital.

First, of course, Hideyoshi's efforts were directed toward restoration. He was engaged both in healing the wounds of war and in reviving, to an extent, the quality of the early city. The care bestowed upon the palace and the major temples was the business of a good custodian intent upon repairing a town rent by invasion and reduced by neglect. As Minamoto no Yoritomo had directed reconstruction after the war of 1180–1185, so Hideyoshi removed the traces of the latest and most terrible of Kyoto's battles. He assumed responsibility for the capital's monuments as part of the burden of national power. He seems additionally to have been interested in a sort of antiquarianism, in accord, perhaps, with his elevation to an ancient court post. The *odoi*, Teramachi, and the planning of streets were faithful to ninth-century prototypes. No major effort was made to bring the original capital back, but insofar as Hideyoshi shared objectives with the city's founders, he built in conformity with their models.

Further, Hideyoshi's walled fortress, his vassal enclave, and his zone of temples imparted to Kyoto the character of a castle town. All these features appeared in daimyo headquarters of the late sixteenth century, and all were symbolic of martial power.[76] Hideyoshi used Jurakutei, in particular, to signal his dominance in the city and his resolve to make Kyoto his personal capital. He employed the conventions of Azuchi to awe his men. Certainly Jurakutei was a stately mansion as well as a castle, just as Kyoto was capital of a regent as well as a lord. But in binding himself to the court, Hideyoshi did not abandon the monumental architecture associated with military glory.

Finally, Hideyoshi built to please himself and to edify his countrymen. Beyond the business of restoration and the affirmation of political primacy, he relished spectacular effects. His wall and his Buddha, whatever their other purposes, were displays of an extravagance that had less to do with politics than a bold temperament.

Conclusion

In reflecting upon the Toyotomi regime some years after Hideyoshi's death, the Portuguese Jesuit João Rodrigues wrote, as we have seen:

> [Hideyoshi] completed the subjugation of the entire country, and there was not a single part of it which did not obey him . . . The laws, administration, customs, culture, trade, wealth and magnificence were restored throughout the kingdom, and populous cities and other buildings were raised everywhere as a result of trade and peace . . . Throughout the kingdom there was a great abundance of money, new mines were opened and the kingdom was well supplied with everything.
>
> Finally they reestablished the ranks and boards of the royal household . . . The [emperor] himself was provided with adequate sustenance . . . and his palace was again renovated in a most magnificent and sumptuous manner.[77]

An old friend and one of the last men to visit Hideyoshi before he died, Rodrigues saw Hideyoshi's career as it was intended to be seen. The respect for tradition, the return to ritual, the introduction of a new splendor and prosperity, the recovery of order and justice—these were the things conveyed by Hideyoshi's conduct and properly celebrated by his sympathizers. An early Tokugawa biographer wrote in the same vein, although he was most arrested by Toyotomi displays of wealth: "Never before had such gold been seen. Even the peasants and the rustics of the time could not have too much gold and silver."[78]

Similar perceptions of the munificence and nobility of Hideyoshi's rule are suggested in his portraits and in the public memory of him as *taikō*. The throne itself served eloquent witness to Hideyoshi's achievement when Emperor Go-Yōzei elevated him as the "Most Shining God of Our Bountiful Country." So well did he perform, so carefully did he project the image of upright governor, that Hideyoshi became for many of his contemporaries what he wanted to be. Astute in self-promotion, he concealed his fear and uncertainty behind the veil of pageantry and baffled his historians no less than his sixteenth-century audience.

The deliberation of his life is as clear in his correspondence as in his deeds. In a letter to the Viceroy of the Indies in 1592 he remarks: "Our realm of more than sixty provinces has experienced for long years many days of disturbance and few days of order . . . I gravely lamented this from the time of my manhood and so gave thought and deep attention to the arts of self-cultivation and the problems of governing the country. Now I nurture the military men and show mercy to the cultivators with humanity, wisdom, and attention to defense. I have made justice correct. I have established security."[79] Hideyoshi is peacemaker, the governor who sets his country upon a firm course, the thoughtful minister who understands the rites. Evoked succinctly in this letter is the conqueror who ennobled himself and his confederates through association with the throne, the unashamed propagandist who confirmed his power through self-glorification, the man of destiny who enjoyed his destiny.

The three elements of Hideyoshi's approach to legitimation—the affirmation of traditional values, the rationalization of Toyotomi power, and the promotion of himself—raise issues of character that we have encountered before. The ambition of the man remains striking; he reached for eminent but unfamiliar roles, and so enlarged himself. He also had the assurance, perhaps the greatness of heart, to find his place among the courtiers—and the *tozama*—whom Nobunaga had despised. There is in his behavior an acceptance of the past distinction of the court, and of the present achievements of his confederates, that his status as parvenu alone cannot explain. He was able to look beyond himself for a governing settlement, and that explains much of his success. Finally, though, his excesses are disturbing. The moderation of his treatment of the daimyo hardly precluded the flamboyance of his ceremonial or of his building projects. Yet his appetite for adulation and his disposition toward too many overblown acts begin to belie the image of a fully confident and secure ruler. The portrait he pressed so successfully upon many of his contemporaries would be tarnished by wars and by murders that were subtly prefigured in his consuming passion for adulation.

8

THE LAST YEARS

HIDEYOSHI WAS fifty-four years old when Odawara castle fell and his domestic wars came to an end. Many of the men close to him were a similar age: Kobayakawa Takakage was fifty-seven, Maeda Toshiie fifty-two, Tokugawa Ieyasu forty-eight. Younger men were coming to power, of course. Katō Kiyomasa and Konishi Yukinaga, vanguards of the Korean campaign, approached thirty in 1590. One of the five magistrates, Ishida Mitsunari, had just reached that age. But the circle of leading daimyo remained largely confined to senior warriors who had helped make the peace after surviving a good part of the warring-states era. These daimyo were not yet old men by the standards of their *sengoku* peers, for those who escaped death in battle often lived long lives. Like their predecessors in houses such as the Hōjō and the Shimazu, members of Hideyoshi's coterie would pass comfortably into old age. Date Masamune would die at sixty-nine, Ukita Hideie at eighty-two, Mōri Terumoto at seventy-two, Tokugawa Ieyasu at seventy-four.[1]

Despite the reassuring signs of longevity about him, there were warnings of passage to make Hideyoshi sensitive to his years. In the two years after the siege of Odawara, he buried his first son, his stepbrother, and his mother. As his eyes and his appetite began to fail, Hideyoshi's letters turned increasingly to the problem of health.[2] And if age and gradual weakening did not of themselves mark the passage of time, the steady transformation of the world around him provided ample evidence that Hideyoshi, and his country, had gone through a sea change.

The physical symbols of that change were plentiful. The refurbished palace and the renewed ceremonial of court life eroded memories of imperial distress. The location of the Honganji headquarters in southern Kyoto signaled the pacification of the militant churches of the sixteenth century. Jurakutei commanded the capital's landscape while Ashikaga residences crumbled. As the work of construction proceeded, other and more important activities seemed to confirm the advent of peace and to quiet fears of rebellion. Hideyoshi's cadastral surveyors routinely entered once hostile domains. The collection of weapons from farming communities continued. Orderly trading ventures began to supplant piracy. And the formal investiture of the nation's daimyo with fiefs granted by the imperial regent converted the lords of the warring states into a federation of Toyotomi vassals.

As we have seen, the refinement of Hideyoshi's political settlement and the definition of his legitimacy concerned him throughout the last decade of his life. But two other, and often transcendent, interests concerned him as well. These were the preoccupations of an aging ruler: the establishment of a successor and the immortalization of his own "name and fame." In both pursuits, Hideyoshi abandoned the judicious conduct of much of his career to threaten not only his reputation but his government. He immortalized himself, to be sure, yet as a vainglorious despot. The expedition to Korea, designed to inspire awe throughout Asia and to fix Hideyoshi's greatness for posterity, ended in humiliation. The elevation of his young son as the Toyotomi heir was accompanied by mass executions that suggest a loss of control, perhaps of sanity.

Each of these events invites inquiry into Hideyoshi's character and the deeper motivations underlying his political decisions. In a sense, his last actions were provoked by unique crises. They also seem to indicate, however, a steady disposition that changed less in substance than in manifestation. Hideyoshi's ambition was never free of arrogance, his pride always linked to vanity, and his power ever vulnerable to corruption.

The Invasion of Korea

Years before Japanese warships set sail for Korea, Hideyoshi made his interest in foreign expansion clear. We have noted the letter to his wife, sent after the conquest of Kyushu, revealing his concern with the continent: "By fast ships I have dispatched [orders] to Korea to serve the throne of Japan. Should [Korea] fail to serve [our throne], I have dispatched [the message] by fast ships that I will punish [that country] next year. Even China will enter my grip; I will command it during my lifetime."[3] Somewhat earlier, in 1586, he made a terse announcement to Mōri Terumoto: "I shall extend my conquest to China." The best-known report of Hideyoshi's ambitions comes from Luis Frois. He recounts a conversation held at Osaka castle during the same year.

> He also said that he had reached the point of subjugating all Japan; whence his mind was not set upon the future acquisition of more kingdoms or more wealth in it, since he had enough, but solely upon immortalizing himself with the name and fame of his power; in order to do which he was resolved to reduce the affairs of Japan to order, and to place them on a stable basis;

and, this done, to entrust them to his brother Minodono [Hidenaga], while he himself should pass to the conquest of Korea and China . . . And if he met his death in that undertaking he did not mind, inasmuch as it would be said that he was the first Lord of Japan who had ventured on such an enterprise.[4]

Similar allusions to expansion recur throughout his correspondence, even as the domestic wars continued, and overtures to the Koreans began in earnest during 1587.

At that time Hideyoshi ordered Sō Yoshishige, daimyo of Tsushima, to demand tribute and hostages from the Korean court. When the Sō envoy returned with a rebuff, he was accused of complicity with the Koreans and executed. A second mission from the Sō house crossed to the peninsula in 1588 with a more insistent message. The Korean king countered with his own ultimatum: no official relations between the two nations could be resumed until Korean collaborators of Japanese pirates were returned for punishment. Despite his peremptory demands, Hideyoshi delivered over 160 Korean sailors to their homeland. Hence two Korean ambassadors arrived at Jurakutei in the eleventh month of 1590 to pay their compliments and congratulate Hideyoshi upon his military success.[5]

Just back from his campaign in Mutsu and Dewa, Hideyoshi received the visitors with what Korean accounts describe as considerable informality and some disdain. There may well have been a certain chilliness, for the envoys represented no tributary but a friendly neighbor ready to announce good wishes to a peer. Before their departure, Hideyoshi prepared a message for the Korean king.

> My object is to enter China, to spread the customs of our country to the four hundred and more provinces of that nation, and to establish there the government of our imperial city even unto all the ages. As your country has taken the lead and visited Japan, thus displaying deference, you need have no anxiety . . . On the day I enter China, I shall be leading my soldiers and shall review my military headquarters; then we shall renew our alliance. My wish is nothing other than that my name be known throughout the three countries [of Japan, China, and India].[6]

The letter characteristically blends intimidation with assurance. Hideyoshi identifies China as his target and chooses to assume that Korea—both ally and vassal of Japan—will ease his progress. Not surprisingly, the Koreans made no response. Two more missions by the Sō, in the third and sixth months of 1591, failed to secure consent to Hideyoshi's implicit demand for safe passage through the peninsula to China. In the seventh month of 1591, then, Hideyoshi began preparations for the war with Korea. In the ninth month he ordered his daimyo to mass troops. And in the tenth month he commanded Katō Kiyomasa to initiate work on a castle in northwest Kyushu—in Nagoya of Hizen province—from which the attack could be launched. Hideyoshi described the campaign not as an offensive against Korea but as the entry to China (*Kara iri*).[7]

The troop levies that followed the declaration of war are exceptional proof of Hideyoshi's command of the country. He mobilized his men as efficiently for the foreign invasion as for domestic battles. Thirty-two daimyo raised as many as 158,700 soldiers, divided into nine brigades, for the main attack; four daimyo commanded a navy of approximately 9,200 sailors; other daimyo brought more than 100,000 troops to Nagoya to serve as a back-up force.[8] Neither resistance to Hideyoshi's call for soldiers nor significant disturbance in the domains left under deputy rule while their lords departed for Kyushu gave evidence of discord and political instability.

The conduct of the "entry to China" is well known and requires little comment. The first and more important phase of the campaign lasted about a year. It began in the fourth month of 1592 when Konishi Yukinaga's army took Pusan (map 3). Within three weeks Konishi had reached Seoul, where he was joined by other Japanese brigades. They surveyed a city deserted by its king and burned and looted by native troops who had abandoned their capital before the invaders' arrival. The generally effortless progress of Hideyoshi's men sent the stunned Koreans into retreat.[9]

The initial reaction of the Koreans might have been foreseen. With no recent experience of warfare, unequipped with firearms, and lacking a reliable conscription system, the Koreans were powerless before their war-seasoned neighbors. There is some suggestion, too, that the various interlocutors of the Sō house had neglected to portray accurately the intentions of Hideyoshi. Ever placatory because of the proximity and trading importance of Korea, the Tsushima envoys may have cut the edge from the imperious messages they were charged to deliver and thus encouraged the complacency of the Korean court.[10]

Hideyoshi's elation at the success of his troops was not dampened by apprehensions over a second and stronger Korean reaction. He allocated administrative responsibility for the eight Korean circuits to his brigade commanders, ordered Ukita Hideie to govern Seoul and to prepare for his arrival, and then began to broadcast victory. On the sixth day of the fifth month he wrote to his mother: "I shall take China about the ninth month, and I shall receive [your gift of] formal clothing for the festival of the ninth month in the Chinese capital ... Having taken China, I shall dispatch an envoy to meet you."[11] He wrote in a similar vein to his wife. But it is in a long communication to his nephew that Hideyoshi made his most daring projections. Sent from

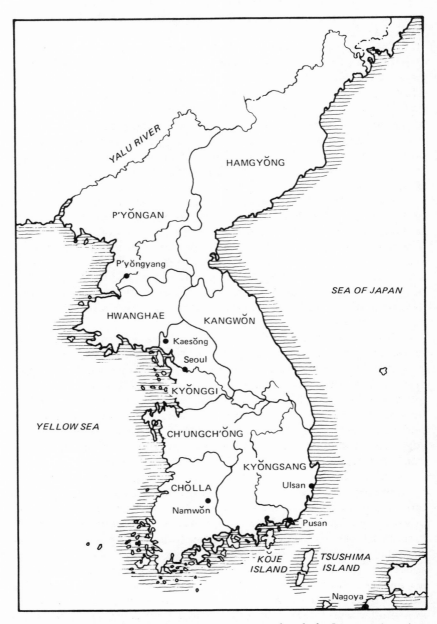

Map 3. The provinces of Korea and sites associated with the Japanese invasions

Nagoya on the sixteenth day of the fifth month, 1592, the document takes the conquest of Korea for granted and proceeds to discuss ceremonial and administrative matters pertinent to the submission of China. The last seven items are the most interesting.

Item: Our sovereign shall move to the Ming capital, and there should be proper arrangements for this. The imperial progress (*gyōkō*) will occur during the year after next. Accordingly, we shall present the emperor with ten provinces around the Ming capital. All courtiers should be awarded fiefs within this holding . . .

Item: The regent (*kampaku*) of China shall, as we have mentioned, be Hidetsugu. One hundred provinces around the capital shall be transferred to him. The regent of Japan shall be either the Yamato Chūnagon [Toyotomi Hideyasu] or the Bizen Saishō [Ukita Hideie], in accord with their readiness.

Item: The throne of Japan shall be occupied by either the young prince or Prince Hachijō.

Item: Korea shall be in the charge of either the Gifu Saishō [Hashiba Hidekatsu] or the Bizen Saishō. Accordingly, the Tamba Chūnagon [Kobayakawa Hideaki] shall be assigned to Kyushu.

Item: When the emperor goes to China, the ceremonies should [conform to] the proper *gyōkō* form. Places for his lodging shall be prepared along the route of the current campaign. Men and horses [for the purpose] shall be called from the countries through which the emperor passes.

Item: Korea and China will be taken without trouble. As there will not be the slightest disturbance to either high or low, and as there should not be any flight by the lowly, recall the magistrates from the provinces and order preparations for the [continuing] campaign.

Item: I shall make an announcement concerning the deputy of Heian and Jurakutei in the future.[12]

Hideyoshi's expedition to Korea is one of those subjects in Japanese history that has provoked divergent but equally passionate interpretations in different periods. Certain Meiji commentators, for example, found it inevitable, even laudatory, and concentrated upon its heroic aspects; historians writing since World War II have returned to the critical tone of Tokugawa scholars. Beyond moral judgment, disagreements over Hideyoshi's motives have occurred as well. The early nineteenth-century scholar Rai San'yō saw the Korean war as a military exercise—an opportunity to employ a vast army unneeded at home and to expand the reward bank for men whose loyalty was a function of returns in land. Other writers argue that the invasion was designed to force Japan's neighbors into the regular, direct trading relationships that Korea and China had renounced. Hideyoshi's decision to control Japanese ports, his initiation of the red-seal ship system, the emphasis on trade in his eventual peace proposals—all suggest his interest in economic ventures abroad.[13]

These explanations of the expedition tend to disregard, however, the message to Hidetsugu and the other correspondence. Hideyoshi did develop strong interests in trade; he did test fealty on the battleground. Yet if his letters are to be believed—and it is difficult to dismiss their consistent strain of glory—he was also reaching for an empire. Personal fame was at stake, and control of China was a part of his plans. And Hideyoshi did not confine his aspirations to the continent. In the second month of 1590 he sent a member of the Shimazu house to the Ryukyu court with gifts and a letter acknowledging the recent receipt of tribute from the island kingdom. "Throughout our nation of more than sixty provinces, I have pacified all people and governed with mercy and affection. Everything—excepting no foot or inch of land—has entered my grasp . . . Consequently, it is [now] my basic desire to spread my administration to other regions . . . Henceforth, even if a land be thousands of miles distant, I shall deeply achieve amity and so build with foreign lands the spirit of the four seas as one family."[14] The document was dispatched to confirm Hideyoshi's dominion over the Ryukyus—a position he exploited by raising troops and supplies there for the Korean campaign—but is interesting primarily because of its intimations of expansion. Just over a year later, in the seventh month of 1591, Hideyoshi wrote in the same fashion to the Viceroy of the Indies. "My country is already secure. Nonetheless, it is my intention to govern China. To sail in my tower-ship for a few days and reach the Middle Kingdom will be as easily done as pointing to the palm of my hand."[15]

He strikes a still bolder note in a letter sent to Manila in the ninth month of the year: "The Ryukyus, [other] distant countries, and foreign regions have submitted and I have received them. Now I desire to subjugate China . . . As I shall be in Hizen province of Kyushu next spring directing [the invasion], and shall not move for some time, you should bear the banner of surrender and come to submit [to me there]. If, creeping and crawling along, there is any delay [in your arrival], it will be necessary promptly to attack [your country]."[16] A demand for tribute from Taiwan made in the eleventh month of 1593 includes an announcement already familiar to us: "At the time my mother conceived me, she had an auspicious dream. That night, a ray of the sun filled the room as if it were noontime. All were overcome with astonishment and fright and when the diviners had gathered, they interpreted the event, saying: when he reaches the prime of life, his virtue will illumine the four seas, his authority shall emanate to the myriad peoples."[17]

Hideyoshi's declarations do not always mean what they say. From the Ryukyus he wanted an amicable relationship with overtones of Japanese suzerainty. There is no evidence that Hideyoshi intended to extend his administration to that chain of islands through cadastral surveys or local enfeoffment. What deference he desired from Taiwan, including such tokens of vassalage as tribute and hostages, he was not prepared to elicit with anything more than threatening letters. The bombast directed to the Philippines had a variety of objectives: stimulation of economic ties, warning to Europeans with religious designs upon Japan, discouragement of Spanish intrusion in Japanese politics.[18]

Yet even as saber rattling, the letters are unique in Japanese history and nearly unparalleled elsewhere. The ambitions Hideyoshi describes are boundless, and his need to command foreign homage—through letters grandiloquent to the point of comedy—troubling. It is true that his experiences gave some foundation to his aspirations: he had unified his own country, commanded one of the greatest armies in Asia, participated in trade that was linking the Pacific nations more closely, and observed the first phase of European colonialism. Such developments conspired to encourage Hideyoshi's pretensions to empire, pretensions that the Spaniards in the Philippines, at least, took seriously.[19]

It is also true, however, that Hideyoshi lacked the resources to make his goals remotely feasible. He knew little in detail about continental geography, had a small fleet inexperienced in combat and unsupported by adequate numbers of able navigators and builders, and he led unenthusiastic vassals.[20] Daimyo such as the Tokugawa and Maeda remained neutral about the Korean campaign from its inception. They discouraged Hideyoshi from crossing to the peninsula himself, pressed moderate peace terms upon him, and withdrew quickly from Korea after Hideyoshi's death.[21]

Thus while it is helpful to put Hideyoshi's correspondence and his invasion of Korea into the unusual context of the times, it is necessary to return to Luis Frois for their meaning. The individual architect of a foreign campaign dictated by no urgent incentives, Hideyoshi was interested in "immortalizing himself with the name and fame of his power," in being "the first Lord of Japan who had ventured on such an enterprise."

For a time after the occupation of Seoul by his troops in the fifth month of 1592, the confidence of Hideyoshi's letter to Hidetsugu seemed justified. By the seventh month his daimyo had advanced from Kaesŏng to P'yŏngyang to the Yalu River. But also around this time, the counteroffensive began to form. The Korean admiral Yi Sun-sin decimated the Japanese navy and stalled the transfer of fresh troops and supplies for the Toyotomi brigades. Korean guerrillas burned crops to deny food to the invaders and preyed upon daimyo camps. Finally, Chinese soldiers crossed the Yalu to push the Japanese force south of P'yŏngyang. Following a fifty-day armistice in the autumn of 1592, a continental army estimated at 40,000 men moved into the vicinity of Seoul in the first month of 1593.[22]

While Ukita Hideie and Konishi Yukinaga encouraged a policy of defense and negotiation, Katō Kiyomasa and others—taking the lead of Hideyoshi's forceful commands from Nagoya—tried to retain the offensive. By the fifth month of 1593, however, negotiation appeared the only alternative to a slow defeat. After the Chinese agreed to dispatch three ambassadors to Nagoya, most of Hideyoshi's men came home. Konishi built a string of fortifications along the coast of Kyŏngsang to maintain a Japanese presence on the peninsula, but for most purposes Hideyoshi's first Korean war had come to an end by the seventh month of 1593.[23] Before departure, Hideyoshi's daimyo left the Chinese with Hideyoshi's seven stipulations for peace.

Item [1]: As we pledge that, without violation, there shall be no transgression throughout the realm, the daughter of the Ming emperor shall be given as consort to the emperor of Japan.

Item [2]: Licensed trade will be arranged.

Item [3]: The ministers of China and Japan will exchange oaths [of peace].

Item [4]: In regard to Korea, the previous dispatch of many [of our troops there], and our disposition of all [local affairs]: we sent many men and ordered [affairs] in order to achieve peace for the farmers and other peoples throughout the years and months. As the articles [of peace] proclaimed to China are now settled, the king of Korea—although he has not been submissive to us—shall be entrusted to China; further, since on one previous occasion the king offered his respects [to us], the capital of Korea and the four [northern] provinces will be given over to him.

Item [5]: Insofar as these provinces will be released, a prince and several accompanying elders shall be presented [to us] as hostages.

Item [6]: The two princes taken alive by us previously, as they are not lowly men, were received by our four men without harm or molestation; we shall now give them over to Shen Wei-ching and return them to Korea.

Item [7]: The elders of Korea shall swear eternally that there will be no violation [of the peace].[24]

There is a certain moderation in these peace proposals. Abandoning the rhetoric of the letter to Hidetsugu, Hideyoshi makes no mention of an "entry to China" or a Japanese administration there. He now portrays the Chinese as partners of a sort, both in trade and in the governance of Korea, where he outlines dual spheres of influence. And he is eager to confirm a fraternity of interest by arranging an imperial marriage between two courts. Hideyoshi is negotiating with the emperor of China in the same manner he had negotiated with rival daimyo. As he had moved Tokugawa Ieyasu to peace by threatening a war of attrition, so he lays claim to four Korean provinces and leaves a brigade in the south to demonstrate the tenacity of Japanese interests in the peninsula. As he had taken hostages from Ieyasu and confirmed Ieyasu's holdings, so he offers to share Korean jurisdiction with the Chinese in exchange for ample assurances of goodwill. Hideyoshi acknowledges no difference between the sovereignty of states and the hegemony of a provincial daimyo; he approaches international diplomacy from the vantage of *sengoku* arbitration.

Yet in any but the most generous terms, of course, these proposals were not moderate. The call for royal hostages and a partitioning of Korea was outrageous, particularly from an outmaneuvered invader. Designed to conceal the reality of retreat, at least from Hideyoshi himself, the proposals took on the tone of the jubilant letters to his family that had exalted the victories and ignored the defeats of the Toyotomi forces. Throughout the waning months of the expedition he promised his correspondents that he would sail victoriously to Korea were it not for rough seas or entreaties from the emperor or, finally, the death of his mother. He seized upon her last illness to leave Nagoya for several months in the latter part of 1592 and let personal grief disguise a national tragedy.[25]

Hideyoshi's conviction—repeatedly expressed in his later correspondence—that achievements at home were harbingers of greater glory recall the ambition conveyed in his earliest letters after Nobunaga's death. His rapid fulfillment of the promise to create a government superior to anything since Yoritomo converted bravado into prophecy. The outcome of his determination that even China would enter his grip revealed a confidence that had become hubris. It is well to consider, however, that the same daring inspired both the war with Shibata Katsuie and the war with the Koreans. Hideyoshi rose to power not because he was called to it by peers or optimal circumstances, but because he was talented and driven enough to act on his own vision of the possible. In neither his domestic nor his foreign encounters was a wise accounting of events notably more important than the will to succeed. What we perceive as shrewdness in one circumstance we may see as megalomania in the other, while acknowledging in both the ambition that has led the rare individual to goals much beyond normal reckoning.

The pursuit of homage was also common to both Hideyoshi's foreign and domestic politics. He was clearly less interested in military dominion abroad than in fame. Conquest became the vehicle of fame, to be sure, but Luis Frois probably read Hideyoshi's intentions correctly when he remarked that: "If he succeeded, and the Chinese rendered obedience to him, he would not deprive them of their country, or remain in it himself . . . because he only wished them to recognize him for their lord."[26] Hideyoshi said much the same thing in his letter to the Korean king: "My wish is nothing other than that my name be known throughout the three countries." The communications dispatched throughout Asia—which were not followed by military action and which, if they were serious, only undercut his purpose by giving ample warning of invasion—suggested again that Hideyoshi wanted homage rather than control.

A similar search for acclamation from the *tozama* daimyo had made Hideyoshi gracious in alliance, fair to those who honored him, and sensible of his peacetime responsibilities. Yet once defeat in Korea had robbed him not so much of political gains, which were never paramount, but of his pride, Hideyoshi seemed beyond temperate reaction. Incapable of judicious retreat because he had put a premium on his honor rather than on defensible goals that could survive assault, Hideyoshi salvaged his self-respect with peace proposals that twisted reality. There can be little doubt that those proposals, and his letter to Hidetsugu, display a warped judgment. While the steady progress of conquest and alliance in Japan had encouraged conciliation, defeat abroad—really Hideyoshi's first defeat—drove him to apparent self-deceit. Graceful in victory, he flouted the consequences of a foolish invasion.

Hideyoshi's behavior suggests that he had few of the leveling virtues to halt excess, little of an unassailable self-esteem to protect him against vainglory. His strengths were corrupted in the pursuit of empire. Those who find madness in his foreign expedition—and certainly his documents have a crazed intensity—overlook the sustained sense of a limitless destiny which made him both a good general and an unprincipled invader. Corruption is not madness.

As long as defeat was clouded by flattering terms of peace, Hideyoshi was able to tolerate long and inconclusive negotiations. The Chinese ambassadors who traveled to Nagoya for a settlement returned to the continent with Hideyoshi's terms to continue discussions there with Naitō Joan, a vassal of Konishi Yukinaga. Not until the end of

1596, more than three years after the first Korean campaign was concluded, would a Chinese delegation return to Japan with a response. Doubtless aware of Chinese incredulity over his proposals and of Yukinaga's efforts to reach a milder accommodation, Hideyoshi waited. There is little reason to believe that he was displeased by the absence of a resolution. Ambiguity was preferable to an unbecoming settlement. By the close of 1593, in any case, Hideyoshi's energies and interests were elsewhere. The preoccupations of a distant campaign were dismissed when Hideyoshi turned to the problem of the future of his house.

Succession

Hideyoshi was not fortunate in his heirs. During the last decade of his life he coped with crises of succession that were far more important to the fate of Toyotomi rule than the conduct of the foreign campaign. Some have even suggested that the invasion was a diversion for an aging Hideyoshi, pessimistic over the transfer of power and the future of his family, who sought a final and irrevocable distinction abroad.[27] If this view inclines toward the romantic, it is nonetheless true that peace negotiations were allowed to lag and thoughts of new engagements eclipsed when succession again became an urgent matter at the time of Hideyori's birth in the eighth month of 1593. Until Hideyoshi's own death five years later, his concerns would revolve primarily around his son.

Hideyori was Hideyoshi's second and last child. Both he and his brother, Tsurumatsu, were born to Hideyoshi's principal concubine, Chacha.[28] Her more familiar names, Yodo-dono and Yodo-gimi, are taken from the castle on the Yodo River that she received from Hideyoshi during her first pregnancy. Regularly a companion to Hideyoshi in his campsites and tenderly addressed in a long series of letters, Yodo-dono had been a favorite in Hideyoshi's entourage since she entered it, still an adolescent, after a tumultuous childhood. She was the daughter of Oda Nobunaga's sister, Oichi, and Asai Nagamasa. When Nobunaga destroyed the Asai, Chacha moved with her mother and her two sisters first to Nobunaga's castle at Kiyosu and later to Echizen, upon the marriage of Oichi and Shibata Katsuie. Hideyoshi recovered the three girls in 1583, following the suicides of Oichi and Katsuie, while Toyotomi troops stormed their fortress. He arranged the marriage of one of the sisters to Tokugawa Ieyasu's heir, and of a second to Kyōgoku Takatsugu.

Chacha he kept as one of his *sokushitsu*, his "side chambers." The mother of his only children, she acquired sufficient influence to attract, and possibly to manipulate, ambitious men seeking Hideyoshi's attention. Allusions in his correspondence to factions among his intimates, as well as Yodo-dono's volatile defense of Hideyori's succession claims after Hideyoshi's death, have given substance to legends representing her as a canny conspirator who learned how to protect her own interests. Hideyoshi's failure to produce offspring other than her two sons, despite the existence of numerous concubines, and his advanced age at the time of Hideyori's birth, have encouraged the inquiry into Chacha's enterprise.

Hideyoshi's first son and heir, Tsurumatsu, was born to Yodo-dono in 1589 but died in the eighth month of 1591. Decisions on succession were complicated by the death, during the same year, of Hideyoshi's younger stepbrother Hidenaga. Hidenaga had been a leader in all the Toyotomi campaigns, a counselor to his brother, a guardian of Tsurumatsu, and, at one time, a likely heir himself.[29] After Hidenaga's interment, Hideyoshi settled upon his eldest nephew—the son of his sister and Miyoshi Yoshifusa—as successor. He transferred the title of *kampaku* to the twenty-three-year-old Hidetsugu in the twelfth month of 1591 and established him at Jurakutei. Hideyoshi then assumed the title *taikō*. Signs of unease over his decision persisted, however. He continued to assess the talents of his two younger nephews and wrote of an adopted daughter, one of Maeda Toshiie's children, that "were she a man, I would make her *kampaku*."[30] Hidetsugu's position was most gravely threatened, of course, by the successful delivery of Yodo's second son.

Once he learned of Hideyori's birth at Osaka castle, Hideyoshi returned promptly from his Kyushu headquarters to greet the child and to celebrate the event with banquets and nō presentations at the imperial palace. He was seldom very far from his son thereafter, and when separations occurred he dispatched entreaties to Yodo-dono and others to watch constantly against hazards. "While recently I have been far away, I have known only a longing [for home]. I cannot describe the endless tedium, as if I were guarding an empty house, when Hideyori is not here with me. I say again, strictly order that all be vigilant against fire. Each night have someone make the rounds of the rooms two or three times. Do not be negligent in this."[31] He asked repeatedly about Hideyori's health and his appetite. He presented him to visitors, showered him with gifts. He also sent letters directly to the child: "You have assembled a linen kimono (*katabira*) and other garments (*dōfuku*) [for me] for the festival. This is most propitious. I shall wear them, praying that you will live a long life. I shall certainly come [to you] at the time of the festival and I shall kiss you [then]. For such an auspicious occasion, I shall come without fail."[32]

Despite Hideyoshi's pleasure in Hideyori, he continued to treat

Hidetsugu with a certain deference. Hidetsugu was included in the great pilgrimage to Mount Kōya in 1594 when Hideyoshi dedicated his mother's mortuary temple. And he was left secure at Jurakutei where he maintained an active ceremonial life as *kampaku*.[33] In the seventh month of 1595, however, almost two years after Hideyori's birth, Hidetsugu was abruptly ordered into exile at Mount Kōya, where he received a command to take his own life. Some of his retainers died with him, and others—Hidetsugu's chief vassals—were compelled to commit suicide shortly thereafter. The Jesuit Luis Frois continues the story:

> It mighte seame that the rigour, furye, and indignation of [Hideyoshi] were alreadei come to [their] full periode, and heighte of crueltie [with the death of Hidetsugu], but so far was he transported with an unsatiable, and devilishe mynde of destroienge, and rootinge upp of all those that anie wayes had belonged unto Hidetsugu that his butcherlie crueltie surpassed all the bowndes of Tirannie. for his purpose was to destroye the woemen, wyves and children of all those that he had alreadie murthered ... and to the ende that there deathe mighte be more infamous, and dishonorable, he commanded them to be drawen throughe all the cheife streates of [the capital] in cartes, and so to be ledde to the publicke place of execution, where malefactours were put to deathe ... When then the bloudie and black daye came that [Hideyoshi's] commandment must be exequuted, there were drawen alonge in the streates in cartes to the open view of the world 31 Ladies and gentlewoemen, with the two sonnes and one daughter of [Hidetsugu] the eldest of whiche was not above five yeares olde. how greivous a spectacle this was unto the beholders eyes everie man maie imagyne. nothinge was there hard but sighinges, and groanes, able to have mooved not onlie men but stoanes into compassion and mercie, and suche as pearced the verie bowels of the most barbarous beholders ...
>
> When the cartes were come to the place of exequution, behold there a hangman ... [Hidetsugu's] thre children were first murthered, and then all the other Ladies in ranke one after an other were taken out of the carte; and ... theire owne headdes were stricken of.
>
> All theire boddies by order from [Hideyoshi] were throwne into a pitte, made for the nonce, over the whiche he caused to be buylded a little Chappell with a Tombe in it with this inscription: The Tombe of the Traitors.[34]

Although this is the most vivid account of the executions, it is substantially corroborated by the Tamon'in diarist and contemporary observers. Ōta Gyūichi's *Taikō gunki* confirms that Hidetsugu's head was on display throughout the proceedings. In the following weeks Hideyoshi had the castle of Jurakutei leveled and elicited from his major vassals an oath of loyalty to Hideyori, who, needless to say, became his sole heir.[35]

Hideyoshi's documents do not shed much light on his attitude toward his nephew. We know that Hidetsugu, sixteen at the time, participated in Hideyoshi's offensive against Tokugawa Ieyasu in 1584 and took charge of the Toyotomi complement at the battle of Nagakute in Mikawa where the Tokugawa won a decisive victory. Hideyoshi made a slighting reference to Hidetsugu's survival of this encounter in a letter to the mother of an important general who died at Nagakute. He also dispatched an excoriating criticism directly to his nephew after the defeat which threatened his life as well as his inheritance.[36]

Despite the Nagakute debacle, Hideyoshi advanced his nephew in succeeding years. Hidetsugu was enfeoffed in Ōmi and later in Owari, where he took command of the Tōkaidō. He participated with distinction in the Shikoku and Kantō campaigns. And finally he was named the Toyotomi heir. But beyond an oath of loyalty that Hideyoshi had his nephew sign, and the announcement of plans for the administration of China which we have already seen, we know of few exchanges between the two men after Hidetsugu's appointment as *kampaku*. That oath deserves brief consideration:

> Item: Although the provinces are at peace, I will be prudent with regard to martial affairs—weapons and provisions—without any negligence. Should there be a deployment of troops, I will make provisions and be in readiness for a long campaign in accord with Hideyoshi's orders.
>
> Item: I will strictly proclaim the law. Should there be the slightest violation [of it], I will conduct a searching examination without prejudice or partiality . . .
>
> Item: I will act faithfully toward the court and render service to it . . .
>
> Item: I will not follow Hideyoshi's example in the tea ceremony, in hawking, or in the courtship of women . . .[37]

It was not so odd, perhaps, to exact such conditions of an heir, although suspicion ripples on the surface of the words. Yet with its assertion of Hidetsugu's subordination to his uncle, the oath becomes one more indication that Hidetsugu enjoyed no real authority or independence during his tenure as regent. Land documents and most other forms of official communication continued to appear with Hideyoshi's seal. The Korean expedition was solely under his command. City and *kenchi* magistrates received appointment from the *taikō*. Hidetsugu was not his own man.[38]

If Hideyoshi's record is too limited to allow a neat untangling of his emotions toward Hidetsugu, other sources are somewhat more helpful in explaining the intercourse between the two men after Hideyori's birth. They describe a predictable tale of collision. The Tokitsugu diary suggests that Hideyoshi proposed a division in national jurisdiction between Hidetsugu and Hideyori. The Komai diary reports that Hideyoshi pressed Hidetsugu to marry his daughter to Hideyori, to adopt Hideyori then as his own heir, and subsequently to transfer the title of *kampaku* to him.[39] These and similar allusions to negotiations designed to guarantee Hideyori a place of prominence or even superiority in Hidetsugu's regime help explain certain defensive acts on Hidetsugu's part that his uncle chose to perceive as treacherous.

Two popular, and often sensational, accounts of these events—the *Taikō gunki* and Oze Hoan's *Taikō-ki*—note that Hidetsugu increased his personal guard and sought oaths of allegiance to himself from a number of powerful daimyo following Hideyori's birth. Frois, too, comments upon Hidetsugu's attempts to secure his place. Such acts apparently provoked Hideyoshi's suspicions.[40] Shortly before Hidetsugu was sent under guard to Mount Kōya, he was interrogated by the five *bugyō* and forced to justify the expansion of his guard and his subversive overtures to daimyo allies. These imputations of disloyalty became the grounds of Hidetsugu's death sentence.[41]

Beyond his real or contrived doubts about Hidetsugu's fidelity, Hideyoshi had reason to suspect that his nephew had a vicious character. Although Hidetsugu is often described as a learned man by the standards of his day—he wrote acceptable poetry and studied the classics—the *Taikō gunki* has this to say about him: "In order to practice with his muskets, he would go to the Kitano area where, having spied farmers in their fields, he would shoot them. Once, practicing archery . . . he summoned a passing traveler and slew him."[42] Frois corroborates the allegations in lurid detail:

> He was so bent, and inclined to shedd mennes bloode that he mighte well be thoughte to have sucked that brutishe minde together with his mothers milke. and in this he was so well inured that one of his cheifest delightes was to see poore men slaine and cruellie butchered: wherfor dailie at an accustomes houre, for his pastime, and recreation, he played the parte of an executioner, in killinge, and muthering condemned persons . . . he tooke exceedinge delighte to cutt them in peices with suche dexteritie, as yf they had bene but little birdes. otherwhiles he wold have them for a iyvelie marke to ayme at, either with darte or gunne: sometymes like unto a yonge Nero he opened and ripped upp woemen to see their entrailes and place of conception.[43]

Hidetsugu's end may well have been brought on by an unstable character, a resistance to compromise over Hideyori's claims, and Hideyoshi's preference—and growing affection—for his own child. But we have no account of that end from Hidetsugu himself, from Hideyoshi, or from their intimates to help sort out the emotions at work. The interesting point is that Hideyoshi chose to keep veiled the troubling events of his late life. His private letters, although continuing in a warm-hearted vein until his death, abandon political subjects by 1593. Hideyoshi's once digressive official correspondence grows thinner and thinner as he moves into the 1590s. And his personally commissioned biography, the *Tenshō-ki*, concludes with the year 1592, thus avoiding discussion of both the uncertain course of the Korean engagement and the Hidetsugu episode.

Perhaps Hideyoshi recoiled against discussion of the unhappy events in his life. The absence of a chronicle for his last years and the absence, too, of a revealing correspondence after 1593 may certainly be the result of many factors, including the ravages of time. But Hideyoshi's decision to begin his biography only with the Tenshō period, when his great successes occurred, and the omission of dark strains in all of his communications suggest that Hideyoshi was a censorial historian, or at least a selective one, and that failure moved him to silence.

While the emotional dimensions of the Hidetsugu affair are difficult to explore, the principal motivation for the execution is not so elusive. Hideyoshi may have distrusted his nephew and cherished his son, but Hidetsugu was surely destroyed, in the last instance and regardless of personal attachments, to protect the logical transfer of authority. Hideyoshi had witnessed enough fratricide and patricide in *sengoku* society to acquaint him with the dangers of unclear or contested succession arrangements. Quarrels between heirs were endemic, ferocious, and the cause of the destruction of major and minor families alike. Hideyoshi knew his own rise to be predicated upon succession problems within the Oda establishment following the simultaneous elimination of Nobunaga and his first son. Persuaded that any negotiated settlement between Hidetsugu and Hideyori would splinter upon his own death or would move other pretenders to a challenge, Hideyoshi annihilated Hidetsugu in so dramatic a fashion as to burn his will into the contemporary consciousness.

It is certainly possible to regard Hideyoshi's elevation of his young son as a foolish act, though not as an irrational one. Hideyoshi promoted Hideyori not because he felt the promotion to be without its hazards—the pathos of his deathbed appeals for devotion to Hideyori are evidence enough of his distress—but because he felt that promotion to be unavoidable. A divided house was a more fearful prospect than a house governed by a minor. Hideyori, buffered by powerful *tozama* with interests sufficiently competitive to frustrate a coalition among them against the heir, appeared to Hideyoshi a more welcome successor than the uneasy and possibly dangerous Hidetsugu.

For all his concern with imperial sanction, Hideyoshi continued to place trust in the bonds of fealty. He assumed that power would pass to the hereditary head of his house, that power was bestowed by, and exercised through, the relationship between lord and vassal, and that essentially private contracts—ideally durable through generations—formed the basis of government. Court appointment could reinforce, never bestow, the authority of lordship. Confusion over the transfer of that authority consequently threatened the entire polity. The urgency of controversies over succession has often moved men to extraordinary behavior, and Hideyoshi finds company with many others in the anguish, as well as the bizarre resolutions, attending the troubled transfer of power.

The savage execution of Hidetsugu's women and family members, however, remains beyond the limits of rational political conduct. It is well to remember the brutality of warring-states society: the defeat of vanquished daimyo was often finalized by the elimination of major vassals and descendants. It is also well to remember the desperation of Hideyoshi's position. He was almost sixty in 1595 and unwell. Although the elimination of a rival heir clarified the succession, it carried little of the force of the execution of an entire household in public. That deed left no doubt about the strength of Hideyoshi's will or his determination to enforce it. Much more was at stake for an aging Hideyoshi with a child heir in 1595 than had been at stake earlier, when he could afford mercy to the Shimazu or the Chōsokabe. But the margin had narrowed in his late life.

The family executions were such a departure from Hideyoshi's customarily temperate pattern of behavior, though, that they require further explanation. Death sentences were unusual in his regime, and such public shows of cruelty were largely unknown. Two other brutal deeds accomplished after 1590 deserve consideration before we assess the motivation behind the murder of Hidetsugu's intimates.

The Rikyū Affair and the Crucifixion of the Christians

The condemnation of the tea master Sen no Rikyū is interesting because of Rikyū's artistic eminence and intimacy with Hideyoshi, the sensational nature of his death, and the widespread speculation of contemporaries over the reasons for his fate. Suitable provocation has never been uncovered.

Sen no Rikyū is best known as the master who codified the rubrics of the tea ceremony and defined a training schedule for serious practitioners of the art. As a connoisseur and designer of tea implements and tea houses, he also had a decisive influence upon the aesthetics of the ceremony. Reacting against the gilded tradition of his society, he effected a revolution in taste. Rikyū's tea rooms were made of reeds and plaster; his vessels of wood, bamboo, and clay.[44]

The tea ceremony absorbed the military community and became its most common, and competitive, form of entertainment. An occasion to display personal cultivation, beautiful wares, good gardens, and artful tea houses, the tea service became the measure of the gentleman. Nobunaga's interest in the art led him to call distinguished masters into his service at high stipends, and Hideyoshi too employed teachers—eight of them, including Rikyū—to preside over his constant parties. Sen no Rikyū performed ceremonies at the imperial court for Hideyoshi, designed his tea houses, and purchased his vessels. He was sufficiently important to require a residence within the walls of Jurakutei.[45]

Rikyū may also have become an important advisor to Hideyoshi. Ōtomo Sōrin, the Kyushu daimyo, reports a conversation with Hideyoshi's stepbrother Hidenaga that produced this disclosure: "In all private affairs it is Sōeki [Rikyū], in public affairs it is myself, Hidenaga, who knows."[46] Some substance is given to the claim by Rikyū's participation in peace negotiations with the Shimazu, the Ōtomo, and the Date. His letters indicate that he handled financial transactions for Hideyoshi and that he occasionally had charge of Osaka castle.[47]

After years of close association, nonetheless, Hideyoshi sent Rikyū into a brief exile in Sakai and then recalled him to Kyoto to receive a sentence of death. Rikyū prepared tea for several friends before taking his own life, in the second month of 1591, at the advanced age of sixtynine. Hideyoshi surrounded the tea master's home and lined neighboring streets with over three thousand soldiers while the sentence was executed. Later he hauled a statue of Rikyū from its place at a Zen temple and put it on a crucifix for public view.[48]

The statue had apparently been a sore point. Rikyū himself had ordered it carved and enclosed in the second story of a gate at Daitokuji. A history of the Sen house continues: "Denouncing the placement of a wooden statue of Rikyū wearing straw sandals above the main gate of Mount Ryūhō—where emperors and retired emperors came in imperial processions and where members of the Fujiwara house and other great nobles would pass—as an unseemly and improper act that should not have been carried out, [Hideyoshi] condemned Rikyū."[49] Other commentators assumed that Rikyū had been condemned for creating confusion in the pottery market: "In new vessels he has willfully declared good points bad and bought them for mean prices. In rough vessels he has declared bad points good and bought them at high prices. He has called new pieces old and old pieces new. Bad he has called good, false he has called genuine."[50] Still others wondered whether

Rikyū was a secret Christian, or whether he had denied his desirable daughter to Hideyoshi.

More recently, scholars have argued that Rikyū was a political scapegoat. He had joined a group of "moderates" who urged negotiation rather than war with the Hōjō and the Date. Although the proponents of severe reprisals prevailed in the Hōjō case, the Date were brought into the Toyotomi federation. Some claim that Ishida Mitsunari, leader of the "hard-liners," fastened his rage against this act of conciliation upon Rikyū, who was sacrificed to appease the radicals.[51]

Like all explanations for Rikyū's end, this one too is unsatisfactory. It is not described in contemporary records and discounts both the utility of the Date to Hideyoshi and Rikyū's support from the Maeda, Tokugawa, and Asano in advocating arbitration. The execution remains one of the most mysterious acts in Hideyoshi's career. Before drawing a meaning from it, let us consider the last of Hideyoshi's unseemly shows of force.

The crucifixion of the Christians was unremarkable to Japanese observers. The event barely receives mention in the popular histories of the period and is recorded briefly, and as a matter of fact, in the diary literature.[52] Hideyoshi's contemporaries understood it for what it apparently was, a rebuke to aggressive foreigners who had threatened the peace. The missionaries, of course, saw it as a more bewildering departure from Hideyoshi's peaceable conduct toward the Catholic church. The proscription edict of 1587 was not energetically enforced, and the Franciscans, new to Japan in 1592, were allowed to proselytize and to build churches. Hideyoshi continued to receive the priests with courtesy and cordially greeted the ambassador of the Viceroy of the Indies, Father Valignano, in 1591.[53]

The missionaries were able to agree with native commentators, however, that the executions were provoked by the *San Felipe* incident. Loaded with silver and bound from Manila to Acapulco, the Spanish galleon *San Felipe* was wrecked on the coast of Shikoku during the ninth month of 1596. Representatives of the captain, including Franciscan countrymen of the sailors, then began negotiations with Hideyoshi to recover the cargo. But not only did Hideyoshi refuse to restore the silver to the Spaniards, he arrested six Franciscans, three Japanese lay brothers in the Jesuit order, and seventeen Japanese Christians who were sent to Nagasaki for crucifixion.

The events preceding the execution have been discussed at length elsewhere.[54] What is interesting for our purpose is the emergence of fierce debates between the Franciscans and the Jesuits regarding responsibility for Hideyoshi's decision. The Portuguese Jesuits accused the Spanish Franciscans of provoking fears of armed foreign aggression in Japan and the emergence of a "fifth column" among native converts incited by their missionary teachers. The Jesuit Bishop Martins also blamed the Franciscans for aggressive evangelism that affronted and alarmed their Japanese hosts. The Franciscans, for their part, found the Jesuits guilty of slander. They concluded that Hideyoshi responded to insinuations by the Portuguese of Spanish adventurism and ill intentions.

The rivalry between the two orders may have been sufficient to move Hideyoshi to chastise the Christians. Further, the conjunction of religious, trading, and political interests revealed by the *San Felipe* negotiations raised once more the image of a martial church. Unwarned by either the fate of their Buddhist counterparts or the proscription edict of 1587, the Christians had again intervened in affairs of state. The missionaries themselves saw a certain logic behind the executions that they put down to political harassment following the wreck of the *San Felipe*. Like the edict of 1587, the executions were acts of redress, not the initiation of a "final solution." The missionaries were allowed to remain in Japan, and trade with the foreigners went on without incident. The crucifixions were part of a pattern of reprisal against militant sectarians, whatever their creed, who chose to invade the realm of politics.[55]

Yet the speed of Hideyoshi's reaction, the murder of blameless individuals who had not been party to the *San Felipe* quarrels, and the discrepancy between the harsh punishment and the not-so-startling crime are peculiar. Why, after fifteen years of friendly relations, did Hideyoshi seize upon a dispute over a shipwreck to give a ferocious warning to the Christians? Why did grisly punishments supplant other solutions?

The Question of Madness

It is often easy, particularly in the case of a man remote in time, either to exaggerate or to rationalize disturbing behavior. Thus Hideyoshi's expedition to Korea as well as the sordid executions might be seen as aberrant to the point of hysteria. If other phenomena are considered— Hideyoshi's extreme grief over the deaths of Hidenaga and his mother, his distraction over his son, his growing preoccupation, to the exclusion of other interests, with dancing, tea, and designing gardens—signs of imbalance seem apparent. Hideyoshi begins to appear an old warrior, removed from the battlefield and unhinged by his success, a warrior who has been released from the demands of the military challenge that led him to greatness and then baffled him.

On the other hand, cleverness and control might be detected in his brutal actions. Not only was the elimination of a violent and subversive Hidetsugu sensible, the elevation of Hideyori resulted in a clear succession during a time of potential upheaval. The other executions served warning to possible adversaries. Rikyū was an arrogant counselor who could encourage others to disobedience or self-promotion and hence was a logical sacrifice. The crucifixions, hardly as severe as the leveling of Hiei and Negoro, humbled an aggressive church and the adventurers associated with it. The continental campaign, further, was ill judged but adventurous, an outlet for the ambition of a peerless victor who came surprisingly close to conquering Korea.

There is a middle ground between madness and full self-possession, however, where Hideyoshi probably stood. It is difficult to find, since Hideyoshi surely was the archetypal man of action who defined himself in decisions alone. No introspective literature reveals the quick of his mind. His family letters, too often brief, banal, and repetitive, seal off his interior life. Yet clues to his motivations in the 1590s are offered both by the character of his suddenly peaceful society and his unusual place in it.

Until 1590 Hideyoshi and his vassals were confronted by domestic military problems that were familiar and concrete. The strains of peace were new and subtle. The firmness of wartime alliances had yet to be proven, and the sort of crisis that might explode the federal settlement was unknown. Concerned about his fragile peace, then, and determined to extirpate the causes of discord, Hideyoshi began to react abruptly and decisively to perceived threats. Neither the *San Felipe* incident nor the presence of Hidetsugu's family was critical in itself. Yet continued mildness toward a foreign doctrine and foreign interlopers might open the way to graver encounters. Similarly, Hidetsugu's relatives—as living symbols of the controversy over succession—could become the focus of future rebellions. It was the possibility for upheaval implicit in the *San Felipe* and Hidetsugu events, rather than immediate hazard, that seems to have inspired Hideyoshi's responses. Conciliatory in the straightforward situation of war, Hideyoshi became violent in his attempt to hold the peace.

At the deepest level, moreover, the Toyotomi federation was secured by the ties of lord to vassal. Lacking the momentum of a dynastic tradition, unprotected by a history of legal or bureaucratic development, and only symbolically fortified by the court, the federation continued to center on one strong and personal leader. Thus as he faced the challenges of the 1590s, Hideyoshi relied upon the force of his personality and demonstrations of will to maintain order. He had few other resources. Attainder alone could not quiet the Hidetsugu threat; trade sanctions against the Europeans would have punished the Japanese as well. Perhaps the execution of Rikyū best illustrated the purpose of Hideyoshi's brutal actions. Whether he was abrasively independent, politically unpopular, unscrupulous, or inclined to acts of lese majesty, Rikyū threatened Hideyoshi personally in some fashion to emerge as a symbol of disorder in the vassal corps. Hence just as the domestic campaigns ended and the vigilance of war relaxed, Hideyoshi may have chosen to remove this obstreperous official to remind others that the discipline of wartime command would survive. One extreme punishment from a determined leader had to substitute for the resources of law and tradition that the new regime lacked to protect itself. The very arbitrariness of the execution gave it strength as a warning.

But why did Hideyoshi feel driven to such ruthless displays of power? Age played a part, of course; inexperience played a part too. It is also possible that Hideyoshi was locked into a battle with the future. To some extent, that future involved his own reputation, one he imagined in graver jeopardy from unfinished or weakly defended policies, perhaps, than from ruthlessness. That future may also have involved Hideyori. The executions of Hidetsugu's family and of the Christians, as well as another invasion of Korea, occurred after the aging Hideyoshi had a second child he did not expect to have, a son he loved and an heir who might continue his line. Dynastic ambitions, unthought of or repressed when he lacked a healthy son, may have begun to overwhelm him. We can see every show of force, then, as an assertion of the absolute primacy of the leader over his confederates and as a deterrent to either present or future rebellion; that is, as an action designed to assure the primacy and security less of Hideyoshi himself than of Hideyori. Once he became a father, the moderate federalist had suddenly divided interests. Hideyoshi's last experiences, at Fushimi castle, show him pulled in both old and new directions.

Fushimi

Fushimi castle, Hideyoshi's last residence, was conceived as a rather simple sanctuary in the eighth month of 1592 after Hideyoshi returned to the capital from Nagoya for his mother's funeral rites. Hidetsugu was still established in Jurakutei, and Osaka castle—perhaps the logical retreat for Hideyoshi—seems to have had little appeal for him. He never spent much time there in any case. Kyoto remained his center, with its courtly diversions, its daimyo enclave, and its lively traffic. He settled consequently upon Fushimi, just southeast of the capital, for his headquarters as *taikō*.

As he had erected Osaka castle upon the site of Emperor Nintoku's palace and Jurakutei upon the site of Kyoto's first imperial complex, Hideyoshi built his last home in an area equally rich in noble associations. Fushimi was the burial place of Emperor Kammu, founder of Kyoto, and a popular location for aristocratic villas since the tenth century. When Hideyoshi ordered work begun on his own retreat, he envisioned it as a place of retirement and entrusted to Maeda Gen'i the responsibility to construct a modest compound. We have little information about the original plan other than Hideyoshi's instructions that building of the tea houses proceed "in accordance with Rikyū's taste. This I earnestly demand."[56]

Gen'i and his carpenters visited Hideyoshi at Nagoya to review the progress of the work, but their planning radically changed direction toward the end of 1593. Once Hideyoshi was back in the capital following the birth of Hideyori and the suspension of peace negotiations with the Chinese ambassadors, his conception of the Fushimi villa changed. He may have wished to receive his son in proper circumstances or to erect a castle to impress the Chinese envoys. Further, if he was going to press Hideyori's suit with Hidetsugu, Hideyoshi needed a stronger presence in the capital than that conveyed by a retirement home. Thus he turned over the Osaka complex to Hideyori and his attendants and began to plan at Fushimi a suitable headquarters for himself.

Largely completed by the middle of 1594, the more boldly drawn Fushimi castle spread over eleven enclosures facing south toward the Uji River. Hoan's *Taikō-ki* reports that 250,000 men worked there under six magistrates and that materials were brought from areas as distant as Akita and Tosa. The donjon rose to five stories. After Hideyoshi condemned Hidetsugu to death, he enlarged the Fushimi complex by transporting some of Jurakutei's buildings, and its daimyo residences, to the new Toyotomi capital.[57] Much of the Fushimi area was destroyed by earthquake in 1596, however, and so Hideyoshi drew together another massive labor force, which reputedly worked day and night on new buildings somewhat to the north of the original site.[58]

Fushimi's most distinctive feature was not the great keep but the Yamazato, or "Mountain Village," enclave. A park and recreational area, the Yamazato contained two thatched tea houses in addition to nō stages, moonviewing platforms, arbors of fruit trees, and gardens of tropical foliage. A small waterway connected it to the Uji River, permitting pleasure seekers to boat out to small islands planted with cherry orchards. Designed to bring the countryside to the interior of the fortress, the Yamazato was an innovation that later became a staple in castle landscapes.[59]

Fushimi's Yamazato compound suggests rather well the changing tenor of Hideyoshi's aesthetic pursuits in the 1590s, when he turned to a more serious education in the art forms of his day. Although his attention to the arts—all the while his Korean war raged and his succession problems reached their height—might indicate the unhealthy distraction of a man at odds with himself, there is also in Hideyoshi's affairs the theme of private cultivation in retirement. Hideyoshi was served by a tradition we have noted before, the pursuit in military circles of a felicitous union of *bun*—the civil arts—and *bu*—the arts of war. Long before injunctions to master both *bun* and *bu* became commonplace in the codes of the Tokugawa and their vassals, warriors had emulated their betters in seeking to acquire a range of civilizing embellishments. While *bun* came to signify skill in Chinese and some mastery of the Confucian corpus in the Tokugawa period, it continued to embrace a broader concept of gentility familiar to Hideyoshi and his predecessors—grace in the performing arts and poetry.

Exemplary military gentlemen were rare enough, to be sure, yet it is unusual to examine a biography of a warrior that lacks some mention of his cultivation. Mōri Motonari, for example, was a poet and patron of *sarugaku* (a prototype of nō drama). Shimazu Narihisa received esoteric instruction in the Japanese poetic tradition from the courtier Konoe Sakihisa. Hosokawa Yūsai wrote critical works on the *Tale of Ise* and other literary subjects. Akechi Mitsuhide's skill in linked verse is almost as notable as his treachery against Oda Nobunaga. Perhaps more interesting than individual instances of scholarship are indications of a communal concern with the classics. The following account was posted at a Gion shrine in the Mōri domain during 1577: "From the twelfth month of the fourth year of Tenshō until the first month of the following year, Lord Kujō of Kyoto was present in the main hall of this shrine. Praiseworthy men came through the snow to gather at this place day after day and listen to the *Tale of Genji*. [Lord Kujō] read only the *Genji*. [Thus] it became clear in detail."[60] There appears in Hideyoshi's later artistic life a similar concern with the nurturing of the private man. He began to conform to this older ideal of cultivation and, in the process, to reaffirm its importance for a generation of warriors much in need of peacetime retooling. Jurakutei was the headquarters of a *kampaku* interested in the projection of authority through grand behavior; Fushimi was the headquarters of a *taikō* exploring the inner dimension of gentility.

Hideyoshi's chief artistic interest in the 1590s was nō drama. Nō had remained a fixture in the ceremonial life of the military throughout the period of warring states, despite the disappearance of Ashikaga financial support for the leading schools of players and the growing dependence of the actors upon urban audiences for survival. Thus Nobunaga and Hideyoshi, as well as their fellow daimyo, routinely included nō performances in events of significance. Hideyoshi's enthusiasm for the art became most marked during his sojourn in Nagoya. He brought the four main schools of actors to his camp for the entertainment of his men and then detained their leaders to instruct himself and his principal retainers in the techniques of chanting and dance. By the early months of 1593 Hideyoshi was assuming the lead role in plays from the classical repertoire, and soon he was able to write his wife that he had learned fifteen or sixteen plays within the previous fifty days. Komparu Ansho and Kurematsu Shinkyuro appear to have been his major teachers, although he sought coaching from members of each of the main schools and from the female no players and other musicians whom he also called to Nagoya.[61]

Hideyoshi did not confine his appearances to Nagoya audiences, needless to say. When he visited the palace in the tenth month of 1593 to celebrate Hideyori's birth, he acted before the emperor in eleven plays over a period of three days. The critic Konoe Sakihisa was able to muster the remark that "the *taiko's* performance conveys the impression of enormous development."[62] Scant praise was praise enough, and in the following months Hideyoshi appeared at Osaka castle and Juraku-tei. Early in 1594, he was ready to make his most curious foray into the world of no by commissioning his secretary, Omura Yuko, to write a cycle of new plays founded upon his own life. Komparu Ansho composed the music. Although the ten plays share with the *Tensho-ki* a preoccupation with Hideyoshi's military triumphs—over Akechi Mitsuhide, Shibata Katsuie, and Hojo Ujimasa—they also describe his journey to view the cherries at Yoshino and the visit to his mother's mortuary temple.[63]

Hideyoshi played the lead in five of these dramas at Osaka castle in the third month of 1594. He was not to perform these plays again, yet he did regularly summon audiences to see him in classical roles until the end of his life. The connoisseur Shimatsuma Shoshin was called to Fushimi to evaluate his work during several days in 1595; leading no actors and Toyotomi vassals made the trek to Fushimi several times in each succeeding year for similar festivities in the Yamazato enclave.[64] Hideyoshi's fascination with the art and his pleasure in being admired were sufficiently well known to inspire this apocryphal story: "One day when the *taiko* was passing on horseback through Karasuma Street on his way to the palace, four or five women in red aprons went out to watch him near some newly built houses. Seeing them, the *taiko* spoke from his horse: 'I am just now on my way to the palace where all of you must come to watch me perform no.' "[65]

It is impossible to ignore the exhibitionism and the need for flattery in Hideyoshi's interest in no. In choosing an artistic discipline, he characteristically selected a form of public presentation. But the nice point, of course, is that Hideyoshi began to present himself as the gentleman artist rather than as the benefactor host. The pageantry available to any bold and powerful man was replaced by the performance of a cultivated practitioner of the arts. Thus just as Hideyoshi's acts of restoration—in the capital, at the major monasteries—satisfied his interest in lordly behavior while they revealed certain assumptions about the business of the good lord, so his turn to active practice of nō afforded him the pleasures of center stage while it disclosed a belief that art was at least as admirable as show.

Fushimi was not only the site of Hideyoshi's attempted transformation into a gentleman, however. It also became the command post for resumed war with Korea. Regardless of the lessons of the first engagement, Hideyoshi committed reluctant soldiers to new battles. In his own eyes, at least, the provocation was formidable. In the sixth month of 1596, Chinese ambassadors finally arrived in Sakai to deliver their court's response to Hideyoshi's peace overtures. Detained by the earthquake of that year while Hideyoshi made repairs to his Fushimi residence, they were received at Osaka castle on the first day of the ninth month. There they presented Hideyoshi with gold, silk robes, and other gifts. On the second day, after an entertainment of nō, a monk from Shōkokuji was charged to read out the message from the Ming emperor. The essential sentence was brusque and uncompromising: "We hereby declare that you are invested as the king of Japan."

Ashikaga Yoshimitsu had accepted a similar pronouncement in the early fifteenth century as a condition for restoring official trade with the continent. Although later excoriated by native commentators for this deference to a foreign throne, Yoshimitsu established a precedent, in the eyes of the Chinese, for dealings with Japanese rulers. It appears, too, that Konishi Yukinaga and Naitō Joan acceded to the declaration during their negotiations with China in 1594 and 1595. They may also have promised that all Japanese soldiers would depart Korea and that a renewed offensive would not take place.[66]

For Hideyoshi, confirmation of his power by the Ming emperor was a humiliation exacerbated by the absence of any concession to his own terms of peace. He had set the stakes foolishly high and thus invited both an imperious rejoinder from China and personal shame. The message of the Ming court slighted Hideyoshi himself while mocking his briefly successful effort at foreign conquest. Unable to live with the insult and to dismiss the first expedition as a closed and now meaningless matter, Hideyoshi opened a new war on the peninsula. There was a certain constancy in the decision, a determination to guard the honor of himself and his army. But there was also the familiar incapacity for moderation when his name, and possibly the dignity of his heir, was injured.

In the beginning of 1597, the Katō, Konishi, and Nabeshima armies returned to Korea to join a small force that had remained there around Pusan. In the second month of the year, Hideyoshi issued levies for additional soldiers—totaling over 140,000 men—to resume a full-scale offensive. They initially met success. The armies of the Ukita, Konishi, and Shimazu moved into Namwŏn by the eighth month, and Kuroda Nagamori defeated a Chinese contingent in Ulsan. In the seventh month the Japanese navy overpowered the Korean fleet at Kŏje Island. Hideyoshi received some of the gorier, and most notorious, trophies of the war—a cache of noses taken from the Korean dead—in the ninth month.[67]

Although Hideyoshi suggested that he might cross to Korea himself should the Chinese join the war in large numbers, he never went so far as Nagoya to direct the second campaign. Indeed, a chronology of his life in 1597 and 1598 shows limited attention to affairs abroad. While his navy defended Kŏje, Hideyoshi and Hideyori played with an elephant, delivered by the Spanish, at Osaka castle and the palace. Hideyoshi visited his Great Buddha in Kyoto, made repairs to the Fushimi complex, added to his collection of tea vessels, and began preparations for the entertainment at Daigoji. In the ninth month of 1597 he arranged for Hideyori's coming-of-age ceremony and his promotion to the office of *sakon'e gon-shōshō* at the junior fourth rank, lower grade. The ceremony, which took place at the imperial palace, was premature but urgent as Hideyoshi sought to enhance his heir's position. In the fourth month of 1598, Hideyoshi arranged his son's promotion to the office of *gon-chūnagon* at the junior second rank.[68]

Increasingly, the Korean situation gave cause for alarm. Yi Sun-sin resumed command over the Korean navy and initiated a series of successful attacks on Japanese bases. As supply problems became acute, the Chinese army marched south. And by the fifth month of 1598 Hideyoshi ordered Kuroda Nagamasa to hold the Pusan area while he recalled Ukita Hideie, Mōri Hidemoto, Hachisuka Iemasa, and other leaders of the campaign home to Japan.[69] Although the last battles and the full return of Japanese troops would take place after Hideyoshi's death, this recall signaled the effective end to a war that had followed much the same course as the earlier offensive. Once more Hideyoshi's army had demonstrated an ability to move quickly into the peninsula and to hold strategic points. Once more Hideyoshi had responded to stiff counterattack by retiring enough soldiers from the engagement to avoid conclusive defeat.

Hideyoshi probably achieved what he wanted from the second invasion of Korea. He displayed the firmness of his will, showed again that his army could challenge China, and took a gruesome toll in Korean casualties for the slight to his honor. No rhetoric comparable to his letters of 1592 suggested that he really envisioned conquest. He was simply mounting—for himself, his men, and foreign leaders—a final demonstration of personal power and unsatiated ambition. Anything less, perhaps, he would have seen as a failure of resolve that would undermine his house as well as his political settlement. In redeeming his reputation, of course, Hideyoshi did grave damage. And he also evinced once more that obsession with his image that pushed him to infamous acts. He responded to frustration as if it eroded his soul, to failure as a negation of all previous achievements.

Yet what must now appear as compulsive behavior may help explain Hideyoshi's hold over his men. One remarkable feature of his career is his ability to command obedience in difficult circumstances. Why did powerful *tozama* sail to Korea? Certainly Hideyoshi's force of will had a mesmerizing impact upon his vassals. Never ambiguous in his decisions, Hideyoshi acted with a conviction that stilled dissent and inspired action.

Dying

Even as many of his generals returned home, Hideyoshi entered his final illness. At the request of his wife, the court sponsored a presentation of sacred dance (*kagura*), in the sixth month of 1598, to pray for his recovery. The ceremonies were repeated in the seventh month. *Kagura* performances were also offered in Hideyori's name, and the emperor dispatched messengers to most of the temples and shrines of Kyoto to request continuing invocations for Hideyoshi's safety. Toward the end of the seventh month, Hideyoshi sent off parting gifts of gold, silver, swords, and robes to the emperor, the high-ranking nobility, and his own major vassals.[70]

His essential concern was with his son. Under order, senior daimyo gathered at Maeda Toshiie's residence in Fushimi to renew their oaths of loyalty to Hideyori on the fifteenth day of the seventh month. Mōri Terumoto signed this pledge:

Item: I will serve Hideyori. [My] service [to him], just like [my service to] the *taikō*, shall be without negligence. Addendum: I will know no duplicity or other thoughts at all.

Item: As for the laws and [Hideyoshi's] orders as they have been declared up to the present time, I will not violate them in the slightest.

Item: Inasmuch as I understand it to be for the sake of public affairs, I will discard personal enmities toward my peers and will not act on my own interests.

Item: I will not establish factions among [my] associates. Even if there are lawsuits, quarrels, or disputes and [they involve] parents and children, brothers, or complainants whom I know, I resolve, knowing no partiality, [to act] in conformity with the law.

Item: I will not return willfully to my fief without asking leave.[71]

Shortly thereafter, on the fifth day of the eighth month, Hideyoshi issued these orders to the elders:

Item: Of the five magistrates (*bugyō*), Tokuzen'in [Maeda Gen'i] and Natsuka-dai [Natsuka Masaie] will constitute the first guard. One of the remaining three men shall act as the absentee representative at Fushimi castle. The *naifu* [Tokugawa Ieyasu] shall be the general absentee representative.

Item: Two of the magistrates shall act as the absentee representative at Osaka castle.

Item: Once Hideyori has entered Osaka castle, the various generals, their wives, and their children shall [also] go to Osaka.[72]

He elaborated upon this message with a personal plea to the elders—Tokugawa Ieyasu, Maeda Toshiie, Uesugi Kagekatsu, Mōri Terumoto, and Ukita Hideie: "I appeal to you addressed here to establish Hideyori. Nothing weighs on my mind other than this. Again and again I appeal to you over Hideyori. I state my appeals [also] to the five men [magistrates]. I have communicated the particulars to the five [magistrates]. I grieve at this parting."[73]

On the eighth day of the eighth month Tokugawa Ieyasu and his son, Hidetada, as well as Maeda Toshiie and his son, Toshinaga, joined Ukita Hideie in delivering further oaths of loyalty to Hideyori. The magistrates took oaths before Ieyasu and Maeda Toshiie on the eleventh day of the eighth month. After the tenth, however, Hideyoshi was seldom conscious. He died on the eighteenth day of the eighth month, 1598, at Fushimi castle. He was sixty-three years old.

Before he died, Hideyoshi composed a poem of parting.

My life
Came like dew
Disappears like dew.
All of Naniwa
Is dream after dream.[74]

The poem is very much what a last poem should be, and many find there that sense of transience and humility that an audacious man might properly discover as he dies. But the poem is as wry as it is melancholy. Close to death, Hideyoshi sent gifts to princes and generals and then wrote the appropriate poem. He retained that polite interest in the behavior becoming a ruler that runs throughout his career. The poem strikes so false, and so reproaches a life of seminal action, that one is reminded again that Hideyoshi shaped himself to many roles and could die in the style required. Until the end, a part of his soul remained in the control of his audience.

AFTERWORD

HIDEYOSHI'S LAST appeals for loyalty to his five-year-old son were not successful. Months after his interment, strains within the council of regents and within the larger body of daimyo had become apparent. While one faction continued to support the child-heir, another formed around that wily ally, first of the Oda and later of the Toyotomi, Tokugawa Ieyasu. The split among Hideyoshi's confederates ran deep, often unpredictably: the Mōri and the Uesugi, for example, rallied behind the heir; the Maeda and the Date turned to the challenger.

The first battle between the opponents, fought on the plain of Sekigahara in Mino during 1600, gave a decisive advantage to Ieyasu. He received the title of *sei-i tai-shōgun* from the court in 1603 and, after years of resolute consolidation, overcame the last remnant of opposition during the siege of Osaka castle in 1614–15. The heir and his mother, Yodo-dono, took their own lives.

Although crisis within the Toyotomi federation is unsurprising, the form it took is revealing. Hideyoshi's daimyo did not respond to his death by reopening regional contests for ascendancy; nor did they reverse his basic policies by renouncing the edicts on arms and class or invading cities under the regents' control. Instead, they went to war, and then only twice, over the question of leadership. Implicit in their search for a head was assent to the notion of central authority. In the critical years after Hideyoshi died, domainal lords challenged Toyotomi primacy while maintaining the Toyotomi political course.

Discussion of the persistence of Hideyoshi's settlement over a longer time is hazardous, for the discontinuities between the Toyotomi and Tokugawa regimes are often as striking as the continuities. In the first instance, the actions pursued by Ieyasu and his immediate successors to assure the precedence of the Tokugawa house departed significantly in scope, if not always in kind, from those of Hideyoshi. By the time of the third shogun's death in 1651, the new administration had purged or enfeebled threatening daimyo through the attainder of 213 domains and the transfer of 281. Accompanying these land transactions was a grave tightening of control on the conduct of local lords. They were restricted to one castle each, routinely examined by spies and inspectors, and compelled to spend one of every two years in Edo. This elaborate hostage policy, together with a foreign policy that prohibited all overseas travel by Japanese and confined Dutch and Chinese traders to a single port controlled by the shogunate, became defining characteristics of Tokugawa government.

Various controls upon the daimyo did relax after 1651, fresh assaults upon their freedom became rare, and attainders slowed to a trickle. The turn toward moderation during the administration of the fourth shogun gives the first half-century of Tokugawa rule an aberrant quality; it appears a period of postwar adjustment, ferocious certainly but not significant of political transformation. Even so, the changes in landholding during those years had almost doubled the wealth of the shogunal house and resulted, as well, in the investiture of scores of new daimyo from the Tokugawa ranks. The controls on daimyo behavior tilted the balance of power toward the center, securing a regime that few would contest as the most authoritarian in premodern Japanese history. The early gains of the Tokugawa in wealth and power, if not succeeded by continuing improvements, permanently set their government apart from Hideyoshi's.[1]

Discontinuity between the Toyotomi and Tokugawa eras is more apparent in society and the economy. The burgeoning of cities, the growth and increasing commercialization of agriculture, the ascendancy of popular culture, the intensity of philosophical debate, the expansion of literacy, of banking, of transportation and communication—these and related developments marked formidable boundaries not only between the periods of Toyotomi and Tokugawa rule but between the many phases of the shogunate's experience. While most such changes were consequences of political actions taken by Hideyoshi and Ieyasu, they gradually shaped a society that neither man would have recognized.

Finally, Hideyoshi's relationship to his successors is complicated by questions of motive and perception that we can only raise here. Even when Toyotomi and Tokugawa policies were congruent, the conditions that fostered them and the objectives they served need hardly have been the same. From the decision to govern under the title of shogun to their promiscuous use of attainder, from their choice of an eastern capital to their retreat into a national seclusion policy, the Tokugawa followed very different paths from Hideyoshi. Their rule, in intention and formulation, is best explored on its own terms.

We are left, nonetheless, with the extraordinary fact that the con-

tours of Hideyoshi's settlement were still easy to detect when the fifteenth and last Tokugawa shogun resigned his post to the emperor in
1867. The separation of classes, the regulation of movement, the monopolization of political power by the military, the restriction on
arms—these policies, if sometimes laxly enforced, remained law in
mid-nineteenth-century Japan. The distribution of land, too, followed a
familiar pattern. While the shogunate controlled 16 percent of registered resources directly (and the bannermen an additional 10 percent),
280 domainal lords held the remainder. Despite the tumultuous attainders of the seventeenth century, 108 of these lords, with 37 percent of
the nation's resources, were *tozama;* that is, descendants of those Toyotomi confederates who had made their peace, not always readily, with
the Tokugawa. Included among them were the Mōri and the Shimazu,
opponents of Ieyasu at Sekigahara. Collaterals and *fudai* of the Tokugawa, largely the successors of house vassals raised to lordship by the
first three shogun, comprised a majority of the daimyo group and held
the final 37 percent of registered resources.[2] Their numbers, however,
are no more significant than the fact that their very investiture represented a continuing division, not a concentration, of power. Regardless
of their origins, these daimyo acquired separate land bases like those of
the *tozama.*

While there can be no doubt that increased vulnerability to attainder, harsh hostage laws, and exclusion from foreign trade deeply altered daimyo roles, many of the critical privileges of domainal rule
during the Toyotomi era had survived into the mid-nineteenth century:
freedom from central taxation, authority over the resident military population, control of local justice, commerce, and agriculture. In the seventeenth century, with the creation of a council of elders as the shogunate's primary policy organ, daimyo participation in central
government was also institutionalized. The occasional eclipse of the
council by strong shogun or their favorites, as well as the restriction of
membership to *fudai,* could not vitiate the importance of routine management of national affairs by daimyo. Thus Tokugawa government
retained the federal character of the Toyotomi settlement.

Tenacious and conducive to stable rule as elements of Hideyoshi's
policy proved to be, by 1850 many were exhausted and others put to
different purposes. Yet in at least two areas—political philosophy and
the relations of the domain to the center—the experience of the Toyotomi years opened issues that remained vital until the close of Tokugawa rule. And it may be in these areas, rather than in particular forms
of rule which were losing their meaning, that we might best seek out
the relationship between the late *sengoku* and the Tokugawa eras.

A characteristic of Tokugawa intellectual life, one which set it off definitively from the past, was extensive and sustained inquiry into an essentially new question: What is the proper role of government? To ask the question is not only to convey a dilemma but to assume that government's function is definable and therefore particular or limited. The question rejects the right of fiat. To begin to define the role of government, further, is to establish a standard against which performance can be measured, and therefore to imply the notion of accountability. To grapple with the notion of accountability is to raise the possibility that government can be judged for failure, and therefore be reformed or rejected. And to explore the possibility of rejection is to see government as a system made and potentially remade by men of new vision.

The question occupying Tokugawa thinkers, and its implications, seems necessarily linked to the climax of the civil war—when men who had rejected the medieval order to create independent domains forged an accommodation with each other and a leader. The absence of a precedent for their resolution, the deliberateness of their action, their mutual distrust, and the federal quality of their agreement gave new urgency to matters of political philosophy that had rarely been of more than passing or perfunctory interest to their predecessors. The role of government needed explication; it was not a given.

If the Tokugawa inherited a question from the Toyotomi, they inherited the beginnings of an answer as well. The orthodox response, framed by tutors to the shogun, observed that government existed to preserve harmony through humane and benevolent rule. Mediated by Confucian thought, that response reflected the Toyotomi preoccupation with order and the formulation of *kōgi* as the public trust. This definition of government's role became little more than a frame for political discourse, however, as generations of Tokugawa thinkers explored its consequences. Together with the critics and petitioners of the regime, they held the shogunate to account for a mission that was more perilous for its vague, encompassing definition. As surely as the Tokugawa confronted questions about the function of authority, they created a legitimate context for reformist debate. Thus at the same time that he attacked a Neo-Confucian shibboleth by describing government as the creation and instrument of man, the eighteenth-century philosopher Ogyū Sorai excoriated the shogunate for condemning samurai to a parasitic existence in cities. Insofar as we can associate the developments of the late sixteenth century with such loosening of political thought and its dynamic linkage to criticism in both official and unofficial circles, the Toyotomi legacy surpasses matters of policy.

The possibility that government might be rejected rather than reformed came alive in the mid-nineteenth century after the intrusion of western powers threw the shogunate into chaos. Critics of many leanings—those who accused the Tokugawa of disregard for the throne, of failure to protect the nation from foreign barbarians, of violation of domainal interests—used charges of malfeasance either as motive or rationalization for rebellion. Violent action took place within the framework of ideology as men of new, if still cloudy, vision began to remake government once again.

The seat of their rebellion was the domain. More subordinate to central government in some ways than they had been in Hideyoshi's day, a number of domains had enhanced their independence in others. Certain local governments had developed stronger, more resilient economies than the regime's; some served as havens for unorthodox scholars and centers of Dutch studies; two, Tsushima and Satsuma, maintained relations with Korea and the Ryukyus; and most—whether by issuing their own paper currency, protecting local monopolies, or supporting some landed retainers—deviated clearly from shogunal guidelines of rule. Both the primary locus of identity for most Japanese and a political entity separable from the shogunate, the domain long stabilized the regime by deflecting pressure from the center, only to help topple it by serving as the logical stage for rebellion. The domainal order, flexible and dangerous from the start, revealed its vitality less in lists of daimyo landholdings than in its adroit changes and its survival of the shogunate.

The relationship of Hideyoshi's settlement to political philosophy and to domainal development in the Tokugawa era is broad and problematic, hardly as simple as its links to certain shogunal policies, and one we have only begun to explore here. That relationship could not, however, be broken by closing Hideyoshi's shrine. Storytellers may have preserved his legend. But the Tokugawa themselves had to struggle in ever renewed form with the meaning of the unification movement. Even the shrine had a revival. Restored by the Meiji government in the late nineteenth century, it has become a good place to greet the New Year in the company of a persistent ghost.

NOTES

1. The Toyotomi Peace

1. The original shrine buildings, and the festivities accompanying the ceremonies marking the seventh anniversary of Hideyoshi's death, are known to us from several pairs of screens depicting those memorial services. The most famous pair, by Kanō Naisen (1570–1616), is in the collection of Hōkoku shrine in Kyoto. Although the shrine now stands within the precincts of Hōkōji, the original site was closer to the entrance to Hideyoshi's mausoleum on Amidagasaki. See Kyōto-shi, comp., *Kyōto no rekishi*, 10 vols. (Tokyo: Gakugei Shorin, 1970–78), IV, 594–600, 610–611, 620–622, 644–645; Tanaka Toyozō, "Hōkoku-sai no byōbu ni tsuite," in *Nihon bijutsu no kenkyū* (Tokyo: Nigen-sha, 1960), pp. 291–300; and Kyōto Kokuritsu Hakubutsukan, *Rakuchū rakugai zu* (Tokyo: Kadokawa Shoten, 1966), pp. 44–48.

2. The two most important and formative of Hideyoshi's early biographies are: Oze Hoan, *Taikō-ki*, ed. Kuwata Tadachika (Tokyo: Shinjimbutsu Ōrai-sha, 1971); and Ōta Gyūichi, *Taikō gunki*, included in Kuwata Tadachika, ed., *Taikō shiryō-shū* (Tokyo: Shinjimbutsu Ōrai-sha, 1971). Hoan (1564–1640) probably completed his twenty-two chapter biography of Hideyoshi around 1625. A doctor and scholar by profession, he apparently used a variety of records in preparing his work: the documents of the Maeda house, Hideyoshi's letters, records relating to the land survey, and previous biographies. His *Taikō-ki* is nonetheless replete with apocrypha, moralistic tales, and elaborate, fictionalized descriptions of important events. Most of the later Tokugawa-period biographies of Hideyoshi—the *Ehon taikō-ki*, *Shinsho taikō-ki*, the *ukiyo-zōshi*, *kibyōshi*, and *sharebon* concerning the Toyotomi—improvised upon Hoan's work. See Kuwata Tadachika, *Taikō-ki no kenkyū* (Tokyo: Tokuma Shoten, 1965), pp. 135–149 and the afterword to the *Taikō-ki*, pp. 610–642. The *Taikō gunki* is a two-chapter work, written in colloquial Japanese, which covers the later period of Hideyoshi's life and was probably completed within the first decade of his death. Gyūichi served both Nobunaga and Hideyoshi and composed a biography of Nobunaga as well. See Kuwata, *Taikō-ki no kenkyū*, pp. 96–119.

3. Quoted from the *Ōnin-ki* by Akeda Tetsuo in *Ransei Kyōto* (Kyoto: Shirakawa Shoin, 1969), I, 224.

4. Rodrigues (1561–1634), born in Portugal, arrived in Japan in 1566, and entered the Society of Jesus there in 1580. He served both Hideyoshi and Ieyasu as interpreter. After his expulsion from Japan in 1610, he wrote a history

of the church in that country (*História da Igreja do Japão*) as well as the first grammar of the Japanese language (*Arte da Lingoa de Iapam*). For a partial translation of the former work, and an introduction to Rodrigues' life, see Michael Cooper, trans. and ed., *This Island of Japon* (Tokyo and New York: Kodansha International, 1973). This quotation appears on p. 78.

5. Although I shall refer to my subject as Toyotomi Hideyoshi throughout this work, he did not begin to use the name Toyotomi until 1586, when it was awarded to him by the court. He affected the surname Kinoshita during his early career as a soldier and later, around 1573, assumed the surname Hashiba. As a child, he may have used the personal name Hiyoshimaru. He used the personal name Tokichirō in his early manhood and switched to Hideyoshi while serving Oda Nobunaga. He signed one of his first extant letters (third month, 1571) Kinoshita Tokichirō; by the tenth month of 1573 he was signing Hashiba Chikuzen no Kami Hideyoshi. Chikuzen no Kami was an honorary court title. For the correspondence, see Kusaka Hiroshi, ed., *Hōkō ibun* (Tokyo: Hakubunkan, 1914), pp. 1–3. Also see Kuwata Tadachika, *Toyotomi Hideyoshi kenkyū* (Tokyo: Kadokawa Shoten, 1975), pp. 121–127.

6. For the quotation, see Kuwata, *Toyotomi Hideyoshi kenkyū*, pp. 252–253.

7. For the Yoritomo quotation, see Kuwata Tadachika, *Taikō no tegami* (Tokyo: Bungei Shunjū-sha, 1959), p. 76; for the Ryukyu quotation, see Kuwata, *Toyotomi Hideyoshi kenkyū*, pp. 251–252.

8. Tōkyō Daigaku Shiryō Hensanjo, comp., *Hō taikō shinseki-shū*, 3 vols. (Tokyo: Tōkyō Daigaku Shuppan-kai, 1938), I, document 18.

9. Oze Hoan, *Taikō-ki*, p. 554.

2. A World without a Center

1. The *Taikō sujōki*, composed by the Tokugawa *hatamoto* Tsuchiya Yasutada who came from Hideyoshi's birthplace, is one of the most influential, though less well known, of the Hideyoshi genealogies. Find a discussion of this work and Hideyoshi's early biography in Suzuki Ryōichi, *Toyotomi Hideyoshi* (Tokyo: Iwanami Shoten, 1971), pp. 3–6. Tsuchiya's genealogy includes the anomalous references to Yaemon's service as a *teppō ashigaru* (musket-carrying foot soldier). He also gives Hideyoshi's family the surname Kinoshita. The name, affected by Hideyoshi himself after he joined the Imagawa retainer Matsushita Yukitsuna, may have been a gesture of homage to his lord (Matsushita means "under the pine"; Kinoshita means "under the tree") or, more plausibly, borrowed from his wife's brothers, who bore that surname. Bestowal of the name on Hideyoshi's parents is merely a courtesy. For other biographical discussion, see Oze Hoan, *Taikō-ki*, pp. 31–34, and Hayashi Razan, *Toyotomi Hideyoshi-fu* (in the collection of the Kyoto University Library, Bungaku-bu). A remarkably thorough chronology of Hideyoshi's life, including general citations of sources, may be found in *Toyotomi Hideyoshi* (*Rekishi tokuhon: Denki shirīzu*, 8; Tokyo: Shinjimbutsu Ōrai-sha, July 1978), vol. III, no. 3, pp. 114–127. This work suggests that Hideyoshi was born in 1537, a date preferred by some scholars to 1536. Compare the treatments of the temple sojourns of Hideyoshi and Minamoto no Yoshitsune in Helen C. McCullough, *Yoshitsune* (Stanford: Stanford University Press, 1966), pp. 79–81, and Oze Hoan, *Taikō-ki*, p. 31.

2. Oze Hoan, *Taikō-ki*, p. 31.

3. *Hōkō ibun*, pp. 490–491.

4. The oldest of Hideyoshi's votive portraits, and the one that serves as the frontispiece, is in the collection of Kōdaiji, a Rinzai Zen monastery affiliated with Kenninji that was founded by Ieyasu in 1605 for the repose of Hideyoshi's soul. Hideyoshi's widow resided there until the time of her own death in 1624. It bears an inscription by the Myōshinji monk Nanka Genkō, dated the eighteenth day of the eighth month, 1598, the day of Hideyoshi's death. It was commissioned by the Toyotomi retainer Tanaka Yoshimasa as a commemorative portrait. Seventeen similar portraits, most completed before the fall of Osaka castle (1615), also survive. (Two of the better known are in the Hatakeyama Museum, Tokyo, and in Saikyōji, Ōtsu.) See Kameda Tsutomu, Men to shōzō (Genshoku Nihon no bijutsu, no. 23; Tokyo: Shōgaku-kan, 1971), pp. 95, 188; Shirahata Yoshi, Shōzō-ga (Nihon no bijutsu, no. 8; Tokyo: Shibundō, 1966), p. 106; and Shirahata Yoshi, "Ransei no gazō," in Sengoku hyakunin (Taiyō, no. 2; Spring, 1973), p. 177. See chapter 3, n. 30 for the reference to "bald rat." The other reference comes from an anonymous graffito: "With the last age / There is no difference, / Even fixing our gaze / On the Monkey Regent / Kinoshita." See Fukuo Takeichirō, "Rakushu ni arawareta Hideyoshi seiken hihan," in Toyotomi Hideyoshi (Rekishi tokuhon: Denki shirīzu, 8), pp. 198–200.

5. This section contains my own characterization of a very long period of time. Useful background reading includes: John W. Hall, Government and Local Power in Japan (Princeton: Princeton University Press, 1966); Hall and Jeffrey P. Mass,. eds., Medieval Japan: Essays in Institutional History (New Haven: Yale University Press, 1974); Mass, Warrior Government in Medieval Japan (New Haven: Yale University Press, 1974); Hall and Toyoda Takeshi, eds., Japan in the Muromachi Age (Berkeley and Los Angeles: University of California Press, 1977); and Peter Judd Arnesen, The Medieval Japanese Daimyo (New Haven: Yale University Press, 1979).

6. An emperor's accession ceremony (senso), which involves transfer of the imperial regalia, takes place soon after the death or abdication of his predecessor. The enthronement ceremony (sokui)—something of a misnomer in English since no throne is used—is a larger and more public ceremony that follows later. The best chronology of Kyoto's history, including general citations of primary sources, constitutes most of vol. X of Kyōto-shi, comp., Kyōto no rekishi (Tokyo: Gakugei Shorin, 1976). It is often well, however, to check critical dates for this period in Tōkyō Daigaku Shiryō Hensanjo, comp., Shiryō sōran (Tokyo: Tōkyō Daigaku Shuppan-kai, 1953–54), XI–XIII. Kyōto no rekishi, X, contains occasional errors in dates and other facts—for example, it gives both 1526 and 1536 as the dates of Go-Nara's senso. It was the sokui ritual that took place in 1536. The contributions of Shōnyo, Ōuchi Yoshitaka, and others to the sokui ceremonies are discussed in Richard Ponsonby-Fane, Kyoto: The Old Capital of Japan (Tokyo: Kenkyū-sha, 1956), p. 271. Also see Suzuki Ryōichi, Oda Nobunaga (Iwanami Shinsho, 649; Tokyo: Iwanami Shoten, 1967), p. 4. The last extant documents concerning Ashikaga support of senso or sokui rituals date from 1500—when the bakufu tried to levy special house taxes (munebechisen) in Kyoto and its environs for the accession ceremony of Go-Kashiwabara. See Kyōto-shi, comp., Shiryō Kyōto no rekishi (Tokyo: Heibon-sha, 1979), III, 312–313 (documents 11 and 12).

7. Kyōto no rekishi, IV, 58.

8. For lists and an analysis of imperial holdings during the period of mili-

tary ascendancy, see Teishitsu Rin'ya Kyoku, comp., *Go-ryōchi shikō* (Tokyo: Kunaishō, 1937), pp. 171–235.

9. See the *Tokitsugu kyō-ki* (Tokyo: Zoku Gunsho Ruijū Kansei-kai, 1965) for an account by Yamashina Tokitsugu—the imperial treasurer—of class mix and convergence in wartime Kyoto. Also see *Kyōto no rekishi*, III, 333–352, 429–480, 591–598.

10. See *Shiryō Kyōto no rekishi*, III, 309–331 for extant documents concerning the relations between the shogun, the *kanrei*, and their deputies in the Miyoshi and Matsunaga houses.

11. *Kyōto no rekishi*, III, 482–502.

12. *Kyōto no rekishi*, X, 223–272; *Shiryō Kyōto no rekishi*, III, 309–370.

13. *Shugo* families that had long histories of service to the Ashikaga and that survived well into the *sengoku* period include the Imagawa, Takeda, Ōuchi, Shimazu, Rokkaku, Sō, Satake, and Kyōgoku. The Utsunomiya and the Yūki had served as *shugo* somewhat more sporadically than these other houses. They were also warring-states lords. Several branches of the Hosokawa *shugo* house succeeded as *sengoku* daimyo, although the regental line was overpowered in 1549. The Uesugi survived until the 1550s, and in name into the Tokugawa period. A member of a deputy *shugo* house, the Nagao, took over Uesugi leadership around 1560. The Toki and the Shōni *shugo* houses also survived until mid-century. The greatest difficulty in determining the continuity of *shugo* households (throughout the Ashikaga period and into the *sengoku* period), and in calculating the numbers of *shugo* acting at any one time, is the lack of thorough documentation of *shugo* appointments. Satō Shin'ichi, after collating extant records, has published a careful list of *shugo* for the Nambokuchō period (1336–1392) in *Muromachi bakufu shugo seido no kenkyū* (Tokyo: Tōkyō Daigaku Shuppan-kai, 1976), pp. 105–153. (Volume II of the work, concerning the latter part of the Ashikaga period, has not yet appeared.) A fuller list of Ashikaga-period *shugo* does appear in Takayanagi Mitsutoshi and Takeuchi Rizō, *Kadokawa Nihon-shi jiten* (Tokyo: Kadokawa Shoten, 1966), pp. 1002–17. Because sources for the information are not cited, this list must be used with great caution. It mentions fewer than twenty-five *shugo* serving at the time of the Ōnin war. The number was probably larger, although documentation problems remain formidable. The histories of *sengoku* daimyo are best checked in Takayanagi Mitsutoshi and Matsudaira Toshikazu, eds., *Sengoku jimmei jiten* (Tokyo: Yoshikawa Kōbunkan, 1962).

14. See Kawai Masaharu, "Shogun and Shugo: The Provincial Aspects of Muromachi Politics," in Hall and Toyoda, eds., *Japan in the Muromachi Age*, pp. 65–86, for a general discussion of shogunal controls on the *shugo*. Kawai is representative of those historians who emphasize the weakness of *shugo* and their prompt collapse in the *sengoku* era. As n. 13 suggests, however, a fair number of *shugo* did survive.

15. The *Kadokawa Nihon-shi jiten* lists thirty-two individuals in forty provinces who received appointment as *shugo* after 1500. See pp. 1002–17.

16. For discussion of the *sengoku* village, see Nagahara Keiji, "Village Communities and Daimyo Power," in Hall and Toyoda, eds., *Japan in the Muromachi Age*, pp. 107–123, and Nagahara Keiji, "Daimyō ryōgoku seika no nōmin shihai gensoku," in Nagahara Keiji, ed., *Sengoku-ki no kenryoku to shakai* (Tokyo: Tōkyō Daigaku Shuppan-kai, 1976), pp. 105–153.

17. This discussion of Kamikuze-no-shō is based on Araki Moriaki, *Taikō*

kenchi to kokudaka-sei (*NHK Bukkusu*, 93; Tokyo: Nippon Hōsō Shuppan Kyōkai, 1969), pp. 38–63. Also see Nagahara, "Village Communities and Daimyo Power," for comments on Kamikuze-no-shō in 1357 and 1458.

18. Although words like *jizamurai* and *dogō* are imprecise and can refer to a variety of armed men, *jizamurai* will be used here for armed cultivators essentially outside the proprietary class. For a good definition of terms, see Nagahara Keiji et al., eds., *Chūsei-shi handobukku* (Tokyo: Kondō Shuppan-sha, 1973), and Nihon-shi Yōgo Daijiten Henshū Iinkai, ed., *Nihon-shi yōgo daijiten* (Tokyo: Hakushobō, 1978).

19. The two articles by Nagahara Keiji cited in n. 16 illustrate the first position. Katsumata Shizuo ("Sengoku daimyō kenchi ni kan suru ikkōsatsu," in Nagahara, ed., *Sengoku-ki no kenryoku to shakai*, pp. 3–34) espouses the second position. Katsumata uses the Takeda surveys, which resulted in the expropriation of *myōshu* gains, to rebut claims that *myōshu* were real powers able to bargain for, and win, considerable concessions from military authorities. It must be remembered, though, that evidence from the larger and stronger domains cannot be perceived as typical. The Shinshū sectarians, whom I shall discuss in the following chapter, as well as villagers in poorly consolidated domains, were often successful antagonists against local daimyo.

20. The best available list of *sengoku* daimyo is in Nagahara et al., eds., *Chūsei-shi handobukku*, pp. 397–402. Any such list is necessarily difficult to compile and estimates of daimyo numbers during one particular decade must be rough. The list in this handbook does not include some smaller and transient houses, nor does it mention leading retainers of great lords who might qualify as daimyo under a definition that stressed the area of land controlled rather than the autonomy of rule.

21. See n. 13 for a list of *shugo* houses that survived into the *sengoku* era.

22. Like *jizamurai*, *kokujin* is a word of many meanings. It is used here to designate warriors from the proprietary class. For further definition, see the sources mentioned in n. 18. For a detailed and highly informative case study of one *kokujin*, see Bitō Sakiko, "Kinai shoryōshu no seiritsu," in Hōgetsu Keigo Sensei Kanreki Kinen-kai, ed., *Nihon shakai keizai-shi kenkyū: chūsei* (Tokyo: Yoshikawa Kōbunkan, 1967). Also see Miyagawa Mitsuru, "From Shōen to Chigyō: Proprietary Lordship and the Structure of Local Power," in Hall and Toyoda, eds., *Japan in the Muromachi Age*, pp. 89–105.

23. See Hayashiya Tatsusaburō, *Tenka ittō* (*Nihon no rekishi*, 12; Tokyo: Chūō Kōron-sha, 1971), pp. 77–78.

24. For a history of Imagawa development, see Wakabayashi Atsushi, *Shizuoka-ken no rekishi* (Tokyo: Yamakawa Shuppan-sha, 1970), pp. 114–154. The Imagawa served as *shugo* in Tōtōmi from 1352 to 1401, from 1407 to 1413, and from 1511 to 1560.

25. See Miyagawa, "From Shōen to Chigyō," pp. 89–105, for discussion of the range and use of *shugo* privileges. Also see Satō Shin'ichi, "Muromachi bakufu-ron," in *Iwanami kōza: Nihon rekishi* (Tokyo: Iwanami Shoten, 1963), VII, 3–48, and Tanuma Mutsumi, "Muromachi bakufu to shugo ryōgoku," in Rekishigaku Kenkyū-kai, ed., *Hōken shakai no tenkai* (*Kōza Nihon-shi*, 3; Tokyo: Tōkyō Daigaku Shuppan-kai, 1978), pp. 85–115. See Nagahara et al., eds., *Chūsei-shi handobukku*, p. 414, for a list of estates in Suruga and the extant documentation. The number of estates listed for the Muromachi period is five.

26. The discussion of the Imagawa land surveys is based on Arimitsu

Yūgaku, "Sengoku daimyō Imagawa-shi no rekishi-teki seikaku," in Nihon-shi Kenkyū-kai, ed., *Nihon-shi kenkyū*, no. 138 (January, 1974), pp. 1–43. Of the sixty-six surveys, thirty-nine covered temple and shrine holdings, thirteen the holdings of the Imagawa themselves, and fourteen the holdings of *kokujin*. Institutional continuity doubtless accounts for the survival of numerous documents concerning religious properties. It need not be assumed that temples and shrines controlled an inordinate amount of property or that inspection of their lands was any more frequent than inspection of Imagawa or *kokujin* holdings.

27. Katsumata Shizuo argues, in opposition to Arimitsu, that the later Imagawa surveys were prompted not by judicial actions but by an interest in rigorous reporting of all village resources. He also argues that the Imagawa were less concerned with converting the *myōshu* into retainers than they were in confiscating *myōshu* revenues, an attitude somewhat different from their attitude toward *kokujin*. See "Sengoku daimyō kenchi ni kan suru ikkōsatsu," pp. 33–34. Both criticisms help refine the Arimitsu thesis without refuting its basic premises that many of the early Imagawa surveys were responses to judicial appeals, and that control of *myōshu* incomes led to the investiture of *myōshu* retainers as well as the appropriation of a good share of *myōshu* rents.

28. Satō Shin'ichi, Ikeuchi Yoshisuke, and Momose Kesao, *Buke kahō* (*Chūsei hōsei shiryō-shū*, pt. 3; Tokyo: Iwanami Shoten, 1969), I, 115.

29. See Arimitsu, "Sengoku daimyō Imagawa-shi rekishi-teki seikaku," p. 20, for a list of *zōbun* resulting from the Imagawa surveys.

30. For lists and discussions of *zōbun* in the Hōjō and Takeda domains, see Nagahara Keiji, "Daimyō ryōgoku seika no kandaka-sei," in Nagahara Keiji, John W. Hall, and Kozo Yamamura, eds., *Sengoku jidai* (Tokyo: Yoshikawa Kōbunkan, 1978), pp. 5–8; and Katsumata, "Sengoku daimyō kenchi ni kan suru ikkōsatsu," especially pp. 4–14. Nagahara and Katsumata discuss various sources for the new tax increments: production increases, rents, and daimyo claims to lands outside the estate and *kokugaryō* systems that had been held by minor officials. Katsumata, and Arimitsu, find the expropriation of landlords' rents (*myōshu kajishi tokubun*) to be the critical source of the increases.

31. See Arimitsu, "Sengoku daimyō Imagawa-shi no rekishi-teki seikaku," pp. 28–42, for analysis of such investitures and the changing definition of *myōshu* from landlord to retainer. In one particularly clear case discussed by Arimitsu, that of the *myōshu* Sugiyama Zenjirō, the Imagawa claimed 200 *hyō* of additional taxes (probably former rental fees), and invested in him 10 *koku*, 1 *to* of rice, and 5 *kammon* in cash. The investiture was a reward for Zenjirō's assistance in the surveying of his village and assumed continuing service to the Imagawa. The investiture document concludes: "Should there be a disagreement between farmers and managers [over tax adjustments in times of natural disaster], and should there be [consequent] demands on your duly invested *myōshiki*, we shall strictly forbid it." Find the document in Kodama Kōta et al., eds., *Shiryō ni yoru Nihon no ayumi: kinsei* (Tokyo: Yoshikawa Kōbunkan, 1955), p. 5.

32. This cadastre resulted from a survey of the Erinji holdings, lands covering several villages in the province of Kai, that was conducted in 1563. The discussion is based on Sugiyama Hiroshi, *Sengoku daimyō* (*Nihon no rekishi*, 11; Tokyo: Chūō Kōron-sha, 1970), pp. 219–223, and Katsumata, "Sengoku daimyō kenchi ni kan suru ikkōsatsu," pp. 3–34. Find the relevant documents in Miyagawa Mitsuru, *Taikō kenchi-ron* (Tokyo: Ochanomizu Shobō, 1963), III,

55–91. (Volumes I and II of this work were first published in 1957 and 1959.) For discussion of typical tax exemptions and their function during the *sengoku* period, see Nagahara, "Daimyō ryōgoku seika no kandaka-sei," pp. 8–10, and Araki, *Taikō kenchi to kokudaka-sei*, pp. 63–72. Araki's analysis proceeds from a study of a village in the Hōjō domain and parallels our survey of Kamikuze and the Erinji holdings.

33. Find lists of sixteenth-century land surveys in Takayanagi and Takeuchi, *Kadokawa Nihon-shi jiten*, pp. 1027–28, and Kodama et al., eds., *Shiryō ni yoru Nihon no ayumi: kinsei*, p. 6. Neither list is authoritative. Both must be checked against studies, such as Arimitsu's, of individual domains.

34. See Ikegami Hiroko, "Sengoku daimyō ryōgoku ni okeru shoryō oyobi kashindan hensei no tenkai," in Nagahara, ed., *Sengoku-ki no kenryoku to shakai*, pp. 35–103, particularly pp. 60–85, for discussion of recruitment by the Hōjō and the organization of the basic vassal corps. The size of the vassal investitures varied significantly: 11 of the 556 housemen held land parcels valued at over 1,000 *kammon* each, 228 held land parcels valued at under 50 *kammon* each (p. 68). Ikegami argues that the Hōjō controlled their housemen by keeping fiefs generally small and scattered. Ikegami assumes that the Hōjō were able to assemble troops greatly in excess of the regular troops attached to their vassals by forgiving various agricultural taxes in exchange for emergency military duty.

35. Arimitsu, Katsumata, and Nagahara all conclude that the significant increases in *zōbun* in the Imagawa, Takeda, and other domains reflect real and continuing tax gains. See Nagahara, "Daimyō ryōgoku seika no kandaka-sei," pp. 4–8, and Sugiyama, *Sengoku daimyō*, pp. 223–225, for a discussion of tax rates.

36. See the Imagawa and Takeda laws on *munebechisen* and *tansen* in Satō, Ikeuchi, and Momose, *Buke kahō*, I, 130 (article 20) and 209–210 (articles 32–37). A clear description of the Hōjō levy appears in Sugiyama, *Sengoku daimyō*, pp. 228–230. For the labor taxes, see Sugiyama, pp. 234–236, and Satō, Ikeuchi, and Momose, I, 203 (article 13). For a more general analysis of tax burdens, see Nagahara, "Daimyō ryōgoku seika no kandaka-sei," pp. 10–13; Sugiyama, pp. 225–228; Araki, *Taikō kenchi to kokudaka-sei*, pp. 77–82.

37. House codes were issued in the *sengoku* period by the Ōuchi (between 1492 and 1500), Imagawa (1526, additions 1553), Date (1536), Takeda (1547), Sagara (completed 1555), Yūki (1556), Miyoshi (c. 1560), and Rokkaku (1567). The Chōsokabe code of 1597 really postdates the era of warring states. The Date, Sagara, Miyoshi, and Chōsokabe houses had not provided *shugo* during the Ashikaga period. Find these codes in Satō, Ikeuchi, and Momose, *Buke kahō*, I. The original and supplementary statutes of the Imagawa appear on pp. 115–131.

38. The numerically most significant statutes govern violent crimes (items, 7, 8, 9, 10, 11, 12, and 25) and loans and mortgages (items 13, 14, 16, 18, 19, and 20—also supplementary item 9).

39. The procedural laws appear in Satō, Ikeuchi, and Momose, *Buke kahō*, I, 131–134. Items 2, 4, and 17 of the original statutes, as well as items 1, 2, 4, and 19 of the supplementary statutes, also concern procedure.

40. See particularly items 5 and 6 of the original statutes; item 21 of the supplementary statutes.

41. Wakita Osamu, *Oda seiken no kiso kōzō* (*Shokuhō seiken no bunseki*, 1; Tokyo: Tōkyō Daigaku Shuppan-kai, 1975), pp. 41–47; Suzuki, *Oda Nobunaga,* pp. 1–13.

42. Suzuki, *Oda Nobunaga,* pp. 1, 11–12; Wakabayashi, *Shizuoka-ken no re-kishi,* pp. 143–146.

43. Wakabayashi, *Shizuoka-ken no rekishi,* pp. 142–147.

44. For description of the battle of Okehazama and its prelude, see Haya-shiya, *Tenka ittō,* pp. 78–81; Wakabayashi, *Shizuoka-ken no rekishi,* pp. 146–147; Yamaga Sokō, *Buke jiki* (Tokyo: Shinjimbutsu Ōrai-sha, 1969), pp. 753–758.

45. Hayashiya, *Tenka ittō,* pp. 82–85, 90–92.

46. The first book of Oze Hoan's *Taikō-ki* covers Hideyoshi's youth and early military career. See pp. 40–48 for the account of the Saitō campaign. Also see Suzuki, *Oda Nobunaga,* pp. 21–28. Saitō Yoshitatsu died in 1561 and it was his son, Tatsuoki, whom Nobunaga fought.

47. The letter is quoted in Teishitsu Rin'ya Kyoku, *Go-ryōchi shikō,* p. 237. Also see *Kyōto no rekishi,* IV, 46–47, for discussion of the "other matters." The emperor first made requests to Nobunaga to restore estates in his domain in 1564. See Suzuki, *Oda Nobunaga,* p. 21.

48. See Ponsonby-Fane, *Kyoto,* p. 271, and Suzuki, *Oda Nobunaga,* p. 4, for discussion of the donations that made Ōgimachi's enthronement ceremony possible.

49. Okuno Takahiro, *Ashikaga Yoshiaki* (Tokyo: Yoshikawa Kōbunkan, 1960), pp. 107–139; *Shiryō Kyōto no rekishi,* III, 373 (documents 1–3). Yoshiaki's initial overtures to Nobunaga occurred in 1566 and were renewed thereafter.

3. The Terror

1. Nobunaga may have planned to build a personal residence in Kyoto during 1573, but the project was never completed. See *Shiryō Kyōto no rekishi,* III, 375 (document 9). Around 1576 he did build a mansion, the Nijō *shin-gosho,* but turned it over to the crown prince. See Asao Naohiro, " 'Shōgun kenryoku' no sōshutsu," pt. 2, in *Rekishi hyōron* (August, 1972), pp. 50–53.

2. Most accounts suggest that Nobunaga took his own life. For three de-scriptions of the Honnōji affair, see *Shiryō Kyōto no rekishi,* III, 378 (document 16); Ōmura Yūko, *Tenshō-ki,* in Kuwata, ed., *Taikō shiryō-shū,* pp. 28–30; and Tsuji Zennosuke, ed., *Tamon'in nikki* (Tokyo: Kadokawa Shoten, 1967), III, 224–225. Also see Kuwata Tadachika, *Sadō no rekishi* (Tokyo: Tōkyō-dō Shup-pan-sha, 1972), pp. 115–117.

3. See Sassa Katsuaki, *Oda Nobunaga* (Tokyo: Shinjimbutsu Ōrai-sha, 1973), pp. 248–255, and Takayanagi Mitsutoshi, *Akechi Mitsuhide* (Tokyo: Yo-shikawa Kōbunkan, 1958), pp. 212–226.

4. Yūda Yoshio, ed., *Bunraku jōruri-shū* (*Nihon koten bungaku taikei,* 99; Tokyo: Iwanami Shoten, 1965), p. 364.

5. Okuno Takahiro, ed., *Oda Nobunaga monjo no kenkyū,* 2 vols. (Tokyo: Yoshikawa Kōbunkan, 1969–1970), II, 239–243. The sixteen statutes include nine main articles and seven supplementary articles. The statute cited is main article six. It is interesting that Nobunaga followed the pattern of the Hoso-kawa and the Miyoshi in channeling major documents through the shogun.

6. Okuno, *Ashikaga Yoshiaki,* pp. 142–159.

7. The best known of the Ashikaga residences, Yoshimitsu's *Hana no gosho*, fell in the fifteenth century, and a more recent headquarters was destroyed during the raids of the Miyoshi and Matsunaga against the thirteenth shogun, Yoshiteru. For a brief history of Ashikaga palaces, see Ponsonby-Fane, *Kyoto*, pp. 186–192. Ponsonby-Fane claims that Yoshiteru committed suicide, although some historians believe he was killed by the Matsunaga. For descriptions of the Nijō *gosho*, which stood between Karasuma and Shimmachi, Kasuga and Konoe streets, see *Kyōto no rekishi*, IV, 50–53; Toba Masao, *Nihon jōkaku jiten* (Tokyo: Tōkyō-dō Shuppan-sha, 1971), pp. 243–244; and *Shiryō Kyōto no rekishi*, III, 374–375 (documents 6 and 7). The garden, and Nobunaga's interest in gardening, are discussed in Shigemori Mirei and Shigemori Kanto, *Momoyama no niwa* (*Nihon teien-shi taikei*, 11; Tokyo: Shakai Shisō-sha, 1971), I, 63.

8. Okuno, ed., *Oda Nobunaga monjo no kenkyū*, II, 343–346.

9. Cited in Kuwata, *Taikō no tegami*, p. 14.

10. A detailed study of Nobunaga's use of muskets, including discussion of supply problems, the numbers involved, and the extent of the Oda monopoly on Sakai's production, has yet to be undertaken. For one brief and characteristic analysis of the problem, see Imai Rintarō, "Nobunaga no shutsugen to chūsei-teki ken'i no hitei," in Fujiki Hisashi and Kitajima Manji, eds., *Shokuhō seiken* (*Ronshū Nihon rekishi*, 6; Tokyo: Yūseidō, 1974), pp. 62–63.

11. The letter was written to Imai Sōkyū, a Sakai merchant who had cautioned his peers against resistance to the Oda and had made an early overture to Nobunaga, before his attack on the city, by dispatching a precious tea vessel to him. In return for Sōkyū's support, Nobunaga made him a municipal official and settled an annual rice allowance of 2,200 *koku* upon him. See Toyoda Takeshi, *Sakai* (1957, Tokyo: Shibundō, 1978), pp. 73–90. Also see Fujimoto Atsuchi, *Ōsaka-fu no rekishi* (Tokyo: Yamakawa Shuppan-sha, 1969), pp. 106–108. Nobunaga levied extraordinary taxes not only in Sakai but in Settsu, Yamato, and Izumi as well. He also demanded 5,000 *kammon* from Ishiyama Honganji.

12. Basic narrative accounts of Nobunaga's campaigns after 1570 can be found in Suzuki, *Oda Nobunaga*, pp. 64–106, Imai, "Nobunaga no shutsugen," pp. 50–57, and Kuwata, *Taikō no tegami*, pp. 14–24. Yamaga Sokō provides one of the earliest and most detailed analyses of these campaigns and focuses upon major battles such as Anegawa and Mikatagahara in the *Buke jiki*, pp. 777–814. Maps are included in this study. These and other histories rely heavily upon the *Shinchō kōki*, ed. Kuwata Tadachika (Tokyo: Shinjimbutsu Ōrai-sha 1965), a biography of Nobunaga written about 1600 by one of his secretaries, Ōta Gyūichi. Although Gyūichi is frequently imprecise and capable of fictional elaboration, the main elements of the biography appear trustworthy.

13. Kuwata, *Taikō no tegami*, pp. 19–20. This book contains a good summary of the Ōmi and Echizen campaigns on pp. 13–25.

14. Translated from the *Nobunaga-ki* (*Dai Nihon shiryō*, pt. 10, vol. 6, pp. 871–874) in Ryusaku Tsunoda et al., comps., *Sources of Japanese Tradition* (New York: Columbia University Press, 1958), p. 316.

15. See the sources mentioned in n. 12 for description of this campaign.

16. See Okuno, *Ashikaga Yoshiaki*, pp. 216–227, and *Shiryō Kyōto no rekishi*, III, 377 (document 13). *Kyōto no rekishi*, IV, 88–89, describes Nobunaga's raid upon the northern capital.

17. Owada Tetsuo, *Ōmi Asai-shi* (Tokyo: Shinjimbutsu Ōrai-sha, 1973),

pp. 247–250; Kuwata Tadachika, *Yodogimi* (Tokyo: Yoshikawa Kōbunkan, 1958), pp. 19–24.

18. Although we cannot catalogue Oda brutalities in detail here, we might note that an attack upon the Shinshū sectarians of Ise during 1574 concluded with the burning of a Shinshū fortress said to have held over 20,000 people and with the massacre of those who attempted to flee. Another 20,000 or more people may have died during the campaign against the sectarians in Echizen in 1575. See Okuno Takahiro, *Nobunaga to Hideyoshi* (Tokyo: Shibundō, 1972), p. 36, and Okuno, ed., *Oda Nobunaga monjo no kenkyū*, II, 66–70.

19. Imai, "Nobunaga no shutsugen," p. 59, and Wakita, *Oda seiken no kiso kōzō*, pp. 41–47. This figure probably reflected not the total productivity of the land (*seisandaka*), but its yield in taxes (*nengudaka*). Wakita Osamu argues that all valuations of land before Hideyoshi's period were probably *nengudaka*; see *Kinsei hōken-sei seiritsu shiron* (Tokyo: Tōkyō Daigaku Shuppan-kai, 1977), pp. 7–53. Also see chapter 5, n. 27, below.

20. See Wakita, *Oda seiken no kiso kōzō*, pp. 48–59, and Imai, "Nobunaga no shutsugen," pp. 58–61. The best biographical reference work on major warring-states figures is Takayanagi and Matsudaira, *Sengoku jimmei jiten*.

21. The Owari men included Gamō Ujisato, Horio Hidemasa, Katō Kiyomasa, Fukushima Masanori, Katō Yoshiaki, and Horio Yoshiharu. The Mino men included Inaba Sadasuke, Aoyama Hidemasa, Kajita Hidemasa, Tsubouchi Toshisada, and Takenaka Shigeharu. For discussion of Hideyoshi's vassals, see Kuwata Tadachika, *Toyotomi Hideyoshi kenkyū*, pp. 331–340, and Kuwata, *Taikō kashindan* (Tokyo: Shinjimbutsu Ōrai-sha, 1971), which covers the Yellow Shields and the Tsukubushima records on pp. 61–69, 113–120. The *Tenshōki* includes no full account of Hideyoshi's early vassal corps. Asao Naohiro discusses the problem of fief transfers and the status of previous investitures in " 'Shōgun kenryoku' no sōshutsu," pt. 3, in *Rekishi hyōron* (September, 1974), pp. 34–35. Nobunaga's specific requirement that the Maeda surrender all Echizen claims before the move to Noto may suggest that earlier transfers did not necessarily involve the forfeiture of previous holdings.

22. Okuno, ed., *Oda Nobunaga monjo no kenkyū*, II, 702–703. See articles 3, 5, and 6. Also see Imai, "Nobunaga no shutsugen," pp. 61–62.

23. Kuwata, *Taikō no tegami*, pp. 26–27. See pp. 27–29 for a brief account of city building in Nagahama.

24. Ibid., pp. 28–29.

25. See Wakita, *Oda seiken no kiso kōzō*, p. 132, for a recent list of land registrations carried out by Nobunaga and his daimyo. The list is a conservative one that relies primarily upon daimyo and temple records (the *Shinchō kōki* is cited only once) and therefore tends toward greater accuracy than more speculative surveys of the subject.

26. Kunitomo in the Sakada district of Ōmi was a traditional center of metal work that, during the mid-sixteenth century, became one of the first areas to produce muskets in Japan. The Asai and the Ashikaga collaborated in its development, and the weapons produced there were critical to the defense of Odani castle. Muskets were also forged in some quantity at Negoro temple in Kii, an area brought under Hideyoshi's control in 1585.

27. The *Oda jinja monjo* and the *Shibata Katsuie shimatsuki* describe Katsuie's seizure of weapons in Echizen from 1576 to 1578. See Kuwata, *Toyotomi Hideyoshi kenkyū*, pp. 269–270.

28. Okuno, ed., *Oda Nobunaga monjo no kenkyū*, II, 87–92. See similar laws for Kai and Shinano on pp. 702–703. The Echizen code makes another important point that might be overlooked. Item 4 indicates that Nobunaga would protect only those estates that were actively and consistently administered by their proprietors. In general, he was disposed to honor claims that had been successfully defended during the twenty-year period preceding his ascent.

29. The item recalls the conclusion of the "Laws Governing the Military Households" issued by the Tokugawa in 1635: "In all things, follow the rules of Edo in all provinces and places." See Ishii Shirō, *Kinsei buke shisō* (*Nihon shisō taikei*, 27; Tokyo: Iwanami Shoten, 1974), p. 547. Perhaps closer to Nobunaga's statute is the statement contained in an oath required of daimyo in 1611 that "when laws are issued from Edo, they shall be strictly observed." See Ishii, p. 455.

30. Okuno, ed., *Oda Nobunaga monjo no kenkyū*, II, 189–191.

31. Translated from *Cartas que os Padres y Hermanos de la Compañia de Jesus que andan en los Reynos de Japon escrivieron* . . . (Alcalá, 1575), p. 287, in Michael Cooper, *They Came to Japan: An Anthology of European Reports on Japan, 1543–1640* (Berkeley and Los Angeles: University of California Press, 1965), p. 93.

32. See Asao, " 'Shōgun kenryoku' no sōshutsu," pt. 2, pp. 48–51, for a discussion of Nobunaga's titles and his attitudes toward them.

33. See Okuno Takahiro, *Kōshitsu gokeizai-shi no kenkyū* (Tokyo: Chūō Kōron-sha, 1944), II, 210–224, for a detailed analysis of attempts to recover imperial estates during Nobunaga's period in power. Estate income remained erratic. A *shōen* in Ise, for example, paid taxes in 1567, but no further mention of income from this province occurs until 1580, when the throne received a gift of gold. Two parcels of land in Wakasa delivered taxes until 1580, but sporadically and in varying amounts. Estates were not restored in Nobunaga's provinces of Owari and Mino.

34. *Kyōto no rekishi*, IV, 60–62; Okuno, *Kōshitsu gokeizai-shi no kenkyū*, pp. 225–227. The amount of five hundred twenty *koku* of rice was originally levied. The neighborhood associations were to render three-tenths of this capital to the court each year, in monthly installments. Southern Kyoto may have made payments until 1576, but payments from northern Kyoto came to an end in 1573 after Nobunaga carried out a raid against its residents for refusing to pay him a special military tax. See *Kyōto no rekishi*, IV, 88–89.

35. Teishitsu Rin'ya Kyoku, *Go-ryōchi shikō*, pp. 239–241; Okuno, *Kōshitsu gokeizai-shi no kenkyū*, pp. 227–238. Nobunaga's other gifts to the throne and the work on the palace are described in *Kyōto no rekishi*, IV, 56–60. His father, Nobuhide, had earlier assisted in the repair of the palace and the Ise shrine. See *Go-ryōchi shikō*, p. 237.

36. *Kyōto no rekishi*, IV, 229–232.

37. The Frois report is cited at length, and the argument described in this paragraph is advanced in the fascinating article by Asao Naohiro, " 'Shōgun kenryoku' no sōshutsu," pt. 2, pp. 46–59. After his death, Nobunaga was elevated to the position of *daijō daijin*.

38. Ōta Gyūichi, *Shinchō kōki*, pp. 197–200. Also see Shun'ichi Takayanagi, "The Glory That Was Azuchi," in *Monumenta Nipponica*, vol. 32, no. 4 (Winter, 1977), pp. 515–524.

39. Nobunaga was an avid, and calculating, student of tea. He patronized

a number of tea masters, including Sen no Rikyū, Imai Sōkyū, and Tsuda Sōkyū—all men of influence in Sakai. He bought or confiscated important tea vessels in Kyoto and Sakai that he displayed at gatherings of connoisseurs and occasionally gave to his vassals as rewards. Hideyoshi received his first tea vessels from Nobunaga after the conquest of the Bessho at Miki castle. Nobunaga also "bestowed permission" upon his generals to practice the way of tea, much as he invested them with fiefs. He understood tea as a gentlemanly art, an entry into mercantile circles, and an embellishment to the craft of politics. See *Kyōto no rekishi*, IV, 65–67, 659–662; Kuwata, *Sadō no rekishi*, pp. 111–117; and Murai Yasuhiko, *Sen no Rikyū* (Tokyo: Nippon Hōsō Shuppan Kyōkai, 1973), pp. 136–155.

40. See Okuno, ed., *Oda Nobunaga monjo no kenkyū*, I, 184–185 for the Gifu laws; and II, 300–304 for the Azuchi laws.

41. Murai governed under the title of *shoshidai*. During the Ashikaga period, the head (*shoshi*) of the Board of Retainers (*samuraidokoro*) generally acted concurrently as the military governor (*shugo*) of Yamashiro province. The responsibility for Kyoto that derived from being *shugo* was delegated to a deputy (*shoshidai*). Thus Murai's title conformed to the historical nomenclature for his job. For discussion of his rule in the capital, see *Kyōto no rekishi*, IV, 61–62, 91–94, 375–376, 510–514. Although few documents survive from the Murai administration, references to his decisions are frequent in a collection of seventy documents dating from the first years of his successor's administration. See Maeda Gen'i, "Gen'i hōin gejijō," in *Zoku gunsho ruijū* (Tokyo: Zoku Gunsho Ruijū Kansei-kai, 1961), ser. 23, pt. 2, *kan* 666, pp. 329–342.

42. Okuno, ed., *Oda Nobunaga monjo no kenkyū*, II, 547–552; Tsuji, ed., *Tamon'in nikki*, 126–131. Also see pp. 552–553 for an accounting from Hōryūji.

43. See Asao, " 'Shōgun kenryoku' no sōshutsu," pts. 2 and 3, particularly pp. 25–35 of pt. 3, for an excellent discussion of the vocabulary of Nobunaga's rule. Asao argues that Nobunaga's increasing use of words such as *kōgi*, and his allusions to the future, display a broadening sense of legitimacy. Also see Wakita Osamu, "Oda seiken," in Wakita Osamu, moderator, *Shokuhō seiken-ron* (*Shimpojiumu Nihon rekishi*, 10; Tokyo: Gakusei-sha, 1972), pp. 85–92.

44. For a description of the Takeda campaign, see Yamaga Sokō, *Buke jiki*, pp. 806–814.

45. Inoue Toshio, *Ikkō ikki no kenkyū* (Tokyo: Yoshikawa Kōbunkan, 1968), pp. 256–648, and Suzuki, *Oda Nobunaga*, pp. 107–115, 123–152.

46. Imai, "Nobunaga no shutsugen," pp. 53–56. Following defeat at the hands of the Mōri navy in 1574, probably the first important sea battle in his career, Nobunaga commissioned Takigawa Kazumasu and others to construct a small fleet (reportedly seven ships) of armored vessels. Formidable enough to impress the Portuguese, these ships sailed in 1578 from Ise to Osaka, where they set up a blockade of the harbor.

47. Okuno, ed., *Oda Nobunaga monjo no kenkyū*, II, 508–510.

48. While the conflict between daimyo and the Shinshū sectarians can be easily traced, it is less easy to document the relationship between theoretical and practical politics within the Shinshū community itself. The extent to which "self rule" in the community's strongholds brought an egalitarian departure from prevailing forms of military administration has still to be demonstrated. Yet it remains important to some historians that the sect looked to an ideal at odds with the goals of the warlords. See, for example, Asao Naohiro, " 'Shōgun kenryoku' no sōshutsu," pt. 1, *Rekishi hyōron* (August, 1970), pp. 70–78. Also

see Stanley Weinstein, "Rennyo and the Shinshū Revival," in Hall and Toyoda, eds., *Japan in the Muromachi Age*, pp. 331–358, for an exceedingly interesting discussion of Shinshū beliefs and Rennyo's reforms in the late fifteenth century.

49. For description of the San'yō campaign, see Tanaka Yoshinari, *Toyotomi jidai-shi* (Tokyo: Meiji Shoin, 1934), pp. 12–20; and Kuwata, *Taikō no tegami*, pp. 34–49. See Hall, *Government and Local Power in Japan*, pp. 268–270, for an analysis of the relations between the Oda and the Ukita.

50. Ōmura Yūko, *Tenshō-ki*, p. 22.

4. Conquest and Conciliation

1. See Yamaga Sokō, *Buke jiki*, pp. 814–858, for discussion of Hideyoshi's major campaigns. A seventeenth-century work by a Confucian scholar and samurai, the *Buke jiki* also covers the major campaigns of the Oda and Tokugawa and includes biographical discussions of leading military figures and their retainers. There is also a section on castles. Based on the various *gunki-mono*, contemporary documents, letters, and family records, it is a scholarly account, largely reliable, which has become the foundation of most military history of the period. Maps accompany Sokō's tactical commentary.

2. For a discussion of *Tendō* (the Way of Heaven, or destiny), see, for example, Kuwata, *Taikō-ki*, pp. 628–633, and *Kyōto no rekishi*, IV, 718–719.

3. The list appears in *Hōkō ibun*, pp. 627–640. The nine opponents were: Tokugawa Ieyasu, 2,402,000 *koku*; Mōri Terumoto, 1,125,000 *koku*; Uesugi Kagekatsu, 919,000 *koku*; Date Masamune, 614,000 *koku*; Shimazu Yoshihiro, 559,-530 *koku*; Satake Yoshinobu, 530,000 *koku*; Ukita Hideie, 474,000 *koku*; Nabeshima Naoshige, 320,000 *koku*; Kobayakawa Hideaki, 300,000 *koku*. The Oda vassals were: Maeda Toshiie and his sons Toshinaga and Toshimasa, with 235,-000 *koku*, 320,000 *koku*, and 210,000 *koku* respectively; Hori Hideharu, 200,000 *koku*; Ikeda Nagayoshi, the son of Ikeda Tsuneoki, 200,000 *koku*. Hideyoshi's own retainers were: Fukushima Masanori, 200,000 *koku*; Mashita Nagamori, 200,000 *koku*. There are several problems with the list in *Hōkō ibun*. It includes the name of a deceased daimyo (Hori Hidemasa with 550,000 *koku*, whom I have eliminated from the above list), and the figures on income it includes are sometimes incorrect (Hori Hideharu, for example, had 300,000 *koku* according to his investiture document). Three daimyo listed in the *Hōkō ibun* document with under 200,000 *koku* had larger investitures than the document acknowledges: Chōsokabe Motochika, 220,000 *koku*; Ishida Mitsunari, 200,000 *koku*; Katō Kiyomasa, 200,000 *koku*. The first was an opponent of Hideyoshi, the others were his vassals. If we amend the above tally to include these men, nineteen daimyo had investitures of 200,000 *koku* or more: ten were opponents; five were Oda vassals; and four were Toyotomi vassals. Some scholars might wish to identify the sons of Maeda Toshiie and Ikeda Nagayoshi with the Toyotomi rather than the Oda camp. There is difficulty, further, with the size of Kobayakawa Hideaki's fief. Although Hideaki was transferred in 1598 from a domain in Kyushu valued at over 300,000 *koku* to one in Echizen valued at 120,000 *koku*, Hideyoshi decided to restore him to his original holding about the time of Hideyoshi's death. I have consequently left Hideaki on my list with a fief of 300,-000 *koku*. Such matters of judgment, and the errors in the *Hōkō ibun* list, make an authoritative analysis of the daimyo corps difficult. The document in *Hōkō ibun* is the only one of its kind, however, and invaluable in assessing the size and wealth of the group of Hideyoshi's daimyo.

4. A list of Hideyoshi's holdings appears in Araki, *Taikō kenchi to koku-daka-sei*, pp. 118–119. For a map of these holdings, see Asao Naohiro, "Toyotomi seiken-ron," in *Iwanami kōza: Nihon rekishi* (Tokyo: Iwanami Shoten, 1963), IX, 189.

5. My identification of the status of Toyotomi daimyo relies on Yamaga Sokō, *Buke jiki*, pp. 495–567; Kuwata, *Toyotomi Hideyoshi kenkyū*, pp. 329–340; and Kuwata, *Taikō kashindan*, pp. 61–243. While the terms *fudai* and *tozama* are used here for convenience, they are not strictly accurate. The word *fudai* in particular, implying hereditary vassalage, is inappropriate in the history of a regime that lasted only one generation. Kuwata prefers the terms *jikisanshū* (for *fudai*), *shinzan* (for former vassals of rival daimyo who entered Hideyoshi's service following the collapse of the original house or as the result of some other enticement), and *tozama* (rival daimyo who accepted Hideyoshi's suzerainty). See *Taikō kashindan*, pp. 59, 180.

6. See Tsuji, ed., *Tamon'in nikki*, III, 225–226. The annual Gion festival was even canceled following the Honnōji attack. Such cancellations were virtually unknown after the beginning of the sixteenth century.

7. *Kyōto no rekishi*, IV, 229–231; Kuwata, *Toyotomi Hideyoshi kenkyū*, pp. 156–160.

8. Okuno, *Nobunaga to Hideyoshi*, pp. 21–22; Kuwata, *Toyotomi Hideyoshi kenkyū*, pp. 160–168.

9. Ōmura Yūko, *Tenshō-ki*, pp. 34–36; Yamaga Sokō, *Buke jiki*, pp. 814–819.

10. *Kawasumi taikō-ki*, in Kuwata, ed., *Taikō shiryō-shū*, pp. 237–247.

11. Okuno, *Nobunaga to Hideyoshi*, p. 15.

12. *Hōkō ibun*, p. 1.

13. Eight letters from Hideyoshi to Kobayakawa Takakage, written prior to Nobunaga's death, are extant. See *Hōkō ibun*, pp. 1–7.

14. For descriptions of the Kiyosu conference, see Ōmura Yūko, *Tenshō-ki*, p. 38, and the *Kawasumi taikō-ki*, pp. 274–281. Also see Tanaka, *Toyotomi jidai-shi*, pp. 23–25, and Kuwata, *Toyotomi Hideyoshi kenkyū*, pp. 165–166.

15. The Hideyoshi apocrypha represents him as the dominant personality at both the Kiyosu conference and at Nobunaga's memorial service. He emerges in the *Taikō-ki* as the clear leader, who prevails by virtue of a strong character. For an interesting English version of such representations, see Walter Dening, *The Life of Toyotomi Hideyoshi* (Kobe: J. L. Thompson and Co., 1930; rpt. New York: AMS Press, 1971), pp. 194–200.

16. *Kyōto no rekishi*, IV, pp. 255–258, 367.

17. Shimonaka Yasaburō, comp., *Nihon shiryō shūsei* (Tokyo: Heibon-sha, 1956), p. 255.

18. *Asano-ke monjo* (*Dainihon komonjo, Iewake monjo*, ser. 2, comp. Tōkyō Teikoku Daigaku Shiryō Hensanjo; Tokyo: Tōkyō Teikoku Daigaku, 1906), pp. 15–23.

19. Kuwata, *Toyotomi Hideyoshi kenkyū*, pp. 168–175; Tanaka, *Toyotomi jidai-shi*, pp. 27–36.

20. Yamaga Sokō, *Buke jiki*, pp. 819–833.

21. *Hōkō ibun*, p. 34.

22. Ōmura Yūko, *Tenshō-ki*, p. 62.

23. See Kuwata, *Taikō no tegami*, pp. 86–87, for a remarkable letter of condolence sent by Hideyoshi to Tsuneoki's mother. The campaign is described in Yamaga Sokō, *Buke jiki*, pp. 833–856; Kuwata, *Toyotomi Hideyoshi kenkyū*, pp. 175–190. Nobukatsu is sometimes called Nobuo.

24. Okuno, *Ashikaga Yoshiaki*, pp. 271–272.

25. Yamaga Sokō, *Buke jiki*, pp. 822–823; Kuwata, *Taikō kashindan*, pp. 61–75, 161–165. Kuwata's work is largely based upon the *Buke jiki* and, like its source, is unable to describe recruitment, numbers, and the chain of command with precision. Hideyoshi's letters (for example, *Hōkō ibun*, pp. 33–36) very occasionally mention troop numbers and division commanders, but do not permit detailed assessments of these matters. The *Taikō-ki* (for example, pp. 134–136, 170–173) and the *Buke jiki* rely upon the *Tenshō-ki* data and, to some extent, information from other war tales, such as the *Taikō gunki*.

26. Kuwata, *Toyotomi Hideyoshi kenkyū*, pp. 336–337; Kuwata, *Taikō kashindan*, pp. 206–217.

27. *Asano-ke monjo*, pp. 28–38.

28. Kuwata, *Toyotomi Hideyoshi kenkyū*, pp. 168–169.

29. *Kawasumi taikō-ki*, pp. 323–326.

30. Any list of leading daimyo and competitors for national power is necessarily somewhat arbitrary. (Nobunaga, for example, would not be on such a list for 1565; Hideyoshi himself would be properly subsumed under the Oda house in a 1580 list.) Other than the Oda, however, the great houses in 1580 would include the Date, Hōjō, Takeda, Uesugi, Tokugawa, Mōri, Chōsokabe, Ōtomo, Ryūzōji, and Shimazu. John W. Hall identifies thirteen houses that, in 1572, controlled "over two-thirds of Japan": the Hōjō, Takeda, Uesugi, Asakura, Tokugawa, Oda, Asai, Mōri, Yamana, Chōsokabe, Ōtomo, Ryūzōji, and Shimazu; see *Government and Local Power*, p. 272. By 1580, of course, Nobunaga had destroyed the Asai and the Asakura; the Mōri had destroyed the Yamana. A list for 1585 would also exclude the Takeda (defeated by Nobunaga in 1582) and the Ryūzōji (defeated by the Shimazu in 1584).

31. Kuwata, *Taikō no tegami*, p. 76.

32. Ōmura Yūko, *Tenshō-ki*, pp. 62–64. This list, although the most reliable of its kind, is incomplete. For further discussion, see Tanaka, *Toyotomi jidai-shi*, pp. 39–41; Hanami Sakumi, *Azuchi Momoyama jidai*, in *Sōgō Nihon-shi taikei* (Tokyo, 1929), VIII, 376–379.

33. The identification as well as the characterization of daimyo as *fudai* or Oda men throughout this section relies upon Yamaga Sokō, *Buke jiki*, pp. 495–567, and Kuwata, *Taikō kashindan*, pp. 61–243.

34. *Hōkō ibun*, p. 53. As an indication of the limitations of the *Tenshō-ki* list of 1584 investitures, this grant is not mentioned there.

35. Of these thirty-seven provinces, five had come through recent wars: Tamba fell with the defeat of Mitsuhide; Ōmi, Echizen, Mino, and Ise were largely taken during the Shibata campaign. Three other provinces, Kaga, Noto, and Etchū, were acquired indirectly through the Shibata offensive. Once conquered by Shibata Katsuie and held by his vassals, this territory entered Hideyoshi's sphere following a Toyotomi alliance with the former Shibata vassal Maeda Toshiie and a truce with the Uesugi that guaranteed its boundaries. The ten San'in and San'yō provinces included Bitchū, Harima, and Awaji (Hideyoshi's last conquests for Nobunaga, seized during the Mōri campaign); Bizen

and Mimasaka (gained through alliance with the Ukita and secured through the Mōri treaty); and Wakasa, Hōki, Tango, Tajima, and Inaba (taken by Mitsuhide and Hideyoshi after 1577, during their drive to the Mōri stronghold). The Kinai and Iga came with Hideyoshi's acquisition of Yamashiro at Kiyosu, his move into Osaka in 1584, and his careful treatment of local Oda vassals. Hideyoshi controlled Owari after Oda Nobukatsu's surrender in 1584. The Tokugawa peace gave him influence in Mikawa, Tōtōmi, Suruga, Shinano, and Kai. The Uesugi alliance protected his interests in Echigo. The Mōri alliance protected his interests in Bingo, Iwami, Aki, Nagato, and Suō.

36. The *Hōkō ibun*, although it is not complete, contains very few investiture documents for the first eight years of Hideyoshi's tenure. See the principal examples on pp. 49, 51–52, 53, 70, 143, 147, 148, 157, 169, 187, 235, 238.

37. Ōmura Yūko, *Tenshō-ki*, pp. 36, 60, 113–114; *Kawasumi taikō-ki*, pp. 316, 324.

38. Hideyoshi adopted sons from the Oda, Maeda, Ukita, and Kobayakawa houses. For discussion of his *ichimon-shū*, see Kuwata, *Taikō kashindan*, pp. 33–39; Shiba Ryōtarō, *Toyotomi-ke no hitobito* (Tokyo: Kadokawa Shoten, 1971), pp. 51–140, 155–194.

39. Tanaka, *Toyotomi jidai-shi*, pp. 78–85; Kuwata, *Toyotomi Hideyoshi kenkyū*, pp. 193–195; *Kawasumi taikō-ki*, pp. 339–349; Ōmura Yūko *Tenshō-ki*, pp. 98–99. Also see Tanaka, p. 79, for discussion of possible negotiations between Hideyoshi and the Chōsokabe preceding the invasion.

40. Tanaka, *Toyotomi jidai-shi*, p. 84.

41. See Marius B. Jansen, "Tosa in the Sixteenth Century: The 100 Article Code of Chōsokabe Motochika," in John W. Hall and Marius B. Jansen, eds., *Studies in the Institutional History of Early Modern Japan* (Princeton: Princeton University Press, 1968), pp. 89–114, for an excellent and brief study of Chōsokabe administration.

42. Kuwata, *Taikō no tegami*, p. 101. For discussion of the campaign, see Tanaka, *Toyotomi jidai-shi*, pp. 67–73. As we shall see, Narimasa was later enfeoffed in Kyushu, only to cause additional problems for Hideyoshi there. Both of the Sassa uprisings are sometimes characterized as "rebellions," the only such incidents in Hideyoshi's tenure prior to 1590.

43. Hideyoshi arranged for Toshiie's promotion to the position of *sangi*, eventually appointed him one of the *go tairō*, and frequently relied upon his counsel—particularly during the Korean campaign. Hideyoshi took one of Toshiie's daughters as a concubine and adopted a second, for whom he developed sufficient respect to write: "Were she a man, I would make her *kampaku.*" See Kuwata, *Taikō no tegami*, p. 201.

44. Ōmura Yūko, *Tenshō-ki*, pp. 67–69; Tanaka, *Toyotomi jidai-shi*, pp. 73–78.

45. Kuwata, *Toyotomi Hideyoshi kenkyū*, pp. 273–274; Kodama et al., eds., *Shiryō ni yoru Nihon no ayumi: kinsei*, pp. 46–47.

46. Kuwata, *Toyotomi Hideyoshi kenkyū*, pp. 274–275.

47. See *Kyōto no rekishi*, IV, 519–520.

48. See Kodama et al., eds., *Shiryō ni yoru Nihon no ayumi: kinsei*, p. 47; *Kyōto no rekishi*, IV, 175, 188–190; Tanaka, *Toyotomi jidai-shi*, pp. 150–153.

49. For a fine treatment of Christianity in Japan, particularly in Kyushu, see Charles Boxer, *The Christian Century in Japan* (Berkeley and Los Angeles:

University of California Press, 1951), especially pp. 91–187. A standard Japanese study is Okamoto Yoshitomo, *Jūroku seiki Nichiō kōtsū-shi no kenkyū* (Tokyo: Rokkō Shobō, 1942). Also see Matsuda Kiichi, *Hideyoshi no namban gaikō* (Tokyo: Shinjimbutsu Ōrai-sha, 1972).

50. See George Elison, *Deus Destroyed* (Cambridge: Harvard University Press, 1973), particularly the translation of "Ha Daisu," pp. 259–291.

51. See, for example, Boxer, *The Christian Century in Japan*, pp. 137–138.

52. For discussion of warfare in Kyushu prior to Hideyoshi's entry, as well as for description of the Toyotomi campaign in the island, see Hayashiya, *Tenka ittō*, pp. 361–384; *Kawasumi taikō-ki*, pp. 341–358.

53. Kuwata, *Toyotomi Hideyoshi kenkyū*, pp. 209–211.

54. Hayashiya, *Tenka ittō*, pp. 377–378.

55. *Hōkō ibun*, pp. 138–140.

56. For discussion of the Kyushu investitures, see Kuwata, *Toyotomi Hideyoshi kenkyū*, pp. 219, 222–223.

57. *Hōkō ibun*, pp. 138–140.

58. Translated by George Elison in *Deus Destroyed*, pp. 115–116.

59. See Elison, *Deus Destroyed*, pp. 115–125.

60. See Boxer, *The Christian Century in Japan*, pp. 91–136.

61. See Elison, *Deus Destroyed*, pp. 112–115, and Boxer, *The Christian Century in Japan*, pp. 140–142, for discussion of an offer by the Jesuit Vice-Provincial Coelho of mercenaries for Hideyoshi's campaigns. Clearly the offer deepened Hideyoshi's suspicions of the Church.

62. Quoted by Diego Pacheco in Michael Cooper, ed., *The Southern Barbarians* (Tokyo: Kodansha International, 1971), p. 73.

63. Hayashiya, *Tenka ittō*, p. 412.

64. For discussion of the campaign, see Ōmura Yūko, *Tenshō-ki*, pp. 140–145; Kuwata, *Toyotomi Hideyoshi kenkyū*, pp. 228–235; Hayashiya, *Tenka ittō*, pp. 408–420.

65. *Hōkō ibun*, pp. 213–231.

66. Kuwata, *Taikō no tegami*, pp. 155–156.

67. Kuwata, *Taikō no tegami*, pp. 159–160.

68. See Hayashiya, *Tenka ittō*, pp. 420–426; Tanaka, *Toyotomi jidai-shi*, 220–231.

69. Tanaka, *Toyotomi jidai-shi*, p. 215.

70. Ibid., pp. 215–216.

5. Toyotomi Policy: Shaping the New Order

1. Oze Hoan, *Taikō-ki*, p. 334.

2. There is neither a complete edition nor a complete directory of the voluminous Toyotomi papers. The *Hō taikō shinseki-shū*, 3 vols., Tōkyō Daigaku Shiryō Hensanjo, comp. (Tokyo: Tōkyō Daigaku Shuppan-kai, 1938), contains photostatic reproductions and annotations of documents written in the hands of Hideyoshi and his son, Hideyori. The *Hōkō ibun* is a far larger collection of both private and official documents of the Toyotomi, yet it is neither inclusive of all the Toyotomi papers nor annotated. It also fails to mention the original source of the documents it does include. For documents issued before Hideyo-

shi's appointment as *kampaku, see Hōkō ibun,* pp. 1–58; for the *kampaku* papers, see pp. 59–320 of the same volume; and for the *taikō* papers, see pp. 321–624. Documents of unclear date, as well as the list of vassals, are included in an appendix in *Hōkō ibun,* pp. 625–640. The records of Oda Nobunaga and Tokugawa Ieyasu have been published in full editions. See Okuno Takahiro, ed., *Oda Nobunaga monjo no kenkyū,* 2 vols. (Tokyo: Yoshikawa Kōbunkan, 1969–70); and Nakamura Kōya, ed., *Tokugawa Ieyasu monjo no kenkyū,* 5 vols. (Tokyo: Nihon Gakujutsu Shinkō-kai, 1958–71). For an analysis of the types of documents issuing from military houses in the Oda and Toyotomi periods, see Ijichi Tetsuo et al., *Nihon komonjo-gaku teiyō* (Tokyo: Shinsei-sha, 1966–69), I, 535–544. Hideyoshi apparently used a single seal throughout his tenure. For English translations of letters written in Hideyoshi's own hand, see Adriana Boscaro, *101 Letters of Hideyoshi* (Tokyo: Sophia University, 1975).

3. Two contemporary paraphrases of the original edict—from the Kikkawa and Date houses—indicate that orders to conduct a national census were relayed in individual letters. See *Kikkawa-ke monjo,* 3 vols. (*Dainihon komonjo, Iewake monjo,* ser. 9 [1925, 1926, 1932]), II, document 975; and Aida Jirō, "Futatabi Toyotomi Hideyoshi no kokō chōsa ni tsuite," in *Rekishi chiri,* vol. 47, no. 4 (April, 1926), p. 303.

4. See *Mōri-ke monjo,* 4 vols. (*Dainihon komonjo, Iewake monjo,* ser. 8, [1920, 1922, 1922, 1924]), III, document 900, for one variation on a set of instructions Hideyoshi dispatched to several generals in Korea. The first article of the document, addressed to Mōri Terumoto, requires the recipient to place his seal on the orders, and the closing remarks state: "Although these articles have [already] been ordered and dispatched to the *bugyō* [Hideyoshi's three magistrates in Korea], I [repeat them] in this fashion to inform you individually of my commands."

5. For an overview of the anomalies in Hideyoshi's legal language, see the Toyotomi documents in Kodama et al., eds., *Shiryō ni yoru Nihon no ayumi: kinsei,* pp. 31–71. While there are often reasonable distinctions between *sadame* and *oboe,* for example, the detection of real consistency in the use of such headings would require a somewhat forced logic.

6. *Hōkō ibun,* pp. 201–202.

7. A comparison of the sword-collection edicts in the Katō house papers (cited in Miyagawa, *Taikō kenchi-ron,* III, 358), the Kobayakawa house papers (2 vols., *Dainihon komonjo, Iewake monjo,* ser. 11 [1927], I, document 503), and the archives of the Ōsaka-jō Tenshukaku (no. A 115) reveals few and minor variations in language. All lack specific addressees and show the same date. Like the edicts prohibiting change of class (see Kodama et al., eds., *Shiryō ni yoru Nihon no ayumi: kinsei,* pp. 40–41) or Christian proselytism (see Kodama, pp. 50–51), the sword-collection orders appeared on *tategami.* This formal style, employed during Hideyoshi's time for general statutes, contrasts with the style of *origami*—sheets of paper, folded horizontally, carrying their message first in vertical lines along the upper half of the paper, then in vertical lines along the lower half of the paper, and finally in lines filling the margins in front of the opening of the missive and separating the continuing lines of the message. Used for personal correspondence, and always addressed to a specific recipient or recipients, *origami* were often preferred by Hideyoshi. As the photographs in the *Hō taikō shinseki-shū* demonstrate, communications written in Hideyoshi's own hand normally appeared in this form. The *Hōkō ibun* does not indicate distinctions between *tategami, origami,* and *kirigami* (*tategami* from which unused por-

tions have been cut). Since the distinctions are meaningful, it is well to examine critical documents in the original. The most easily consulted collection of Hideyoshi's documents may be found in the Ōsaka-jō Tenshukaku. A partial catalogue of holdings has been published in two special editions of the *Ōsaka-jō tenshukaku kiyō* under the title *Ōsaka-jō tenshukaku shozō shiryō mokuroku* (an original list plus a supplement, *zoku*, covering acquisitions and entries between 1967–1973).

8. Kodama et al., eds., *Shiryō ni yoru Nihon no ayumi: kinsei*, p. 51.

9. See Kuwata, *Toyotomi Hideyoshi kenkyū*, pp. 273–280, for a discussion of arms seizures in the monasteries, and p. 286 for documentary references to arms seizures among the townsmen.

10. Ibid., pp. 267–270. See pp. 266–289 of this volume for general coverage of the collection of arms.

11. Kodama et al., eds., *Shiryō ni yoru Nihon no ayumi: kinsei*, pp. 38–39.

12. Kuwata, *Toyotomi Hideyoshi kenkyū*, p. 283.

13. Fukuo Takeichirō, "Rakushu ni arawareta Hideyoshi seiken hihan," p. 200. (See chapter 2, n. 4, for the full citation.)

14. Kuwata, *Toyotomi Hideyoshi kenkyū*, pp. 286–287. Also see pp. 280–288 for discussion of the conduct of the *katana-gari* in the domains.

15. *Hōkō ibun*, pp. 311–312. As early as his Nagahama period, Hideyoshi issued his first laws concerning class movement. See Nakabe Yoshiko, *Kinsei toshi no seiritsu to kōzō* (Tokyo: Shinsei-sha, 1967), p. 243.

16. Nakabe, *Kinsei toshi no seiritsu to kōzō*, pp. 290–293, is particularly interested in the distinctions between Hideyoshi's urban and agrarian policies and the consistent favoritism for city dwellers displayed in the Toyotomi administration.

17. See Conrad Totman, *Politics in the Tokugawa Bakufu* (Cambridge: Harvard University Press, 1967), pp. 8–31, and Hall, *Government and Local Power in Japan*, pp. 238–270, for two discussions of the rationalization of military command in the *sengoku* era.

18. Hirasawa Kiyoto, *Kinsei sonraku e no ikō to heinō bunri* (Tokyo: Azekura Shobō, 1973), pp. 96–133, particularly pp. 96–100, 129–133. This study of Shinano from the *sengoku* to the early Tokugawa period traces the impact of Hideyoshi's reforms upon Shinano villages and draws into question the extent of his cadastral surveys in the province, as well as the immediate influence of his sword-collection and class-separation edicts.

19. See Miyagawa, *Taikō kenchi-ron*, III, 365–368, for laws issued by Ishida Mitsunari in lands specified as *kyūnin-chi* and *kurairi-chi*.

20. See Ishii, *Kinsei buke shisō*, pp. 454–455, for the Tokugawa law. The fact that subinfeudation in Kyushu and parts of the Tōhoku survived during the Tokugawa period is well known. For a discussion of Kyushu, see Robert Sakai, "The Consolidation of Power in Satsuma-Han," in Hall and Jansen, eds., *Studies in the Institutional History of Early Modern Japan*, pp. 133–139.

21. Miyagawa, *Taikō kenchi-ron*, III, 357 (articles 8–11 of document 45).

22. Items 6–9 of the "Hundred Article Code" of the Chōsokabe, translated by Marius Jansen, "Tosa in the Sixteenth Century: The 100 Article Code of Chōsokabe Motochika," in Hall and Jansen, eds., *Studies in the Institutional History of Early Modern Japan*, pp. 89–114. Also see Satō, Ikeuchi, and Momose, *Buke kahō*, I, 285–302.

23. Hirasawa, *Kinsei sonraku e no ikō to heinō bunri*, p. 10.

24. Miyagawa, *Taikō kenchi-ron*, III, 357 (article 4 of document 45). Also see p. 367 (article 7 of document 62): "Should there be any farmer who—since the time of the Odawara campaign—has deserted his fields and become a military retainer, a town dweller, or a tradesman, you shall inquire into his present position and inform us through our representatives."

25. *Kikkawa-ke monjo*, II, document 975. I have not translated the final two articles that deal with the conduct of this particular census in the Kikkawa domain. Aida Jirō ("Toyotomi Hideyoshi no kokō chōsa") argues that these orders were designed to gauge manpower strength in preparation for the Korean offensive. He finds the emphasis in the articles on full registration, not on the prohibition against movement. In a sequel to the essay ("Futatabi Toyotomi Hideyoshi no kokō chōsa ni tsuite"), he both reconsiders an earlier contention that a partial census was definitely carried out and concedes that these orders sought to control population movement as well as to measure manpower resources. He continues, however, to regard the latter objective as the critical one.

26. See Miyagawa, *Taikō kenchi-ron*, III, 4–270, for a number of *sengoku* cadastres that reveal such problems. Arimitsu argues ("Sengoku daimyō Imagawa-shi rekishi-teki seikaku," p. 13) that only the Hōjō house conducted uniform and well-organized *kenchi* in the era of warring states.

27. See Iinuma Jirō, *Kokudaka-sei no kenkyū* (Kyoto: Minerubua Shobō, 1974), pp. 25–64, for an analysis of patterns of land evaluation prior to Nobunaga's emergence. Iinuma argues (pp. 64–76) that land was evaluated in rice, and in terms of its total productivity (*kokudaka*), only in Ōmi before Oda rule. Nobunaga and Hideyoshi, he concludes, adopted their own evaluation practices from the Kyōgoku, Asai, and Rokkaku houses of this province. Nobunaga did continue to evaluate certain provinces (for example, Owari and Mino) in terms of cash. In some cases he also used tax figures, rather than total production figures, to express value. Also see n. 19, p. 252.

28. Wakita Osamu argues (*Oda seiken no kiso kōzō*, pp. 131–138) that six out of twelve documented surveys carried out under Nobunaga's orders were of the *kenchi* rather than the *sashidashi* variety. That is, they involved the active inspection of land by surveyors. This trend toward physical examination of fields was new, however, and cannot be reliably traced back into the *sengoku* period.

29. Katsumata ("Sengoku daimyō kenchi ni kan suru ikkōsatsu," pp. 33–34) makes the startling conclusion that some farmers were compiling *sashidashi* reports themselves. The prevailing assumption, which proceeds from study of the better-documented surveys such as the one at Kōfukuji, is that the proprietary class prepared the land reports.

30. See two lists of cadastral surveys during Hideyoshi's period in Miyagawa, *Taikō kenchi-ron*, I, 315, and in Iinuma, *Kokudaka-sei no kenkyū*, pp. 76–77, which also contains a partial list of surveys conducted directly under Hideyoshi's supervision (pp. 126–127). It is not clear that *kenchi* occurred in Inaba, Tajima, Iga, Etchū, Awaji, Tsushima, Iki, and parts of the Tōhoku during the Toyotomi tenure. On occasion Hideyoshi specifically exempted areas from registration. See Miyagawa, p. 329, concerning the exemption of Ise shrine.

31. *Kyōto no rekishi*, IV, 279.

32. Miyagawa, *Taikō kenchi-ron*, III, 328–329. The complete set of instructions includes five other items. Item 5: "Use previous evaluations when they

are higher than the rates indicated here." Item 6: "Determine the annual tax after ordering strict reports concerning, and after examining, the miscellaneous tax yields on mountain and sea [products]." Item 8: "Place stakes at village boundaries and position them so as to avoid intermingling [or confusion due to the scattering of holdings of farmers of different villages]. If there is confusion over the current [boundary] stakes, consult officials of the neighboring districts and determine new boundaries." Item 11: "In conformity with our orders, you shall provide for your own upkeep. You may request *sōji* [washing?], firewood, rice bran, and straw from the villagers." Item 12: "Should there be an individual who [commits] a violation by taking money or presents pressed upon him by farmers or stipendiaries (*kyūnin*), a searching examination of both parties shall be conducted as soon as we hear of it. If the bearers of measuring rods [*kenchi* officials] fail to report [the matter], they too shall be brought to judgment. Lest there be any confusion among the authorities, you shall declare that there is to be no negligence in this." While it is odd that these instructions contain no standard evaluations for dry fields, orders for the *kenchi* magistrates of Ise, issued around the same time and including the same statements on paddies and residence plots, declare: "Order that superior dry fields [be registered with a value of] one *koku*, two *to* [per *tan*], medium dry fields [with a value of] one *koku*, inferior dry fields [with a value of] eight *to*, and very inferior [dry fields] upon examination." Iinuma, *Kokudaka-sei no kenkyū*, p. 16.

33. Miyagawa, *Taikō kenchi-ron*, III, 170. The complete register is on pp. 170–217. I have converted all measurements into *bu*, although the original uses *tan* and *se* (1 *tan* = 10 *se* = 300 *bu*) as well. While some registers list fields in order of their type (paddy, dry, residential), or group together all the holdings of an individual cultivator, this cadastre follows the more conventional pattern of noting plots in the order of their appearance in the smaller geographical units (*ko-aza*) that made up Tenkawa.

34. The name of the *kenchi* magistrate appeared on the cover sheet of the cadastre together with the date of completion and the name of the village, district, and province involved. For the Tenkawa example, see Miyagawa, *Taikō kenchi-ron*, III, 170, 217. Copies went to the villagers, to Hideyoshi, and to the imperial court. Also see Iinuma, *Kokudaka-sei no kenkyū*, pp. 126–127, for a list of Hideyoshi's principal cadastral magistrates.

35. Hideyoshi fixed the *ken*, the basic unit of length, at 6 *shaku*, 3 *sun*, although it had generally been measured—with significant variations—at 6 *shaku*, 5 *sun* in the warring-states period. The *bu* remained, as always, 1 square *ken*. The greatest change was made in the *tan*. Averaging 360 *bu* throughout the war years, Hideyoshi reduced it to 300 *bu*. The *Kyō-masu* was a wooden box that measured volumes up to 10 *gō*; theoretically it was made to a standard specification and approved by Maeda Gen'i, the Toyotomi magistrate in Kyoto.

A *ken* of 6 *shaku*, 3 *sun* was in use in Kaga and Noto by 1583, but most of Hideyoshi's instructions regarding this standard date from the 1590s. They were issued in the Tōhoku, for example, in 1590, in Ōmi in 1591, in Bungo in 1593. For a fuller list, see Iinuma, *Kokudaka-sei no kenkyū*, p. 128. Even before 1573, a *tan* of 300 *bu* was known in Mino, Hida, Echizen, Ōmi, Ise, and Kii. Both Nobunaga and Hideyoshi adopted this standard, as well as the calculation of 1 *se* as 30 *bu*, after their entry into Ōmi where these definitions were current. See Iinuma, pp. 128–129; also see pp. 130–133 for a chart of measurement practices in the various provinces. For discussion of the *Kyō-masu*, see *Kyōto no rekishi*, IV, 378–380.

36. The *kenchi* magistrates in Ise were ordered to leave behind their *ken* rods, as well as their *masu*. See Iinuma, *Kokudaka-sei no kenkyū*, p. 16.

37. In Tenkawa, for example, it becomes apparent that superior paddy was registered at 1.4 *koku* per *tan*, medium at 1.2 *koku* per *tan*, and inferior at 1 *koku* per *tan*; dry fields were registered at 1.2 and 1 and .8 *koku* per *tan*. I arrive at these standard values by dividing the registered value by the registered size of a sample number of wet and dry fields. A close inspection of any of Hideyoshi's cadastres, however, will show that computation errors by the magistrates occurred from time to time. In the Tenkawa cadastre, computations of the value of inferior paddy seem particularly erratic.

See Miyagawa, *Taikō kenchi-ron*, III, 324–327, for instructions to *kenchi* magistrates in different provinces concerning the standard values to be assigned the various categories of paddy and dry field.

38. Iinuma, *Kokudaka-sei no kenkyū*, pp. 15–16. Also see Miyagawa, *Taikō kenchi-ron*, III, 367–368 (article 13 of document 62), for an injunction to inspect the fields at harvest time.

39. Iinuma, *Kokudaka-sei no kenkyū*, p. 17.

40. Miyagawa, *Taikō kenchi-ron*, III, 326–327.

41. For a basic discussion of the *kokudaka-sei*, see Iinuma, *Kokudaka-sei no kenkyū*, pp. 64–76, 134–140.

42. For fuller discussion of these and other arguments, see Araki, *Taikō kenchi to kokudaka-sei*, pp. 195–219, Wakita Osamu, "The *Kokudaka* System: A Device for Unification," in the *Journal of Japanese Studies*, vol. 1, no. 2 (Spring, 1975), pp. 312–313, and Iinuma, *Kokudaka-sei no kenkyū*, pp. 134–139. Iinuma emphasizes the importance of the muddled currency situation in the decision to fix upon a rice base. Araki, and other scholars such as Nagahara Keiji, are more concerned with the pervasiveness of a natural economy in late sixteenth-century Japan. These historians are trying to correct popular impressions that a market economy was strong and widespread at this time. It should be remembered that while many *sengoku* daimyo were evaluating and trying to tax land in cash—in order to raise money for arms and other wartime supplies—economically prosperous areas such as the Kinai continued to use rice evaluations before the rise of Nobunaga and Hideyoshi. There are various explanations for this fact. Nagahara ("Daimyō ryōgoku seika no kandaka-sei," p. 2) tends to see the practice as a simple holdover from the *shōen* system. Proprietors in the capital, he argues, taxed distant estates in cash (hence the emergence of cash evaluations in areas like the Kantō) and nearby estates in rice (hence the survival of rice evaluations in the Kinai). Iinuma (pp. 64–68) portrays the use of a rice standard in Ōmi, combined with early decisions to evaluate land in terms of its total product, as a progressive development that overcame the problems inherent in cash calculations (given the underdevelopment of the market, the currency situation, and the continuing valuation, under the *kandaka* system, of land in terms of its tax burden alone).

43. Miyagawa, *Taikō kenchi-ron*, III, 364. Also see Araki, *Taikō kenchi to kokudaka-sei*, pp. 201–208 for a number of annual tax statements from Hideyoshi's holdings. Like similar, though far more plentiful, statements from the early Tokugawa period (see Miyagawa, *Taikō kenchi-ron*, III, 388), these documents indicate that most taxes were rendered in rice but that payment in soybeans, gold, and silver was significant and routine. For discussion of the wide-scale

return to rice payments in tax and trade dealings, and of Nobunaga's opposition to the practice, see *Kyōto no rekishi*, IV, 381-385.

44. In only one case, a memorandum from Ishida Mitsunari to inspectors of the Shimazu domain, do we find a sustained discussion of products other than rice and dry grains. Mitsunari's notes on cotton, bamboo, iron, tea, lacquer, lumber, and other harvests from rivers, mountains, and the sea identify taxable and nontaxable items and comment, too, on the method of tax payment. Yet this memorandum is primarily concerned with the annual statement of land dues and not with data appropriate for inclusion in the *kenchi* registry. The cadastres' entries were usually limited to wet and dry fields and residential plots, while the tax statements included information on the *komononari* (supplementary imposts). Mitsunari's notes do not, incidentally, urge the conversion of miscellaneous products into a rice value but simply note that taxes on most items can be rendered in kind, in cash, or in rice. See Miyagawa, *Taikō kenchi-ron*, III, 327-328.

45. Araki, *Taikō kenchi to kokudaka-sei*, pp. 132-139.

46. Miyagawa, *Taikō kenchi-ron*, III, 329-330. This translation includes seven of the original fourteen articles.

47. Iinuma, *Kokudaka-sei no kenkyū*, pp. 128-133.

48. Miyagawa, *Taikō kenchi-ron*, III, 367 (article 6). The major, and continuing, problem with the *masu* was that the Japanese did not command the technology to construct uniform measures of volume at this time.

49. Iinuma, *Kokudaka-sei no kenkyū*, 125-127. See Miyagawa, *Taikō kenchi-ron*, III, 324-325, for Hideyoshi's orders concerning the Tōhoku registrations. The various categories of fields were to be evaluated in differing amounts of Eiroku *zeni*; superior paddy, for example, was to be valued at 200 *mon* (units of copper cash) per *tan*.

50. Miyagawa discusses these problems at length in *Taikō kenchi-ron*, II, 45-283. No trend—whether toward an increase in cultivators' names in the cadastres, a gradual reduction of large holdings, or an increase in the number of registered households with separate residences—can be traced conclusively. Indeed, contrary evidence is plentiful once seventeenth-century documents are surveyed. Since much of Miyagawa's evidence necessarily comes from the Tokugawa period, distinctions between the *kenchi* practices of Hideyoshi and his successors, although important, are not easily established. See p. 158 for one interesting chart showing substantial increases in registrants. Also see Araki, *Taikō kenchi to kokudaka-sei*, pp. 144-170. Araki attempts to define the registrants in Hideyoshi's cadastres by using legal documents as well as the registries themselves (which form the basis of Miyagawa's analysis). Wakita ("The *Kokudaka* System: A Device for Unification," p. 315) argues that virtually all registrants in Nobunaga's cadastres were *myōshu* (owners or landlords).

51. Araki, *Taikō kenchi to kokudaka-sei*, pp. 155-162.

52. Miyagawa, *Taikō kenchi-ron*, III, 367 (article 3).

53. Araki, *Taikō kenchi to kokudaka-sei*, pp. 155-158; Miyagawa, *Taikō kenchi-ron*, III, 361, 400.

54. Miyagawa, *Taikō kenchi-ron*, III, 357 (article 5 of document 45). Ishida Mitsunari also advised his vassals that they should "not pursue any action which interferes with farming or involves an impermissible action" (p. 367, the

end of article 2 of document 62). Hideyoshi ordered Sassa Narimasa, when he took over a fief in Kyushu, "It is important that there be no hardship for the farmers." Further, "You are to be careful that uprisings do not occur." Oze Hoan, *Taikō-ki*, p. 196.

55. See Miyagawa's breakdown of the Tenkawa cadastres in *Taikō kenchiron*, II, 251. According to one registry, twenty-eight individuals retained holdings of 10 to 14 *tan* each; thirty-six individuals retained 3 to 10 *tan* each; sixty-one individuals retained 1 to 3 *tan* each; sixty-three individuals retained less than 1 *tan* each. Miyagawa (*Taikō kenchi-ron*, II, 60 and 113) also uses charts to compare the number of names listed in certain official cadastres (*kenchi-chō*) with the number of names listed in the *nayose-chō* derived from them. *Nayose-chō* were the village documents, listing taxpayers and their holdings, which became the basis for most economic and political decisions within the village. In the Imazaike example, the *kenchi-chō* for 1598 lists eighty cultivators working land valued at 213.963 *koku*; the *nayose-chō* of 1598 for the same village lists forty cultivators working land valued at 213.896 *koku* (Miyagawa, p. 113).

56. An important debate continues among Japanese historians concerning whether or not Hideyoshi really intended to promote tenants to the status of cultivator and so alleviate inequalities and dependency within the village. For two introductions to this debate see Miyagawa Mitsuru, "Taikō kenchi-ron," in *Shokuhō seiken-ron* (*Shimpojiumu Nihon rekishi*, 10; Tokyo: Gakusei-sha, 1972), pp. 187–194 (with a discussion of the essay, on pp. 194–237); and Wakita, "The *Kokudaka* System: A Device for Unification," pp. 297–300. For sustained analysis of the critical arguments see Araki, *Taikō kenchi to kokudaka-sei*; Miyagawa, *Taikō kenchi-ron*; and Wakita, *Kinsei hōken-sei seiritsu shiron*. Araki and Miyagawa emphasize the liberal elements of the *kenchi*, Wakita its oppressive dimension. Wakita (see especially *Shimpojiumu Nihon rekishi*, 10, pp. 194–195) observes that even if tenants were recognized as village holders, the continued primacy of economically and politically powerful farmers—combined with the general repressiveness of Hideyoshi's laws on arms and class—leaves the question of the registries' leveling of status unimportant.

57. Miyagawa, *Taikō kenchi-ron*, III, 357 (article 1 of document 46). Asao ("Toyotomi seiken-ron," p. 161) emphatically makes the point concerning the provider-consumer division.

58. *Hōkō ibun*, p. 53.

59. Miyagawa, *Taikō kenchi-ron*, III, 385. For similar documents, see *Shimazu-ke monjo*, 3 vols. (*Dainihon komonjo, Iewake monjo*, ser. 16 [1942, 1953, 1966]), II, document 1095; *Uesugi-ke monjo*, 3 vols. (*Iewake monjo*, ser. 12 [1931, 1935, 1963]), II, document 832; *Kobayakawa-ke monjo*, 2 vols. (*Iewake monjo*, ser. 11 [1926]), I, document 180.

60. *Hōkō ibun*, pp. 627–640.

61. A number of historians (such as, Araki, *Taikō kenchi to kokudaka-sei*, pp. 139–144) find the specification of the allowances of collaterals in these investiture documents particularly important. Like Nobunaga, Hideyoshi chose to control subinvestiture decisions within the domains and therefore, in this respect at least, to exert greater influence on his principal daimyo than would the Tokugawa.

62. *Hōkō ibun*, p. 235.

63. Miki Seiichirō ("Chōsen-eki ni okeru gun'yaku taikei ni tsuite," in *Shigaku zasshi*, vol. 75, no. 2 (February, 1966), pp. 129–154, has done the basic

analysis of recruitment practices for the first Korean campaign. Despite his general conclusions, stated here, he points out that calculation of the *gun'yaku* for the fourth contingent and for the three back-up contingents (numbers seven to nine) is quite speculative. Other problems—differences between the Mōri and the Kobayakawa musters, uneven rates of exemption, our ignorance of the size of many fiefs in 1592—also make his conclusions tentative.

64. Miyagawa, *Taikō kenchi-ron*, III, 358. The total levy called for one man for every 200 *koku* of taxable land in the Kinai; four men for every 100 *koku* in the Chūgoku; six men for every 100 *koku* in the area from Shikoku to Owari; and six and one-half men for every 100 *koku* in the Hokkoku.

65. See Wakita, *Kinsei hōken-sei seiritsu shiron*, pp. 229–237, for a fuller analysis of Hideyoshi's *gun'yaku* practices.

66. See the references in n. 59, also the *Mōri-ke monjo*, III, document 957.

67. Kuwata, *Toyotomi Hideyoshi kenkyū*, p. 223; Tanaka, *Toyotomi jidai-shi*, pp. 118–123, 246–266; Ebisawa Arimichi, *Takayama Ukon* (Tokyo: Yoshikawa Kōbunkan, 1958), pp. 137–152. The following orders had been issued by Hideyoshi to Sassa Narimasa when Narimasa received his fief in Kyushu: "Item: You are to invest the fifty-two local warriors (*kokujin*) with the fiefs they held previously. Item: You are not to conduct a land survey for three years. Item: It is important that there be no hardship for the farmers. Item: You are to be careful that uprisings (*ikki*) do not occur. Item: You shall be excused from construction responsibilities in the Kamigata [Kyoto-Osaka area] for three years." See Oze Hoan, *Taikō-ki*, p. 196.

68. The discussion of Hideyoshi's attainders and fief reductions after 1593 is based on a detailed chart compiled by Nakabe Yoshiko in *Kinsei toshi no seiritsu to kōzō*, pp. 281–283. Those figures which Nakabe has not included (the size of the Utsunomiya fief, for example) come from Takayanagi and Matsudaira, *Sengoku jimmei jiten*. Although Nakabe portrays the transfers and attainders as part of a new, harsh policy toward the daimyo, I do not think the evidence warrants such a conclusion.

69. See *Hōkō ibun*, pp. 538–544, for documents concerning the accounting and transfer of the Gamō fief.

70. See n. 68. Nakabe attributes (p. 280) some of these additions to those increases in productivity noted in new cadastral surveys, increases which Hideyoshi formally invested in the daimyo concerned.

71. Perhaps the nearest Hideyoshi ever came to an official indictment of one of his daimyo is a series of letters in which he itemizes Sassa Narimasa's offenses. See, for example, Araki, *Taikō kenchi to kokudaka-sei*, pp. 129–130. A letter from four of the *bugyō* to the Kikkawa, announcing Hidetsugu's exile, pointedly ignores any discussion of the motives for the punishment. See *Hōkō ibun*, pp. 544–545. It is interesting that none of Hideyoshi's biographers, from Ōmura Yūko to Kuwata Tadachika, deals with the problem of legal conduct in this period. Particularly for the authors of the *Tenshō-ki* and the *Taikō-ki*, it was not a separate and significant issue. While they are normally careful to mention the provocation for acts of discipline, Hideyoshi's right of fiat is taken for granted.

72. See Araki, *Taikō kenchi to kokudaka-sei*, pp. 118–119, and Miyagawa, *Taikō kenchi-ron*, I, 359, for lists of the total *kokudaka* and Hideyoshi's holdings in each province around 1598. I have used the figures in these lists, rather than those cited in Nakabe's chart, to describe Hideyoshi's gains in Bungo, Echizen,

and Chikuzen. Nakabe's figures do not allow for the grants and land adjustments made toward the end of Hideyoshi's life. Even the figures in the Araki and Miyagawa lists must be used with caution, of course, since they do not always correspond with the figures in contemporary investiture and cadastral documents. After Hideyoshi's death and by his wish, a domain in Chikuzen and Chikugo was restored to Kobayakawa Hideaki. See Chapter 4, n. 3.

73. These figures are based on *Hōkō ibun*, pp. 627–640. As I mentioned in chapter 4, n. 3, the document in *Hōkō ibun* presents a number of problems that make such calculations imperfect. My tally is based on several adjustments to the document: I have deleted Hori Hidemasa, with 550,000 *koku* from the list; calculated Hori Hideharu's fief at 300,000 *koku*, and both Ishida Mitsunari's and Katō Kiyomasa's fiefs at 200,000 *koku*; and added Chōsokabe Motochika, with 220,000 *koku*, and Asano Nagamasa, with 120,000 *koku*, to the list. The errors in the document, and the imprecision of our knowledge concerning the distribution and value of land, preclude perfect calculations. Yet the general revelations of the document—that leading *tozama* held about half the nation's wealth and leading *fudai* strikingly less—seem clear.

74. Mashita Nagamori, Ishida Mitsunari, Konishi Yukinaga, and Asano Nagamasa joined the Toyotomi; Hori Hideharu, Fukushima Masanori, Mogami Yoshiaki, Katō Kiyomasa, Katō Yoshiaki, and Tanaka Yoshimasa joined the Tokugawa; Nakagawa Hideshige turned from the Toyotomi to the Tokugawa; the sons of Hachisuka Iemasa and Ikoma Chikamasa joined the Tokugawa while the fathers remained remote from the fray; Horio Yoshiharu also took no action. Harold Bolitho makes an eloquent case to the effect that, in the Tokugawa period, the distinction between *fudai* and *tozama* was not deeply meaningful (in *Treasures among Men: The Fudai Daimyo in Tokugawa Japan* [New Haven: Yale University Press, 1974]).

75. Ōmura Yūko, *Tenshō-ki*, p. 65. We have few details concerning the construction of Osaka castle. Historians therefore rely, although reluctantly, upon the *Tenshō-ki* account.

76. Oze Hoan, *Taikō-ki*, pp. 262, 452–455.

77. *Hōkō ibun*, pp. 197–201.

78. *Hōkō ibun*, pp. 528–529.

79. For a discussion of *sengoku* mining, see Kobata Atsushi et al., comps., *Dokushi sōran* (Tokyo: Jimbutsu Ōrai-sha, 1966), pp. 845–849; Kobata Atsushi, "Kōgyō" in *Azuchi Momoyama jidai* (*Nihon bunka-shi taikei*, vol. 8; Tokyo: Shōgaku-kan, 1968), pp. 156–159; and Kobata, *Kingin bōeki-shi no kenkyū* (Tokyo: Hōsei Daigaku Shuppan Kyoku, 1976), pp. 109–110. A list of Hideyoshi's gold and silver income appears in Miyagawa, *Taikō kenchi-ron*, I, 359. The estimation of 1 *mai* at 165 grams is *very* tentative, and is derived from the fact that Hideyoshi's extant coins of 1 *mai* (1 *mai* = 10 *ryō* = 44 *momme* of gold, 43 *momme* of silver) tend to weigh about 165 grams. It is not clear, though, that this equivalence applied both to coins and to the slugs and bars of metal that were more commonly used. For a discussion of some of the problems of measurement, see Nihon Ginkō Chōsa Kyoku, ed., *Zuroku Nihon no kahei* (Tokyo: Tōyō Keizai Shimpō-sha, 1972), vol. 1, pp. 89–120, 299–320.

Although Hideyoshi authorized five mintings of special gold coins and four mintings of silver coins, he did not use his near monopoly of precious metals to impose order upon the deeply confused currency situation. Each of his mintings was small and was commissioned for private use. The Tenshō *ōban*, for instance, were large disks, weighing ten *ryō*, of unusual purity—70 to 75 percent pure gold. The rough equivalent of forty to fifty *koku* of rice each, the coins were intended as gifts or rewards. See Miyamoto Matao, "Hideyoshi no kahei," in *Toyotomi Hideyoshi (Rekishi tokuhon: Denki Shirīzu*, 8), p. 191; *Kyōto no rekishi*, IV, 386–388; Kuwata, *Toyotomi Hideyoshi kenkyū*, pp. 326–328.

80. Kuwata, *Toyotomi Hideyoshi kenkyū*, p. 295. See pp. 292–302 for a general discussion of Hideyoshi's castle-leveling program.

81. Shimonaka, ed., *Nihon shiryō shūsei*, p. 255.

82. For maps of castles in the Hōjō holdings and in the Yamato area, see Toyoda Takeshi, "Gun'yū kakkyo," in *Azuchi Momoyama jidai*, pp. 51–54. Also see Kuwata, *Toyotomi Hideyoshi kenkyū*, pp. 298–300.

83. *Mōri-ke monjo*, II, document no. 502.

84. Kodama et al., eds., *Shiryō ni yoru Nihon no ayumi: kinsei*, p. 51.

85. Kodama et al., eds., *Shiryō ni yoru Nihon no ayumi: kinsei*, p. 55. While Kuwata (*Toyotomi Hideyoshi kenkyū*, pp. 256–257) tends to take this account at face value, many discussions of the document are more skeptical. See, for example, *Kyōto no rekishi*, IV, 445–446. Asao Naohiro drew my attention to an article by Maruyama Tsuneo ("Toyotomi-ki kaigai bōeki keitai," in *Tōkai daigaku bungaku-bu kiji*, no. 8) that discusses a document in which Katō Kiyomasa turns over one of Hideyoshi's red-seal permits for trade to a merchant associate.

86. See references in n. 22.

87. Iinuma, *Kokudaka-sei no kenkyū*, pp. 126–127.

88. Kuwata, *Toyotomi Hideyoshi kenkyū*, pp. 280–288; the Kōya oath is in Kodama et al., eds., *Shiryō ni yoru Nihon no ayumi: kinsei*, pp. 46–47.

89. See the references in n. 3. Also see Jansen, "Tosa in the Sixteenth Century," article 23.

90. Kobata, "Kōgyō," p. 158; Kuwata, *Toyotomi Hideyoshi kenkyū*, pp. 324–326; Miyagawa, *Taikō kenchi-ron*, I, 358–361. In his discussion, Kuwata includes several of Hideyoshi's documents of receipt for silver.

91. See n. 87; also Guy Moréchand, "Taiko kenchi: Le Cadastre de Hideyoshi Toyotomi," in *Bulletin de l'École Française d'Extrême-Orient*, 53 (1966), 54–55.

92. See Izumi Chōichi, *Sakai to Hakata* (Tokyo: Sōgen-sha, 1976), pp. 99–124 and 169–204, for an introduction to Hideyoshi's relations with the leading merchants of these two cities.

93. *Hōkō ibun*, pp. 545–547.

94. Ibid., pp. 616, 621–622. Kobayakawa Takakage died in 1597, reducing the group of *tairō* to five members. Certain *tairō* papers are signed by only four men, excluding Uesugi Kagekatsu. See pp. 619–620, 622–624.

95. The most important document signed by the *tairō*, and the one that conventionally serves to identify the group, is the oath of loyalty to Hideyori taken at Hideyoshi's deathbed. See *Hōkō ibun*, p. 616.

96. Supplementary article 6 of the code (Ibid., pp. 546–547) states that: "If a complaint is made, it should first be addressed to the ten men." The ten men were probably the six *tozama* signatories of the code plus Ishida, Mashita, Natsuka, and Maeda Gen'i. Asano Nagamasa, who was closely identified with the camp of Hidetsugu in 1595, may have been excluded from the group mentioned in the code.

97. Oze Hoan, *Taikō-ki*, pp. 177–178.

98. Kuwata Tadachika, "Toyotomi-shi no go-bugyō seido ni kan suru kōsatsu," in *Shigaku zasshi*, vol. 46, no. 9 (1935), pp. 1032–80, and Kuwata, *Toyotomi Hideyoshi kenkyū*, pp. 359–364. Kuwata concentrates upon the absence of any documentary proof for the creation of such a body before the later 1590s as well as upon the impossibility—given biographical details about these five men in the 1580s—of the formation of this particular group into a vassal council so early in the Toyotomi tenure.

99. See the principal documents of the *bugyō* in *Hōkō ibun*, pp. 543–544 (concerning the Gamō fief); 544–545 (Hidetsugu's exile to Kōya); 575–576 (the five- and ten-man groups); 593 (the Korean campaign); 594 (the demands for hostages during the Korean campaign); 620–622 (the loyalty oaths of the *tairō* that were addressed to the *bugyō*). Also see Miyagawa, *Taikō kenchi-ron*, III, 364 (management of Hideyoshi's income) and 401 (tax matters in a daimyo fief). See *Kyōto no rekishi*, IV, 333, for discussion of the dismantlement of Jurakutei. Kuwata, *Toyotomi Hideyoshi kenkyū*, pp. 364–374, discusses the general functions of the *bugyō*. Although most of the documents cited here were issued by, or addressed to, the five *bugyō*, several involved only three or four members of the council (see, for example, *Hōkō ibun*, pp. 544–545, 593).

100. Kodama et al., eds., *Shiryō ni yoru Nihon no ayumi: kinsei*, pp. 32–33.

101. Cited in Nakabe, *Kinsei toshi no seiritsu to kōzō*, p. 296.

102. Kodama et al., eds., *Shiryō ni yoru Nihon no ayumi: kinsei*, p. 32. Also see Nakabe, *Kinsei toshi no seiritsu to kōzō*, pp. 295–300, for discussion of earlier requests for hostages.

103. Sakurai Narihiro, *Toyotomi Hideyoshi no kyojō* (Tokyo: Nihon Jōkaku Shiryō-kan Shuppan-kai, 1970–71), vol. I (*Ōsaka-jō*), pp. 309–322; vol. II (*Jurakutei, Fushimi-jō*), pp. 137–158, 348–363. Also see *Kyōto no rekishi*, IV, 339–342.

104. See Nakabe, *Kinsei toshi no seiritsu to kōzō*, p. 300 (n. 59), regarding the special allowances Hideyoshi made to some daimyo to underwrite the cost of residing in Kyoto. Some grants were very large—the Tokugawa received 30,-000 *koku* in Ōmi for expenses in the capital. The award of lands close to Kyoto to daimyo in residence there is another indication of the limited development of markets.

105. Oaths concerning the administration of Hideyoshi's properties may be found in Miyagawa, *Taikō kenchi-ron*, III, 364. Mōri Terumoto's oath of loyalty to Hideyori, similar to those taken by other members of the *go-tairō* and *go-bugyō* though more elaborate than the oaths taken earlier by approximately thirty of the Toyotomi daimyo, is in *Hōkō ibun*, p. 615. See the *Mōri-ke monjo*, II, document 502, for the edict on piracy.

106. Ōmura Yūko, *Tenshō-ki*, pp. 113–114.

107. *Hōkō ibun*, pp. 545–547.

6. Federation and Its Motives

1. The debate over Japanese feudalism, which began in the early decades of this century, has focused not upon whether the Toyotomi and Tokugawa regimes *were* feudal (a point that has been assumed) but upon what *stage* in feudal development these regimes represent. Arguments largely begin with different readings of the Muromachi and *sengoku* evidence, rather than with the late sixteenth-century evidence. Disagreements over the motives behind Hideyoshi's cadastral policy, though fierce, are eclipsed by disagreements over the status of cultivators in earlier years. For an introduction to the debates and

their literature, beginning with the *Rōnō-ha Kōza-ha* controversy, as well as for remarks on the discussion of absolutism that follows below, see Wakita, "The *Kokudaka* System: A Device for Unification," Nagahara et al., eds., *Chūsei-shi handobukku*, p. 133, and Kodama Kōta et al., eds., *Kinsei-shi handobukku* (Tokyo: Kondō Shuppan-sha, 1972), pp. 1–9.

2. Perry Anderson coined the phrase "parcellized sovereignty" in *Lineages of the Absolutist State* (Thetford and Norfolk, England: Lowe and Brydone Printers, 1974; verso ed. 1979).

3. Ibid., p. 417.

4. Edwin O. Reischauer popularized the expression "centralized feudalism" in his essay, "Japanese Feudalism," in Rushton Coulborn, ed., *Feudalism in History* (Princeton: Princeton University Press, 1956). Also see Reischauer and John K. Fairbank, *East Asia: The Great Tradition* (Boston: Houghton Mifflin Co., 1958), p. 579. John W. Hall observes that the Tokugawa regime "kept alive a dynamic tension between feudal and bureaucratic techniques and between decentralized and centralized authority" (*Japan: From Prehistory to Modern Times* [Tokyo: Charles E. Tuttle, 1971], p. 165). For a fuller treatment of the problem, see John W. Hall, "Feudalism in Japan—A Reassessment," in Hall and Jansen, eds., *Studies in the Institutional History of Early Modern Japan*, pp. 15–51. Both Conrad Totman (*Politics in the Tokugawa Bakufu*, pp. 235–261) and Harold Bolitho (*Treasures among Men*) explore reasons for the unusual shape that Tokugawa government took, although they do not commit themselves to characterizing it as "centralized feudalism." Totman is concerned with the absence of a precedent for a more highly centralized government; Bolitho attributes the strength of the domains to the appointment by the bakufu of daimyo administrators at the center. He does not, however, engage at length the problem of *why* daimyo administrators were appointed.

5. Quoted by Asao in "Toyotomi seiken-ron," p. 167.

6. See, for example, Nakamura, ed., *Tokugawa Ieyasu monjo no kenkyū*, I, 767 (for use of the title *uesama*), 768 (for use of the title *kampaku*), and 775 (for use of the title *denka*).

7. See the *Sengoku hyakunin* issue of *Taiyō* (cited in chapter 2, n. 4) for these and other portraits; Takeda Toshikuni, "Rakuchū rakugai shoshū no tatchū to sono seiritsu," in Dōshisha Daigaku Jimbun Kagaku Kenkyūjo, ed., *Kyōto shakai-shi kenkyū* (Kyoto: Hōritsu Bunka-sha, 1971), pp. 266–67, for discussion of the building of monasteries; Kawai Masaharu, *Chūsei buke shakai no kenkyū* (Tokyo: Yoshikawa Kōbunkan, 1973), pp. 172–180, 203–290, for discussion of warrior pursuit of the traditional arts; Kyōto Kokuritsu Hakubutsukan, *Rakuchū rakugai zu*, pp. 3–16, for discussion of the paintings of the capital.

8. See Satō, Ikeuchi, and Momose, *Buke kahō*, I, 121–122 (items 30, 31, 33) for Imagawa proscriptions against marriages, alliances, and mercantile agreements formed beyond domainal boundaries.

9. See, for example, Ōmura Yūko, *Tenshō-ki*, p. 144. For a more general discussion of the word *kōgi*, see Fukaya Katsumi, "Kōgi to mibun-sei," in Sasaki Junnosuke et al., eds., *Taikei Nihon kokka-shi: kinsei* (Tokyo: Tōkyō Daigaku Shuppan-kai, 1975), pp. 149–172, and Nagahara Keiji, "Sengoku daimyō ni okeru 'kōgi' kannen no kisei," in *Chūsei nairan-ki no shakai to minshū* (Tokyo: Yoshikawa Kōbunkan, 1977), pp. 295–300. Discussion of the meaning of the term is made difficult, for the *sengoku* era no less than for the Toyotomi era, by the infrequency of its usage. Current arguments that the daimyo used it to de-

scribe themselves as well as a certain abstract notion of the public domain cannot be made conclusively.

10. Jansen, "Tosa in the Sixteenth Century," p. 102; *Hōkō ibun*, p. 615; *Shiryō Kyōto no rekishi*, III, 397 (document 42).

11. See Kuwata, *Toyotomi Hideyoshi kenkyū*, pp. 252 and 253, for the letter to the Viceroy of the Indies and the comments on his birth; Kuwata, *Taikō no tegami*, p. 76, for the reference to Yoritomo; *Hōkō ibun*, pp. 138–140, for the remarks on China. Twenty-one of Hideyoshi's personal letters close with the signature *tenka*; for a convenient synopsis of such information, see Boscaro, *101 Letters of Hideyoshi*, appendix III, pp. 92–100.

12. Such matters are treated in chapter 8.

13. Hideyoshi's important concubines were Yodo (daughter of Asai Nagamasa), Tora (daughter of Gamō Katahide), Matsu-maru (daughter of Kyōgoku Takayoshi), and Gō and Maa (daughters of Maeda Toshiie).

14. *Hō taikō shinseki-shū*, documents 52, 57, 41; Kuwata, *Taikō shoshin* (Tokyo: Chijin Shokan, 1943), p. 34; Kuwata, *Taikō no tegami*, pp. 86–87.

7. The Pursuit of Legitimacy

1. Refer to chapter 1, n. 2 for a discussion of the *Taikō-ki* genre. Although *taikō* was originally used as a term of respect for the *sesshō* or the *daijō daijin*, it gradually came to designate a retired *kampaku*. This chapter has been influenced by the work of Tanaka Yoshinari, who argues that Hideyoshi sought court titles because he had no interest in promotion as shogun. Tanaka's thesis was doubtless influenced by his personal view of the respective stature of the throne and the *bakufu*, for Tanaka was born in the Meiji period and shared his contemporaries' perception of the obvious superiority of courtly positions to military ones. See *Toyotomi jidai-shi*, pp. 43–45.

2. The resemblance between this portrait and those of the imperial family may be confirmed by perusing Tani Shin'ichi et al., eds., *Kokushi shōzō shūsei* (Tokyo: Meguro Shoten, 1970), vol. I. The stylistic conventions portraying the nobility had, of course, been used by military men ever since the Heian period. See Kameda Tsutomu, *Men to shōzō*, plates 17, 18, 19, 44, 45.

3. One of the more convenient lists of these appointments may be found in Kobata et al., eds., *Dokushi sōran*, p. 107. For confirmation, see Kuroita Katsumi, ed., *Kugyō bunin*, in *Shintei zōho kokushi taikei* (Tokyo: Kokushi Taikei Kankō-kai, 1934–1938), vols. 53–57. For the appointments made during Hideyoshi's tenure (1582–1598) by Emperors Ōgimachi and Go-Yōzei, see LV, 486–514.

4. Mass, *Warrior Government in Medieval Japan*, pp. 123–142. Part 1 of this volume is a fine study of the growth of military power prior to the Gempei war.

5. While the *Gukanshō* and the *Masukagami* both treat court-*bakufu* relations in a fashion ultimately unbecoming to the throne, the most critical presentation of imperial politics is found in the catalogue of ill-advised actions attributed to Go-Daigo following the Kemmu restoration in the *Taiheiki*, Gotō Tanji and Kamada Kisaburō, eds., in *Nihon koten bungaku taikei*, vols. 34–36 (Tokyo: Iwanami Shoten, 1960–1962). For the essential section, see Helen C. McCullough, trans., *The Taiheiki: A Chronicle of Medieval Japan* (New York: Columbia University Press, 1959), pp. 340–387.

6. Both the *Go-seibai shikimoku* and the *Kemmu shikimoku* expressly limit the

authority of the military deputies. See Satō, Ikeuchi, and Momose, *Kamakura bakufu hō* (*Chūsei hōsei shiryō-shū*, pt. 1), pp. 37-55; and *Muromachi bakufu hō* (*Chūsei hōsei shiryō-shū*, pt. 2), pp. 3-10 (Tokyo: Iwanami Shoten, 1955, 1957).

7. Elizabeth Sato provides one of the clearest defenses of the legality of the *shōen* system in "The Early Development of the *Shōen*," in Hall and Mass, eds., *Medieval Japan: Essays in Institutional History*, pp. 99-108.

8. A punctilious portrait of Yoritomo as a loyal and legitimate governor emerges, of course, in the *Azuma kagami*, particularly in the sections covering the years 1185-1186. See Kuroita Katsumi, ed., *Shintei zōho kokushi taikei*, XXXII (1932), 131-250.

9. See Kobata et al., eds., *Dokushi sōran*, pp. 107-113.

10. For some idea of the mixed loyalties of courtiers and military men in 1221, see William H. McCullough, "Shōkyūki: An Account of the Shōkyū War of 1221," in *Monumenta Nipponica*, vol. 19, nos. 1-2, 3-4 (1964), pp. 163-215, 186-221.

11. Delmer M. Brown and Ichirō Ishida, trans. and eds., *The Future and the Past: A Translation and Study of the Gukanshō, an Interpretative History of Japan Written in 1219* (Berkeley and Los Angeles: University of California Press, 1979), p. 210.

12. Ibid., p. 228.

13. Satō, Ikeuchi, and Momose, *Buke kahō*, I, 115-131. Item 22 of the original statutes does uphold a limited immunity for estates, except in cases of negligent administration. Item 20 of the supplementary statutes, however, terminates immunity and declares all domainal land subject to Imagawa taxation and jurisdiction.

14. Tanaka, *Toyotomi jidai-shi*, pp. 41-46; Ōmura Yūko, *Tenshō-ki*, pp. 75-77.

15. Ōmura Yūko, *Tenshō-ki*, pp. 77-79.

16. *Kyōto no rekishi*, IV, 46-50.

17. Kuwata, *Toyotomi Hideyoshi kenkyū*, pp. 262-264; *Kyōto no rekishi*, IV, 263-264.

18. Ōmura Yūko, *Tenshō-ki*, pp. 80-82.

19. Tanaka, *Toyotomi jidai-shi*, pp. 46-47.

20. Watanabe Yosuke's classic study of Hideyoshi's family members, *Hō taikō to sono kazoku* (Tokyo: Nihon Gakujutsu Fukyū-kai, 1919), is the readiest source for biographical information of this nature.

21. *Kyōto no rekishi*, IV, 230-232.

22. For the titles of Hideyoshi's vassals in 1598, see *Hōkō ibun*, pp. 627-640. A review of various forms of correspondence in the same collection will confirm Hideyoshi's preference for courtly forms of address.

23. See, for example, *Kyōto no rekishi*, IV, 299, 729-730.

24. Teishitsu Rin'ya Kyoku, *Go-ryōchi shikō*, pp. 239-241; Okuno, *Kōshitsu go-keizai-shi*, pp. 227-241.

25. *Kōshitsu go-keizai-shi*, pp. 248-250; *Go-ryōchi shikō*, pp. 242-246.

26. *Kōshitsu go-keizai-shi*, pp. 250-259.

27. *Kōshitsu go-keizai-shi*, pp. 241-248. Maeda Gen'i made some efforts on

Hideyoshi's behalf to recover other parts of the traditional imperial benefice, but these actions ceased by 1585.

28. *Kyōto no rekishi,* III, 273-276.

29. *Kyōto no rekishi,* IV, 256.

30. Kuwabara Sadanari served as Hideyoshi's *daikan* in Kyoto for less than a month in 1582. He was apparently discharged for causing "unpleasantness to the citizens" and for interfering in the administration of *kuge* properties. *Kyōto no rekishi,* IV, 514.

31. See Herschel Webb, *The Japanese Imperial Institution in the Tokugawa Period* (New York: Columbia University Press, 1958), pp. 126-128. It is, as Webb points out, often difficult and inappropriate to compare court and daimyo incomes. In Hideyoshi's day, however, the court did not even come very close to the lowest level of daimyo grants.

32. Ōmura Yūko, *Tenshō-ki,* pp. 78-79, 112. This brief mention of the more spectacular gifts overlooks the routine, but nonetheless lavish, presentation of coins, foodstuffs, silks, fans, and other exotica on festival days and formal occasions.

33. *Kyōto no rekishi,* IV, 57-60, 286-290; Tsuji, ed., *Tamon'in nikki,* II, 174.

34. An excellent description of the Heian *daidairi* may be found in *Kyōto no rekishi,* I, 268-299. During the Kamakura period, the imperial house used a number of different residences, including the popular Kan'in *dairi.* See Ponsonby-Fane, *Kyoto,* pp. 133-147.

35. Following the enthronement of Emperor Kōmyō in the Tsuchimikado *dairi* in 1337, this palace had become the regular domicile of the reigning monarch. For discussion and an illustration of the compound, see *Kyōto no rekishi,* III, 42-44. The Tsuchimikado *dairi* is also represented in the earliest extant *rakuchū rakugai zu byōbu,* dated roughly 1520. See Kyōto Kokuritsu Hakubutsukan, *Rakuchu rakugai zu,* color plate 3.

36. Watanabe Yosuke, *Hō taikō no shiteki seikatsu* (Tokyo: Sōgen-sha, 1939), p. 75.

37. The following discussion is based upon the "Juraku gyōkō-ki," in Ōmura Yūko, *Tenshō-ki,* pp. 101-139, and *Kyōto no rekishi,* IV, 267-272.

38. Ōmura Yūko, *Tenshō-ki,* pp. 113-114.

39. Ibid., pp. 117-134. See the first exchange on p. 120; the Nobufusa and Ieyasu poems on p. 123.

40. See the "Juraku gyōkō-ki" entry in Kokusho Kenkyūshitsu, ed., *Kokusho sōmokuroku* (Tokyo: Iwanami Shoten, 1963-1972), IV, 327.

41. H. H. Gerth and C. Wright Mills, trans. and eds., *From Max Weber: Essays in Sociology* (New York: Oxford University Press, 1946; rpt. 1958), pp. 77-80.

42. This topic has recently been explored by Paul Varley, "Ashikaga Yoshimitsu and the World of Kitayama: Social Change and Shogunal Patronage in Early Muromachi Japan," in Hall and Toyoda, eds., *Japan in the Muromachi Age,* pp. 183-204.

43. *Hōkō ibun,* p. 160.

44. Accounts of the party by tea masters from Kyoto and Sakai may be found in Nagashima Fukutarō, *Chūsei bunkajin no kiroku* (Tokyo: Tankō-sha, 1972), pp. 85-100. The Kitano tea party was discontinued after the first day,

probably because of Sassa Narimasa's rebellion in Higo. A partial seating and display chart for the occasion is reproduced in *Kyōto no rekishi*, IV, 666-667.

45. *Kyōto no rekishi*, IV, 665. The Kitano shrine was also the scene of *dengaku* and *renga* (linked verse) parties during Yoshimochi's tenure.

46. Gien's journal, which details Hideyoshi's reconstruction of the temple, is excerpted in Shigemori Mirei and Shigemori Kanto, *Momoyama no niwa*, I, 117-130. Also see pp. 62-81 of the same volume for an analysis of the project.

47. A fold-out sketch of the Sambōin garden is attached as an end paper to *Momoyama no niwa*. Plates 48-76 of that volume also represent parts of the landscape.

48. For descriptions of this party, see Oze Hoan's *Taikō-ki*, pp. 455-463, and *Kyōto no rekishi*, IV, 490-492.

49. See Oze Hoan's *Taikō-ki*, pp. 437-449.

50. Tanaka, *Toyotomi jidai-shi*, pp. 140-141.

51. The two nō plays—*Yoshino mōde* and *Kōya mōde*—may be found in Nonomura Kaizō, ed., *Yōkyoku sambyaku gojū-ban shū* (Tokyo: Nihon Meicho Zenshū Kankō-kai, 1928), pp. 675-676, 704-706. Kanō Mitsunobu's pair of screens, "Yoshino no hanami," is in the Hosomi collection, Osaka. "Daigo no hanami," a single anonymous screen, remains at Daigoji in Kyoto.

52. The best general reference regarding city development during this period is Nakabe, *Kinsei toshi no seiritsu to kōzō*.

53. Population estimates for the sixteenth century are, of course, extremely speculative. By mid-century, Sakai and Nara probably had populations somewhat under 10,000 (Nakabe, *Chūsei toshi no seiritsu to kōzō*, p. 61), and Kamakura and Hakata (and possibly Funai) may have approached that figure. Estimates of Kyoto's population range from 150,000 upwards (*Kyōto no rekishi*, III, 33-41), but are based on such soft evidence that a fraction of that number seems a safer estimate. Indeed, the evidence for all population estimates is so scarce as to discourage sustained discussion. See *Iwanami kōza Nihon rekishi*, IX (1963), 14, 120-121.

54. For a discussion of Kyoto-centered trade, see *Kyōto no rekishi*, III, 503-539.

55. *Kangin-shū*, in Asano Kenji, ed., *Shintei chūsei kayō-shū* (Nihon koten zensho; Tokyo: Asahi Shimbun-sha, 1973), pp. 62-63.

56. See *Kyōto no rekishi*, III, 663-675; Miyata Teru, ed., *Shō-Kyōto hyakusen* (Tokyo: Akita Shoten, 1975).

57. See Takeda Chōshū, "Rakuchū rakugai shoshū no tatchū to sono seiritsu," pp. 266-267, for a list of sub-monasteries in Kyoto built during the Momoyama period. (See chapter 6, n. 7 for the full citation.)

58. Regarding the location of Jurakutei, see Tsuji, ed., *Tamon'in nikki*, IV, 9-10. The complex is described in Ōmura Yūko, *Tenshō-ki*, pp. 102-103; *Kyōto no rekishi*, IV, 267-270, 331-334. Also see Sakurai, *Toyotomi Hideyoshi no kyojō*, II, 39-190. The front matter of this volume contains maps and illustrations of Jurakutei. The mansion is also called Jurakudai, the term used in map 2.

59. See Kyōto Kokuritsu Hakubutsukan, *Rakuchū rakugai zu*, color plate 4. This screen is in the collection of the Mitsui Bunko of Tokyo.

60. Oze Hoan, *Taikō-ki*, p. 262.

61. *Nihon seikyō-shi*, quoted in *Kyōto no rekishi*, IV, 616.

62. Sakurai, *Toyotomi Hideyoshi no kyojō*, II, 137–158; *Kyōto no rekishi*, IV, 354.

63. Oze Hoan, *Taikō-ki*, pp. 179–182; *Kyōto no rekishi*, IV, 274–276. Regarding the recruitment of workers, see *Hōkō ibun*, pp. 197–201. For one of many paintings of the Daibutsu and its construction, see Kyōto Kokuritsu Hakubutsukan, *Rakuchū rakugai zu*, monochrome plate 35. The Daibutsu, represented on the right member of pairs of screens depicting Kyoto during the Tokugawa period, provides the counterpoint to Nijō castle—represented on the left member of such pairs. It was doubtless juxtaposed against paintings of Jurakutei in earlier sets, now lost.

64. *Hōkō ibun*, pp. 201–202.

65. For this quotation and other commentary upon the *odoi*, see *Kyōto no rekishi*, IV, 294–301. The quote is on p. 294. Also see Fujita Motoharu, *Heian-kyō hensen-shi* (Kyoto: Suzukake, 1930), p. 43, and Ponsonby-Fane, *Kyoto*, pp. 243–253.

66. *Kyōto no rekishi*, I, 253–259.

67. *Kyōto no rekishi*, IV, 299, 729–730.

68. For this quotation and a general discussion of the temple relocations, see *Kyōto no rekishi*, IV, 301–307; Fujita, *Heian-kyō hensen-shi* pp. 43–44.

69. Even Niigata, a port rather than a military capital, located its temples in a sort of semicircle under the ridge of mountains that enclose the harbor. See the reproductions of Edo-period maps in Nishikawa Kōji and Harada Tomohiko, eds., *Nihon no shigai kozu: higashi Nihon* (Tokyo: Kashima Kenkyūjo Shuppan-kai, 1973).

70. For this quotation and a general discussion of the relocation of part of the population of commoners, see *Kyōto no rekishi*, IV, 288–294. The quote is on p. 291.

71. *Kyōto no rekishi*, IV, 299–300; Fujita, *Heian-kyō hensen-shi*, p. 45.

72. *Kyōto no rekishi*, IV, 307–311.

73. *Kyōto no rekishi*, IV, 179–188.

74. *Kyōto no rekishi*, IV, 188–193.

75. Kodama et al., eds., *Shiryō ni yoru Nihon no ayumi: kinsei*, p. 47.

76. See the map reproductions in Nishikawa and Harada, *Nihon no shigai kozu*. For an excellent treatment of the zoning question, see Matsumoto Toyotoshi, *Jōkamachi no rekishi-chiri-gaku-teki kenkyū* (Tokyo: Yoshikawa Kōbunkan, 1967).

77. Rodrigues, trans. Cooper, *This Island of Japon*, pp. 77–78.

78. Ōta Gyūichi, *Taikō gunki*, pp. 149–150.

79. Kuwata, *Toyotomi Hideyoshi kenkyū*, pp. 253–254.

8. The Last Years

1. The longevity of major sixteenth-century daimyo is consistently surprising. Shimazu Yoshihisa, for example, died at the age of seventy-eight, Mōri Motonari at seventy-four, Chōsokabe Motochika at sixty-one, Uesugi Kagekatsu at sixty-eight.

2. After 1587 Hideyoshi's constant inquiries into the health of his intimates are combined with comments upon his own health, particularly his fail-

ing appetite. See, for example, *Hō taikō shinseki-shū*, documents 18, 25, 31. The first letter notes that "My white hairs have increased during this last campaign [in Kyushu]. I can no longer pull them all out. I can show myself only to you [his wife] without suffering. Even this will be troubling." His eye problems, which caused him to postpone departure for Nagoya and supervision of the Korean campaign in 1592, caused him the greatest difficulty, although we know little about them in detail. See Boscaro, *101 Letters of Hideyoshi*, p. 22.

3. *Hō taikō shinseki-shū*, document 18.

4. Quoted in James Murdoch, *A History of Japan*, 3 vols. (London: Kegan Paul, Trench, Trubner, 1925-1926), II, 305.

5. Hayashiya, *Tenka ittō*, pp. 457-458.

6. Kuwata, *Toyotomi Hideyoshi kenkyū*, p. 239.

7. Hayashiya, *Tenka ittō*, pp. 458-461. Also see Oze Hoan, *Taikō-ki*, p. 334, and Ōta Gyūichi, *Taikō gunki*, p. 192.

8. *Hōkō ibun*, pp. 334-339. Also see Miki, "Chōsen eki ni okeru gun'yaku taikei ni tsuite," especially pp. 136-137, for collation and analysis of all extant lists of troop levies for this campaign.

9. Hayashiya, *Tenka ittō*, pp. 461-462; Miki, "Chōsen eki ni okeru gun'yaku taikei ni tsuite," pp. 140-141. James Murdoch's colorful but basically sound account of the campaign is still the major English description of Hideyoshi's Korean war. See *A History of Japan*, especially II, 302-359. George Sansom, *A History of Japan, 1334-1615* (Stanford: Stanford University Press, 1961), pp. 352-361, should also be consulted. Oze Hoan's history (*Taikō-ki*, pp. 334-436) has influenced later Japanese writing on the campaign. More recently, however, Japanese historians have turned to Korean and Chinese sources for their accounts. Among the leading histories is Nakamura Hidetaka, *Nihon to Chōsen* (Tokyo: Shibundō, 1966). Matsuda includes a detailed chronology of the campaign in *Hideyoshi no namban gaikō*, pp. 142-145, 172-174. Two short and clear descriptions of the war may be found in Fujiki Hisashi, *Oda Toyotomi seiken* (Tokyo: Shōgaku-kan, 1975), pp. 318-374, and Hayashiya, *Tenka ittō*, pp. 462-480. Also see Nakamura, *Nitchō kankei-shi no kenkyū* (Tokyo: Yoshikawa Kōbunkan, 1962-1969), vol. 2.

10. The Koreans were, of course, familiar with firearms but apparently had no significant supply and were not manufacturing them. See Hayashiya, *Tenka ittō*, pp. 457, 463-464, for discussion of the Korean context and the role of the Sō negotiators.

11. *Hō taikō shinseki-shū*, document 31.

12. *Hōkō ibun*, pp. 356-359. The articles cited here are numbers 18 to 24 of a twenty-four-item letter.

13. Find a survey of the historical treatment of this campaign in Ishihara Michihiro, *Bunroku Keichō no eki* (Tokyo: Hanawa Shobō, 1963), pp. 19-27. Also see Kuwata, *Toyotomi Hideyoshi kenkyū*, pp. 236-237, and Asao Naohiro, "Toyotomi seiken-ron," in Wakita, *Shokuhō seiken-ron*, pp. 147-156. Asao sees the foreign campaign as an opportunity for Hideyoshi to confirm his power over the daimyo, to make real the symbolic authority conveyed by his court promotions, and to assert, in uncompromising terms, the rights of the center. Also see Nakamura Hidetaka, "Taigai sensō ni okeru Toyotomi Hideyoshi no mokuteki," in Fujiki and Kitajima, eds., *Shokuhō seiken*, pp. 277-305.

14. Kuwata, *Toyotomi Hideyoshi kenkyū*, pp. 251-252.

15. Ibid., pp. 253–254.

16. Ibid., p. 255.

17. Ibid., pp. 252–253; *Hōkō ibun*, pp. 490–491.

18. See Boxer, *The Christian Century in Japan*, pp. 160–162, for discussion of Harada Magoshichirō's influence upon Japanese relations with the Philippines.

19. For commentary on Spanish reactions to Hideyoshi's threats against the Philippines, see Antonio de Morga, *History of the Philippine Islands*, E. H. Blair and J. A. Robertson, trans. (Cleveland: A. H. Clark Co., 1907), VIII, 256–261, 284–296; IX, 24–57, 122–134, 140–149, 262–264, 301–307; X, 45–50, 168–172, 210–212. Due in part to Spanish fears that Hideyoshi would invade Taiwan and use that island as a steppingstone to the Philippines, the Spaniards sent a ship to Taiwan in 1597 to chart the island, find a good base, and make a defensive alliance with China against the Japanese. I am indebted to Peter Kozumplick for this reference.

20. The debate concerning Hideyoshi's grasp of Chinese geography cannot be resolved. He did have a famous fan with a very general map of China painted on one surface and, as he was able to refer to the "four hundred and more provinces" of that nation, he evidently had some elementary grasp of its size. He had access to information from the Tsushima daimyo, the *wakō* (pirate traders), and the missionaries (and from Ashikaga records as well), but the precision of that information and Hideyoshi's use of it remain unclear. There is no evidence that he systematically researched either the geographical problem or the problem of Chinese military organization.

21. Kuwata, *Toyotomi Hideyoshi kenkyū*, pp. 248–251; Hayashiya, *Tenka ittō*, pp. 465–466. The only clear incident of resistance to Hideyoshi's call for troops involved a Shimazu vassal, Umekita Kunikane, who refused to participate in the Korean offensive and then planned an attack upon Nagoya castle in Hizen in 1592. He was killed in Higo, enroute to Nagoya, and his leading sympathizer, Shimazu Toshihisa, was forced to commit suicide. Despite the absence of active resistance to the war, a ground swell of support never occurred either. Not only did Ieyasu and Toshiie restrain Hideyoshi when he planned to cross to the peninsula to support his troops, they and their peers—Uesugi Kagekatsu and Date Masamune, for example—pointedly declined to go themselves.

22. For a continuing description of the campaign, see Fujiki, *Oda Toyotomi seiken*, pp. 353–374. For description of the sea battles, see A. L. Sadler, "The Naval Campaign in the Korean War of Hideyoshi, 1592–1598," in *Transactions of the Asiatic Society of Japan*, ser. 2. vol. 14 (June, 1937), pp. 178–208; and Nakamura, *Nitchō kankei-shi no kenkyū*, II, 197–240.

23. Hayashiya, *Tenka ittō*, pp. 469–471.

24. *Mōri-ke monjo*, III, document 929.

25. *Hō taikō shinseki-shū*, documents 31, 32, 33, 35, 36, 37, 38. Go-Yōzei's intervention is described in Hayashiya, *Tenka ittō*, p. 467. Ōmandokoro's death and Hideyoshi's reaction, treated as important events in virtually all diaries and early histories of the period, are described in Ōta Gyūichi, *Taikō gunki*, pp. 212–216.

26. See n. 4 for the reference.

27. Kuwata, *Toyotomi Hideyoshi kenkyū*, p. 236. It is interesting, in this connection, that Hideyoshi issued his first orders concerning the Korean offensive only eight days after Hidetsugu was named as the Toyotomi heir. Following

Hideyoshi's return to the area of the capital upon Hideyori's birth, he was never to go back to Nagoya castle, even while the second Korean offensive was being waged.

28. See Watanabe, *Hō taikō no shiteki seikatsu*, pp. 173–208, for a biographical discussion of Chacha, or Yodo-dono.

29. Ibid., pp. 244–254. Raised to the position of *dainagon* at the junior second rank, and enfeoffed, according to some accounts, with as much as 1,000,-000 *koku*, Hidenaga died around the age of fifty after several years of illness. Hideyoshi led a frenzied round of prayers at capital-area temples for his recovery.

30. Kuwata, *Taikō no tegami*, pp. 201–202.

31. *Hō taikō shinseki-shū*, document 56.

32. Ibid., document 54.

33. On the twenty-sixth day of the first month, 1592, Hidetsugu had entertained the emperor in his own version of Hideyoshi's earlier Juraku *gyōkō*.

34. An excerpt from "The Second Epistle of the deathe of the Quabacondono, Written by F. Aloysius Frois, one of the Societye of Jesus, From Japania in the moneth of October, An. Do: 1595," in a contemporary translation by Frederica Oldach; held by the Houghton Library, Harvard University, MS Jap 3.1, pp. 68–69. Cited by permission of the Houghton Library. Professor George Elison has prepared a yet unpublished edition of the manuscript.

35. Ōta Gyūichi, *Taikō gunki*, pp. 161–168. Immediately after Hidetsugu's death, Hideyoshi elicited oaths of loyalty to Hideyori from the Tokugawa, Mōri, Kobayakawa, Maeda, and Oda. Oaths from most other daimyo followed within the year.

36. See Kuwata, *Taikō no tegami*, pp. 86–87, for Hideyoshi's letter to the mother of Ikeda Tsuneoki concerning the Nagakute battle. The letter to Hidetsugu is cited on pp. 88–90 and in Watanabe, *Hō taikō no shiteki seikatsu*, pp. 68–69. The letter cannot, however, be authenticated.

37. Watanabe, *Hō taikō no shiteki seikatsu*, pp. 75–76.

38. Among the more important of Hidetsugu's documents are a series of regulations concerning the encampment in Nagoya in preparation for the first Korean campaign (*Mōri-ke monjo*, I, document 260) and a series of instructions, very similar to those of Hideyoshi, concerning the *kenchi* (Miyagawa, *Taikō kenchi-ron*, III, 325–326). Because of a confusion over the date on which the orders to conduct a national census were issued, it is possible that Hidetsugu promulgated those statutes as well. See Miki Seiichirō, "Hito barai-rei o megutte," in Nagoya Daigaku Bungaku Kokushi Kenkyūshitsu, ed., *Nagoya Daigaku Nihonshi ronshū* (Tokyo: Yoshikawa Kōbunkan, 1975), II, 99–136. Miki argues that Hidetsugu did issue the census orders, that some censuses were prepared, and that Hidetsugu intended to use them to exploit manpower resources for the center. He attributes to Hidetsugu an understanding of central power, and an intention to use it fully, that contrasts with Hideyoshi's feudal conception of government. Asao ("Toyotomi seiken-ron," pp. 153–156) sees Hidetsugu and his daimyo supporters as a countervailing force to the centrists in Hideyoshi's camp. The power split implicit in Hidetsugu's promotion to *kampaku* while Hideyoshi governed as *taikō*, he suggests, prevented an aggrandizement of central powers by Hideyoshi. Asao also sees Toyotomi failures in the Korean campaign, and the selection of a child heir who required the support of powerful

tozama, as the final checks on Hideyoshi's ambitions at home. The differences in the Miki and the Asao analyses reflect the poor documentary record left by Hidetsugu and a consequent reliance on informed speculation. Even if Hidetsugu was responsible for the census order, however, his autonomy from his uncle is profoundly suspect. His extant documents mirror those of Hideyoshi; they never involve basic powers such as the recruitment of the Toyotomi daimyo for warfare. Needless to say, Hidetsugu was also powerless once Hideyoshi decided to advance the claims of Hideyori.

39. Find a discussion of these and other reports in Watanabe, *Hō taikō shiteki seikatsu*, pp. 78–82.

40. Oze Hoan, *Taikō-ki*, pp. 468–477; Ōta Gyūichi, *Taikō gunki*, pp. 150–155; Frois, "The Second Epistle of the deathe of the Quabacondono."

41. See Watanabe, *Hō taikō shiteki seikatsu*, pp. 89–95; Oze Hoan, *Taikō-ki*, pp. 468–472.

42. Ōta Gyūichi, *Taikō gunki*, p. 151.

43. Frois, "The Second Epistle of the deathe of the Quabacondono," pp. 50–51.

44. In a schema borrowed from Zeami's *Fūshi kadensho*, Rikyū outlined the training of tea devotees: from the ages of fifteen to thirty, the student must be submissive to the teacher in all things; during the following ten years the student may explore his own tastes but must be careful to alter only half of what he has learned; in the next decade the student must turn to rebellion: "Should the teacher go west, I shall turn toward the east . . ."; from the ages of fifty to sixty, the practitioner should discover harmony with the teacher's Way. Rikyū the historian also defined three ranks of proficiency in tea to which he assigned his predecessors. Kuwata, *Sadō no rekishi*, pp. 87–94. See Kuwata Tadachika, ed., *Cha ni ikita hito* (*Zusetsu sadō taikei*, 6; Tokyo: Kadokawa Shoten, 1970), I, 123–178, for discussion and illustration of Rikyū's vessels. Also see Kuwata, *Sadō no rekishi*, pp. 85–90, 97–107.

45. For discussion of Nobunaga's interest in tea, see *Kyōto no rekishi*, IV, 65–67, 659–662, and Kuwata, *Sadō no rekishi*, 111–117. Murai, *Sen no Rikyū*, pp. 65–135, outlines the general relations between merchant tea men and their military patrons. Hideyoshi received permission from Nobunaga to practice tea at Azuchi castle in 1578 after his conquest of the Bessho. In a later letter he mentions: "Impossible to forget in this life or the next is the permission to practice the tea ceremony." (Kuwata, *Taikō no tegami*, p. 58.) Hideyoshi's principal instructors in the tea ceremony were Rikyū, Imai Sōkyū, and Tsuda Sōkyū (Kuwata, *Sadō no rekishi*, p. 118).

46. *Kyōto no rekishi*, IV, 321.

47. See Beatrice M. Bodart, "Tea and Counsel: The Political Role of Sen Rikyū," in *Monumenta Nipponica*, vol. 32, no. 1 (Spring, 1977), pp. 49–74, for one assessment of Rikyū's role in Toyotomi politics.

48. Haga Kōshirō, *Sen no Rikyū* (Tokyo: Yoshikawa Kōbunkan, 1963), pp. 259–272; Murai, *Sen no Rikyū*, p. 230.

49. Cited in Murai, *Sen no Rikyū*, p. 231.

50. Ibid., p. 235.

51. *Kyōto no rekishi*, IV, 321–322.

52. Mention is made of the crucifixions in the *Tokitsugu kyō-ki* and the *Gien jugō nikki* (entries Keichō 1.11.15), but virtually all other sources (including the *Tamon'in nikki*) overlook the episode.

53. Boxer, *The Christian Century in Japan*, pp. 137–179, and Elison, *Deus Destroyed*, pp. 109–141, discuss the course of Hideyoshi's relations with the missionaries in detail.

54. The incident is discussed in Matsuda, *Hideyoshi no namban gaikō*, pp. 212–234, 254–295; Elison, *Deus Destroyed*, pp. 136–141; and Boxer, *The Christian Century in Japan*, pp. 163–167, 416–418, 420–424.

55. The Tokugawa would be the first to introduce trade constraints upon the Europeans when they closed Japanese ports to vessels from Portugal and from Spain.

56. In a letter to Maeda Gen'i (*Hō taikō shinseki-shū*, document 136) written in the twelfth month of 1592, after Hideyoshi had returned to Nagoya, he instructs Gen'i and his carpenters to join him in Kyushu with plans for the castle. Neither these plans, nor other details concerning Hideyoshi's first conception of the Fushimi residence, remain.

57. Find discussion of the construction of the castle and the circumstances surrounding it in Oze Hoan, *Taikō-ki*, pp. 452–455; *Kyōto no rekishi*, IV, 326–349.

58. See Sakurai, *Toyotomi Hideyoshi no kyojō*, II, 264–347.

59. Oze Hoan, *Taikō-ki*, p. 600; Sakurai, *Toyotomi Hideyoshi no kyojō*, II, 331–345; Hayashiya, *Tenka ittō*, pp. 483–485.

60. Kawai Masaharu, *Chūsei buke shakai no kenkyū*, p. 278. For a broader discussion of military men and the arts, see Kawai, pp. 271–280, and *Kyōto no rekishi*, IV, 717–741.

61. For discussion of Hideyoshi's interest in nō, see Morisue Yoshiaki, "Nō to hogosha," in Nogami Toyoichirō, ed., *Nōgaku zensho* (Tokyo: Sōgen-sha, 1942), II, 361–388, especially pp. 379–380, regarding the Nagoya period; and Watanabe, *Hō taikō no shiteki seikatsu*, pp. 318–326. See Oze Hoan, *Taikō-ki*, pp. 387–390, concerning Hideyoshi's performances at Nagoya castle; and *Kyōto no rekishi* IV, 692, concerning his study of the fifteen or sixteen plays.

62. *Kyōto no rekishi*, IV, 692; Morisue, "Nō to hogosha," p. 383.

63. Morisue, "Nō to hogosha," pp. 372–376. Four of the five extant plays may be found in Nonomura, ed., *Yōkyoku sambyaku gojū-ban shū*, pp. 675–676, 684–689, 704–706.

64. See Morisue, "Nō to hogosha," p. 384, and *Kyōto no rekishi*, IV, 694, for description of the Osaka performance; Morisue, pp. 386–387, for description of the performance for Shōshin.

65. Morisue, "Nō to hogosha," p. 385.

66. See Kuwata, *Toyotomi Hideyoshi kenkyū*, pp. 249–251, and Hayashiya, *Tenka ittō*, pp. 472–475, for discussion of these negotiations and Hideyoshi's response.

67. See *Hōkō ibun*, pp. 569–574, for a list of the warrior levies, and Hayashiya, *Tenka ittō*, pp. 480–482, for an account of the campaign. The noses of the Korean dead are reputedly buried in the "Ear Mound" located in southern Kyoto. See *Kyōto no rekishi*, IV, 336–337.

68. For an excellent chronology of Hideyoshi's activities during these years, with citations, see Okada Masato, ed., "Toyotomi Hideyoshi gekidō no

rokujū-ni nen," in *Toyotomi Hideyoshi* (*Rekishi tokuhon: Denki shirīzu*, 8) especially pp. 126–127.

69. Hayashiya, *Tenka ittō*, p. 482. It is interesting that Hideyoshi did go so far as to begin a cadastral survey of Korea in preparation for making enfeoffments. See Wakita, *Kinsei hōken-sei seiritsu shiron*, p. 39, and *Hōkō ibun*, pp. 140, 143.

70. Ōta Tōshirō, ed., *Oyu-dono no ue no nikki* (Tokyo: Zoku Gunsho Ruijū Kansei-kai, 1935), IX, 48–51.

71. *Mōri-ke monjo*, III, document 962.

72. Kodama et al., eds., *Shiryō ni yoru Nihon no ayumi: kinsei*, p. 32.

73. Cited in Kuwata, *Taikō no tegami*, p. 274.

74. Ibid., p. 275.

Afterword

1. Harold Bolitho discusses the early increase in power and subsequent moderation of controls in *Treasures among Men*, pp. 1–41. He sees the latter phase as aberrant, however, and attributes the moderation to *fudai* involvement in government.
2. Totman, *Politics in the Tokugawa Bakufu*, p. 33.

INDEX

Harvard East Asian Monographs